The Complete
AIR FRYER
Cookbook

1000 Recipes For Easy & Delicious Air Fryer Homemade Meals

Olivia Miller

CONTENTS

SNACKS & APPETIZERS 35

MEAT RECIPES **108**

VEGETABLES & SIDES **126**

LUNCH 141

SWEETS 155

INTRODUCTION

The air fryer. It's been the subject of life-changing anecdotes, memes, and it's developed a big following. Seriously, though, the air fryer is quite incredible. This little device can cook almost anything you throw at it, delivering you some yummy food in less time and with fewer calories than sticking it in a vat of grease.

Yes, that's right. It is worth the hype. However, if you're new to the air fryer world, you may be confused as to how an air fryer works, and you may be prone to mistakes. These mistakes can ruin your experience and turn you off from what is otherwise a fantastic invention. Luckily, air fryers are easy to use if you know what you're doing.

This intro will explain what the air fryer is, its benefits, and give you some valuable tips and tricks. Let's begin.

WHAT IS AN AIR FRYER? HOW DOES IT WORK?

If you ask several people this question, you may come up with several different answers. Some say it's like a deep fryer, but without the extra calories. Others claim it's just a portable oven. And some will say it was delivered personally by the cooking gods to your front door.

Let's give you the actual answer. An air fryer cooks your food by surrounding it with hot air that comes from convection heating. In simple terms, the air fryer heats hot air, which rises and pushes the cold air away. Because the hot air covers your food from all angles, it can cook it similarly to deep-frying it.

An air fryer is different from an oven in that it cooks the food much faster due to how quickly it heats up. It also evenly cooks your food more than an oven due to its small size.

The air fryer is different from a deep fryer in that you use little to no cooking oil, and you can do a lot more with foods besides deep frying them. An air fryer can also bake or grill your food too. Also, a deep fryer can make food crispier, but there are ways to get your food as close to that deep-fried taste as possible without the extra calories.

There are many sizes, types, and combinations of air fryers available for purchase. Some can hold more food, while others have more preset cooking options. In addition, some air fryers combine with other appliances. For example, combination microwaves/air fryers exist, helping you to save countertop space.

While people have been using convection ovens for decades, the modern air fryer was created by Philips in 2010. In recent years, the air fryer's popularity has exploded. One try, and it's easy to see why.

New Lifestyle and How to Convert Traditional Recipes to Air Fryer

The air fryer is said to be lifestyle-changing. So many people stop using their ovens and swear by the air fryer, and it's easy to see why. Thanks to the air fryer, people can save time, eat healthier, and learn to cook at home more.

However, one roadblock you may have is converting traditional recipes to the air fryer. First, let's say that there are plenty of websites, cookbooks, and other media explicitly designed around the air fryer, which can help you make your favorite recipes without having to convert it.

- **If Using it Like an Oven**

An air fryer can give you that oven experience, but the cooking times and temperatures may differ. One method to try is to lower the temperature by 25 F, or a little under 1 C. As for the cooking time, reduce it by 20 percent. So, for example, if you cook food for 20 minutes in the oven, try 16 minutes in the air fryer.

- **If Using it Like a Deep Fryer**

Deep frying can depend on how much food you have and what type it is. A good rule of thumb is to fry it at about 390 F or 199 C. Then, about halfway, shake the basket to even out the food, or flip it over if it's something like a piece of fried chicken.

- **Every Fryer is Different**

With that said, how long you have to cook your food can depend on what type of air fryer you have. Start with these two rules, then adjust if needed. You may need more or less time and temperature to get your food to the perfection it deserves. The air fryer can be a trial and error device. Of course, all cooking has an element of trial and error, but an air fryer may require a bit of experimentation and trials to get right.

Benefits of Using an Air Fryer

» **Crispy Taste Without the Added Calories and Fat**

Many people love fried foods, but we're all aware that they add unneeded calories or fat due to being dunked in hot oil. So if you're on a diet, deep-fried foods are something to avoid except for special occasions. With that said, baked, broiled, or grilled foods may not have the same appeal.

An air fryer can be a good compromise between crispy deliciousness and being health conscious.

» **Easier to Portion**

Another benefit the air fryer offers is portioning your food is much easier. Due to the baskets having less space than an oven or deep fryer, you tend to eat fewer portions. When trying to lose fat, it's all about how much you eat.

» **It's Small**

If you live in an area with little space, an air fryer works great, especially if combined with other appliances such as a microwave. Its size also makes it so you can take it with you while traveling. Bring it on a vacation or camping to eat well while you're out of your home.

» **It's Cooler**

An oven or air fryer can get quite hot. If you're cooking during a hot day and your AC isn't keeping up, an air fryer can prevent making your home even more sizzling.

» **It's Safer**

A deep fryer can pop, and it has hot oils that burn if touched. An air fryer lacks all of that, so it's much safer for you to use. With that said, be sure to check all the safety tips on your air fryer through its manual.

» **It's Inexpensive**

Air fryers can differ in price, but they can cost around $80 to a few hundred dollars. The more expensive ones may add additional features or have more space, but a cheaper air fryer can still give you quality cooking. It pays for itself when you buy an air fryer and use it more instead of eating out.

» **It Works Great For a Smaller Family**

Air fryers can be problematic if you have a larger family, as even the bigger ones may require more than one cooking session. However, if you have a smaller household then you're in luck. Air fryers are excellent for a small family.

Consider buying a bigger air fryer, an air fryer with more than one basket, or multiple fryers for a larger family.

» **Cooking is Faster**

An air fryer heats up faster and requires less cooking time than an oven. So if you're a workaholic, busy parent, or have another situation where you don't have the time, the air fryer makes it so you can cook delicious meals without the wait. Instead of going to a fast-food restaurant, which adds extra calories and costs more, you can air fryer some food on the go!

Top 5 Tips for a Better Experience With Your Air Fryer

1. **Use a Bit of Oil to Make the Food Crispier**

If the foods you're cooking with your air fryer seem dry and lack the crispiness you want, use a bit of oil. You can brush each side with oil or mist them using a spray bottle. Aerosol sprays can chip your basket, so avoid that if you're using a traditional basket air fryer.

Misting oil on your food adds only a negligible amount of calories to it. Remember, a little cooking oil goes a long way with the air fryer. So you can get your food as close to deep-fried as possible without having to worry about the extra calories.

2. **Making Fries or Wings? Shake the Basket Every Few Minutes**

To promote even cooking, be sure to take out the basket every couple of minutes and give it a good shake.

3. Preheat if Needed

An air fryer heats fast, but you may want to preheat it before cooking. Run the air fryer for a couple of minutes, then add the food. With that said, you don't need to preheat all of the time.

4. Use Foil to Catch Drippings

You can use some aluminum foil on the bottom to catch any drippings. You can even use something like bread to catch the drippings. With foil, be sure that it's not in the way of the air fryer's heating element.

5. Read the Manual

Like we said, every air fryer is different. The air fryer you have can offer additional features or require adjustments to the cooking times due to its size. Read the manual on your specific model to ensure you didn't miss anything.

Top 7 Mistakes to Avoid When Cooking

1. Overcrowding the Fryer

Your air fryer isn't a party. When making fries, wings, or similar foods, give them room to breathe. Putting too much in the air fryer can cause your foods to feel soggy or undercooked. Remember, less is more. Try using a serving of the food first, then adjust if needed.

2. Not Cleaning it

Like every appliance, an air fryer needs cleaning. You don't need to give it the whole nine yards after every single cleaning, but you do want to wipe it down with a sponge and soapy water occasionally or after a messy meal. Be sure to remove the basket before you clean. Not cleaning your air fryer can lead to clogs or the food tasting odd.

3. Not Rotating Meats or Proteins Halfway Through

To ensure even cooking, one thing you should do is to rotate your proteins when they're halfway done cooking. Since they're on the bottom, they may not get that even cooking they deserve.

4. Not Giving Your Air Fryer Space

Since the air fryer uses the air around it, be sure to give it enough space to breathe. If you overcrowd the air fryer, it may end up undercooking your foods. Be sure to put the fryer 5 inches of space on all sides and put it on a flat, even service.

5. Using Wet Foods

If your food has too much moisture, the air frier may not get rid of it, and your foods may turn out not the way you want them. Use foods that are dry. Pat down any excess moisture before cooking if needed.

6. Not Checking the Temperature After Cooking

Some foods, especially frozen, may be hot on the outside but undercooked on the inside. Use a meat thermometer on your foods to check the temperature internally before serving. Eating undercooked food, as you probably know, can make you sick.

7. Not Experimenting and Having Fun

Finally, you have to remember that an air fryer is a learning experience. If the food doesn't turn out the way you expected, adjust the temperature, consider adding a bit of oil and try again.

Above all else, have fun! Experiment with different recipes. See what you can cook in the air fryer. It can cook pretty much anything, from baking cakes to grilling food to perfection.

Yes, the air fryer is well worth the hype. It can cook almost any food you throw at it, all with less time and calories than the traditional oven. While it is a learning experience, reading this book will help you get adjusted to the air fryer.

BREAKFAST RECIPES

Avocado Toasts with Poached Eggs

Serves: 4 | Total Time: 15 minutes

4 eggs	1 pitted avocado, sliced
Salt and pepper to taste	½ tsp chili powder
4 bread pieces, toasted	½ tsp dried rosemary

Preheat air fryer to 320°F. Crack 1 egg into each greased ramekin and season with salt and black pepper. Place the ramekins into the air frying basket. Bake for 6-8 minutes.

Scoop the flesh of the avocado into a small bowl. Season with salt, black pepper, chili powderp and rosemary. Using a fork, smash the avocado lightly. Spread the smashed avocado evenly over toasted bread slices. Remove the eggs from the air fryer and gently spoon one onto each slice of avocado toast. Serve and enjoy!

Tri-Color Frittata

Serves: 4 | Total Time: 30 minutes

8 eggs, beaten	1 garlic clove, minced
1 red bell pepper, diced	½ tsp dried oregano
Salt and pepper to taste	½ cup ricotta

Preheat air fryer to 360°F. Place the beaten eggs, bell pepper, oregano, salt, black pepper, and garlic and mix well. Fold in ¼ cup half of ricotta cheese.

Pour the egg mixture into a greased cake pan and top with the remaining ricotta. Place into the air fryer and Bake for 18-20 minutes or until the eggs are set in the center. Let the frittata cool for 5 minutes. Serve sliced.

Mushroom & Cavolo Nero Egg Muffins

Serves: 6 | Total Time: 20 minutes

8 oz baby Bella mushrooms, sliced	
6 eggs, beaten	½ tsp chili powder
1 garlic clove, minced	1 cup cavolo nero
Salt and pepper to taste	2 scallions, diced

Preheat air fryer to 320°F. Place the eggs, garlic, salt, pepper, and chili powder in a bowl and beat until well combined. Fold in the mushrooms, cavolo nero, and scallions. Divide the mixture between greased muffin cups. Place into the air fryer and Bake for 12-15 minutes, or until the eggs are set. Cool for 5 minutes. Enjoy!

Flank Steak with Caramelized Onions

Serves: 2 | Total Time: 30 minutes

½ lb flank steak, cubed	2 eggs
1 tbsp mustard powder	1 onion, sliced thinly
½ tsp garlic powder	Salt and pepper to taste

Preheat air fryer to 360°F. Coat the flank steak cubes with mustard and garlic powders. Place them in the frying basket along with the onion and Bake for 3 minutes.

Flip the steak cubes over and gently stir the onions and cook for another 3 minutes. Push the steak and onions over to one side of the basket, creating space for a heat-safe baking dish. Crack the eggs into a ceramic dish. Place the dish in the fryer. Cook for 15 minutes at 320°F until the egg whites are set, and the onion is caramelized. Season with salt and pepper. Serve warm.

Herby Parmesan Pita

Serves: 2: | Total Time: 15 minutes

1 whole-wheat pita	¼ tsp dried tarragon
2 tsp olive oil	¼ tsp dried thyme
¼ sweet onion, diced	⅛ tsp salt
¼ tsp garlic, minced	3 tsp grated Parmesan cheese
1 egg	

Preheat air fryer to 380°F. Lightly brush the top of the pita with olive oil, then top with onion and garlic. Crack the egg into a small bowl and sprinkle it with tarragon, thyme, and salt. Place the pita in the frying basket and gently pour the egg onto the top of the pita. Sprinkle with cheese over the top. Bake for 6 minutes. Leave to cool for 5 minutes. Cut into pieces and serve.

Easy Caprese Flatbread

Serves: 2 | Total Time: 15 minutes

1 fresh mozzarella ball, sliced	
1 flatbread	¼ cup diced tomato
2 tsp olive oil	6 basil leaves
¼ garlic clove, minced	½ tsp dried oregano
1 egg	½ tsp balsamic vinegar
⅛ tsp salt	

Preheat air fryer to 380°F. Lightly brush the top of the bread with olive oil, then top with garlic. Crack the egg into a small bowl and sprinkle with salt. Place the bread into the frying basket and gently pour the egg onto the top of the pita. Top with tomato, mozzarella, oregano and basil. Bake for 6 minutes. When ready, remove the pita pizza and drizzle with balsamic vinegar. Let it cool for 5 minutes. Slice and serve.

Canadian Bacon & Cheese Sandwich

Serves: 1 | Total Time: 30 minutes

1 English muffin, halved	1 Canadian bacon slice
1 egg	1 slice provolone cheese

Preheat air fryer to 350°F. Put the muffin, crusty side up, in the frying basket. Place a slice of bacon next to the muffins and Bake for 5 minutes. Flip the bacon and muffins, and lay a slice of provolone cheese on top of the muffins. Beat the egg in a small heatproof bowl.

Add the bowl in the frying basket next to the bacon and muffins and Bake for 15 minutes, or until the cheese melts, bacon is crispy and eggs set. Remove the muffin to a plate, layer a slice of bacon, then the egg and top with the second toasted muffin.

Mediterranean Granola

Serves: 6 | Total Time: 40 minutes

1 cup rolled oats	1 tbsp olive oil
¼ cup dried cherries, diced	1 tsp ground cinnamon
¼ cup almond slivers	¼ tsp ground nutmeg
¼ cup hazelnuts, chopped	¼ tsp salt
¼ cup pepitas	2 tbsp dark chocolate chips
¼ cup hemp hearts	3 cups Greek yogurt
3 tbsp honey	

Preheat air fryer to 260°F. Stir the oats, cherries, almonds, hazelnuts, pepitas, hemp hearts, 2 tbsp of honey, olive oil, cinnamon, nutmeg, and salt in a bowl, mixing well. Pour the mixture onto the parchment-lined frying basket and spread it into a single layer. Bake for 25-30 minutes, shaking twice. Let the granola cool completely. Stir in the chocolate chips. Divide between 6 cups. Top with Greek yogurt and remaining honey to serve.

Sweet Potato & Mushroom Hash

Serves: 6 | Total Time: 35 minutes

2 peeled sweet potatoes, cubed
4 oz baby Bella mushrooms, diced

½ red bell pepper, diced	1 garlic clove, minced
½ red onion, diced	Salt and pepper to taste
2 tbsp olive oil	½ tbsp chopped marjoram

Preheat air fryer to 380°F. Place all ingredients in a large bowl and toss until the vegetables are well coated. Pour the vegetables into the frying basket. Bake for 8-10 minutes, then shake the vegetables. Cook for 8-10 more minutes. Serve and enjoy!

Cinnamon Banana Bread with Pecans

Serves: 6 | Total Time: 35 minutes

2 ripe bananas, mashed	1 cup flour
1 egg	¼ tsp salt
¼ cup Greek yogurt	¼ tsp baking soda
¼ cup olive oil	½ tsp ground cinnamon
½ tsp peppermint extract	¼ cup chopped pecans
2 tbsp honey	

Preheat air fryer to 360°F. Add the bananas, egg, yogurt, olive oil, peppermint, and honey in a large bowl and mix until combined and mostly smooth.

Sift the flour, salt, baking soda, and cinnamon into the wet mixture, then stir until just combined. Gently fold in the pecans. Spread to distribute evenly into a greased loaf pan. Place the loaf pan in the frying basket and Bake for 23 minutes or until golden brown on top and a toothpick inserted into the center comes out clean. Allow to cool for 5 minutes. Serve.

Banana-Strawberry Cakecups

Serves: 6 | Total Time: 25 minutes

½ cup mashed bananas	½ cup Greek yogurt
¼ cup maple syrup	1 tsp vanilla extract
1 egg	½ tsp baking powder
1 ½ cups flour	½ tsp salt
1 tbsp cornstarch	½ cup strawberries, sliced
½ tsp baking soda	

Preheat air fryer to 360°F. Place the mashed bananas, maple syrup, yogurt, vanilla, and egg in a large bowl and mix until smooth. Sift in 1 ½ cups of the flour, baking soda, baking powder, and salt, then stir to combine.

In a small bowl, toss the strawberries with the cornstarch. Fold the mixture into the muffin batter. Divide the mixture evenly between greased muffin cups and place them into the air frying basket. Bake for 12-15 minutes until golden brown on top and a toothpick inserted into the middle of one of the muffins comes out clean. Leave to cool for 5 minutes. Serve and enjoy!

Honey Oatmeal

Serves: 6 | Total Time: 35 minutes

2 cups rolled oats	1 tsp vanilla extract
2 cups oat milk	½ tsp ground cinnamon
¼ cup honey	¼ tsp salt
½ cup Greek yogurt	1 ½ cups diced mango

Preheat air fryer to 380°F. Stir together the oats, milk, honey, yogurt, vanilla, cinnamon, and salt in a large bowl until well combined. Fold in ¾ cup of the mango and then pour the mixture into a greased cake pan. Sprinkle the remaining mango across the top of the oatmeal mixture. Bake in the air fryer for 30 minutes. Leave to set and cool for 5 minutes. Serve and enjoy!

English Breakfast

Serves: 2 | Total Time: 30 minutes

6 bacon strips	½ tbsp flour
1 cup cooked white beans	Salt and pepper to taste
1 tbsp melted butter	2 eggs

Preheat air fryer to 360°F. In a second bowl, combine the beans, butter, flour, salt, and pepper. Mix well. Put the bacon in the frying basket and Air Fry for 10 minutes, flipping once. Remove the bacon and stir in the beans. Crack the eggs on top and cook for 10-12 minutes until the eggs are set. Serve with bacon.

Pumpkin Empanadas

Serves: 4 | Total Time: 30 minutes

1 (15-oz) can pumpkin purée

¼ cup white sugar	¼ tsp vanilla extract
2 tsp cinnamon	2 tbsp butter
1 tbsp brown sugar	4 empanada dough shells
½ tbsp cornstarch	

Place the puree in a pot and top with white and brown sugar, cinnamon, cornstarch, vanilla extract, 1 tbsp of water and butter and stir thoroughly. Bring to a boil over medium heat. Simmer for 4-5 minutes. Allow to cool.

Preheat air fryer to 360°F. Lay empanada shells flat on a clean counter. Spoon the pumpkin mixture into each of the shells. Fold the empanada shells over to cover completely. Seal the edges with water and press down with a fork to secure. Place the empanadas on the greased frying basket and Bake for 15 minutes, flipping once halfway through until golden. Serve hot.

Fruity Blueberry Muffin Cups

Serves: 2 | Total Time: 30 minutes

½ cup white sugar	¼ cup unsweetened yogurt
1 ½ cups all-purpose flour	2 tsp vanilla extract
2 tsp baking powder	1 cup blueberries
½ tsp salt	1 banana, mashed
1/3 cup vegetable oil	1 tbsp brown sugar
1 egg	

Preheat air fryer to 350°F. In a bowl, add 1 tbsp of flour and throw in the blueberries and bananas to coat. In another bowl, combine white sugar, baking powder, remaining flour, and salt. Mix well. In a third bowl, add oil, egg, yogurt, and vanilla. Beat until well combined.

Add the wet into the dry mixture and whisk with a fork. Put in the blueberries-banana mix and stir. Spoon the batter into muffin cups, 3/4th way up. Top with brown sugar and Bake for 10-12 minutes until a toothpick inserted comes out clean.

Spring Vegetable Omelet

Serves: 4 | Total Time: 20 minutes

¼ cup chopped broccoli, lightly steamed	
½ cup grated cheddar cheese	
6 eggs	1 green onion, chopped
¼ cup steamed kale	Salt and pepper to taste

Preheat air fryer to 360°F. In a bowl, beat the eggs. Stir in kale, broccoli, green onion, and cheddar cheese. Transfer the mixture to a greased baking dish and Bake in the fryer for 15 minutes until golden and crisp. Season to taste and serve immediately.

Meaty Omelet

Serves: 4 | Total Time: 20 minutes

6 eggs	8 bacon strips, sliced
½ cup grated Swiss cheese	Salt and pepper to taste
3 breakfast sausages, sliced	

Preheat air fryer to 360°F. In a bowl, beat the eggs and stir in Swiss cheese, sausages, and bacon. Transfer the mixture to a baking dish and set in the fryer. Bake for 15 minutes or until golden and crisp. Season and serve.

Apple French Toast Sandwich

Serves: 1 | Total Time: 30 minutes

2 white bread slices	½ peeled apple, sliced
2 eggs	1 tbsp brown sugar
1 tsp cinnamon	¼ cup whipped cream

Preheat air fryer to 350°F. Coat the apple slices with brown sugar in a small bowl. Whisk the eggs and cinnamon into a separate bowl until fluffy and thoroughly blended. Coat the bread slices with the egg mixture, then place them on the greased frying basket. Top with apple slices and Air Fry for 20 minutes, flipping once until the bread is brown nicely and the apple is crispy.

Place one French toast slice onto a serving plate, then spoon the whipped cream on top and spread evenly. Scoop the caramelized apple slices onto the whipped cream, and cover with the second toast slice. Serve.

Easy Corn Dog Cupcakes

Serves: 6 | Total Time: 30 minutes

1 cup cornbread Mix	1 egg
2 tsp granulated sugar	¼ cup minced onions
Salt to taste	1 tsp dried parsley
3/4 cup cream cheese	2 beef hot dogs, sliced and
3 tbsp butter, melted	cut into half-moons

Preheat air fryer to 350°F. Combine cornbread, sugar, and salt in a bowl. In another bowl, whisk cream cheese, parsley, butter, and egg. Pour wet ingredients to dry ingredients and toss to combine. Fold in onion and hot dog pieces. Transfer it into 8 greased silicone cupcake liners. Place it in the frying basket and Bake for 8-10 minutes. Serve right away.

Banana Muffins with Chocolate Chips

Serves: 8 | Total Time: 25 minutes

1 cup flour	½ tsp vanilla extract
½ tsp baking soda	1 egg
1/3 cup brown sugar	1 tbsp vegetable oil
¼ tsp salt	¼ cup chocolate chips
1/3 cup mashed banana	1 tbsp powdered sugar

Preheat air fryer to 375°F. Combine dry ingredients in a bowl. In another bowl, mix wet ingredients. Pour wet ingredients into dry ingredients and gently toss to combine. Fold in chocolate chips. Do not overmix.

Spoon mixture into 8 greased silicone cupcake liners, place them in the frying basket, and Bake for 6-8 minutes. Let cool onto a cooling rack. Serve right away sprinkled with powdered sugar.

Blueberry Pannenkoek (Dutch Pancake)

Serves: 4 | Total Time: 30 minutes

3 eggs, beaten	½ tsp vanilla
½ cup buckwheat flour	1 ½ cups blueberries, crushed
½ cup milk	2 tbsp powdered sugar

Preheat air fryer to 330°F. Mix together eggs, buckwheat flour, milk, and vanilla in a bowl. Pour the batter into a greased baking pan and add it to the fryer. Bake until the pancake is puffed and golden, 12-16 minutes. Remove the pan and flip the pancake over onto a plate. Add blueberries and powdered sugar as a topping and serve.

Nordic Salmon Quiche

Serves: 4 | Total Time: 30 minutes

¼ cup shredded mozzarella cheese
¼ cup shredded Gruyere cheese

1 refrigerated pie crust	1 tsp dry dill
2 eggs	5 oz cooked salmon
¼ cup milk	1 large tomato, diced

Salt and pepper to taste

Preheat air fryer to 360°F. In a baking dish, add the crust and press firmly. Trim off any excess edges. Poke a few holes. Beat the eggs in a bowl. Stir in the milk, dill, tomato, salmon, half of the cheeses, salt, and pepper. Mix well as break the salmon into chunks, mixing it evenly among other ingredients. Transfer the mix to the baking dish.

Bake in the fryer for 15 minutes until firm and almost crusty. Slide the basket out and top with the remaining cheeses. Cook further for 5 minutes, or until golden brown. Let cool slightly and serve.

Egg & Salmon Croissant Sandwich

Serves: 1 | Total Time: 30 minutes

1 croissant, halved	1 smoked salmon slice
2 eggs	Salt and pepper to taste
1 tbsp guacamole	

Preheat air fryer to 360°F. Place the croissant, crusty side up, in the frying basket side by side. Whisk the eggs in a small ceramic dish until fluffy. Place in the air fryer. Bake for 10 minutes. Gently scramble the half-cooked egg in the baking dish with a fork. Flip the croissant and cook for another 10 minutes until the scrambled eggs are cooked, but still fluffy, and the croissant is toasted.

Place one croissant on a serving plate, then spread the guacamole on top. Scoop the scrambled eggs onto guacamole, then top with smoked salmon. Sprinkle with salt and pepper. Top with the second slice of toasted croissant, close sandwich, and serve hot.

Breakfast Sausage Bites

Serves: 4 | Total Time: 30 minutes

1 lb ground pork sausages	½ tsp fennel
¼ cup diced onions	¼ tsp garlic powder
1 tsp rubbed sage	2 tbsp parsley, chopped
¼ tsp ground nutmeg	Salt and pepper to taste

Preheat air fryer to 350°F. Combine all ingredients, except the parsley, in a bowl. Form mixture into balls. Place them in the greased frying basket and Air Fry for 10 minutes, flipping once. Sprinkle with parsley and serve immediately.

Cream Cheese Deviled Eggs

Serves: 4 | Total Time: 20 minutes

2 cooked bacon slices, crumbled

4 whole eggs	2 tbsp mayonnaise
1 tsp yellow mustard	Salt and pepper to taste
½ tsp dill pickle juice	2 tbsp cream cheese
1 tsp diced sweet pickles	Parsley for sprinkling

Preheat air fryer to 250°F. Place egg in the frying basket and Air Fry for 15 minutes. Then place them immediately into a bowl with ice and 1 cup of water to stop the cooking process. Let chill for 5 minutes, then carefully peel them. Cut egg in half lengthwise and spoon yolks into a bowl. Arrange the egg white halves on a plate.

Mash egg yolks with a fork. Stir in mayonnaise, mustard, pickle juice, diced pickles, salt, pepper, and cream cheese. Pour 1 tbsp of the mixture into egg white halves, scatter with crumbled bacon and parsley and serve.

Pesto Egg & Ham Sandwiches

Serves: 2 | Total Time: 20 minutes

4 sandwich bread slices	2 Colby cheese slices
2 tbsp butter, melted	4 tsp basil pesto sauce
4 eggs, scrambled	¼ tsp red chili flakes
4 deli ham slices	¼ sliced avocado

Preheat air fryer to 370°F. Brush 2 pieces of bread with half of the butter and place them, butter side down, into the frying basket. Divide eggs, chili flakes, sliced avocado, ham, and cheese on each bread slice.

Spread pesto on the remaining bread slices and place them, pesto side-down, onto the sandwiches. Brush the remaining butter on the tops of the sandwiches and Bake for 6 minutes, flipping once. Serve immediately.

Fun Fruity Pebble French Toast Sticks

Serves: 3 | Total Time: 20 minutes

4 sandwich bread slices	½ tsp ground cinnamon
2 eggs, beaten	½ tsp vanilla extract
1/3 cup milk	1 cup crushed fruity pebbles
½ pinch of salt	¼ cup honey

Preheat air fryer to 375°F. Cut each bread slice into 4 sticks. Whisk the eggs, milk, salt, cinnamon, and vanilla in a bowl. Put the crushed cereal on a plate. Submerge the sticks into the egg mixture, then coat them in the fruity pebbles. Place the breadsticks in the greased frying basket and Air Fry for 5-6 minutes, flipping once. Serve immediately with honey as a dip.

Avocado Toast with Smoked Salmon

Serves: 2 | Total Time: 20 minutes

2 tbsp minced green chili pepper

1 avocado, pressed	2 bread slices
1 garlic clove, minced	2 plum tomatoes, sliced
¼ tsp lemon juice	4 oz smoked salmon
Salt and pepper to taste	¼ diced peeled red onion

Preheat air fryer to 350°F. Combine the avocado, garlic, lemon juice, and salt in a bowl until you reach your desired consistency. Spread avocado mixture on the bread slices.

Top with tomato slices and sprinkle with black pepper. Place bread slices in the frying basket and Bake for 5 minutes. Transfer to a plate. Top each bread slice with salmon, green chili pepper, and red onion. Serve.

Orange Trail Oatmeal

Serves: 4 | Total Time: 20 minutes

1 ½ cups quick-cooking oats	2 tbsp butter, melted
1/3 cup light brown sugar	2 tsp dried cranberries
1 egg	1 tsp dried blueberries
1 tsp orange zest	1/8 tsp ground nutmeg
1 tbsp orange juice	Salt to taste
2 tbsp whole milk	¼ cup pecan pieces
2 tbsp honey	

Preheat air fryer to 325°F. Combine the oats, sugar, egg, orange zest, orange juice, milk, honey, butter, dried cranberries, dried blueberries, nutmeg, salt, and pecan in a bowl. Press mixture into a greased cake pan. Place cake pan in the frying basket and Roast for 8 minutes. Let cool for 5 minutes before slicing. Serve.

Healthy Granola

Serves: 4 | Total Time: 10 minutes

¼ cup chocolate hazelnut spread	
1 cup chopped pecans	¼ cup maple syrup
1 cup quick-cooking oats	1 tbsp light brown sugar
1 tbsp chia seeds	½ tsp vanilla extract
1 tbsp flaxseed	¼ cup hazelnut flour
1 tbsp sesame seeds	2 tbsp cocoa powder
1 cup coconut shreds	Salt to taste

Preheat air fryer to 350°F. Combine the pecans, oats, chia seeds, flaxseed, sesame seeds, coconut shreds, chocolate hazelnut spread, maple syrup, sugar, vanilla extract, hazelnut flour, cocoa powder, and salt in a bowl. Press mixture into a greased cake pan. Place cake pan in the frying basket and Bake for 5 minutes, stirring once. Let cool completely before crumbling. Store it in an airtight container for up to 5 days.

Almond-Pumpkin Porridge

Serves: 4 | Total Time: 10 minutes

1 cup pumpkin seeds	1 tsp dried berries
2/3 cup chopped pecans	2 tbsp butter
1/3 cup quick-cooking oats	2 tsp pumpkin pie spice
¼ cup pumpkin purée	¼ cup honey
¼ cup diced pitted dates	1 tbsp dark brown sugar
1 tsp chia seeds	¼ cup almond flour
1 tsp sesame seeds	Salt to taste

Preheat air fryer to 350°F. Combine the pumpkin seeds, pecans, oats, pumpkin purée, dates, chia seeds, sesame seeds, dried berries, butter, pumpkin pie spice, honey, sugar, almond flour, and salt in a bowl. Press mixture into a greased cake pan. Place cake pan in the frying basket and Bake for 5 minutes, stirring once. Let cool completely for 10 minutes before crumbling.

Lorraine Egg Cups

Serves: 6 | Total Time: 30 minutes

3 eggs	1 tbs dried parsley
2 tbsp half-and-half	3 oz cooked bacon, crumbled
Garlic salt and pepper to taste	¼ cup grated Swiss cheese
2 tbsp diced white onion	1 tomato, sliced

Preheat air fryer to 350°F. Whisk the egg, half-and-half, garlic sea salt, parsley and black pepper in a bowl. Divide onion, bacon, and cheese between 6 lightly greased silicone cupcakes. Spread the egg mixture between cupcakes evenly. Top each cup with 1 tomato slice. Place them in the frying basket and Bake for 8-10 minutes. Serve immediately.

Coconut & Peanut Rice Cereal

Serves: 4 | Total Time: 15 minutes

4 cups rice cereal	1 tbsp light brown sugar
1 cup coconut shreds	2 tsp ground cinnamon
2 tbsp peanut butter	¼ cup hazelnut flour
1 tsp vanilla extract	Salt to taste
¼ cup honey	

Preheat air fryer to 350°F. Combine the rice cereal, coconut shreds, peanut butter, vanilla extract, honey, brown sugar, cinnamon, hazelnut flour, and salt in a bowl. Press mixture into a greased cake pan. Place cake pan in the frying basket and Air Fry for 5 minutes, stirring once. Let cool completely for 10 minutes before crumbling. Store it in an airtight container for up to 7 days.

American Biscuits

Serves: 4 | Total Time: 30 minutes

2 cups all-purpose flour	½ tsp sugar
1 tbsp baking powder	4 tbsp cold butter, cubed
½ tsp baking soda	1 ¼ cups buttermilk
½ tsp cornstarch	1/2 tsp vanilla extract
½ tsp salt	1 tsp finely crushed walnuts

Preheat air fryer to 350°F. Combine dry ingredients in a bowl. Stir in the remaining ingredients gradually until a sticky dough forms. Using your floured hands, form dough into 8 balls. Place them into a greased pizza pan. Place pizza pan in the frying basket and Bake for 8 minutes. Serve immediately.

Morning Apple Biscuits

Serves: 6 | Total Time: 15 minutes

1 apple, grated	¼ cup peanut butter
1 cup oat flour	1/3 cup raisins
2 tbsp honey	½ tsp ground cinnamon

Preheat air fryer to 350°F. Combine the apple, flour, honey, peanut butter, raisins, and cinnamon in a bowl until combined. Make balls out of the mixture. Place them onto parchment paper and flatten them. Bake for 9 minutes until slightly brown. Serve warm.

Favorite Blueberry Muffins

Serves: 8 | Total Time: 25 minutes

1 cup all-purpose flour	¼ cup milk
½ tsp baking soda	½ tsp vanilla extract
1/3 cup granulated sugar	1 egg
¼ tsp salt	1 tbsp vegetable oil
1 tbsp lemon juice	¼ cup halved blueberries
1 tsp lemon zest	1 tbsp powdered sugar

Preheat air fryer to 375°F. Combine dry ingredients in a bowl. Mix ¼ cup of fresh milk with 1 tsp of lemon juice and leave for 10 minutes. Put it in another bowl with the wet ingredients. Pour wet ingredients into dry ingredients and gently toss to combine. Fold in blueberries. Spoon mixture into 8 greased silicone cupcake liners and Bake them in the fryer for 6-8 minutes. Let cool onto a cooling rack. Serve right away sprinkled with powdered sugar.

Egg & Bacon Pockets

Serves: 4 | Total Time: 50 minutes

2 tbsp olive oil	1 ½ tsp baking powder
4 bacon slices, chopped	½ tsp salt
¼ red bell pepper, diced	1 cup Greek yogurt
1/3 cup scallions, chopped	1 egg white, beaten
4 eggs, beaten	2 tsp Italian seasoning
1/3 cup grated Swiss cheese	1 tbsp Tabasco sauce
1 cup flour	

Warm the olive oil in a skillet over medium heat and add the bacon. Stir-fry for 3-4 minutes or until crispy. Add the bell pepper and scallions and sauté for 3-4 minutes. Pour in the beaten eggs and stir-fry to scramble them, 3 minutes. Stir in the Swiss cheese and set aside to cool.

Sift the flour, baking powder, and salt in a bowl. Add yogurt and mix together until combined. Transfer the dough to a floured workspace. Knead it for 3 minutes or until smooth. Form the dough into 4 equal balls. Roll out the balls into round discs. Divide the bacon-egg mixture between the rounds. Fold the dough over the filling and seal the edges with a fork. Brush the pockets with egg white and sprinkle with Italian seasoning.

Preheat air fryer to 350°F. Arrange the pockets on the greased frying basket and Bake for 9-11 minutes, flipping once until golden. Serve with Tabasco sauce.

English Muffin Sandwiches

Serves: 4 | Total Time: 25 minutes

4 English muffins	4 cheddar cheese slices
8 pepperoni slices	1 tomato, sliced

Preheat air fryer to 370°F. Split open the English muffins along the crease. On the bottom half of the muffin, layer 2 slices of pepperoni and one slice of cheese and tomato. Place the top half of the English muffin to finish the sandwich. Lightly spray with cooking oil. Place the muffin sandwiches in the air fryer. Bake for 8 minutes, flipping once. Let stand for 10 minutes before serving.

Mascarpone Iced Cinnamon Rolls

Serves: 6 | Total Time: 40 minutes

¼ cup mascarpone cheese, softened	
9 oz puff pastry sheet	¼ tsp salt
3 tbsp light brown sugar	2 tbsp milk
2 tsp ground cinnamon	1 tbsp lemon zest
2 tsp butter, melted	¼ cup confectioners' sugar
¼ tsp vanilla extract	

Preheat air fryer to 320°F. Mix the brown sugar and cinnamon in a small bowl. Unroll the pastry sheet on its paper and brush it with melted butter. Then sprinkle with cinnamon sugar. Roll up the dough tightly, then cut into rolls about 1-inch wide. Put into a greased baking pan with the spiral side showing. Put the pan into the air fryer and Bake until golden brown, 18-20 minutes. Set aside to cool for 5-10 minutes.

Meanwhile, add the mascarpone cheese, vanilla, and salt in a small bowl, whisking until smooth and creamy. Add the confectioners' sugar and continue whisking until fully blended. Pour and mix in 1 tsp of milk at a time until the glaze is pourable but still with some thickness. Spread the glaze over the warm cinnamon rolls and scatter with lemon zest. Serve and enjoy!

Bacon & Egg Quesadillas

Serves: 4 | Total Time: 30 minutes

8 flour tortillas	1 tsp chopped chives
½ lb cooked bacon, crumbled	1 tsp parsley
6 eggs, scrambled	Black pepper on taste
1 ½ cups grated cheddar	

Preheat air fryer to 350°F. Place 1 tortilla in the bottom of a cake pan. Spread ¼ portion of each crumbled bacon, eggs, chives, parsley, pepper and cheese over the tortilla and top with a second tortilla.

Place cake pan in the frying basket and Bake for 4 minutes. Set aside on a large plate and repeat the process with the remaining ingredients. Let cool for 3 minutes before slicing. Serve right away.

Pumpkin Bread with Walnuts

Serves: 6 | Total Time: 30 minutes

½ cup canned pumpkin purée	
1 cup flour	1 egg
½ tsp baking soda	1 tbsp vegetable oil
½ cup granulated sugar	1 tbsp orange juice
1 tsp pumpkin pie spice	1 tsp orange zest
¼ tsp nutmeg	¼ cup crushed walnuts
¼ tsp salt	

Preheat air fryer to 375°F. Combine flour, baking soda, sugar, nutmeg, pumpkin pie spice, salt, pumpkin purée, egg, oil, orange juice, orange zest, and walnuts in a bowl. Pour the mixture into a greased cake pan. Place cake pan in the frying basket and Bake for 20 minutes. Let sit for 10 minutes until slightly cooled before slicing. Serve.

Home-Style Pumpkin Crumble

Serves: 6 | Total Time: 60 minutes + chilling time

¾ cup canned pumpkin puree

½ cup whole-wheat flour	1 tbsp orange zest
5 tbsp sugar	1 tbsp butter, melted
¼ tsp baking soda	1 egg
¼ tsp baking powder	¾ tsp vanilla extract
1 tsp pumpkin pie spice	2 tbsp light brown sugar
⅛ tsp ground cinnamon	½ tbsp cornflour
⅛ tsp ground nutmeg	⅛ tsp ground cinnamon
⅛ tsp salt	½ tbsp cold butter

Combine all dry ingredients in a bowl with a whisk. In a large bowl, combine pumpkin puree, butter, egg, and vanilla. Beat these ingredients in a mixer at medium speed until thick. Slowly add 1/3 cup of the flour mixture to the pumpkin mixture at a low speed until it is combined. Pour batter into a greased baking dish.

Prepare the crumb topping by combining brown sugar, cornflour, and cinnamon in a small bowl. Using a fork, cut in the cold butter until the mixture is coarse and crumbly. Sprinkle over the batter evenly.

Preheat air fryer to 300°F. Put the pan in the frying basket. Bake until a toothpick in the center comes out clean, 40-45 minutes. Allow to cool for 30 minutes before cutting and serving.

Apple & Turkey Breakfast Sausages

Serves: 4 | Total Time: 15 minutes

½ tsp coriander seeds, crushed

1 tbsp chopped rosemary	½ tsp garlic powder
1 tbsp chopped thyme	½ tsp shallot powder
Salt and pepper to taste	⅛ tsp red pepper flakes
1 tsp fennel seeds, crushed	1 pound ground turkey
¾ tsp smoked paprika	½ cup minced apples

Combine all of the seasonings in a bowl. Add turkey and apple and blend seasonings in well with your hands. Form patties about 3 inches in diameter and ¼ inch thick.

Preheat air fryer to 400°F. Arrange patties in a single layer on the greased frying basket. Air Fry for 10 minutes, flipping once until brown and cooked through. Serve.

Effortless Toffee Zucchini Bread

Serves: 6 | Total Time: 30 minutes

1 cup flour	1 egg
½ tsp baking soda	1 tbsp olive oil
½ cup granulated sugar	1 tsp vanilla extract
¼ tsp ground cinnamon	2 tbsp English toffee bits
¼ tsp nutmeg	2 tbsp mini chocolate chips
¼ tsp salt	1/2 cup chopped walnuts
1/3 cup grated zucchini	

Preheat air fryer to 375°F. Combine the flour, baking soda, toffee bits, sugar, cinnamon, nutmeg, salt, zucchini, egg, olive oil, vanilla and chocolate chips in a bowl. Add the walnuts to the batter and mix until evenly distributed.

Pour the mixture into a greased cake pan. Place the pan in the fryer and Bake for 20 minutes. Let sit for 10 minutes until slightly cooled before slicing. Serve immediately.

Mashed Potato Taquitos with Hot Sauce

Serves: 4 | Total Time: 30 minutes

1 potato, peeled and cubed	2 tbsp minced scallions
2 tbsp milk	4 corn tortillas
2 garlic cloves, minced	1 cup red chili sauce
Salt and pepper to taste	1 avocado, sliced
½ tsp ground cumin	2 tbsp cilantro, chopped

In a pot fitted with a steamer basket, cook the potato cubes for 15 minutes on the stovetop. Pour the potato cubes into a bowl and mash with a potato masher. Add the milk, garlic, salt, pepper, and cumin and stir. Add the scallions and cilantro and stir them into the mixture.

Preheat air fryer to 390°F. Run the tortillas under water for a second, then place them in the greased frying basket. Air Fry for 1 minute. Lay the tortillas on a flat surface. Place an equal amount of the potato filling in the center of each. Roll the tortilla sides over the filling and place seam-side down in the frying basket. Fry for 7 minutes or until the tortillas are golden and slightly crisp. Serve with chili sauce and avocado slices. Enjoy!

Vegetarian Quinoa Cups

Serves: 6 | Total Time: 25 minutes

1 carrot, chopped	2 tbsp lemon juice
1 zucchini, chopped	¼ cup nutritional yeast
4 asparagus, chopped	¼ tsp garlic powder
¾ cup quinoa flour	Salt and pepper to taste

Preheat air fryer to 340°F. Combine the vegetables, quinoa flour, water, lemon juice, nutritional yeast, garlic powder, salt, and pepper in a medium bowl, and mix well. Divide the mixture between 6 cupcake molds. Place the filled molds into the air fryer and Bake for 20 minutes, or until the tops are lightly browned and a toothpick inserted into the center comes out clean. Serve cooled.

Banana-Blackberry Muffins

Serves: 6 | Total Time: 20 minutes

1 ripe banana, mashed	2 tbsp coconut sugar
½ cup milk	¾ cup flour
1 tsp apple cider vinegar	1 tsp baking powder
1 tsp vanilla extract	½ tsp baking soda
2 tbsp ground flaxseed	¾ cup blackberries

Preheat air fryer to 350°F. Place the banana in a bowl. Stir in milk, apple vinegar, vanilla extract, flaxseed, and coconut sugar until combined. In another bowl, combine flour, baking powder, and baking soda. Pour it into the banana mixture and toss to combine. Divide the batter between 6 muffin molds and top each with blackberries, pressing slightly. Bake for 16 minutes until golden brown and a toothpick comes out clean. Serve cooled.

Cherry-Apple Oatmeal Cups

Serves: 2 | Total Time: 20 minutes

2/3 cup rolled oats	½ tsp ground cinnamon
1 cored apple, diced	¾ cup milk
4 pitted cherries, diced	

Preheat air fryer to 350°F. Mix the oats, apple, cherries, and cinnamon in a heatproof bowl. Add in milk and Bake for 6 minutes, stir well and Bake for 6 more minutes until the fruit are soft. Serve cooled.

Blueberry Applesauce Oat Cake

Serves: 4 | Total Time: 65 minutes

1 cup applesauce	1 tbsp honey
2/3 cup quick-cooking oats	1 egg
½ tsp baking powder	1 tsp vanilla extract
A pinch of salt	½ cup blueberries
½ cup almond milk	4 tbsp grape preserves
5 tbsp almond flour	

In a bowl, combine oats, baking powder, and salt. In a larger bowl, combine milk, almond flour, honey, egg, and vanilla with a whisk until well mixed. Add the applesauce until combined, then add the oat mixture. Gently fold in blueberries. Pour the mixture into a greased baking dish. Spoon jelly over the top, but do not stir it in.

Preheat air fryer to 300°F. Put the baking dish into the air fryer. Bake until the top is golden and the oatmeal is set, 25 minutes. Remove and allow to cool for 10-15 minutes. Slice four ways and serve warm.

Lime Muffins

Serves: 6 | Total Time: 30 minutes

1 ½ tbsp butter, softened	1 tsp lime juice
6 tbsp sugar	1 lime, zested
1 egg	5 oz Greek yogurt
1 egg white	¾ cup + 2 tbsp flour
1 tsp vanilla extract	¾ cup raspberries

Beat butter and sugar in a mixer for 2 minutes at medium speed. In a separate bowl, whisk together the egg, egg white and vanilla. Pour into the mixer bowl, add lime juice and zest. Beat until combined. At a low speed, add yogurt then flour. Fold in the raspberries. Divide the mixture into 6 greased muffin cups using an ice cream scoop. The cups should be filled about ¾ of the way.

Preheat air fryer to 300°F. Put the muffins into the air fryer and Bake for 15 minutes until the tops are golden and a toothpick in the center comes out clean. Allow to cool before serving.

Coconut Mini Tarts

Serves: 2 | Total Time: 25 minutes

¼ cup almond butter	½ cup oat flour
1 tbsp coconut sugar	2 tbsp strawberry jam
2 tbsp coconut yogurt	

Preheat air fryer to 350°F. Use 2 pieces of parchment paper, each 8-inches long. Draw a rectangle on one piece. Beat the almond butter, coconut sugar, and coconut yogurt in a shallow bowl until well combined. Mix in oat flour until you get a dough. Put the dough onto the undrawing paper and cover it with the other one, rectangle-side up. Using a rolling pin, roll out until you get a rectangle. Discard top paper.

Cut it into 4 equal rectangles. Spread on 2 rectangles, 1 tbsp of strawberry jam each, then top with the remaining rectangles. Using a fork, press all edges to seal them. Bake in the fryer for 8 minutes. Serve right away.

Cinnamon-Coconut Doughnuts

Serves: 6 | Total Time: 35 minutes

1 egg, beaten	¾ cup coconut sugar
¼ cup milk	2 ½ tsp cinnamon
2 tbsp safflower oil	½ tsp ground nutmeg
1 ½ tsp vanilla	¼ tsp salt
½ tsp lemon zest	¾ tsp baking powder
1 ½ cups all-purpose flour	

Preheat air fryer to 350°F. Add the egg, milk, oil, vanilla, and lemon zest. Stir well and set this wet mixture aside. In a different bowl, combine the flour, ½ cup coconut sugar, ½ teaspoon cinnamon, nutmeg, salt, and baking powder. Stir well. Add this mixture to the wet mix and blend. Pull off bits of the dough and roll into balls.

Place in the greased frying basket, leaving room between as they get bigger. Spray the tops with oil and Air Fry for 8-10 minutes, flipping once. During the last 2 minutes of frying, place 4 tbsp of coconut sugar and 2 tsp of cinnamon in a bowl and stir to combine. After frying, coat each donut by spraying with oil and toss in the cinnamon-sugar mix. Serve and enjoy!

Cheddar & Sausage Tater Tots

Serves: 4 | Total Time: 25 minutes

12 oz ground chicken sausage	
4 eggs	Salt and pepper to taste
1 cup sour cream	1 lb frozen tater tots
1 tsp Worcestershire sauce	¾ cup grated cheddar
1 tsp shallot powder	

Whisk eggs, sour cream, Worcestershire sauce and shallot in a bowl. Add salt and pepper to taste. Coat a skillet with cooking spray. Over medium heat, brown the ground sausage for 3-4 minutes. Break larger pieces with a spoon or spatula. Set aside.

Preheat air fryer to 330°F. Prepare a baking pan with a light spray of cooking oil. Layer the bottom of the pan with tater tots, then place in the air fryer. Bake for 6 minutes, then shake the pan. Cover tater tots with cooked sausage and egg mixture. Continue cooking for 6 minutes. Top with cheese, then cook for another 2-3 minutes or until cheese is melted. Serve warm.

Breakfast Burrito with Sausage

Serves: 6 | Total Time: 35 minutes

2 tbsp olive oil	1 onion, finely chopped
Salt and pepper to taste	8 oz chicken sausage
6 eggs, beaten	½ cup salsa
½ chopped red bell pepper	6 flour tortillas
½ chopped green bell pepper	½ cup grated cheddar

Warm the olive oil in a skillet over medium heat. Add the eggs and stir-fry them for 2-3 minutes until scrambled. Season with salt and pepper and set aside.

Sauté the bell peppers and onion in the same skillet for 2-3 minutes until tender. Add and brown the chicken sausage, breaking into small pieces with a wooden spoon, about 4 minutes. Return the scrambled eggs and stir in the salsa. Remove the skillet from heat. Divide the mixture between the tortillas. Fold up the top and bottom edges, then roll to fully enclose the filling. Secure with toothpicks. Spritz with cooking spray.

Preheat air fryer to 400°F. Bake the burritos in the air fryer for 10 minutes, turning them once halfway through cooking until crisp. Garnish with cheddar cheese. Serve.

Breakfast Potato Patties with Dill

Serves: 6 | Total Time: 50 minutes

4 Yukon Gold potatoes	2 tbsp lime juice
2 cups kale, chopped	2 tsp dill, chopped
1 cup rice flour	2 tsp shallot powder
¼ cup cornstarch	Salt and pepper to taste
¾ cup milk	½ tsp turmeric powder

Preheat air fryer to 390°F. Scrub the potatoes, prick with a fork, and put them in the fryer. Bake for 30 minutes until soft. Let them cool, then chop them into small pieces. Place them in a bowl and mash with a potato masher. Add kale, rice flour, cornstarch, milk, lime juice, dill, shallot powder, salt, pepper, and turmeric. Stir well.

Make 12 balls out of the mixture and smash them lightly with your hands to make patties. Place them in the greased frying basket, and Air Fry for 10-12 minutes, flipping once, until golden and cooked through. Serve.

Chia Seed Banana Bread

Serves: 6 | Total Time: 35 minutes

2 bananas, mashed	¼ cup sugar
2 tbsp sunflower oil	½ tsp cinnamon
2 tbsp maple syrup	1 orange, zested
½ tsp vanilla	¼ tsp salt
½ tbsp chia seeds	¼ tsp ground nutmeg
½ tbsp ground flaxseeds	½ tsp baking powder
1 cup pastry flour	

Preheat air fryer to 350°F. Place the bananas, oil, maple syrup, vanilla, chia, and flaxseeds in a bowl and stir to combine. Add the flour, sugar, cinnamon, salt, nutmeg, baking powder, and orange zest. Stir to combine.

Pour the batter into a greased baking pan. Smooth the top with a rubber spatula and Bake for 25 minutes or until a knife inserted in the center comes out clean. Remove and let cool for a minute, then cut into wedges and serve. Enjoy warm!

Eggless Mung Bean Tart

Serves: 2 | Total Time: 20 minutes

2 tsp soy sauce	½ cup mung beans, soaked
1 tsp lime juice	Salt and pepper to taste
1 large garlic clove, minced	½ minced shallot
½ tsp red chili flakes	1 green onion, chopped

Preheat the air fryer to 390°F. Add the soy sauce, lime juice, garlic, and chili flakes to a bowl and stir. Set aside. Place the drained beans in a blender along with ½ cup of water, salt, and pepper. Blend until smooth. Stir in shallot and green onion, but do not blend.

Pour the batter into a greased baking pan. Bake for 15 minutes in the air fryer until golden. A knife inserted in the center should come out clean. Once cooked, cut the "quiche" into quarters. Drizzle with sauce and serve.

Sausage & Mushroom Strata

Serves: 4 | Total Time: 40 minutes

½ lb sausage links, casings removed and sliced	
1 cup mushrooms, chopped	2 bread slices, cubed
½ onion, sliced	½ cup grated Gruyere cheese
4 eggs	2 tbsp chopped parsley
3 tbsp milk	Salt and pepper to taste

Preheat air fryer to 340°F. Add sausage, asparagus, and onion to a baking pan. Place the pan into the air fryer. Bake for 8-10 minutes until the sausage is browned and the vegetables are softened and lightly browned.

Beat the eggs and milk in a bowl. Then mix in bread cubes, Gruyere cheese, parsley, salt, and pepper. Pour the mixture over the sausages and veggies. Return to the fryer and Bake until eggs are set, and the tops browned, 12-14 minutes. Serve warm and enjoy!

Light Frittata

Serves: 4 | Total Time: 25 minutes

½ red bell pepper, chopped	8 egg whites
1 shallot, chopped	1/3 cup milk
1 baby carrot, chopped	2 tsp grated Parmesan cheese
1 tbsp olive oil	

Preheat air fryer to 350°F. Toss the red bell pepper, shallot, carrot, and olive oil in a baking pan. Put in the fryer and Bake for 4-6 minutes until the veggies are soft. Shake the basket once during cooking. Whisk the egg whites in a bowl until fluffy and stir in milk. Pour the mixture over the veggies. Toss some Parmesan cheese on top and put the pan back into the fryer. Bake for 4-6 minutes or until the frittata puffs. Serve and enjoy!

Seafood Quinoa Frittata

Serves: 4 | Total Time: 30 minutes

½ cup cooked shrimp, chopped
½ cup cooked quinoa
½ cup baby spinach
4 eggs
½ tsp dried basil
1 anchovy, chopped
½ cup grated cheddar

Preheat air fryer to 320°F. Add quinoa, shrimp, and spinach to a greased baking pan. Set aside. Beat eggs, anchovy, and basil in a bowl until frothy. Pour over the quinoa mixture, then top with cheddar cheese. Bake until the frittata is puffed and golden, 14-18 minutes. Serve.

Parma Ham & Egg Toast Cups

Serves: 4 | Total Time: 25 minutes

4 crusty rolls
4 Gouda cheese thin slices
5 eggs
2 tbsp heavy cream
½ tsp dried thyme
3 Parma ham slices, chopped
Salt and pepper to taste

Preheat air fryer to 330°F. Slice off the top of the rolls, then tear out the insides with your fingers, leaving about ½-inch of bread to make a shell. Press one cheese slice inside the roll shell until it takes the shape of the roll.

Beat eggs with heavy cream in a medium bowl. Next, mix in the remaining ingredients. Spoon egg mixture into the rolls lined with cheese. Place rolls in the greased frying basket and Bake until eggs are puffy and brown, 8-12 minutes. Serve warm.

Cherry Beignets

Serves: 4 | Total Time: 25 minutes

2 tsp baking soda
1 ½ cups flour
¼ tsp salt
3 tbsp brown sugar
4 tsp chopped dried cherries
½ cup buttermilk
1 egg
3 tbsp melted lard

Preheat air fryer to 330°F. Combine baking soda, flour, salt, and brown sugar in a bowl. Then stir in dried cherries. In a small bowl, beat together buttermilk and egg until smooth. Pour in with the dry ingredients and stir until just moistened.

On a floured work surface, pat the dough into a square. Divide it by cutting into 16 pieces. Lightly brush with melted lard. Arrange the squares in the frying basket, without overlapping. Air Fry until puffy and golden brown, 5-8 minutes. Serve.

Chorizo Biscuits

Serves: 4 | Total Time: 20 minutes

12 oz chorizo sausage
1 (6-oz) can biscuits
⅛ cup cream cheese

Preheat air fryer to 370°F. Shape the sausage into 4 patties. Bake in the air fryer for 10 minutes, turning once halfway through. Remove and set aside.

Separate the biscuit dough into 5 biscuits, then place in the air fryer for 5 minutes, flipping once. Remove from the air fryer. Divide each biscuit in half. Smear 1 tsp of cream cheese on the bottom half, top with the sausage, and then cover with the top half. Serve warm.

Lemon Monkey Bread

Serves: 4 | Total Time: 15 minutes

1 (8-oz) can refrigerated biscuits
¼ cup white sugar
3 tbsp brown sugar
½ tsp ground cinnamon
1 lemon, zested
¼ tsp ground nutmeg
3 tbsp melted butter

Preheat air fryer to 350°F. Take the biscuits out of the can and separate them. Cut each biscuit into 4 equal pieces. In a bowl, mix white sugar, brown sugar, lemon zest, cinnamon, and nutmeg. Have the melted butter nearby. Dip each biscuit piece into the butter, then roll into the cinnamon sugar until coated. Place in a baking pan. Bake in the air fryer until golden brown, 6-9 minutes. Let cool for 5 minutes before serving as the sugar will be hot.

Zucchini Hash Browns

Serves: 4 | Total Time: 20 minutes

2 shredded zucchinis
2 tbsp nutritional yeast
1 tsp allspice
1 egg white

Preheat air fryer to 400°F. Combine zucchinis, nutritional yeast, allspice, and egg white in a bowl. Make 4 patties out of the mixture. Cut 4 pieces of parchment paper, put a patty on each foil, and fold in all sides to create a rectangle. Using a spatula, flatten them and spread them.

Then unwrap each foil and remove the hash browns onto the fryer and Air Fry for 12 minutes until golden brown and crispy, turning once. Serve right away.

Veggie & Feta Scramble Bowls

Serves: 2 | Total Time: 25 minutes

1 russet potato, cubed
1 bell pepper, cut into strips
½ feta, cubed
1 tbsp nutritional yeast
½ tsp garlic powder
½ tsp onion powder
¼ tsp ground turmeric
1 tbsp apple cider vinegar

Preheat air fryer to 400°F. Put in potato cubes and bell pepper strips and Air Fry for 10 minutes. Combine the feta, nutritional yeast, garlic, onion, turmeric, and apple vinegar in a small pan. Fit a trivet in the fryer, lay the pan on top, and Air Fry for 5 more minutes until potatoes are tender and feta cheese cooked. Share potatoes and bell peppers into 2 bowls and top with feta scramble. Serve.

Bagels with Avocado & Tomatoes

Serves: 2 | Total Time: 35 minutes

2/3 cup all-purpose flour
½ tsp active dry yeast
1/3 cup Greek yogurt
8 cherry tomatoes
1 ripe avocado
1 tbsp lemon juice
2 tbsp chopped red onions
Black pepper to taste

Preheat air fryer to 400°F. Beat the flour, dry yeast, and Greek yogurt until you get a smooth dough, adding more flour if necessary. Make 2 equal balls out of the mixture.

Using a rolling pin, roll each ball into a 9-inch long strip. Form a ring with each strip and press the ends together to create 2 bagels. In a bowl with hot water, soak the bagels for 1 minute. Shake excess water and let rise for 15 minutes in the fryer. Bake for 5 minutes, turn the bagels, top with tomatoes, and Bake for another 5 minutes.

Cut avocado in half, discard the pit and remove the flesh into a bowl. Mash with a fork and stir in lemon juice and onions. Once the bagels are ready, let cool slightly and cut them in half. Spread on each half some guacamole, top with 2 slices of Baked tomatoes, and sprinkle with pepper. Serve immediately.

Crispy Samosa Rolls

Serves: 4 | Total Time: 30 minutes

2/3 cup canned peas	1 tsp curry powder
4 scallions, finely sliced	1 tsp Garam masala
2 cups grated potatoes	¼ cup chickpea flour
2 tbsp lemon juice	1 tbsp tahini
1 tsp ground ginger	8 rice paper wrappers

Preheat air fryer to 350°F. Mix the peas, scallions, potatoes, lemon juice, ginger, curry powder, Garam masala, and chickpea flour in a bowl. In another bowl, whisk tahini and 1/3 cup of water until combined. Set aside on a plate.

Submerge the rice wrappers, one by one, into the tahini mixture until they begin to soften and set aside on a plate.

Fill each wrap with 1/3 cup of the veggie mixture and wrap them into a roll. Bake for 15 minutes until golden brown and crispy, turning once. Serve right away.

Apricot-Cheese Mini Pies

Serves: 6 | Total Time: 35 minutes

2 refrigerated piecrusts	1 oz cream cheese
1/3 cup apricot preserves	1 tsp sugar
1 tsp cornstarch	Rainbow sprinkles
½ cup vanilla yogurt	

Preheat air fryer to 370°F. Lay out pie crusts on a flat surface. Cut each sheet of pie crust with a knife into three rectangles for a total of 6 rectangles. Mix apricot preserves and cornstarch in a small bowl. Cover the top half of one rectangle with 1 tbsp of the apricot mixture. Repeat for all rectangles. Fold the bottom of the crust over the preserve-covered top. Crimp and seal all edges with a fork.

Lightly coat each tart with cooking oil, then place into the air fryer without stacking. Bake for 10 minutes. Meanwhile, prepare the frosting by mixing yogurt, cream cheese, and sugar. When tarts are done, let cool completely in the air fryer. Frost the tarts and top with sprinkles. Serve.

Ham & Cheese Sandwiches

Serves: 2 | Total Time: 15 minutes

1 tsp butter	4 Cheddar cheese slices
4 bread slices	4 thick tomato slices
4 deli ham slices	1 tsp dried oregano

Preheat air fryer to 370°F. Smear ½ tsp of butter on only one side of each slice of bread and sprinkle with oregano. On one of the slices, layer 2 slices of ham, 2 slices of cheese, and 2 slices of tomato on the unbuttered side. Place the unbuttered side of another piece of bread onto the toppings. Place the sandwiches, butter side down into the air fryer. Bake for 8 minutes, flipping once until crispy. Let cool slightly, cut in half and serve.

Avocado & Pepper Egg Burrito

Serves: 4 | Total Time: 15 minutes

2 hard-boiled eggs, chopped	1 avocado, chopped
2 oz grated cheddar cheese	3 tbsp salsa
¼ green bell pepper, diced	4 flour tortillas
½ red bell pepper, chopped	1 pickled jalapeño, sliced

Preheat air fryer to 390°F. Combine the eggs, cheddar cheese, bell peppers, avocado, and salsa in a bowl. Spoon the mixture into the tortillas and top with jalapeño slices. Fold the edges and roll up; poke a toothpick through so they hold. Place the burritos in the frying basket and Air Fry for 3-5 minutes until crispy and golden. Serve hot.

Crispy Chicken Cakes

Serves: 4 | Total Time: 30 minutes

1 peeled Granny Smith apple, chopped	
2 scallions, chopped	2 tbsp apple juice
3 tbsp ground almonds	Black pepper to taste
1 tsp garlic powder	1 lb ground chicken
1 egg white	

Preheat air fryer to 330°F. Combine the apple, scallions, almonds, garlic powder, egg white, apple juice, and pepper in a bowl. Add the ground chicken using your hands. Mix well. Make 8 patties and set four in the frying basket. Air Fry for 8-12 minutes until crispy. Repeat with the remaining patties. Serve hot.

Breakfast Chicken Patties with Apples

Serves: 6 | Total Time: 20 minutes

1 lb ground chicken	½ tsp ground nutmeg
1 cup diced apples	¼ tsp cayenne pepper
1 garlic clove, minced	¼ tsp fennel seed
Salt and pepper to taste	1 tsp chopped onion
½ tsp dried sage	½ tsp brown sugar
½ tsp ginger powder	

Preheat air fryer to 350°F. Combine all of the ingredients in a large bowl until well combined. Shape into thick patties. Transfer patties to the parchment-lined frying basket and Air Fry for 3 minutes. Flip the patties and Air Fry for another 3-4 minutes. Serve hot.

Fluffy Vegetable Strata

Serves: 4 | Total Time: 30 minutes

½ red onion, thickly sliced	2 bread slices, cubed
8 asparagus, sliced	3 eggs
1 baby carrot, shredded	3 tbsp milk
4 cup mushrooms, sliced	½ cup mozzarella cheese
½ red bell pepper, chopped	2 tsp chives, chopped

Preheat air fryer to 330°F. Add the red onion, asparagus, carrots, mushrooms, red bell pepper, mushrooms, and 1 tbsp of water to a baking pan. Put it in the air fryer and Bake for 3-5 minutes, until crispy. Remove the pan, add the bread cubes, and shake to mix. Combine the eggs, milk, and chives and pour them over the veggies. Cover with mozzarella cheese. Bake for 12-15 minutes. The strata should puff up and set, while the top should be brown. Serve hot.

Cinnamon Pumpkin Donuts

Serves: 6 | Total Time: 30 minutes

1/3 cup canned pumpkin purée

1 cup flour	3 tbsp milk
3 tbsp brown sugar	2 tbsp butter, melted
½ tsp ground cinnamon	1 large egg
1/8 tsp ground nutmeg	3 tbsp powdered sugar
1 tsp baking powder	

Combine the flour, brown sugar, cinnamon, nutmeg, and baking powder in a bowl. Whisk the pumpkin, milk, butter, and egg white in another bowl. Pour the pumpkin mixture over the dry ingredients and stir. Add more milk or flour if necessary to make a soft dough. Cover your hands in flour, make 12 pieces from the dough, and form them into balls. Measure the frying basket, then cut foil or parchment paper about an inch smaller than the measurement. Poke holes in it and put it in the basket.

Preheat air fryer to 360°F. Set the donut holes in the basket and Air Fry for 5-7 minutes. Allow the donuts to chill for 5 minutes, then roll in powdered sugar. Serve.

Blueberry French Toast Sticks

Serves: 4 | Total Time: 20 minutes

3 bread slices, cut into strips	1 tbsp sugar
1 tbsp butter, melted	½ tsp vanilla extract
2 eggs	1 cup fresh blueberries
1 tbsp milk	1 tbsp lemon juice

Preheat air fryer to 380°F. After laying the bread strips on a plate, sprinkle some melted butter over each piece. Whisk the eggs, milk, vanilla, and sugar, then dip the bread in the mix. Place on a wire rack to let the batter drip. Put the bread strips in the air fryer and Air Fry for 5-7 minutes. Use tongs to flip them once and cook until golden. With a fork, smash the blueberries and lemon juice together. Spoon the blueberries sauce over the French sticks. Serve immediately.

Orange-Glazed Cinnamon Rolls

Serves: | Total Time: 30 minutes

½ cup + 1 tbsp evaporated cane sugar	
1 cup Greek yogurt	2 tsp ground cinnamon
2 cups flour	4 oz cream cheese
2 tsp baking powder	¼ cup orange juice
½ tsp salt	1 tbsp orange zest
4 tbsp butter, softened	1 tbsp lemon juice

Preheat air fryer to 350°F. Grease a baking dish. Combine yogurt, 1 ¾ cups flour, baking powder, salt, and ¼ cup sugar in a large bowl until dough forms. Dust the rest of the flour onto a flat work surface. Transfer the dough to the flour and roll into a ¼-inch thick rectangle. If the dough continues to stick to the rolling pin, add 1 tablespoon of flour and continue to roll.

Mix the butter, cinnamon, orange zest and 1 tbsp of sugar in a bowl. Spread the butter mixture evenly over the dough. Roll the dough into a log, starting with the long side. Tuck in the end. Cut the log into 6 equal pieces. Place in the baking dish swirl-side up. The rolls can touch each other. Bake in the air fryer for 10-12 minutes until the rolls are cooked through, and the tops are golden. Let cool for 10 minutes. While the rolls are cooling, combine cream cheese, the rest of the sugar, lemon juice, and orange juice in a small bowl. When the rolls are cool enough, top with glaze and serve.

Cinnamon Pear Oat Muffins

Serves: 6 | Total Time: 30 minutes + cooling time

½ cup apple sauce	1 1/3 cups rolled oats
1 large egg	1 tsp ground cinnamon
1/3 cup brown sugar	½ tsp baking powder
2 tbsp butter, melted	Pinch of salt
½ cup milk	½ cup diced peeled pears

Preheat the air fryer to 350°F. Place the apple sauce, egg, brown sugar, melted butter, and milk into a bowl and mix to combine. Stir in the oats, cinnamon, baking powder, and salt and mix well, then fold in the pears.

Grease 6 silicone muffin cups with baking spray, then spoon the batter in equal portions into the cups. Put the muffin cups in the frying basket and Bake for 13-18 minutes or until set. Leave to cool for 15 minutes. Serve.

Parsley Egg Scramble with Cottage Cheese

Serves: 2 | Total Time: 15 minutes

1 tbsp cottage cheese, crumbled

4 eggs	2 tsp heavy cream
Salt and pepper to taste	1 tbsp chopped parsley

Preheat air fryer to 400°F. Grease a baking pan with olive oil. Beat the eggs, salt, and pepper in a bowl. Pour it into the pan, place the pan in the frying basket, and Air Fry for 5 minutes. Using a silicone spatula, stir in heavy cream, cottage cheese, and half of the parsley and Air Fry for another 2 minutes. Scatter with parsley to serve.

Oat Muffins with Blueberries

Serves: 6 | Total Time: 25 minutes

¾ cup old-fashioned rolled oats
1 ½ cups flour
½ cup evaporated cane sugar
1 tbsp baking powder
1 tsp ground cinnamon
¼ tsp ground chia seeds
¼ tsp ground sesame seeds
½ tsp salt

1 cup vanilla almond milk
4 tbsp butter, softened
2 eggs
1 tsp vanilla extract
1 cup blueberries
2 tbsp powdered sugar

Preheat air fryer to 350°F. Combine flour, oats, sugar, baking powder, chia seeds, sesame seeds, cinnamon, and salt in a bowl. Mix the almond milk, butter, eggs, and vanilla in another bowl until smooth. Pour in dry ingredients and stir to combine. Fold in blueberries. Fill 12 silicone muffin cups about halfway and place them in the frying basket. Bake for 12-15 minutes until just browned, and a toothpick in the center comes out clean. Cool for 5 minutes. Serve topped with powdered sugar.

Carrot Muffins

Serves: 4 | Total Time: 35 minutes + cooling time

1 ½ cups flour
½ tsp baking soda
½ tsp baking powder
1/3 cup brown sugar
½ tsp ground cinnamon

2 eggs
2/3 cup almond milk
3 tbsp sunflower oil
½ cup shredded carrots
1/3 cup golden raisins

Preheat air fryer to 320°F. Mix the flour, baking powder, baking soda, brown sugar, and cinnamon in a bowl. Whisk the eggs, almond milk, and oil in a smaller bowl. Combine the mixtures, stir, but leave some lumps in the batter. Add the carrots and raisins and stir. Make 8 foil muffin cups by doubling 16 cups. Set 4 cups in the air fryer and put the batter in the cups until they're ¾ full. Bake in the fryer for 13-17 minutes; the muffin tops should bounce when touched. Repeat until all muffins are done. Let the muffins cool on a rack, then serve.

Orange Cran-Bran Muffins

Serves: 4 | Total Time: 30 minutes

1 ½ cups bran cereal flakes
1 cup flour
3 tbsp granulated sugar
1 tbsp orange zest
1 tsp baking powder

1 cup milk
3 tbsp peanut oil
1 egg
½ cup dried cranberries

Preheat air fryer to 320°F. Combine the cereal, flour, granulated sugar, orange zest, and baking powder in a bowl, and in another bowl, beat the milk, oil, and egg. Add the egg mix to the dry ingredients, stir, and then add the cranberries and stir again. Make 8 foil muffin cups by doubling 16 cups. Set 4 cups in the frying basket and spoon the batter in the cups until they're ¾ full. Bake for 15 minutes or until the tops bounce when touched. Set the muffins on a wire rack for 10 minutes, then serve.

Sugar-Dusted Beignets

Serves: 4 | Total Time: 30 minutes

1 tsp fast active dry yeast
1/3 cup buttermilk
3 tbsp brown sugar
1 egg
½ tsp brandy

1 ½ cups flour
3 tbsp chopped dried plums
3 tbsp golden raisins
2 tbsp butter, melted
2 tbsp powdered sugar

Combine the yeast with 3 tbsp of water and leave it until frothy, about 5 minutes. Add the buttermilk, brown sugar, brandy, and egg and stir. Add the flour and stir again. Use your hands to mix the plums and raisins into the dough. Leave the mix in the bowl for 15 minutes.

Preheat air fryer to 330°F. Shape the dough into a square, then slice it into 16 pieces. Make 16 balls, then drizzle butter over the balls. Put the balls in the air fryer in a single layer, ensuring they don't touch. Air Fry for 5-8 minutes until they puff up and are golden. Repeat until all balls are cooked. Toss in powdered sugar and serve.

Maple Peach & Apple Oatmeal

Serves: 4 | Total Time: 15 minutes

2 cups old-fashioned rolled oats
½ tsp baking powder
1 ½ tsp ground cinnamon
¼ tsp ground flaxseeds
⅛ tsp salt
1 ¼ cups vanilla almond milk

¼ cup maple syrup
1 tsp vanilla extract
1 peeled peach, diced
1 peeled apple, diced

Preheat air fryer to 350°F. Mix oats, baking powder, cinnamon, flaxseed, and salt in a large bowl. Next, stir in almond milk, maple syrup, vanilla, ¾ of the diced peaches, and ¾ of the diced apple. Grease 6 ramekins. Divide the batter evenly between the ramekins and transfer the ramekins to the frying basket. Bake in the air fryer for 8-10 minutes until the top is golden and set. Garnish with the rest of the peaches and apples. Serve.

Smooth Walnut-Banana Loaf

Serves: 4 | Total Time: 40 minutes

1/3 cup peanut butter, melted
2 tbsp butter, melted and cooled
¾ cup flour
½ tsp salt
¼ tsp baking soda
2 ripe bananas
2 eggs

1 tsp lemon juice
½ cup evaporated cane sugar
½ cup ground walnuts
1 tbsp blackstrap molasses
1 tsp vanilla extract

Preheat air fryer to 310°F. Mix flour, salt, and baking soda in a small bowl. Mash together bananas and eggs in a large bowl, then stir in sugar, peanut butter, lemon juice, butter, walnuts, molasses, and vanilla. When it is well incorporated, stir in the flour mixture until just combined. Transfer the batter to a parchment-lined baking dish and make sure it is even. Bake in the air fryer for 30-35 minutes until a toothpick in the middle comes out clean and the top is golden. Serve and enjoy.

Seedy Bagels

Serves: 4 | Total Time: 25 minutes

1 cup flour	½ tsp white sesame seeds
2 tsp baking powder	½ tsp black sesame seeds
½ tsp salt	½ tsp coriander seeds
1 cup plain Greek yogurt	1 tsp cumin powder
1 egg	½ tsp dried minced onion
1 tsp water	1 tsp coarse salt
1 tsp poppy seeds	

Preheat air fryer to 300°F. Sift the flour, baking powder, salt, and cumin in a bowl. Stir in yogurt until a sticky dough forms. Place them on a flour-dusted work surface. Separate the dough into 4 equal portions. Roll out each piece of dough into a 6-inch log. Pull the two ends around to meet and press the ends together to seal.

Whisk egg and water in a small bowl. Prepare the topping in another small bowl by combining poppy seeds, white sesame seeds, black sesame seeds, coriander seeds, minced onion, and salt. Brush the egg wash on the bagel tops and sprinkle with the topping. Transfer to the frying basket and bake for 12 to 15 minutes until the tops are golden. Serve and enjoy.

Shakshuka Cups

Serves: 4 | Total Time: 25 minutes

2 tbsp tomato paste	¼ tsp paprika
½ cup chicken broth	4 eggs
4 tomatoes, diced	Salt and pepper to taste
2 garlic cloves, minced	2 scallions, diced
½ tsp dried oregano	½ cup grated cheddar cheese
½ tsp dried coriander	½ cup Parmesan cheese
½ tsp dried basil	4 bread slices, toasted
¼ tsp red pepper flakes	

Preheat air fryer to 350°F. Combine the tomato paste, chicken broth, tomatoes, garlic, oregano, coriander, basil, red pepper flakes, and paprika. Pour the mixture evenly into greased ramekins. Bake in the air fryer for 5 minutes.

Carefully remove the ramekins, crack one egg in each ramekin, and then season with salt and pepper. Top with scallions, grated cheese, and Parmesan cheese. Return the ramekins to the frying basket and bake for 3-5 minutes until the eggs are set, and the cheese is melted. Serve with toasted bread immediately.

Garlic & Thyme Steak with Fried Eggs

Serves: 1 | Total Time: 25 minutes

2 tsp butter, melted	½ tsp chili powder
½ tsp dry thyme	Salt and pepper to taste
1 garlic clove, minced	2 eggs
1 (8-oz) sirloin steak	2 dill pickles, sliced

Preheat air fryer to 400°F. Combine the butter, thyme, garlic, chili powder, salt, and pepper in a small bowl. Rub the spice mixture on both sides of the sirloin steak. Transfer the steak to the frying basket.

Cook it for 4 minutes. Then flip the steak and cook for another 3 minutes. Remove the steak to a plate and cover loosely with foil. Allow it to rest.

Crack the eggs into a greased ramekin. Season with salt and pepper. Transfer the ramekin to the frying basket and bake for 4-5 minutes until the egg whites are cooked and set. Remove the foil from the steak. Top with fried eggs. Serve with sliced pickles on the side and enjoy!

Cheddar & Egg Scramble

Serves: 4 | Total Time: 20 minutes

8 eggs	3 tbsp butter, melted
¼ cup buttermilk	1 cup grated cheddar
¼ cup milk	1 tbsp minced parsley
Salt and pepper to taste	

Preheat the air fryer to 350°F. Whisk the eggs in a bowl until foamy. Add the buttermilk, milk, salt, and pepper and whisk again. Set aside. Grease a cake pan with some melted butter and pour in the egg mixture. Put the pan in the air fryer and cook for 10 minutes, stirring twice with a spatula. Mix the cheddar cheese with the remaining butter and pour the mixture over the eggs. Stir gently and cook for 3-4 more minutes or until the eggs have set. Remove the cake pan and scoop the eggs into a serving plate. Scatter with freshly minced parsley and serve.

Aromatic Mushroom Omelet

Serves: 4 | Total Time: 30 minutes

6 eggs	1 tsp dried oregano
2 tbsp milk	1 tbsp chopped chives
½ yellow onion, diced	½ tbsp chopped dill
½ cup diced mushrooms	½ cup grated Gruyère cheese
2 tbsp chopped parsley	

Preheat air fryer to 350°F. Beat eggs in a medium bowl, then add the rest of the ingredients, except for the parsley. Stir until completely combined. Pour the mixture into a greased pan and bake in the air fryer for 18-20 minutes until the eggs are set. Top with parsley and serve.

Chicken Scotch Eggs

Serves 4 | Total Time: 25 minutes

1 lb ground chicken	1 lemon, zested
2 tsp Dijon mustard	Salt and pepper to taste
2 tsp grated yellow onion	4 hard-boiled eggs, peeled
1 tbsp chopped chives	1 egg, beaten
1 tbsp chopped parsley	1 cup bread crumbs
⅛ tsp ground nutmeg	2 tsp olive oil

Preheat air fryer to 350°F. In a bowl, mix the ground chicken, mustard, onion, chives, parsley, nutmeg, salt, lemon zest and pepper. Shape into 4 oval balls and form the balls evenly around the boiled eggs. Submerge them in the beaten egg and dip in the crumbs. Brush with olive oil. Place the scotch eggs in the frying basket and Air Fry for 14 minutes, flipping once. Serve hot.

Fancy Cranberry Muffins

Serves: 6 | Total Time: 30 minutes

1 cup all-purpose flour	3 tbsp sugar
2 tbsp whole wheat flour	½ cup dried cranberries
1 tsp baking powder	1 egg
⅛ tsp baking soda	1/3 cup buttermilk
Pinch of salt	3 tbsp butter, melted

Preheat the air fryer to 350°F. Sift together all-purpose and whole wheat flours, baking powder, baking soda, and salt into a bowl and stir in the sugar. Add in the cranberries and stir; set aside. Whisk the egg, buttermilk, and melted butter into a bowl until combined. Fold the egg mixture into the flour mixture and stir to combine.

Grease 6 silicone muffin cups with baking spray. Fill each muffin cup about 2/3, leaving room at the top for rising. Put the muffin cups in the frying basket and bake 14-18 minutes or until a skewer inserted into the center comes out clean. Set on a wire rack for cooling, then serve.

Easy Vanilla Muffins

Serves: 6 | Total Time: 35 minutes + cooling time

1 1/3 cups flour	¼ cup milk
5 tbsp butter, melted	1 large egg
¼ cup brown sugar	1 tsp vanilla extract
2 tbsp raisins	1 tsp baking powder
½ tsp ground cinnamon	Pinch of salt
1/3 cup granulated sugar	

Preheat the air fryer to 330°F. Combine 1/3 cup of flour, 2 ½ tbsp of butter, brown sugar, and cinnamon in a bowl and mix until crumbly. Set aside. In another bowl, combine the remaining butter, granulated sugar, milk, egg, and vanilla and stir well. Add the remaining flour, baking powder, raisins, and salt and stir until combined.

Spray 6 silicone muffin cups with baking spray and spoon half the batter into them. Add a tsp of the cinnamon mixture, then add the rest of the batter and sprinkle with the remaining cinnamon mixture, pressing into the batter. Put the muffin cups in the frying basket and Bake for 14-18 minutes or until a toothpick inserted into the center comes out clean. Cool for 10 minutes, then remove the muffins from the cups. Serve and enjoy!

Breakfast Frittata

Serves: 2 | Total Time: 25 minutes

4 cooked pancetta slices, chopped	
5 eggs	1 tomato, sliced
Salt and pepper to taste	1 cup iceberg lettuce, torn
½ leek, thinly sliced	2 tbsp milk
½ cup grated cheddar cheese	

Preheat air fryer to 320°F. Beat the eggs, milk, salt, and pepper in a bowl. Mix in pancetta and cheddar. Transfer to a greased with olive oil baking pan. Top with tomato slices and leek and place it in the frying basket. Bake for 14 minutes. Let cool for 5 minutes. Serve with lettuce.

Lemon-Blueberry Morning Bread

Serves 2 | Total Time: 15 minutes

½ cup flour	1 egg
¼ cup powdered sugar	½ tsp gelatin
½ tsp baking powder	½ tsp vanilla extract
⅛ tsp salt	1 tsp lemon zest
2 tbsp butter, melted	½ cup blueberries

Preheat air fryer to 300°F. Mix the flour, sugar, baking powder, and salt in a bowl. In another bowl, whisk the butter, egg, gelatin, lemon zest, vanilla extract, and blueberries. Add egg mixture to flour mixture and stir until smooth. Spoon mixture into a pizza pan. Place pan in the frying basket and Bake for 10 minutes. Let sit for 5 minutes before slicing. Serve immediately.

Shakshuka-Style Pepper Cups

Serves 4 | Total Time: 35 minutes

2 tbsp ricotta cheese crumbles	
1 tbsp olive oil	½ tsp granular sugar
½ yellow onion, diced	¼ tsp ground cumin
2 cloves garlic, minced	¼ tsp ground coriander
¼ tsp turmeric	⅛ tsp cayenne pepper
1 (14-oz) can diced tomatoes	4 bell peppers
1 tbsp tomato paste	4 eggs
½ tsp smoked paprika	2 tbsp chopped basil
½ tsp salt	

Warm the olive oil in a saucepan over medium heat. Stir-fry the onion for 10 minutes or until softened. Stir in the garlic and turmeric for another 1 minute. Add diced tomatoes, tomato paste, paprika, salt, sugar, cumin, coriander, and cayenne. Remove from heat and stir.

Preheat air fryer to 350°F. Slice the tops off the peppers and carefully remove the core and seeds. Put the bell peppers in the frying basket. Divide the tomato mixture among bell peppers. Crack 1 egg into tomato mixture in each pepper. Bake for 8-10 minutes. Sprinkle with ricotta cheese and cook for 1 more minute. Let rest 5 minutes. Garnish with fresh basil and serve immediately.

Vodka Basil Muffins with Strawberries

Serves 6 | Total Time: 20 minutes

½ cup flour	¼ tsp vanilla extract
½ cup granular sugar	3 tbsp butter, melted
½ tsp baking powder	2 eggs
⅛ tsp salt	¼ tsp vodka
½ cup chopped strawberries	1 tbsp chopped basil

Preheat air fryer to 375°F. Combine the dry ingredients in a bowl. Set aside. In another bowl, whisk the wet ingredients. Pour wet ingredients into the bowl with the dry ingredients and gently combine. Add basil and vodka to the batter. Do not overmix and spoon batter into six silicone cupcake liners lightly greased with olive oil. Place liners in the frying basket and Bake for 7 minutes. Let cool for 5 minutes onto a cooling rack before serving.

Spiced Apple Roll-Ups

Serves: 8 | Total Time: 40 minutes

2 Granny Smith apples, peeled and cored
3 tbsp ground cinnamon   ½ lemon, juiced and zested
3 tbsp granulated sugar   10 tbsp butter, melted
2 tsp ground nutmeg   2 tbsp brown sugar
1 tsp ground cardamom   8 thin slices white sandwich
½ tsp ground allspice   bread, crusts cut off

Preheat the air fryer to 350°F. Combine the cinnamon, granulated sugar, nutmeg, lemon juice and zest, cardamom, and allspice in a bowl and mix well. Pour the spice mix into a small glass jar and set aside. Cut the apples into ½-inch pieces and put the pieces in a cake pan. Drizzle 2 tbsp of melted butter on top, then sprinkle brown sugar and a tsp of the spice mix; toss.

Put the pan in the frying basket and Bake the apples for 8-12 minutes or until tender without losing their shape. Remove from the air fryer and put them into a bowl to cool. Lay the sandwich bread slices on a clean workspace and roll with a rolling pin to about ¼ inch thickness.

Top the rolled bread with 2 tbsp of the apple mixture, then roll it up. Dip the roll-ups in the melted butter and sprinkle with ½ tsp of the spice mix. Line a pan with round parchment paper, Put the rolls in a parchment-lined baking pan, seam side down, and Air Fry for 6-9 minutes or until brown and crisp. Serve warm.

Chili Hash Browns

Serves: 4 | Total Time: 45 minutes

1 tbsp ancho chili powder   Salt and pepper to taste
1 tbsp chipotle powder   2 peeled russet potatoes,
2 tsp ground cumin   grated
2 tsp smoked paprika   2 tbsp olive oil
1 tsp garlic powder   1/3 cup chopped onion
1 tsp cayenne pepper   3 garlic cloves, minced

Preheat the air fryer to 400°F. Combine chili powder, cumin, paprika, garlic powder, chipotle, cayenne, and black pepper in a small bowl, then pour into a glass jar with a lid and store in a cool, dry place. Add the olive oil, onion, and garlic to a cake pan, put it in the air fryer, and Bake for 3 minutes. Put the grated potatoes in a bowl and sprinkle with 2 tsp of the spice mixture, toss and add them to the cake pan along with the onion mix. Bake for 20-23 minutes, stirring once or until the potatoes are crispy and golden. Season with salt and serve.

Filled French Toast

Serves: 4 | Total Time: 25 minutes

4 French bread slices   1/3 cup milk
2 tbsp blueberry jam   1 tbsp sugar
1/3 cup fresh blueberries   ½ tsp vanilla extract
2 egg yolks   3 tbsp sour cream

Preheat the air fryer to 370°F. Cut a pocket into the side of each slice of bread. Don't cut all the way through.

Combine the blueberry jam and blueberries and crush the blueberries into the jam with a fork. In a separate bowl, beat the egg yolks with milk, sugar, and vanilla until well combined. Smear some sour cream in the pocket of each bread slice and add the blueberry mixture on top. Squeeze the edges of the bread to close the opening. Dip the bread in the egg mixture. Soak for 3 minutes per side. Put the bread in the greased frying basket and Air Fry for 5 minutes in a single layer. Flip the bread and cook for 3-6 more minutes or until golden.

Huevos Rancheros

Serves: 4 | Total Time: 45 minutes + cooling time

1 tbsp olive oil   1 tsp honey
20 cherry tomatoes, halved   ½ tsp salt
2 chopped plum tomatoes   ⅛ tsp cayenne pepper
¼ cup tomato sauce   ¼ tsp grated nutmeg
2 scallions, sliced   ¼ tsp paprika
2 garlic cloves, minced   4 eggs

Preheat the air fryer to 370°F. Combine the olive oil, cherry tomatoes, plum tomatoes, tomato sauce, scallions, garlic, nutmeg, honey, salt, paprika and cayenne in a 7-inch springform pan that has been wrapped in foil to prevent leaks. Put the pan in the frying basket and

Bake the mix for 15-20 minutes, stirring twice until the tomatoes are soft. Mash some of the tomatoes in the pan with a fork, then stir them into the sauce. Also, break the eggs into the sauce, then return the pan to the fryer and Bake for 2 minutes. Remove the pan from the fryer and stir the eggs into the sauce, whisking them through the sauce. Don't mix in thoroughly. Cook for 4-8 minutes more or until the eggs are set. Let cool, then serve.

Morning Loaded Potato Skins

Serves: 4 | Total Time: 55 minutes

2 large potatoes   2 tbsp milk
1 fried bacon slice, chopped   4 eggs
Salt and pepper to taste   1 scallion, sliced
1 tbsp chopped dill   ¼ cup grated fontina cheese
1 ½ tbsp butter   2 tbsp chopped parsley

Preheat air fryer to 400°F. Wash each potato and poke with fork 3 or 4 times. Place in the frying basket and bake for 40-45 minutes. Remove the potatoes and let cool until they can be handled. Cut each potato in half lengthwise. Scoop out potato flesh but leave enough to maintain the structure of the potato. Transfer the potato flesh to a medium bowl and stir in salt, pepper, dill, bacon, butter, and milk until mashed with some chunky pieces.

Fill the potato skin halves with the potato mixture and press the center of the filling with a spoon about ½-inch deep. Crack an egg in the center of each potato, then top with scallions and cheese. Return the potatoes to the air fryer and bake for 3 to 5 minutes until the egg is cooked to preferred doneness and the cheese is melted. Serve immediately sprinkled with parsley.

Green Egg Quiche

Serves: 4 | Total Time: 30 minutes

1 cup broccoli florets	4 eggs
2 cups baby spinach	2 scallions, chopped
2 garlic cloves, minced	1 red onion, chopped
¼ tsp ground nutmeg	1 tbsp sour cream
1 tbsp olive oil	½ cup grated fontina cheese
Salt and pepper to taste	

Preheat air fryer to 375°F. Combine broccoli, spinach, onion, garlic, nutmeg, olive oil, and salt in a medium bowl, tossing to coat. Arrange the broccoli in a single layer in the parchment-lined frying basket and cook for 5 minutes. Remove and set to the side.

Use the same medium bowl to whisk eggs, salt, pepper, scallions, and sour cream. Add the roasted broccoli and ¼ cup fontina cheese until all ingredients are well combined. Pour the mixture into a greased baking dish and top with cheese. Bake in the air fryer for 15-18 minutes until the center is set. Serve and enjoy.

Oat & Nut Granola

Serves: 6 | Total Time: 25 minutes

2 cups rolled oats	2 tbsp light brown sugar
¼ cup pistachios	3 tbsp butter
¼ cup chopped almonds	½ tsp ground cinnamon
¼ cup chopped cashews	½ cup dried figs
¼ cup honey	

Preheat the air fryer to 325°F. Combine the oats, pistachios, almonds, and cashews in a bowl and toss, then set aside. In a saucepan, cook the honey, brown sugar, butter, and cinnamon over low heat, stirring frequently, about 4 minutes. Melt the butter completely and make sure the mixture is smooth, then pour over the oat mix and stir.

Scoop the granola mixture in a greased baking pan. Put the pan in the frying basket and Bake for 7 minutes, then remove the pan and stir. Cook for another 6-9 minutes or until the granola is golden, then add the dried figs and stir. Remove the pan and let cool. Store in a covered container at room temperature for up to 3 days.

Egg & Bacon Toasts

Serves: 4 | Total Time: 25 minutes

4 French bread slices	½ tsp dried thyme
2 tbsp butter, softened	Salt and pepper to taste
4 eggs	4 oz cooked bacon, crumbled
2 tbsp milk	2/3 cup grated Colby cheese

Preheat the air fryer to 350°F. Brush each slice of bread with butter and Bake in the frying basket for 2-3 minutes until light brown; set aside. Beat together the eggs, milk, thyme, salt, and pepper in a bowl. Transfer to a cake pan and place the pan into the fryer. Bake for 7-8 minutes, stirring once or until the eggs are set. Divide the egg mixture between the bread slices.

Top with bacon and Clby cheese. Return to the fryer and Bake for 4-6 minutes or until the cheese melts and browns in spots. Cut diagonally and serve.

Honey Donuts

Serves: 6 | Total Time: 25 minutes + chilling time

1 refrigerated puff pastry sheet	
2 tsp flour	2 tbsp butter, melted
2 ½ cups powdered sugar	½ tsp vanilla extract
3 tbsp honey	½ tsp ground cinnamon
2 tbsp milk	Pinch of salt

Preheat the air fryer to 325°F. Dust a clean work surface with flour and lay the puff pastry on it, then cut crosswise into five 3-inch wide strips. Cut each strip into thirds for 15 squares. Lay round parchment paper in the bottom of the basket, then add the pastry squares in a single layer.

Make sure none are touching. Bake for 13-18 minutes or until brown, then leave on a rack to cool. Repeat for all dough. Combine the sugar, honey, milk, butter, vanilla, cinnamon, and salt in a small bowl and mix with a wire whisk until combined. Dip the top half of each donut in the glaze, turn the donut glaze side up, and return to the wire rack. Let cool until the glaze sets, then serve.

Cheesy Egg Bites

Serves: 6 | Total Time: 35 minutes

½ cup shredded Muenster cheese	
5 eggs, beaten	Salt and pepper to taste
3 tbsp sour cream	1/3 cup minced bell pepper
½ tsp dried oregano	3 tbsp minced scallions

Preheat the air fryer to 325°F. Make a foil sling: Fold an 18-inch-long piece of heavy-duty aluminum foil lengthwise into thirds. Combine the eggs, sour cream, oregano, salt, and pepper in a bowl. Add the bell peppers, scallions, and cheese and stir. Add the mixture to 6 egg bite cups, making sure to get some of the solids in each cup.

Put the egg bite pan on the sling you made and lower it into the fryer. Leave the foil in but bend down the edges, so they fit. Bake the bites for 10-15 minutes or until a toothpick inserted into the center comes out clean. Remove the egg bite pan using the foil sling. Cool for 5 minutes, then turn the pan upside down over a plate to remove the egg bites. Serve warm.

Wake-Up Veggie & Ham Bake

Serves 4 | Total Time: 25 minutes

25 Brussels sprouts, halved	2 tbsp orange juice
2 mini sweet peppers, diced	¼ tsp salt
1 yellow onion, diced	1 tsp orange zest
3 deli ham slices, diced	

Preheat air fryer to 350°F. Mix the sprouts, sweet peppers, onion, deli ham, orange juice, and salt in a bowl. Transfer to the frying basket and Air Fry for 12 minutes, tossing once. Scatter with orange zest and serve.

Thai Turkey Sausage Patties

Serves 4 | Total Time: 30 minutes

12 oz turkey sausage	¼ tsp Thai curry paste
1 tsp onion powder	¼ tsp red pepper flakes
1 tsp dried coriander	Salt and pepper to taste

Preheat air fryer to 350°F. Place the sausage, onion, coriander, curry paste, red flakes, salt, and black pepper in a large bowl and mix well. Form into eight patties. Arrange the patties on the greased frying basket and Air Fry for 10 minutes, flipping once halfway through. Once the patties are cooked, transfer to a plate and serve hot.

Chorizo Sausage & Cheese Balls

Serves 4 | Total Time: 25 minutes

1 egg white	2 tbsp canned green chiles
1 lb chorizo ground sausage	¼ cup bread crumbs
¼ tsp smoked paprika	¼ cup grated cheddar

Preheat air fryer to 400°F. Mix all ingredients in a large bowl. Form into 16 balls. Put the sausage balls in the frying basket and Air Fry for 6 minutes. When done, shake the basket and cook for an additional 6 minutes. Transfer to a serving plate and serve.

Matcha Granola

Serves 4 | Total Time: 15 minutes

2 tsp matcha green tea	⅛ cup flour
½ cup slivered almonds	⅛ cup almond flour
½ cup pecan pieces	1 tsp vanilla extract
½ cup sunflower seeds	2 tbsp melted butter
½ cup pumpkin seeds	2 tbsp almond butter
1 cup coconut flakes	⅛ tsp salt
¼ cup coconut sugar	

Preheat air fryer to 300°F. Mix the green tea, almonds, pecan, sunflower seeds, pumpkin seeds, coconut flakes, sugar, flour, almond flour, vanilla extract, butter, almond butter, and salt in a bowl. Spoon the mixture into an ungreased round 4-cup baking dish. Place it in the fryer and Bake for 6 minutes, stirring once. Transfer to an airtight container, let cool for 10 minutes, then cover and store at room temperature until ready to serve.

Spicy Sausage & Feta Breakfast Casserole

Serves 2 | Total Time: 25 minutes

¼ cup cooked spicy breakfast sausage	
1 (4.5-oz) can green chiles, including juice	
5 eggs	½ cup feta cheese crumbles
2 tbsp heavy cream	1 tomato, diced
½ tsp ground cumin	1 zucchini, diced
Salt and pepper to taste	2 tbsp parsley, chopped

Preheat air fryer to 325°F. Mix all ingredients in a bowl and pour into a greased baking pan. Place the pan in the frying basket and Bake for 12-14 minutes. Let cool for a few minutes before slicing. Serve right away.

Cheesy Egg Popovers

Serves 6 | Total Time: 30 minutes

5 eggs	Salt and pepper to taste
1 tbsp milk	⅛ tsp ground nutmeg
2 tbsp heavy cream	¼ cup grated Swiss cheese

Preheat air fryer to 350°F. Beat all ingredients in a bowl. Divide between greased muffin cups and place them in the frying basket. Bake for 8-10 minutes. Cool slightly before removing from the muffin cups. Serve and enjoy!

Morning Chicken Frittata Cups

Serves 6 | Total Time: 30 minutes

¼ cup shredded cooked chicken breasts	
3 eggs	¼ cup grated Asiago cheese
2 tbsp heavy cream	2 tbsp chives, chopped
4 tsp Tabasco sauce	

Preheat air fryer to 350°F. Beat all ingredients in a bowl. Divide the egg mixture between greased 6 muffin cups and place them in the frying basket. Bake for 8-10 minutes until set. Leave to cool slightly before serving.

Mini Bacon Egg Quiches

Serves 6 | Total Time: 30 minutes

3 eggs	Salt and pepper to taste
2 tbsp heavy cream	3 oz cooked bacon, crumbled
¼ tsp Dijon mustard	¼ cup grated cheddar

Preheat air fryer to 350°F. Beat the eggs with salt and pepper in a bowl until fluffy. Stir in heavy cream, mustard, cooked bacon, and cheese. Divide the mixture between 6 greased muffin cups and place them in the frying basket. Bake for 8-10 minutes. Let cool slightly before serving.

Crunchy Granola Muffins

Serves 4 | Total Time: 15 minutes

1 cup walnut pieces	⅛ cup pecan flour
1 cup sunflower seeds	2 tsp ground cinnamon
1 cup coconut flakes	2 tbsp melted butter
¼ cup granulated sugar	2 tbsp almond butter
⅛ cup coconut flour	⅛ tsp salt

Preheat air fryer to 300°F. In a bowl, mix the walnuts, sunflower seeds, coconut flakes, sugar, coconut flour, pecan flour, cinnamon, butter, almond butter, and salt.

Spoon the mixture into an ungreased round 4-cup baking dish. Place it in the frying basket and Bake for 6 minutes, stirring once. Transfer to an airtight container, let cool for 10 minutes, then cover and store at room temperature until ready to serve.

SNACKS & APPETIZERS

Curried Pickle Chips

Serves: 4 | Total Time: 25 minutes

2 dill pickles, sliced
1 cup breadcrumbs
2 eggs, beaten

A pinch of white pepper
1 tsp curry powder
½ tsp mustard powder

Preheat air fryer to 350°F. Combine the breadcrumbs, curry, mustard powder, and white pepper in a mixing bowl. Coat the pickle slices with the crumb mixture; then dip into the eggs, then dip again into the dry ingredients. Arrange the coated pickle pieces on the greased frying basket in an even layer. Air Fry for 15 minutes, shaking the basket several times during cooking until crispy, golden brown and perfect. Serve warm.

Beer-Battered Onion Rings

Serves: 4 | Total Time: 25 minutes

2 sliced onions, rings separated
1 cup flour
Salt and pepper to taste

1 tsp garlic powder
1 cup beer

Preheat air fryer to 350°F. In a mixing bowl, combine the flour, garlic powder, beer, salt, and black pepper. Dip the onion rings into the bowl and lay the coated rings in the frying basket. Air Fry for 15 minutes, shaking the basket several times during cooking to jostle the onion rings and ensure a good even fry. Once ready, the onions should be crispy and golden brown. Serve hot.

Hot Avocado Fries

Serves: 2 | Total Time: 20 minutes

1 egg
2 tbsp milk
Salt and pepper to taste

1 cup crushed chili corn chips
2 tbsp Parmesan cheese
1 avocado, sliced into fries

Preheat air fryer to 375°F. In a bowl, beat egg and milk. In another bowl, add crushed chips, Parmesan cheese, salt, and pepper. Dip avocado fries into the egg mixture, then dredge into the crushed chips mixture to coat. Place avocado fries in the greased frying basket and Air Fry for 5 minutes. Serve immediately.

Basil Feta Crostini

Serves: 4 | Total Time: 10 minutes

1 baguette, sliced
¼ cup olive oil
2 garlic cloves, minced

4 oz feta cheese
2 tbsp basil, minced

Preheat air fryer to 380°F. Combine together the olive oil and garlic in a bowl. Brush it over one side of each slice of bread. Put the bread in a single layer in the frying basket and Bake for 5 minutes. In a small bowl, mix together the feta cheese and basil. Remove the toast from the air fryer, then spread a thin layer of the goat cheese mixture over the top of each piece. Serve.

Mediterranean Jacket Potatoes

Serves: 4 | Total Time: 50 minutes

2 russet potatoes
3 tbsp olive oil
Salt and pepper to taste
2 tbsp rosemary, chopped

10 Kalamata olives, diced
¼ cup crumbled feta
2 tbsp chopped dill

Preheat air fryer to 380°F. Poke 2-3 holes in the potatoes with a fork. Drizzle them with some olive oil and sprinkle with salt. Put the potatoes into the frying basket and Bake for 30 minutes. When the potatoes are ready, remove them from the fryer and slice in half. Scoop out the flesh of the potatoes with a spoon, leaving a ½-inch layer of potato inside the skins, and set the skins aside.

Combine the scooped potato middles with the remaining olive oil, salt, black pepper, and rosemary in a medium bowl. Mix until well combined. Spoon the potato filling into the potato skins, spreading it evenly over them. Top with olives, dill and feta. Put the loaded potato skins back into the air fryer and Bake for 15 minutes. Enjoy!

Ranch Potato Chips

Serves: 2 | Total Time: 30 minutes

1 tsp dry ranch seasoning
Salt and pepper to taste
2 cups sliced potatoes

2 tsp olive oil
¼ cup white wine vinegar

Preheat air fryer to 400°F. In a bowl, combine ranch mix, salt, and pepper. Reserve ½ tsp for garnish. In another bowl, mix sliced fingerling potatoes with the vinegar and stir around. Let soak in the vinegar water for at least thirty minutes, then drain the potatoes and pat them dry.

Place potato chips and spread with olive oil until coated. Sprinkle with the ranch mixture and toss to coat. Place potato chips in the frying basket and Air Fry for 16 minutes, shaking 4 times. Transfer it into a bowl. Sprinkle with the reserved mixture and let sit for 15 minutes. Serve immediately.

Crab Cake Bites

Serves: 6 | Total Time: 20 minutes

8 oz lump crab meat
1 diced red bell pepper
1 spring onion, diced
1 garlic clove, minced
1 tbsp capers, minced
1 tbsp cream cheese

1 egg, beaten
¼ cup bread crumbs
¼ tsp salt
1 tbsp olive oil
1 lemon, cut into wedges

Preheat air fryer to 360°F. Combine the crab, bell pepper, spring onion, garlic, and capers in a bowl until combined. Stir in the cream cheese and egg. Mix in the bread crumbs and salt. Divide this mixture into 6 equal portions and pat out into patties. Put the crab cakes into the frying basket in a single layer. Drizzle the tops of each patty with a bit of olive oil and Bake for 10 minutes. Serve with lemon wedges on the side. Enjoy!

Cheesy Green Pitas

Serves: 4 | Total Time: 15 minutes

½ cup canned artichoke hearts, sliced

2 whole-wheat pitas	¼ cup green olives
2 tbsp olive oil, divided	¼ cup grated Pecorino
2 garlic cloves, minced	¼ cup crumbled feta
¼ tsp salt	2 tbsp chopped chervil

Preheat air fryer to 380°F. Lightly brush each pita with some olive oil, then top with garlic and salt. Divide the artichoke hearts, green olives, and cheeses evenly between the two pitas, and put both into the air fryer. Bake for 10 minutes. Remove the pitas and cut them into 4 pieces each before serving. Top with chervil. Enjoy!

Roast the shrimp for 4 minutes, then open the air fryer and place the ramekin with oil and garlic in the basket beside the shrimp packet. Cook for 2 more minutes. Place the shrimp on a serving plate or platter with the ramekin of garlic olive oil on the side for dipping.

Spicy Pearl Onion Dip

Serves: 4 | Total Time: 20 minutes+chilling time

2 cups peeled pearl onions	¼ tsp Worcestershire sauce
3 garlic cloves	1 tbsp lemon juice
3 tbsp olive oil	⅛ tsp red pepper flakes
Salt and pepper to taste	1 tbsp chives, chopped
1 cup Greek yogurt	

Preheat air fryer to 360°F. Place the onions, garlic, and 2 tbsp of olive oil in a bowl and combine until the onions are well coated. Pour the mixture into the frying basket and Roast for 11-13 minutes. Transfer the garlic and onions to your food processor. Pulse the vegetables several times until the onions are minced but still have some chunks.

Combine the garlic and onions and the remaining olive oil, along with the salt, yogurt, Worcestershire sauce, lemon juice, black pepper, chives and red pepper flakes in a bowl. Cover and chill for at least 1 hour. Serve with toasted bread if desired.

Chili Black Bean Empanadas

Serves: 4 | Total Time: 20 minutes

½ cup cooked black beans	½ tsp garlic salt
¼ cup white onions, diced	½ tsp ground cumin
1 tsp red chili powder	½ tsp ground cinnamon
½ tsp paprika	4 empanada dough shells

Preheat air fryer to 350°F. Stir-fry black beans and onions in a pan over medium heat for 5 minutes. Add chili, paprika, garlic salt, cumin, and cinnamon. Set aside covered when onions are soft and the beans are hot.

On a clean workspace, lay the empanada shells. Spoon bean mixture onto shells without spilling. Fold the shells over to cover fully. Seal the edges with water and press with a fork. Transfer the empanadas to the foil-lined frying basket and Bake for 15 minutes, flipping once halfway through cooking. Cook until golden. Serve.

Fried String Beans with Greek Sauce

Serves: 4 | Total Time: 10 minutes

1 egg	¼ lemon zest
1 tbsp flour	½ lb whole string beans
¼ tsp paprika	½ cup Greek yogurt
½ tsp garlic powder	1 tbsp lemon juice
Salt to taste	⅛ tsp cayenne pepper
¼ cup bread crumbs	

Preheat air fryer to 380°F. Whisk the egg and 2 tbsp of water in a bowl until frothy. Sift the flour, paprika, garlic powder, and salt in another bowl, then stir in the bread crumbs. Dip each string bean into the egg mixture, then roll into the bread crumb mixture. Put the string beans in a single layer in the greased frying basket. Air Fry them for 5 minutes until the breading is golden brown. Stir the yogurt, lemon juice and zest, salt, and cayenne in a small bowl. Serve the bean fries with lemon-yogurt sauce.

Hot Shrimp

Serves: 4 | Total Time: 15 minutes

1 lb shrimp, cleaned and deveined	
4 tbsp olive oil	½ tsp salt
½ lime, juiced	¼ tsp chili powder
3 garlic cloves, minced	

Preheat air fryer to 380°F. Toss the shrimp with 2 tbsp of olive oil, lime juice, 1/3 of garlic, salt, and red chili powder in a bowl. Mix the remaining olive oil and garlic in a small ramekin. Pour the shrimp into the center of a piece of aluminum foil, then fold the sides up and crimp the edges so that it forms an aluminum foil bowl that is open on top. Put the resulting packet into the frying basket.

Olive Oil Pita Crackers

Serves: 2 | Total Time: 15 minutes

2 pitas, cut into wedges	½ tsp garlic salt
1 tbsp olive oil	¼ tsp paprika

Preheat air fryer to 360°F. Coat the pita wedges with olive oil, paprika and garlic salt in a bowl. Put them into the frying basket and Air Fry for 6-8 minutes. Serve warm.

Olive & Pepper Tapenade

Serves: 4 | Total Time: 10 minutes

1 red bell pepper	1 garlic clove, minced
3 tbsp olive oil	½ tsp dried oregano
½ cup black olives, chopped	1 tbsp white wine juice

Preheat air fryer to 380°F. Lightly brush the outside of the bell pepper with some olive oil and put it in the frying basket. Roast for 5 minutes. Combine the remaining olive oil with olives, garlic, oregano, and white wine in a bowl. Remove the red pepper from the air fryer, then gently slice off the stem and discard the seeds. Chop into small pieces. Add the chopped pepper to the olive mixture and stir all together until combined. Serve and enjoy!

Goat Cheese & Zucchini Roulades

Serves: 6 | Total Time: 20 minutes

½ cup goat cheese
1 garlic clove, minced
2 tbsp basil, minced
1 tbsp capers, minced
1 tbsp dill pickles, chopped
⅛ tsp salt
⅛ tsp red pepper flakes
1 tbsp lemon juice
2 zucchini, cut into strips

Preheat air fryer to 360°F. Place the goat cheese, garlic, basil, capers, dill pickles, salt, red pepper flakes, and lemon juice in a bowl and stir to combine. Divide the filling between zucchini slices, then roll up and secure with a toothpick through the middle. Arrange the zucchini roulades on the greased frying basket. Bake for 10 minutes. When ready, gently remove the toothpicks and serve.

Tasty Roasted Black Olives & Tomatoes

Serves: 6 | Total Time: 25 minutes

2 cups grape tomatoes
4 garlic cloves, chopped
½ red onion, chopped
1 cup black olives
1 cup green olives
1 tbsp thyme, minced
1 tbsp oregano, minced
2 tbsp olive oil
½ tsp salt

Preheat air fryer to 380°F. Add all ingredients to a bowl and toss well to coat. Pour the mixture into the frying basket and Roast for 10 minutes. Stir the mixture, then Roast for an additional 10 minutes. Serve and enjoy!

Tomato & Basil Bruschetta

Serves: 4 | Total Time: 15 minutes

3 red tomatoes, diced
½ ciabatta loaf
1 garlic clove, minced
1 fresh mozzarella ball, sliced
1 tbsp olive oil
10 fresh basil, chopped
1 tsp balsamic vinegar
Pinch of salt

Preheat air fryer to 370°F. Mix tomatoes, olive oil, salt, vinegar, basil, and garlic in a bowl until well combined. Cut the loaf into 6 slices, about 1-inch thick. Spoon the tomato mixture over the bread and top with one mozzarella slice. Repeat for all bruschettas. Put the bruschettas in the foil-lined frying basket and Bake for 5 minutes until golden. Serve.

Oregano Cheese Rolls

Serves: 4 | Total Time: 25 minutes

¼ cup grated cheddar cheese
¼ cup blue cheese, crumbled
8 flaky pastry dough sheets
1 tbsp vegetable oil
1 tsp dry oregano

Preheat air fryer to 350°F. Mix the cheddar cheese, blue cheese, and oregano in a bowl. Divide the cheese mixture between pastry sheets and seal the seams with a touch of water. Brush the pastry rolls with vegetable oil. Arrange them on the greased frying basket and Bake for 15 minutes or until the pastry crust is golden brown and the cheese is melted. Serve hot.

Turkey Spring Rolls

Serves: 4 | Total Time: 20 minutes

1 lb turkey breast, grilled, cut into chunks
1 celery stalk, julienned
1 carrot, grated
1 tsp fresh ginger, minced
1 tsp sugar
1 tsp chicken stock powder
1 egg
1 tsp corn starch
6 spring roll wrappers

Preheat the air fryer to 360°F. Mix the turkey, celery, carrot, ginger, sugar, and chicken stock powder in a large bowl. Combine thoroughly and set aside. In another bowl, beat the egg, and stir in the cornstarch. On a clean surface, spoon the turkey filling into each spring roll, roll up and seal the seams with the egg-cornstarch mixture. Put each roll in the greased frying basket and Air Fry for 7-8 minutes, flipping once until golden brown. Serve hot.

Spanish Fried Baby Squid

Serves: 2 | Total Time: 30 minutes

1 cup baby squid
½ cup semolina flour
½ tsp Spanish paprika
½ tsp garlic powder
2 eggs
Salt and pepper to taste
2 tbsp lemon juice
1 tsp Old Bay seasoning

Preheat air fryer to 350°F. Beat the eggs in a bowl. Stir in lemon juice and set aside. Mix flour, Old Bay seasoning, garlic powder, paprika, salt, and pepper in another bowl. Dip each piece of squid into the flour, then into the eggs, and then again. Transfer them to the greased frying basket and Air Fry for 18-20 minutes, shaking the basket occasionally until crispy and golden brown. Serve hot.

Bacon-Wrapped Shrimp Bites

Serves: 4 | Total Time: 15 minutes

2 jumbo shrimp, peeled
2 bacon strips, sliced
2 tbsp lemon juice
½ tsp chipotle powder
½ tsp garlic salt

Preheat air fryer to 350°F. Wrap the bacon around the shrimp and place the shrimp in the foil-lined frying basket, seam side down. Drizzle with lemon juice, chipotle powder and garlic salt. Air Fry for 10 minutes, turning the shrimp once until cooked through and bacon is crispy. Serve hot.

Cheddar Stuffed Jalapeños

Serves: 5 | Total Time: 15 minutes

10 jalapeño peppers
6 oz ricotta cheese
¼ cup grated cheddar
2 tbsp bread crumbs

Preheat air fryer to 340°F. Cut jalapeños in half lengthwise. Clean out the seeds and membrane. Set aside. Microwave ricotta cheese in a small bowl for 15 seconds to soften. Stir in cheddar cheese to combine. Stuff each jalapeño half with the cheese mixture. Top the poppers with bread crumbs. Place in air fryer and lightly spray with cooking oil. Bake for 5-6 minutes. Serve warm.

Poppy Seed Mini Hot Dog Rolls

Serves: 4 | Total Time: 25 minutes

8 small mini hot dogs	1 tbsp vegetable oil
8 pastry dough sheets	1 tbsp poppy seeds

Preheat the air fryer to 350°F. Roll the mini hot dogs into a pastry dough sheet, wrapping them snugly. Brush the rolls with vegetable oil on all sides. Arrange them on the frying basket and sprinkle poppy seeds on top. Bake for 15 minutes until the pastry crust is golden brown. Serve.

Oyster Spring Rolls

Serves: 4 | Total Time: 20 minutes

¼ cup button mushrooms, diced	
¼ cup bean sprouts	1 tsp Vegeta seasoning
1 celery stalk, julienned	½ tsp oyster sauce
1 carrot, grated	1 egg
1 tsp fresh ginger, minced	1 tsp corn starch
1 tsp sugar	6 spring roll wrappers

Preheat the air fryer to 360°F. Combine the mushrooms, bean sprouts, celery, carrot, ginger, sugar, Vegeta seasoning, oyster sauce and stock powder in a mixing bowl. In a second bowl, beat the egg, and stir in the cornstarch.

On a clean surface, spoon vegetable filling into each roll, roll up and seal the seams with the egg-cornstarch mixture. Put the rolls in the greased frying basket and Air Fry for 7-8 minutes, flipping once until golden brown. Serve hot.

Easy Crab Cakes

Serves: 4 | Total Time: 20 minutes

1 cup lump crab meat	1 tsp fresh grated ginger
2 green onions, minced	½ tsp allspice
3 garlic cloves, minced	½ cup breadcrumbs
½ lime, juiced	2 tsp oyster sauce
2 tbsp mayonnaise	2 tsp spicy mustard
2 eggs, beaten	Pinch of black pepper

Preheat air fryer to 350°F. Place the crab meat, lime juice, mayonnaise, onions, garlic, ginger, oyster sauce, mustard, allspice, and black pepper in a large mixing bowl. Stir thoroughly until all the ingredients are evenly combined.

Form the mixture into patties. Dip the patties into the beaten eggs, and then roll in the breadcrumbs, coating thoroughly on all sides. Place the coated cakes in the lined frying basket and Air Fry for 5 minutes. Flip the cakes over and cook for another 5 minutes until golden brown and crispy on the outside and tantalizingly juicy on the inside. Serve hot.

Cheesy Green Dip

Serves: 6 | Total Time: 30 minutes

½ cup canned artichoke hearts, chopped	
½ cup cream cheese, softened	
2 tbsp grated Romano cheese	½ cup milk
¼ cup grated mozzarella	Salt and pepper to taste
½ cup spinach, chopped	

Preheat air fryer to 350°F. Whisk the milk, cream cheese, Romano cheese, spinach, artichoke hearts, salt, and pepper in a mixing bowl. Pour the mixture into a greased baking pan, and sprinkle the grated mozzarella cheese over the top. Bake in the air fryer for 20 minutes. Serve.

Wrapped Smokies in Bacon

Serves: 4 | Total Time: 15 minutes

8 small smokies	Salt and pepper to taste
8 bacon strips, sliced	

Preheat air fryer to 350°F. Wrap the bacon slices around smokies. Arrange the rolls, seam side down, on the greased frying basket. Sprinkle with salt and pepper and Air Fry for 5-8 minutes, turning once until the bacon is crisp and juicy around them. Serve and enjoy!

Italian Bruschetta with Mushrooms & Cheese

Serves: 4 | Total Time: 25 minutes

½ cup button mushrooms, chopped	
½ baguette, sliced	1 tbsp extra virgin olive oil
1 garlic clove, minced	Salt and pepper to taste
3 oz sliced Parmesan cheese	

Preheat air fryer to 350°F. Add the mushrooms, olive oil, salt, pepper, and garlic to a mixing bowl and stir thoroughly to combine. Divide the mushroom mixture between the bread slices, drizzling all over the surface with olive oil, then cover with Parmesan slices. Place the covered bread slices in the greased frying basket and Bake for 15 minutes. Serve and enjoy!

Black Olive Jalapeño Poppers

Serves: 5 | Total Time: 20 minutes

5 jalapeño peppers, cut lengthwise, seeded	
¼ cup cream cheese, softened	
¼ cup grated cheddar	1 tbsp mayonnaise
1 tbsp chopped black olives	1 tbsp Parmesan cheese
1 tbsp chopped green olives	1 tbsp dried parsley
1 tsp dried oregano	

Preheat air fryer to 350°F. Mix all ingredients, except jalapeños, in a bowl. Add the prepared mixture into each jalapeño half. Lay stuffed peppers in the frying basket and Bake for 8 minutes. Transfer them to a serving plate. Serve right away and sprinkle with dried parsley.

Baby Spinach Quesadillas

Serves: 2 | Total Time: 35 minutes

4 tbsp shredded cheddar cheese	
4 soft corn tortillas	¼ tsp chili powder
1 tsp olive oil	1 cup baby spinach

Preheat air fryer to 360°F. Spread cheese and spinach over 2 tortillas, sprinkle with chili, and top each with the remaining tortillas. Brush the tops with oil. Place quesadillas in the frying basket and Air Fry for 6 minutes.

Buffalo Chicken Wings

Serves: 6 | Total Time: 60 minutes

2 lb chicken wings, split at the joint
1 tbsp butter, softened
½ cup buffalo wing sauce
1 tbs salt
1 tsp black pepper
1 tsp red chili powder
1 tsp garlic-ginger puree

Preheat air fryer to 400°F. Sprinkle the chicken wings with salt, pepper, red chili powder, grated garlic, and ginger. Place the chicken wings in the greased frying basket and Air Fry for 12 minutes, tossing once. Whisk butter and buffalo sauce in a large bowl. Air Fry for 10 more minutes, shaking once. Once done, transfer it into the bowl with the sauce. Serve immediately.

Dijon Chicken Wings

Serves: 6 | Total Time: 60 minutes

2 lb chicken wings, split at the joint
1 tbsp water
1 tbs salt
1 tsp black pepper
1 tsp red chili powder
1 tbsp butter, melted
1 tbsp Dijon mustard
¼ cup honey
1 tsp apple cider vinegar
Salt to taste

Preheat air fryer to 250°F. Pour water in the bottom of the frying basket to ensure minimum smoke from fat drippings. Sprinkle the chicken wings with salt, pepper, and red chili powder. Place chicken wings in the greased frying basket and Air Fry for 12 minutes, tossing once. Whisk the remaining ingredients in a bowl. Add in chicken wings and toss to coat. Serve immediately.

Cheddar-Pimiento Strips

Serves: 4 | Total Time: 35 minutes

8 oz shredded sharp cheddar cheese
1 (4-oz) jar chopped pimientos, including juice
¼ cup mayonnaise
¼ cup cream cheese
Salt and pepper to taste
1 tsp chopped parsley
8 sandwich bread slices
4 tbsp butter, melted

In a bowl, mix the cheddar cheese, cream cheese, pimientos, mayonnaise, salt, parsley and pepper. Let chill covered in the fridge for 30 minutes.

Preheat air fryer to 350°F. Spread pimiento mixture over 4 bread slices, then top with the remaining slices and press down just enough to not smoosh cheese out of the sandwich edges. Brush the top and bottom of each sandwich lightly with melted butter. Place sandwiches in the frying basket and Grill for 6 minutes, flipping once. Slice each sandwich into 16 sections and serve warm.

Thai-Style Crab Wontons

Serves: 4 | Total Time: 20 minutes

4 oz cottage cheese, softened
2 ½ oz lump crabmeat
2 scallions, chopped
2 garlic cloves, minced
2 tsp tamari sauce
12 wonton wrappers
1 egg white, beaten
5 tbsp Thai sweet chili sauce

Using a fork, mix together cottage cheese, crabmeat, scallions, garlic, and tamari sauce in a bowl. Set it near your workspace along with a small bowl of water. Place one wonton wrapper on a clean surface. The points should be facing so that it looks like a diamond. Put 1 level tbsp of the crab and cheese mixture onto the center of the wonton wrapper. Dip your finger into the water and run the moist finger along the edges of the wrapper.

Fold one corner of the wrapper to the opposite side and make a triangle. From the center out, press out any air and seal the edges. Continue this process until all of the wontons have been filled and sealed. Brush both sides of the wontons with beaten egg white.

Preheat air fryer to 340°F. Place the wontons on the bottom of the greased frying basket in a single layer. Bake for 8 minutes, flipping the wontons once until golden brown and crispy. Serve hot and enjoy!

Chicken Wings with Yogurt Dip

Serves: 4 | Total Time: 35 minutes

2 lb chicken wing portions
1 tbsp chili sauce
1 tsp dried oregano
1 tsp smoked paprika
1 tsp garlic powder
½ tsp salt
¼ cup Greek yogurt
¼ cup mayonnaise
1 tbsp lemon juice
2 tbsp chopped parsley
1 cucumber, cut into sticks
2 carrots, cut into sticks

Add the chicken wings, chili sauce, oregano, garlic powder, smoked paprika, and salt to a large bowl. Toss to coat well, then set aside. In a small bowl, mix the mayonnaise and yogurt. Stir in lemon juice and parsley until blended. Refrigerate covered until it is time to serve.

Preheat air fryer to 390°F. Place the chicken in the greased frying basket and Air Fry for 20-25 minutes, flipping the chicken once, until crispy and browned. Serve the chicken with cucumber, carrot sticks, and yogurt dip.

Cajun-Spiced Pickle Chips

Serves: 4 | Total Time: 20 minutes

16 oz canned pickle slices
½ cup flour
2 tbsp cornmeal
3 tsp Cajun seasoning
1 tbsp dried parsley
1 egg, beaten
¼ tsp hot sauce
½ cup buttermilk
3 tbsp light mayonnaise
3 tbsp chopped chives
⅛ tsp garlic powder
⅛ tsp onion powder
Salt and pepper to taste

Preheat air fryer to 350°F. Mix flour, cornmeal, Cajun seasoning, and parsley in a bowl. Put the beaten egg in a small bowl nearby. One at a time, dip a pickle slice in the egg, then roll in the crumb mixture. Gently press the crumbs, so they stick to the pickle. Place the chips in the greased frying basket and Air Fry for 7-9 minutes, flipping once until golden and crispy. In a bowl, whisk hot sauce, buttermilk, mayonnaise, chives, garlic and onion powder, salt, and pepper. Serve with pickles.

Hot Nachos with Chile Salsa

Serves: 4 | Total Time: 20 minutes

½ chile de árbol pepper, seeds removed
1 tbsp olive oil
Salt to taste
1 shallot, chopped
2 garlic cloves
1 can diced tomatoes
2 tbsp fresh cilantro
Juice of 1 lime
¼ tsp chili-lime seasoning
6 corn tortillas

Add the shallot, garlic, chile de árbol, tomatoes, cilantro, lime juice and salt in a food processor. Pulse until combined and chunky. Pour the salsa into a serving bowl and set aside. Drizzle olive oil on both sides of the tortillas. Stack the tortilla and cut them in half with a sharp knife. Continue to cut into quarters, then cut again so that each tortilla is cut into 8 equal wedges. Season both sides of each wedge with chile-lime seasoning.

Preheat air fryer to 400°F. Place the tortilla wedges in the greased frying basket and Air Fry for 4-7 minutes, shaking once until the chips are golden and crisp. Allow to cool slightly and serve with previously prepared salsa.

BBQ Potato Chips

Serves: 2 | Total Time: 30 minutes

1 scrubbed russet potato, sliced
½ tsp smoked paprika
¼ tsp chili powder
¼ tsp garlic powder
1/8 tsp onion powder
¼ tbsp smoked paprika
1/8 tsp light brown sugar
Salt and pepper to taste
2 tsp olive oil

Preheat air fryer to 400°F. Combine all seasoning in a bowl. Set aside. In another bowl, mix potato chips, olive oil, black pepper, and salt until coated. Place potato chips in the frying basket and Air Fry for 17 minutes, shaking 3 times. Transfer it into a bowl. Sprinkle with the bbq mixture and let sit for 15 minutes. Serve immediately.

Rich Clam Spread

Serves: 6 | Total Time: 40 minutes

2 (6.5-oz) cans chopped clams in clam juice
1/3 cup panko bread crumbs
1 garlic clove, minced
1 tbsp olive oil
1 tbsp lemon juice
¼ tsp hot sauce
1 tsp Worcestershire sauce
½ tsp shallot powder
¼ tsp dried dill
Salt and pepper to taste
½ tsp sweet paprika
4 tsp grated Parmesan cheese
2 celery stalks, chopped

Completely drain one can of clams. Add them to a bowl along with the entire can of clams, breadcrumbs, garlic, olive oil, lemon juice, Worcestershire sauce, hot sauce, shallot powder, dill, pepper, salt, paprika, and 2 tbsp Parmesan. Combine well and set aside for 10 minutes. After that time, put the mixture in a greased baking dish.

Preheat air fryer to 325°F. Put the dish in the air fryer and Bake for 10 minutes. Sprinkle the remaining paprika and Parmesan, and continue to cook until golden brown on top, 8-10 minutes. Serve hot along with celery sticks.

Crab-Stuffed Mushrooms

Serves: 4 | Total Time: 20 minutes

½ cup shredded mozzarella cheese
8 portobello mushrooms
1 tbsp olive oil
¼ tsp salt
3 oz lump crabmeat
3 tsp grated Parmesan cheese
¼ cup panko bread crumbs
1 tbsp ground walnuts
3 tsp mayonnaise
2 tbsp chopped chives
1 egg, beaten
1 garlic clove, minced
¼ tsp seafood seasoning
1 tbsp chopped cilantro

Clean the mushrooms with a damp paper towel. Remove stems and chop them finely. Set aside. Take the mushroom caps and brush with oil before sprinkling with salt. Combine the remaining ingredients, excluding mozzarella, in a bowl. Spoon crab filling mixture into each mushroom cap. Top each cap with mozzarella and press down so that it may stick to the filling.

Preheat air fryer to 360°F. Place the stuffed mushrooms in the greased frying basket. Bake 8-10 minutes until the mushrooms are soft and the mozzarella is golden. Serve.

Roasted Tomatillo Salsa Verde

Serves: 4 | Total Time: 35 minutes + cooling time

2 tbsp olive oil
2 serrano peppers
1 small onion, quartered
2 garlic cloves
1 lb tomatillos, husks removed
3 tsp chopped cilantro
1 tsp lime juice
½ tsp salt

Preheat air fryer to 390°F. Place the serrano peppers, onion, garlic, and tomatillos onto a baking sheet pan and lightly drizzle them with olive oil. Insert the sheet in the air fryer and Roast for 13-15 minutes, turning everything halfway through until blistered.

Remove the sheet from the fryer and add the tomatillos, onion, cilantro, lime juice, and salt to your blender. Wrap the peppers in foil and let them cool for a few minutes. Peel and discard the skin of the garlic and unwrap the peppers. Cut the serrano peppers in half and remove the seeds. Add the garlic and peppers to the blender. Pulse until coarsely chopped. Slowly add 2-3 tbsp of water and pulse again to combine until smooth and pureed. Keep in the refrigerator until ready to use.

Bacon-Wrapped Stuffed Dates

Serves: 6 | Total Time: 20 minutes

12 bacon slices, halved
24 pitted dates
3 tbsp crumbled blue cheese
1 tbsp cream cheese

Make a slit lengthways in each date. Mix the blue cheese and cream cheese in a small bowl. Add ½ tsp of cheese mixture to the center of each date. Wrap each date with a slice of bacon and seal with a toothpick.

Preheat air fryer to 400°F. Place the dates on the bottom of the greased frying basket in a single layer. Bake for 6-8 minutes, flipping the dates once until the bacon is cooked and crispy. Allow to cool and serve warm.

Hawaiian Ahi Tuna Bowls

Serves: 4 | Total Time: 20 minutes

8 oz sushi-grade tuna steaks, cubed
½ peeled cucumber, diced   ½ tsp Sriracha sauce
12 wonton wrappers   1 chili, minced
¾ cup dried beans   2 oz avocado, cubed
2 tbsp soy sauce   ¼ cup sliced scallions
1 tsp toasted sesame oil   1 tbsp toasted sesame seeds

Make wonton bowls by placing each wonton wrapper in a foil-lined baking cup. Press gently in the middle and against the sides. Use a light coating of cooking spray. Spoon a heaping tbsp of dried beans into the wonton cup.

Preheat air fryer to 280°F. Place the cups in a single layer on the frying basket. Bake until brown and crispy, 9-11 minutes. Using tongs, carefully remove the cups and allow them to cool slightly. Remove the beans and place the cups to the side. In a bowl, whisk together the chili, soy sauce, sesame oil, and sriracha. Toss in tuna, cucumber, avocado, and scallions. Place 2 heaping tbsp of the tuna mixture into each wonton cup. Top with sesame seeds and serve immediately.

Zucchini Boats with Pancetta

Serves: 4 | Total Time: 35 minutes

1 ¼ cups shredded Havarti cheese
3 pancetta slices   ¼ tsp sweet paprika
2 large zucchini   8 tsp Greek yogurt
Salt and pepper to taste   2 tbsp chives, chopped
¼ tsp garlic powder

Preheat air fryer to 350°F. Place the pancetta in the frying basket and Air Fry it for 10 minutes, flipping once until crisp. Chop the pancetta and set aside. Cut zucchini in half lengthwise and then crosswise so that you have 8 pieces. Scoop out the pulp. Sprinkle with salt, garlic, paprika, and black pepper. Place the zucchini skins in the greased frying basket. Air Fry until crisp-tender, 8-10 minutes. Remove the basket and add the Havarti inside each boat and top with pancetta. Return stuffed boats to the air fryer and fry for 2 minutes or until the cheese has melted. Top with yogurt and chives before serving.

Sausage & Cauliflower Balls

Serves: 4 | Total Time: 30 minutes

2 chicken sausage links, casings removed
1 cup shredded Monterey jack cheese
4 ½ cups riced cauliflower   2 eggs
½ tsp salt   ½ cup breadcrumbs
1 ¼ cups pizza sauce   3 tsp grated Parmesan cheese

In a large skillet over high heat, cook the sausages while breaking them up into smaller pieces with a spoon. Cook through completely for 4 minutes. Add cauliflower, salt, and ¼ cup of pizza sauce. Lower heat to medium and stir-fry for 7 minutes or until the cauliflower is tender. Remove from heat and stir in Monterey cheese. Allow to cool slightly, 4 minutes or until it is easy to handle.

Lightly coat a ¼-cup measuring cup with cooking spray. Pack and level the cup with the cauliflower mixture. Remove from the cup and roll it into a ball in your palm. Set aside and repeat until you have 12 balls. In a bowl, beat eggs and 1 tbsp of water until combined. In another bowl, combine breadcrumbs and Parmesan. Dip one cauliflower ball into the egg mixture, then in the crumbs. Press the crumbs so that they stick to the ball. Put onto a workspace and spray with cooking oil. Repeat for all balls.

Preheat air fryer to 400°F. Place the balls on the bottom of the frying basket in a single layer. Air Fry for about 8-10 minutes, flipping once until the crumbs are golden and the balls are hot throughout. Warm up the remaining pizza sauce as a dip.

Middle Eastern Roasted Chickpeas

Serves: 3 | Total Time: 30 minutes

2 tsp olive oil   1 tsp ground sumac
1 (15-oz) can chickpeas   ¼ tsp garlic powder
Salt to taste   1 tbsp cilantro, chopped
1 tsp za'atar seasoning

Preheat air fryer to 380°F. Combine salt, za´atar, sumac, and garlic powder in a bowl. Put half of the chickpeas in the greased frying basket. Bake for 12 minutes, shaking every 5 minutes, until crunchy and golden brown. Transfer the chickpeas to a bowl. Lightly coat them with olive oil, then toss them with half of the spice mix while they are still hot. Serve topped with cilantro.

Savory Eggplant Fries

Serves: 4 | Total Time: 20 minutes

1 eggplant, sliced   2 tsp onion powder
2 ½ tbsp shoyu   4 tsp olive oil
2 tsp garlic powder   2 tbsp fresh basil, chopped

Preheat air fryer to 390°F. Place the eggplant slices in a bowl and sprinkle the shoyu, garlic, onion, and oil on top. Coat the eggplant evenly. Place the eggplant in a single layer in the greased frying basket and Air Fry for 5 minutes. Remove and put the eggplant in the bowl again. Toss the eggplant slices to coat evenly with the remaining liquid and put back in the fryer. Roast for another 3 minutes. Remove the basket and flip the pieces over to ensure even cooking. Roast for another 5 minutes or until the eggplant is golden. Top with basil and serve.

Thyme Sweet Potato Chips

Serves: 2 | Total Time: 20 minutes

1 tbsp olive oil   ¼ tsp dried thyme
1 sweet potato, sliced   Salt to taste

Preheat air fryer to 390°F. Spread the sweet potato slices in the greased basket and brush with olive oil. Air Fry for 6 minutes. Remove the basket, shake, and sprinkle with thyme and salt. Cook for 6 more minutes or until lightly browned. Serve warm and enjoy!

Korean Brussels Sprouts

Serves: 4 | Total Time: 20 minutes

1 lb Brussels sprouts	1 ½ tsp soy sauce
1 ½ tbsp maple syrup	2 garlic cloves, minced
1 ½ tsp white miso	1 tsp grated fresh ginger
1 tsp toasted sesame oil	½ tsp Gochugaru chili flakes

Preheat air fryer to 390°F. Place the Brussels sprouts in the greased basket, spray with oil and Air Fry for 10-14 minutes, tossing once until crispy, tender, and golden.

In a bowl, combine maple syrup and miso. Whisk until smooth. Add the sesame oil, soy sauce, garlic, ginger, and Gochugaru flakes. Stir well. When the Brussels sprouts are done, add them to the bowl and toss with the sauce. Serve immediately.

Curried Veggie Samosas

Serves: 4 | Total Time: 30 minutes

4 cooked potatoes, mashed	1 tsp ground coriander
¼ cup peas	Salt to taste
2 tsp coconut oil	½ tsp curry powder
3 garlic cloves, minced	¼ tsp cayenne powder
1 ½ tbsp lemon juice	10 rice paper wrappers
1 ½ tsp cumin powder	1 cup cilantro chutney
1 tsp onion powder	

Preheat air fryer to 390°F. In a bowl, place the mashed potatoes, peas, oil, garlic, lemon juice, cumin, onion powder, coriander, salt, curry powder, and cayenne. Stir.

Fill a bowl with water. Soak a rice paper wrapper in the water for a few seconds. Lay it on a flat surface. Place ¼ cup of the potato filling in the center of the wrapper and roll like a burrito or spring roll. Repeat the process until you run out of ingredients. Place the "samosas" inside in the greased frying basket, separating them. Air Fry for 8-10 minutes or until hot and crispy around the edges. Let cool for a few minutes. Enjoy with the cilantro chutney.

Garam Masala Cauliflower Pakoras

Serves: 4 | Total Time: 30 minutes

½ cup chickpea flour	⅛ tsp baking soda
1 tbsp cornstarch	⅛ tsp cayenne powder
Salt to taste	1 ½ cups minced onion
2 tsp cumin powder	½ cup chopped cilantro
½ tsp coriander powder	½ cup chopped cauliflower
½ tsp turmeric	¼ cup lime juice
1 tsp garam masala	

Preheat air fryer to 350°F. Combine the flour, cornstarch, salt, cumin, coriander, turmeric, garam masala, baking soda, and cayenne in a bowl. Stir well. Mix in the onion, cilantro, cauliflower, and lime juice. Using your hands, stir the mix, massaging the flour and spices into the vegetables. Form the mixture into balls and place them in the greased frying basket. Spray the tops of the pakoras in the air fryer with oil and Air Fry for 15-18 minutes, turning once until browned and crispy. Serve hot.

Orange-Glazed Carrots

Serves: 3 | Total Time: 25 minutes

3 carrots, cut into spears	1 tsp clear honey
1 tbsp orange juice	½ tsp dried rosemary
2 tsp balsamic vinegar	¼ tsp salt
1 tsp avocado oil	¼ tsp lemon zest

Preheat air fryer to 390°F. Put the carrots in a baking pan. Add the orange juice, balsamic vinegar, oil, honey, rosemary, salt, and zest. Stir well. Roast for 15-18 minutes, shaking them once or twice until the carrots are bright orange, glazed, and tender. Serve while hot.

Yellow Onion Rings

Serves: 3 | Total Time: 30 minutes

½ sweet yellow onion	Salt and pepper to taste
½ cup buttermilk	¾ tsp garlic powder
¾ cup flour	½ tsp dried oregano
1 tbsp cornstarch	1 cup bread crumbs

Preheat air fryer to 390°F. Cut the onion into ½-inch slices. Separate the onion slices into rings. Place the buttermilk in a bowl and set aside. In another bowl, combine the flour, cornstarch, salt, pepper, and garlic. Stir well and set aside. In a separate bowl, combine the breadcrumbs with oregano and salt.

Dip the rings into the buttermilk, dredge in flour, dip into the buttermilk again, and then coat into the crumb mixture. Put in the greased frying basket without overlapping. Spritz them with cooking oil and Air Fry for 13-16 minutes, shaking once or twice until the rings are crunchy and browned. Serve hot.

Home-Style Turnip Chips

Serves: 2 | Total Time: 20 minutes

1 tbsp olive oil	Salt to taste
1 peeled thinly sliced turnip	½ cup hummus

Preheat air fryer to 325°F. Put the sliced turnip in the greased frying basket, spread the pieces out, and drizzle with olive oil. Air Fry for 10-12 minutes, shaking the basket twice. Sprinkle with salt and serve with hummus.

Herby Breaded Artichoke Hearts

Serves: 6 | Total Time: 25 minutes

12 canned artichoke hearts	1/3 cup panko bread crumbs
2 eggs	½ tsp dried thyme
½ cup all-purpose flour	½ tsp dried parsley

Preheat air fryer to 380°F. Set out three small bowls. In the first, add flour. In the second, beat the eggs. In the third, mix the crumbs, thyme, and parsley.

Dip the artichoke in the flour, then dredge in the egg, then in the bread crumb. Place the breaded artichokes in the greased frying basket and Air Fry for 8 minutes, flipping them once until just browned and crisp. Allow to cool slightly and serve.

Chinese-Style French Fries

Serves: 4 | Total Time: 30 minutes

2 Yukon Gold potatoes, cut into fries
½ tsp Chinese five-spice | Salt to taste
2 tbsp coconut oil | ¼ tsp turmeric
2 tsp coconut sugar | ¼ tsp paprika
1 tsp garlic powder

Preheat air fryer to 390°F. Place the coconut oil, sugar, garlic, Chinese five-spice, salt, turmeric, and paprika in a bowl and add the potatoes; toss to coat. Transfer the to the greased frying basket and Air Fry for 20-25 minutes, tossing twice until softened and golden. Serve warm.

Shiitake Spring Rolls

Serves: 6 | Total Time: 20 minutes

2 cups shiitake mushrooms, thinly sliced
4 cups green cabbage, shredded
4 tsp sesame oil | Salt to taste
6 garlic cloves, minced | 16 rice paper wraps
1 tbsp grated ginger | ½ tsp ground cumin
1 cup grated carrots | ½ tsp ground coriander

Warm the sesame oil in a pan over medium heat. Add garlic, ginger, mushrooms, cabbage, carrots, cumin, coriander, and salt and stir-fry for 3-4 minutes or until the cabbage is wilted. Remove from heat. Get a piece of rice paper, wet with water, and lay it on a flat, non-absorbent surface. Place ¼ cup of the filling in the middle, then fold the bottom over the filling and fold the sides in. Roll up to make a mini burrito. Repeat until you have the number of spring rolls you want.

Preheat air fryer to 390°F. Place the spring rolls in the greased frying basket. Spray the tops with cooking oil and Air Fry for 8-10 minutes until golden. Serve immediately.

Artichoke & Goat Cheese Phyllo Triangles

Serves: 6 | Total Time: 25 minutes

½ cup canned artichoke hearts, chopped
¼ cup goat cheese | 6 phyllo dough sheets
1 egg, beaten | 2 tbsp melted butter
3 tbsp grated mozzarella | 2 tsp chives, chopped
½ tsp mustard powder | Salt and pepper to taste

Preheat air fryer to 400°F. Place the artichoke hearts, goat cheese, egg, mozzarella cheese, mustard powder, chives, salt, and pepper in a bowl and stir to combine.

Unroll one sheet of phyllo and place it on a flat surface. Cut it lengthwise into 3 strips using a pizza cutter. Place 1 heaped tsp of the filling at the base of each strip.

Fold the bottom right-hand tip of the strip over to the left-hand side to make a triangle. Continue flipping and folding the triangle along the strip. Brush the triangle with butter to seal the edges. Repeat the process until you run out of ingredients. Place triangles in the greased frying basket and Bake until golden and crisp, 4-6 minutes. Serve.

Paprika Onion Blossom

Serves: 4 | Total Time: 35 minutes + cooling time

1 large onion | ½ tsp bell pepper powder
1 ½ cups flour | Salt and pepper to taste
1 tsp garlic powder | 2 eggs
1 tsp paprika | 1 cup milk

Remove the tip of the onion but leave the root base intact. Peel the onion to the root and remove skin. Place the onion cut-side down on a cutting board. Starting ½-inch down from the root, cut down to the bottom. Repeat until the onion is divided into quarters. Starting ½-inch down from the root, repeat the cuts in between the first cuts. Repeat this process in between the cuts until you have 16 cuts in the onion. Flip the onion onto the root and carefully spread the inner layers. Set aside.

In a bowl, add flour, garlic, paprika, bell pepper, salt, and pepper, then stir. In another large bowl, whisk eggs and milk. Place the onion in the flour bowl and cover with flour mixture. Transfer the onion to the egg mixture and coat completely with either a spoon or basting brush. Return the onion to the flour bowl and cover completely. Take a sheet of foil and wrap the onion with the foil. Freeze for 45 minutes.

Preheat air fryer to 400°F. Remove the onion from the foil and place in the greased frying basket. Air Fry for 10 minutes. Lightly spray the onion with cooking oil, then cook for another 10-15 minutes. Serve immediately.

Fiery Sweet Chicken Wings

Serves: 4 | Total Time: 30 minutes

8 chicken wings | ½ cup apple cider vinegar
1 tbsp olive oil | ½ tsp Aleppo pepper flakes
3 tbsp brown sugar | Salt to taste
2 tbsp maple syrup

Preheat air fryer to 390°F. Toss the wings with olive oil in a bowl. Bake in the air fryer for 20 minutes, shaking the basket twice. While the chicken is cooking, whisk together sugar, maple syrup, vinegar, Aleppo pepper flakes, and salt in a small bowl. Transfer the wings to a baking pan, then pour the sauce over the wings. Toss well to coat. Cook in the air fryer until the wings are glazed, or for another 5 minutes. Serve hot.

Pigs in Blankets with Honey-Mustard Dip

Serves: 4 | Total Time: 30 minutes

½ (8-oz) can crescent rolls | ¼ cup honey mustard
8 mini smoked hot dogs | ¼ cup mayonnaise

Preheat air fryer to 380°F. Roll out the crescent roll dough and separate into 8 triangles. Cut each triangle in half. Place 1 hot dog at the base of the triangle and roll it up in the dough; gently press the tip in. Repeat for the rest of the rolls. Place the rolls in the greased frying basket. Bake for 8-10 minutes. Mix the honey mustard and mayonnaise in a small bowl. Serve the hot dogs with the dip.

Three Cheese Spinach Dip Bread Ring

Serves: 6 | Total Time: 35 minutes

1 (11-oz) can refrigerated French bread
8 oz feta cheese, cubed   2 green onions, chopped
¼ cup sour cream   2 tbsp melted butter
½ cup baby spinach   4 tsp grated Parmesan cheese
½ cup grated Swiss cheese

Preheat air fryer to 320°F. Blend together feta, sour cream, spinach, Swiss cheese, and green onions in a bowl. Spread the mixture into a greased baking pan and place in the frying basket. Bake in the fryer until hot, 6-8 minutes. Unroll the French bread and cut into 24 slices.

When the dip is ready, remove the pan from the air fryer. Arrange bread slices over the dip in a ring around the edge of the pan. Brush them with melted butter and sprinkle with Parmesan. Bake until the dough is golden brown and dip is bubbly, 10-14 minutes. Serve warm.

Crispy Curried Sweet Potato Fries

Serves: 4 | Total Time: 20 minutes

½ cup sour cream   2 sweet potatoes, julienned
½ cup peach chutney   1 tbsp olive oil
3 tsp curry powder   Salt and pepper to taste

Preheat air fryer to 390°F. Mix together sour cream, peach chutney, and 1 ½ tsp curry powder in a small bowl. Set aside. In a medium bowl, add sweet potatoes, olive oil, the rest of the curry powder, salt, and pepper. Toss to coat. Place the potatoes in the frying basket.

Bake for about 6 minutes, then shake the basket once. Cook for an additional 4-6 minutes or until the potatoes are golden and crispy. Serve the fries hot in a basket along with the chutney sauce for dipping.

Curly Kale Chips with Greek Sauce

Serves: 4 | Total Time: 15 minutes

1 cup Greek yogurt   1 tbsp ground walnuts
3 tbsp lemon juice   1 bunch of curly kale
½ tsp mustard powder   2 tbsp olive oil
½ tsp dried dill   Salt and pepper to taste

Preheat air fryer to 390°F. Mix together yogurt, lemon juice, mustard powder, ground walnuts, and dill until well blended. Set aside. Cut off the stems and ribs from the kale, then cut the leaves into 3-inch pieces.

In a bowl, toss the kale with olive oil, salt, and pepper. Arrange the kale in the fryer and Air Fry for 2-3 minutes. Shake the basket, then cook for another 2-3 minutes or until the kale is crisp. Serve the chips with Greek sauce.

Cinnamon Sweet Potato Fries

Serves: 5 | Total Time: 30 minutes

3 sweet potatoes   1 tsp cinnamon
2 tsp butter, melted   Salt and pepper to taste

Preheat air fryer to 400°F. Peel the potatoes and slice them thinly crosswise. Transfer the slices to a large bowl. Toss with butter, cinnamon, salt, and pepper until fully coated. Place half of the slices into the air fryer. Stacking is ok. Air Fry for 10 minutes. Shake the basket, and cook for another 10-12 minutes until crispy. Serve hot.

Tomato & Halloumi Bruschetta

Serves: 4 | Total Time: 20 minutes

2 tbsp softened butter   ½ cup basil pesto
8 French bread slices   12 chopped cherry tomatoes
1 cup grated halloumi cheese   2 green onions, thinly sliced

Preheat air fryer to 350°F. Spread butter on one side of the bread. Place butter-side up in the frying basket. Bake until the bread is slightly brown, 3-5 minutes. Remove the bread and top it with halloumi cheese. Melt the cheese on the bread in the air fryer for another 1-3 minutes.

Meanwhile, mix pesto, cherry tomatoes, and green onions in a small bowl. When the cheese has melted, take the bread out of the fryer and arrange on a plate. Top with pesto mix and serve.

Honey Tater Tots with Bacon

Serves: 4 | Total Time: 25 minutes

24 frozen tater tots   1 tbsp honey
6 bacon slices   1 cup grated cheddar

Preheat air fryer to 400°F. Air Fry the tater tots for 10 minutes, shaking the basket once halfway through cooking. Cut the bacon into pieces. When the tater tots are done, remove them from the fryer to a baking pan. Top them with bacon and drizzle with honey. Air Fry for 5 minutes to crisp up the bacon. Top the tater tots with cheese and cook for 2 minutes to melt the cheese. Serve.

Canadian-Inspired Waffle Poutine

Serves: 4 | Total Time: 30 minutes

1 cup frozen waffle cut fries 2 green onions, sliced
2 tsp olive oil   1 cup grated mozzarella
1 red bell pepper, chopped   ½ cup beef gravy

Preheat air fryer to 380°F. Toss the waffle fries with olive oil, then place them in the frying basket. Air Fry for about 10-12 minutes, shake the basket once until crisp and lightly golden. Take the fries out of the basket and place in a baking pan. Top with peppers, green onions, and mozzarella cheese. Cook until the vegetables are tender, about 3 minutes. Remove the pan from the fryer and drizzle beef gravy over all of the fries and vegetables. Heat the gravy through for about 2 minutes, then serve.

Cocktail Beef Bites

Serves: 4 | Total Time: 30 minutes

1 lb sirloin tip, cubed   2 tbsp olive oil
1 cup cheese pasta sauce   ½ tsp garlic powder
1 ½ cups soft bread crumbs   ½ tsp dried thyme

Preheat air fryer to 360°F. Toss the beef and the pasta sauce in a medium bowl. Set aside. In a shallow bowl, mix bread crumbs, oil, garlic, and thyme until well combined. Drop the cubes into the crumb mixture to coat. Place them in the greased frying basket and Bake for 6-8 minutes, shaking once, until the beef is crisp and browned. Serve warm with cocktail forks or toothpicks.

Crispy Chicken Bites with Gorgonzola Sauce

Serves: 4 | Total Time: 30 minutes

¼ cup crumbled Gorgonzola cheese
¼ cup creamy blue cheese salad dressing
1 lb chicken tenders, cut into thirds crosswise
½ cup sour cream   1 cup panko bread crumbs
1 celery stalk, chopped   2 tbsp olive oil
3 tbsp buffalo chicken sauce

Preheat air fryer to 350°F. Blend together sour cream, salad dressing, Gorgonzola cheese, and celery in a bowl. Set aside. Combine chicken pieces and Buffalo wing sauce in another bowl until the chicken is coated.

Mix the bread crumbs and olive oil in a shallow bowl. Dip the chicken into the bread crumb mixture, patting the crumbs to keep them in place. Arrange the chicken in the greased frying basket and Air Fry for 8-9 minutes, shaking the basket halfway through cooking until the chicken is golden. Serve with the blue cheese sauce.

Cheesy Zucchini Chips

Serves: 4 | Total Time: 35 minutes

1 lb thin zucchini chips   ½ cup mayonnaise
2 eggs   ½ tbsp olive oil
½ cup bread crumbs   ½ lemon. juiced
½ cup grated Pecorino cheese   1 tsp garlic powder
Salt and pepper to taste   Salt and pepper to taste

Preheat air fryer to 350°F. Beat eggs in a small bowl, then set aside. In another small bowl, stir together bread crumbs, Pecorino, salt, and pepper. Dip zucchini slices into the egg mixture, then in the crumb mixture. Place them in the greased frying basket and Air Fry for 10 minutes. Remove and set aside to cool. Mix the mayonnaise, olive oil, lemon juice, garlic, salt, and pepper in a bowl to make aioli. Serve aioli with chips and enjoy.

Hot Garlic Kale Chips

Serves: 6 | Total Time: 20 minutes

1 tbsp chili powder   3 tsp olive oil
1 tsp garlic powder   Sea salt to taste
6 cups kale, torn

Preheat air fryer to 390°F. Coat the kale with olive oil, chili, and garlic powder. Put it in the frying basket and Air Fry until crispy, about 5-6 minutes, shaking the basket at around 3 minutes. Toss some sea salt on the kale chips once they are finished and serve.

Cheesy Green Wonton Triangles

Serves: 20 Wontons | Total Time: 55 minutes

6 oz marinated artichoke hearts
6 oz cream cheese   5 oz chopped kale
¼ cup sour cream   2 garlic cloves, chopped
¼ cup grated Parmesan   Salt and pepper to taste
¼ cup grated cheddar   20 wonton wrappers

Microwave cream cheese in a bowl for 20 seconds. Combine with sour cream, Parmesan, cheddar, kale, artichoke hearts, garlic, salt, and pepper. Lay out the wrappers on a cutting board. Scoop 1 ½ tsp of cream cheese mixture on top of the wrapper. Fold up diagonally to form a triangle. Bring together the two bottom corners. Squeeze out any air and press together to seal the edges.

Preheat air fryer to 375°F. Place a batch of wonton in the greased frying basket and Bake for 10 minutes. Flip them and cook for 5-8 minutes until crisp and golden. Serve.

Hot Cheese Bites

Serves: 6 | Total Time: 30 minutes + cooling time

1/3 cup grated Velveeta cheese
1/3 cup shredded American cheese
4 oz cream cheese   2 egg whites
2 jalapeños, finely chopped   ½ cup all-purpose flour
½ cup bread crumbs

Preheat air fryer to 400°F. Blend the cream cheese, Velveeta, American cheese, and jalapeños in a bowl. Form the mixture into 1-inch balls. Arrange them on a sheet pan and freeze for 15 minutes.

Spread the flour, egg, and bread crumbs in 3 separate bowls. Once the cheese balls are removed from the freezer, dip them first in flour, then in the egg and finally in the crumbs. Air Fry for 8 minutes in the previously greased frying basket. Flip the balls and cook for another 4 minutes until crispy. Serve warm.

Cinnamon Pretzel Bites

Serves: 6 | Total Time: 40 minutes

1 ½ tsp instant dried yeast   ½ tsp salt
3 tsp light brown sugar   ½ tbsp powdered sugar
½ tsp lemon zest   2 tbsp ground cinnamon
2 cups flour   2 tbsp butter, melted

Preheat air fryer to 380°F. Stir ¾ cup warm water and yeast in a medium bowl. Sit for 5 minutes. Combine yeast water with flour, brown sugar, lemon zest, and salt. Stir until sticky dough forms. Place the dough on a lightly floured work surface and knead it for 2-3 minutes or until it comes together in a smooth ball. Divide the dough into 4 pieces. Roll each section into a log. Cut each log into 5 pieces. Arrange the dough pieces on the greased basket. Bake for 3 minutes, then flip the pretzels. Cook for another 3-4 until browned. Mix the cinnamon and powdered sugar in a bowl. Brush the pretzels with melted butter, then coat them with cinnamon sugar.

Red Potato Chips with Mexican Dip

Serves: 6 | Total Time: 35 minutes

1 tsp smoked paprika	⅛ tsp cayenne pepper
1 tbsp lemon juice	Sea salt to taste
10 purple red potatoes	1 cup Greek yogurt
1 tsp olive oil	2 chipotle chiles, minced
2 tsp minced thyme	2 tbsp adobo sauce

Preheat air fryer to 400°F. Cut the potatoes lengthwise in thin strips and put them in a bowl. Spray olive oil all over them and toss until the strips are evenly coated. Add the potatoes to the frying basket and Air Fry for 10-14 minutes. Use a metal spoon to mix them up at around minute 5. Mix the yogurt, chipotle chiles, adobo sauce, paprika, and lemon juice in a bowl, then put it in the refrigerator. When cooking is finished, put the potatoes on a large plate and toss thyme, cayenne pepper, and sea salt on top. Serve with this Mexican dip. Enjoy!

Shiitake & Cabbage Potstickers

Serves: 6 | Total Time: 30 minutes

1 cup shredded Chinese cabbage
¼ cup chopped shiitake mushrooms

¼ cup grated carrots	2 tsp grated fresh ginger
2 tbsp minced chives	12 dumpling wrappers
2 garlic cloves, minced	2 tsp sesame oil

Preheat air fryer to 370°F. Toss the Chinese cabbage, shiitake mushrooms, carrots, chives, garlic, and ginger in a baking pan and stir. Place the pan in the fryer and Bake for 3-6 minutes. Put a dumpling wrapper on a clean workspace, then top with a tablespoon of the veggie mix.

Fold the wrapper in half to form a half-circle and use water to seal the edges. Repeat with remaining wrappers and filling. Brush the potstickers with sesame oil and arrange them on the frying basket. Air Fry for 5 minutes until the bottoms should are golden brown. Take the pan out, add 1 tbsp of water, and put it back in the fryer to Air Fry for 4-6 minutes longer. Serve hot.

Cheesy Potato Canapés with Bacon

Serves: 4 | Total Time: 35 minutes

4 bacon slices	Salt and pepper to taste
4 russet potatoes, sliced	1 cup grated cheddar
1 tbsp olive oil	2 tsp chopped chives
1 tsp mustard powder	2 tsp chopped scallions

Cook bacon in a skillet for 5 minutes over medium heat. Drain on a paper towel and crumble. Set aside. Add the potatoes to a large bowl and coat them with olive oil, mustard powder, salt, and pepper.

Preheat air fryer to 400°F. Place the potatoes in the greased frying basket. Air Fry for 10 minutes. Shake the basket and cook for another 5-8 minutes or until potatoes are cooked through and edges are crisp. Transfer the potato bites to a serving dish. Serve warm topped with cheese, bacon, chives, and scallions.

Dill Pickle Crisps

Serves: 4 | Total Time: 20 minutes

1 lb dill pickles, sliced	1/3 cup bread crumbs
2 eggs	1 tsp Italian seasoning
1/3 cup flour	

Preheat air fryer to 400°F. Set out three small bowls. In the first bowl, add flour. In the second bowl, beat eggs. In the third bowl, mix bread crumbs with Italian seasoning. Dip the pickle slices in the flour. Shake, then dredge in egg. Roll in bread crumbs and shake excess. Place the pickles in the greased frying basket and Air Fry for 6 minutes. Flip them halfway through cooking and fry for another 3 minutes until crispy. Serve warm.

Italian-Style Fried Olives

Serves: 4 | Total Time: 25 minutes

1 (5½-oz) jar pitted green olives

½ cup all-purpose flour	½ cup bread crumbs
Salt and pepper to taste	1 egg
1 tsp Italian seasoning	

Preheat air fryer to 400°F. Set out three small bowls. In the first, mix flour, Italian seasoning, salt, and pepper. In the bowl, beat the egg. In the third bowl, add bread crumbs. Dip the olives in the flour, then the egg, then in the crumbs. When all of the olives are breaded, place them in the greased frying basket and Air Fry for 6 minutes. Turn them and cook for another 2 minutes or until brown and crispy. Serve chilled.

Buffalo French Fries

Serves: 6 | Total Time: 35 minutes

3 large russet potatoes	2 tbsp extra-virgin olive oil
2 tbsp buffalo sauce	Salt and pepper to taste

Preheat air fryer to 380°F. Peel and cut potatoes lengthwise into French fries. Place them in a bowl, then coat with olive oil, salt, and pepper. Air Fry them for 10 minutes. Shake the basket, then cook for five minutes. Serve drizzled with Buffalo sauce immediately.

Maple Loaded Sweet Potatoes

Serves: 4 | Total Time: 45 minutes

4 sweet potatoes	1 tsp cinnamon
2 tbsp butter	1 tsp lemon zest
2 tbsp maple syrup	½ tsp vanilla extract

Preheat air fryer to 390°F. Poke three holes on the top of each of the sweet potatoes using a fork. Arrange in air fryer and Bake for 40 minutes. Remove and let cool for 5 minutes. While the sweet potatoes cool, melt butter and maple syrup together in the microwave for 15-20 seconds. Remove from microwave and stir in cinnamon, lemon zest, and vanilla. When the sweet potatoes are cool, cut open and drizzle the cinnamon butter mixture over each and serve immediately.

Hot Cauliflower Bites

Serves: 4 | Total Time: 35 minutes

1 head cauliflower, cut into florets
1 cup all-purpose flour   1/3 cup cayenne sauce
1 tsp garlic powder

Preheat air fryer to 390°F. Mix the flour, 1 cup of water, and garlic powder in a large bowl until a batter forms. Coat cauliflower in the batter, then transfer to a large bowl to drain excess. Place the cauliflower in the greased frying basket without stacking. Spray with cooking, then Bake for 6 minutes. Remove from the air fryer and transfer to a large bowl. Top with cayenne sauce. Return to the fryer and cook for 6 minutes or until crispy. Serve.

Tomato & Garlic Roasted Potatoes

Serves: 4 | Total Time: 25 minutes

16 cherry tomatoes, halved   Salt and pepper to taste
6 red potatoes, cubed   1 tsp chopped chives
3 garlic cloves, minced   1 tbsp extra-virgin olive oil

Preheat air fryer to 400°F. Combine cherry potatoes, garlic, salt, pepper, chives and olive oil in a resealable plastic bag. Seal and shake the bag. Put the potatoes in the greased frying basket and Roast for 10 minutes. Shake the basket, place the cherry tomatoes in, and cook for 10 more minutes. Allow to cool slightly and serve.

Rich Egg-Fried Cauliflower Rice

Serves: 4 | Total Time: 45 minutes

2 ½ cups riced cauliflower   2 spring onions
2 tsp sesame oil   Salt and pepper to taste
1 green bell pepper, diced   1 tbsp tamari sauce
1 cup peas   2 eggs, scrambled
1 cup diced carrots

Preheat air fryer to 380°F. Combine riced cauliflower, bell pepper, peas, carrots, and spring onions in a large bowl. Stir in 1 tsp of sesame oil, salt, and pepper. Grease a baking pan with the remaining tsp of sesame oil. Transfer the rice mixture to the pan and place in the air fryer. Bake for 10 minutes. Remove the pan and drizzle with tamari sauce. Stir in scrambled eggs and serve warm.

Chicken Nachos

Serves: 6 | Total Time: 25 minutes

2 oz baked corn tortilla chips
1 cup leftover roast chicken, shredded
½ cup canned black beans   1 jalapeño pepper, minced
1 red bell pepper, chopped   1/3 cup grated Swiss cheese
½ grated carrot   1 tomato, chopped

Preheat air fryer to 360°F. Lay the tortilla chips in a single layer in a baking pan. Add the chicken, black beans, red bell pepper, carrot, jalapeño, and cheese on top. Bake in the air fryer for 9-12 minutes. Make sure the cheese melts and is slightly browned. Serve garnished with tomatoes.

Crispy Okra Fries

Serves: 4 | Total Time: 25 minutes

½ lb trimmed okra, cut lengthways
¼ tsp deggi mirch chili powder
3 tbsp buttermilk   2 tbsp cornmeal
2 tbsp chickpea flour   Salt and pepper to taste

Preheat air fryer to 380°F. Set out 2 bowls. In one, add buttermilk. In the second, mix flour, cornmeal, chili powder, salt, and pepper. Dip the okra in buttermilk, then dredge in flour and cornmeal. Transfer to the frying basket and spray the okra with oil. Air Fry for 10 minutes, shaking once halfway through cooking until crispy. Let cool for a few minutes and serve warm.

Mustard Green Chips with Curried Sauce

Serves: 4 | Total Time: 20 minutes

1 cup plain yogurt   1 bunch of mustard greens
1 tbsp lemon juice   2 tsp olive oil
1 tbsp curry powder   Sea salt to taste

Preheat air fryer to 390°F. Using a sharp knife, remove and discard the ribs from the mustard greens. Slice the leaves into 2-3-inch pieces. Transfer them to a large bowl, then pour in olive oil and toss to coat. Air Fry for 5-6 minutes. Shake at least once. The chips should be crispy when finished. Sprinkle with a little bit of sea salt. Mix the yogurt, lemon juice, salt, and curry in a small bowl. Serve the greens with the sauce.

Artichoke-Spinach Dip

Serves: 4 | Total Time: 25 minutes

4 oz canned artichoke hearts, chopped
½ cup Greek yogurt   1 garlic clove, minced
¼ cup cream cheese   ½ tsp dried oregano
½ cup spinach, chopped   3 tsp grated Parmesan cheese
½ red bell pepper, chopped

Preheat air fryer to 340°F. Mix the yogurt and cream cheese. Add the artichoke, spinach, red bell pepper, garlic, and oregano, then put the mix in a pan and scatter Parmesan cheese on top. Put the pan in the frying basket and Bake for 10-14 minutes. The dip should be bubble and brown. Serve hot.

Balsamic Grape Dip

Serves: 6 | Total Time: 25 minutes

2 cups seedless red grapes   1 cup Greek yogurt
1 tbsp balsamic vinegar   2 tbsp milk
1 tbsp honey   2 tbsp minced fresh basil

Preheat air fryer to 380°F. Add the grapes and balsamic vinegar to the frying basket, then pour honey over and toss to coat. Roast for 8-12 minutes, shriveling the grapes, and take them out of the air fryer. Mix the milk and yogurt together, then gently stir in the grapes and basil. Serve and enjoy!

Jalapeño & Mozzarella Stuffed Mushrooms

Serves: 4 | Total Time: 30 minutes

16 button mushrooms	1 jalapeño pepper, minced
1/3 cup salsa	1/8 tsp cayenne pepper
3 garlic cloves, minced	3 tbsp shredded mozzarella
1 onion, finely chopped	2 tsp olive oil

Preheat air fryer to 350°F. Cut the stem off the mushrooms, then slice them finely. Set the caps aside. Combine the salsa, garlic, onion, jalapeño, cayenne, and mozzarella cheese in a bowl, then add the stems. Fill the mushroom caps with the mixture, making sure to overfill so the mix is coming out of the top. Drizzle with olive oil. Place the caps in the air fryer and Bake for 8-12 minutes. The filling should be hot and the mushrooms soft. Serve warm.

Honey-Lemon Chicken Wings

Serves: 4 | Total Time: 30 minutes

8 chicken wings	2 cloves garlic, minced
Salt and pepper to taste	2 thinly sliced green onions
3 tbsp honey	¾ cup barbecue sauce
1 tbsp lemon juice	1 tbsp sesame seeds
1 tbsp chicken stock	

Preheat air fryer to 390°F. Season the wings with salt and pepper and place them in the frying basket. Air Fry for 20 minutes. Shake the basket a couple of times during cooking. In a bowl, mix the honey, lemon juice, chicken stock, and garlic. Take the wings out of the fryer and place them in a baking pan. Add the sauce and toss, coating completely. Put the pan in the air fryer and Air Fry for 4-5 minutes until golden and cooked through, with no pink showing. Top with green onions and sesame seeds, then serve with BBQ sauce.

Cocktail Chicken Meatballs

Serves: 4 | Total Time: 30 minutes

2 tsp olive oil	1 egg white
¼ cup onion, minced	½ tsp cayenne pepper
¼ red bell pepper, minced	½ tsp dried thyme
3 tsp grated Parmesan cheese	½ lb ground chicken

Preheat air fryer to 370°F. Combine the olive oil, onion, and red bell pepper in a baking pan, then transfer to the air fryer. Bake for 3-5 minutes until tender. Add the cooked vegetables, Parmesan cheese, egg white, ground chicken, cayenne pepper, and thyme to a bowl and stir. Form the mixture into small meatballs and put them in the frying basket. Air Fry for 10-15 minutes, shaking the basket once until the meatballs are crispy and brown on all sides. Serve warm.

Bacon & Blue Cheese Tartlets

Serves: 6 | Total Time: 30 minutes

6 bacon slices	½ cup diced blue cheese
16 phyllo tartlet shells	3 tbsp apple jelly

Preheat the air fryer to 400°F. Put the bacon in a single layer in the frying basket and Air Fry for 14 minutes, turning once halfway through. Remove and drain on paper towels, then crumble when cool. Wipe the fryer clean. Fill the tartlet shells with bacon and the blue cheese cubes and add a dab of apple jelly on top of the filling. Lower the temperature to 350°F, then put the shells in the frying basket. Air Fry until the cheese melts and the shells brown, about 5-6 minutes. Remove and serve.

Asian-Style Shrimp Toast

Serves: 4 | Total Time: 25 minutes

8 large raw shrimp, chopped	1 celery stalk, minced
1 egg white	2 tbsp cornstarch
2 garlic cloves, minced	¼ tsp Chinese five-spice
1 red chili, minced	3 firm bread slices

Preheat air fryer to 350°F. Add the shrimp, egg white, garlic, red chili, celery, corn starch, and five-spice powder in a bowl and combine. Place 1/3 of the shrimp mix on a slice of bread, smearing it to the edges, then slice the bread into 4 strips. Lay the strips in the frying basket in a single layer and Air Fry for 3-6 minutes until golden and crispy. Repeat until all strips are cooked. Serve hot.

Cayenne-Spiced Roasted Pecans

Serves: 4 | Total Time: 15 minutes

¼ tsp chili powder	1/8 tsp garlic powder
Salt and pepper to taste	1/8 tsp onion powder
1/8 tsp cayenne pepper	1 cup raw pecans
1 tsp cumin powder	2 tbsp butter, melted
1 tsp cinnamon powder	1 tsp honey

Preheat air fryer to 300°F. Whisk together black pepper, chili powder, salt, cayenne pepper, cumin, garlic powder, cinnamon, and onion powder. Set to the side. Toss pecans, butter, and honey in a medium bowl, then toss in the spice mixture. Pour pecans in the frying basket and toast for 3 minutes. Stir the pecans and toast for another 3 to 5 minutes until the nuts are crisp. Cool and serve.

Fiery Cheese Sticks

Serves: 4 | Total Time: 20 minutes + freezing time

1 egg, beaten	¼ tsp ground coriander
½ cup dried bread crumbs	¼ tsp red pepper flakes
¼ cup ground peanuts	1/8 tsp cayenne pepper
1 tbsp chili powder	8 mozzarella cheese sticks

Preheat the air fryer to 375°F. Beat the egg in a bowl, and on a plate, combine the breadcrumbs, peanuts, coriander, chili powder, pepper flakes, and cayenne. Dip each piece of string cheese in the egg, then in the breadcrumb mix. After lining a baking sheet with parchment paper, put the sticks on it and freeze them for 30 minutes. Get the sticks out of the freezer and set in the frying basket in a single layer. Spritz them with cooking oil. Air Fry for 7-9 minutes until the exterior is golden and the interior is hot and melted. Serve hot with marinara or ranch sauce.

Beet Fries with Yogurt Dip

Serves: 4 | Total Time: 40 minutes

2 peeled beets	Salt to taste
½ cup plain Greek yogurt	2 eggs, beaten
1 tbsp fresh dill, chopped	1 cup panko bread crumbs
2 tbsp lime juice	½ tsp paprika

Preheat air fryer to 375°F. Mix the yogurt, lime juice, and salt in a bowl, then pour the dip into a serving bowl. Sprinkle with dill, cover, and refrigerate. Slice the beets into 3-inch long sticks that are ½ inch thick. Beat the eggs in a shallow bowl and combine the panko and paprika on a plate. Dip the fries in the egg, then the panko mixture, coating well. Put the beets in the frying basket and spray with cooking oil. Air Fry for 18-23 minutes or until crispy and golden. Serve with yogurt dip.

Enchilada Chicken Dip

Serves 6 | Total Time: 20 minutes

1 cup chopped cooked chicken breasts
1 (4-oz) can diced green chiles, including juice

8 oz cream cheese, softened	1 jalapeño pepper, minced
¼ cup mayonnaise	1 cup shredded mozzarella
¼ cup sour cream	¼ cup diced tomatoes
2 tbsp chopped onion	1 tsp chili powder

Preheat air fryer to 400°F. Beat the cream cheese, mayonnaise, and sour cream in a bowl until smooth. Stir in the cooked chicken, onion, green chiles, jalapeño, and ½ cup of mozzarella cheese. Spoon the mixture into a baking dish. Sprinkle the remaining cheese on top, and place the dish in the fryer. Bake for 10 minutes. Garnish the dip with diced tomatoes and chili powder. Serve.

Hungarian Spiralized Fries

Serves: 4 | Total Time: 30 minutes

2 russet potatoes, peeled	½ tsp garlic powder
1 tbsp olive oil	½ tsp Hungarian paprika
½ tsp chili powder	Salt and pepper to taste

Preheat the air fryer to 400°F. Using the spiralizer, cut the potatoes into 5-inch lengths and add them to a large bowl. Pour cold water, cover, and set aside for 30 minutes. Drain and dry with a kitchen towel, then toss back in the bowl. Drizzle the potatoes with olive oil and season with salt, pepper, chili, garlic, and paprika. Toss well. Put the potatoes in the frying basket and Air Fry for 10-12 minutes, shaking the basket once until the potatoes are golden and crispy. Serve warm and enjoy!

Piri Piri Chicken Drumettes

Serves: 4 | Total Time: 45 minutes

1 cup crushed cracker crumbs	2 tsp onion powder
1 tbsp sweet paprika	1 tsp garlic powder
1 tbsp smoked paprika	2 lb chicken drumettes
1 tbsp Piri Piri seasoning	2 tbsp olive oil
1 tsp sea salt	

Preheat the air fryer to 380°F. Combine the cracker crumbs, paprikas, Piri Piri seasoning, sea salt, onion and garlic powders in a bowl and mix well. Pour into a screw-top glass jar and set aside. Put the drumettes in a large bowl, drizzle with the olive oil, and toss to coat. Sprinkle 1/3 cup of the breading mix over the meat and press the mix into the drumettes. Put half the drumettes in the frying basket and Air Fry for 2025 minutes, shaking the basket once until golden and crisp. Serve hot.

Chili Corn on the Cob

Serves: 4 | Total Time: 30 minutes

Salt and pepper to taste	1 tbsp butter, melted
½ tsp smoked paprika	¼ cup lime juice
¼ tsp chili powder	1 tsp lime zest
4 corn ears, halved	1 lime, quartered

Preheat air fryer to 400°F. Combine salt, pepper, lime juice, lime zest, paprika, and chili powder in a small bowl. Toss corn and butter in a large bowl, then add the seasonings from the small bowl. Toss until coated. Arrange the corn in a single layer in the frying basket. Air Fry for 10 minutes, then turn the corn. Air Fry for another 8 minutes. Squeeze lime over the corn and serve.

Herbed Cauliflower

Serves: 4 | Total Time: 15 minutes

2 cups cauliflower florets	½ tsp dried rosemary
2 tsp olive oil	½ tsp dried thyme
4 garlic cloves, minced	½ tsp dried oregano
Salt and pepper to taste	¼ tsp ground sage
½ tsp onion powder	1 tbsp chopped parsley
1 tsp smoked paprika	

Preheat air fryer to 375°F. Toss cauliflower and all of the ingredients in a large bowl until coated. Arrange the cauliflower on the frying basket in a single layer. Roast for 5 minutes, then shake the basket. Roast for another 5 minutes until fork tender. Serve sprinkled with parsley.

Cheesy Bacon-Spinach Biscuit Cups

Serves: 8 | Total Time: 30 minutes

1 (16.3-oz) can refrigerated biscuit dough

4 oz cream cheese, softened	2 scallions, chopped
¼ cup mayonnaise	2 cups grated Fontina cheese
1 cup spinach	1 cup grated cheddar cheese
3 bacon slices, chopped	½ tsp garlic powder

Preheat the air fryer to 360°F. Cook the bacon in a skillet over medium heat for about 4 minutes Set aside. Separate the dough into 8 biscuits and press them into the bottom and up the sides of the muffin cups. Place the cream cheese and mayonnaise in a bowl and mix until well combined. Stir in spinach, bacon, scallions, cheddar cheese, and garlic powder. Spoon the mixture into the muffin cups and top with Fontina cheese. Bake for 10-14 minutes or until the cheese has melted and the top is golden brown. Remove and let cool on a wire rack. Serve and enjoy!

Carrot & Zucchini Fritters with Green Dip

Serves: 6 | Total Time: 40 minutes

1 grated carrot	Salt and pepper to taste
1 grated medium zucchini	½ tsp ground cumin
1 minced medium onion	1 avocado, peeled and pitted
1 garlic clove, minced	½ cup plain Greek yogurt
1 large egg	1 tsp lime juice
¼ cup flour	1 tbsp white vinegar
¼ cup bread crumbs	¼ cup chopped cilantro

Preheat air fryer to 380°F. Place the carrot, zucchini, onion, garlic, egg, flour, bread crumbs, salt, pepper, and cumin in a large bowl. Mix until well combined. Scoop out equal portions of the vegetable mixture and form them into patties. Arrange the patties on the greased basket. Air Fry them for about 5-6 minutes, flip over, and continue cooking for another 5-6 minutes or until the fritters are golden and crisp.

While the fritters are cooking, prepare the avocado dip. Mash the avocado in a small bowl to the desired texture. Stir in yogurt, white vinegar, chopped cilantro, lime juice, and salt. When the fritters are done, transfer to a serving plate along with the avocado dip. Serve warm and enjoy.

Uncle's Potato Wedges

Serves: 4 | Total Time: 65 minutes

2 russet potatoes, cut into wedges	⅛ tsp cayenne pepper
	Salt and pepper to taste
1 head garlic	½ tsp chili powder
3 tbsp olive oil	¼ tsp ground cumin
¼ cup mayonnaise	1 tbsp dried Italian herbs
½ tbsp lemon juice	½ cup Parmesan cheese
½ tsp Worcestershire sauce	

Preheat air fryer to 400°F. Cut off garlic head top and drizzle with olive oil. Wrap loosely in foil and transfer to the frying basket. Cook for 30 minutes. Remove from air fryer and open the foil. Cook the garlic for 10 minutes, then squeeze the cloves out of their place in the head. Chop and transfer all but ½ teaspoon to a small bowl. Stir in mayonnaise, lemon juice, Worcestershire, and cayenne pepper. Cover and refrigerate.

Toss potatoes with the rest of the olive oil as well as salt, black pepper, Italian herbs, Parmesan cheese, chili powder, cumin, and the remaining chopped garlic. When coated, place the wedges in the frying basket in a single layer. Air Fry for 10 minutes, then shake the basket. Air Fry for another 8-10 minutes until potatoes are tender. Bring out the garlic aioli. Place the potato wedges on a serving dish along with the aioli for dipping. Serve warm.

Brie-Currant & Bacon Spread

Serves: 6 | Total Time: 30 minutes

4 oz cream cheese, softened	4 oz cooked bacon, crumbled
3 tbsp mayonnaise	1/3 cup dried currants
1 cup diced Brie cheese	
½ tsp dried thyme	

Preheat the air fryer to 350°F. Beat the cream cheese with the mayo until well blended. Stir in the Brie, thyme, bacon, and currants and pour the dip mix in a 6-inch round pan. Put the pan in the fryer and Air Fry for 10-12 minutes, stirring once, until the dip is melting and bubbling. Serve warm.

Avocado Balls

Serves: 6 | Total Time: 25 minutes + freezing time

2 avocados, peeled	1 egg, beaten
1 tbsp minced cilantro	1 tbsp milk
1 tbsp lime juice	¼ cup almond flour
½ tsp salt	½ cup ground almonds

Preheat the air fryer to 400°F. Mash the avocados in a bowl with cilantro, lime juice, and salt. Line a baking sheet with parchment paper and form the mix into 12 balls. Use an ice cream scoop or ⅛-cup measure. Put them on the baking sheet and freeze for 2 hours. Beat the egg with milk in a shallow bowl, then combine the almond flour and almonds on a plate. Dip the frozen guac balls in the egg mix, then roll them in the almond mix, coating evenly. Put half the bombs in the freezer while you cook the first group. The other 6 go in the frying basket. Mist with olive oil and Air Fry for 4-5 minutes or until they are golden. Repeat with the second batch and serve. Enjoy!

Prosciutto Polenta Rounds

Serves: 6 | Total Time: 40 minutes + 10 minutes to cool

1 (18-oz) tube precooked polenta	
1 tbsp garlic oil	2 scallions, sliced
4 oz cream cheese, softened	1 tbsp minced fresh chives
3 tbsp mayonnaise	6 prosciutto slices, chopped

Preheat the air fryer to 400°F. Slice the polenta crosswise into 12 rounds. Brush both sides of each round with garlic oil and put 6 of them in the frying basket. Put a rack in the basket over the polenta and add the other 6 rounds. Bake for 15 minutes, flip, and cook for 10-15 more minutes or until the polenta is crispy and golden. While the polenta is cooking, beat the cream cheese and mayo and stir in the scallions, chives, and prosciutto. When the polenta is cooked, lay it out on a wire rack to cool for 15 minutes. Top with the cream cheese mix and serve.

Cholula Fried Avocado

Serves 2 | Total Time: 20 minutes

1 egg, beaten	¼ tsp Cholula sauce
¼ cup flour	Salt to taste
2 tbsp almond flour	2 peeled avocado halves

Preheat air fryer to 380°F. Mix the egg and Cholula sauce in a bowl. In another bowl, combine the remaining ingredients, except for the avocado. Submerge avocado halves in the egg mixture and dredge them into the dry mix to coat. Place them in the lightly greased frying basket and Air Fry for 4-6 minutes. Serve immediately.

Russian Pierogi with Cheese Dip

Serves: 6 | Total Time: 20 minutes

1 (16-oz) package frozen pierogi

1 cup sour cream	3 spring onions, chopped
1 tbsp fresh lemon juice	½ cup shredded carrot
½ chopped red bell pepper	1 tsp dried rosemary

Preheat the air fryer to 400°F. Mix the sour cream and lemon juice in a bowl, then add the bell pepper, spring onions, carrot, and rosemary and mix well. Set the dip aside. Put as many frozen pierogi as will fit in the frying basket in a single layer and spray with cooking oil. Air Fry for 11-14 minutes, rotating pierogis once until golden. Repeat with the remaining pierogi. Serve with the dip.

Seafood Egg Rolls

Serves: 6 | Total Time: 35 minutes

2 tbsp olive oil	1 cup corn kernels
1 shallot, chopped	1/3 cup chopped cashews
2 garlic cloves, minced	1 tbsp soy sauce
½ cup shredded carrots	2 tsp fish sauce
1 lb cooked shrimp, chopped	12 egg roll wrappers

Preheat the air fryer to 400°F. Combine the olive oil, shallot, garlic, and carrots in a 6-inch. Put the pan in the frying basket and Air Fry for 3-5 minutes, stirring once. Remove the pan and put the veggies in a bowl. Add shrimp, corn, cashews, soy sauce, and fish sauce to the veggies and combine. Lay the egg roll wrappers on the clean work surface and brush the edges with water. Divide the filling equally and fill them, then brush the edges with water again. Roll up, folding in the side, enclosing the filling inside. Place 4 egg rolls in the basket and spray with cooking oil. Air Fry for 10-12 minutes, rotating once halfway through cooking until golden and crispy. Repeat with remaining rolls. Serve hot.

Home-Style Reuben Spread

Serves 6 | Total Time: 20 minutes

8 oz cream cheese, softened

1 cup chopped deli corned beef

¼ cup mayonnaise	1 cup grated Gruyère cheese
¼ cup sour cream	1 tsp caraway seeds
1 cup drained sauerkraut	2 tbsp parsley, chopped

Preheat air fryer to 400°F. Add the cream cheese, mayo, and sour cream in a bowl and stir until combined. Add corned beef, sauerkraut, ½ cup of Gruyere cheese, parsley and caraway seeds. Spoon the mixture into a baking dish and top with the remaining cheese Place the dish in the frying basket and Bake for 10 minutes. Serve.

Crunchy Parmesan Edamame

Serves 4 | Total Time: 25 minutes + cooling time

1 cup edamame, shelled	½ tsp salt
1 tbsp sesame oil	½ tsp garlic powder
1 tsp five-spice powder	¼ cup grated Parmesan

Cook the edamame in boiling salted water until crisp-tender, about 10 minutes. Drain and leave to cool. Preheat air fryer to 350°F. Combine edamame, garlic, and sesame oil in a bowl. Place them in the frying basket and Air Fry for 16 minutes, shaking twice. Transfer to a small bowl and toss with five-spice powder and salt. Serve chilled topped with Parmesan cheese. Enjoy!

Rosemary Garlic Cheese Casserole

Serves 4 | Total Time: 20 minutes

2 peeled garlic cloves roasted	1 tbsp olive oil
1 ½ cups goat cheese	1 tbsp apple cider vinegar
½ cup grated Parmesan	Salt and pepper to taste
1 egg, beaten	1 tsp chopped rosemary

Preheat air fryer to 350°F. Carefully squeeze the garlic into a bowl and mash it with a fork until a paste is formed. Stir in goat cheese, Parmesan cheese, egg, olive oil, vinegar, salt, black pepper, and rosemary. Spoon the mixture into a baking dish, and place the dish in the frying basket. Air Fry for 7 minutes. Serve warm.

Spicy Almond & Marmalade Topped Brie

Serves 6 | Total Time: 35 minutes

1 cup almonds	1 tsp ground cinnamon
1 egg white, beaten	¼ tsp powdered sugar
⅛ tsp ground cumin	1 (8-oz) round Brie cheese
⅛ tsp cayenne pepper	2 tbsp orange marmalade

Preheat air fryer to 325°F. In a bowl, mix the beaten egg white and almonds. In another bowl, mix the spices and sugar. Stir in almonds, drained of excess egg white. Transfer the almonds to the frying basket and Bake for 12 minutes, tossing once. Let cool for 5 minutes. When cooled, chop into smaller bits. Adjust the air fryer temperature to 400°F. Place the Brie on a parchment-lined pizza pan and Bake for 10 minutes. Transfer the Brie to a serving plate, spread orange marmalade on top, and garnish with spiced almonds. Serve and enjoy!

Breaded Mozzarella Sticks

Serves 6 | Total Time: 25 minutes

2 tbsp flour	¼ tsp Italian seasoning
1 egg	10 mozzarella sticks
1 tbsp milk	2 tsp olive oil
½ cup bread crumbs	½ cup warm marinara sauce
¼ tsp salt	

Place the flour in a bowl. In another bowl, beat the egg and milk. In a third bowl, combine the crumbs, salt, and Italian seasoning. Cut the mozzarella sticks into thirds. Roll each piece in flour, then dredge in egg mixture, and finally roll in breadcrumb mixture. Shake off the excess between each step. Place them in the freezer for 10 minutes.

Preheat air fryer to 400°F. Place mozzarella sticks in the frying basket and Air Fry for 5 minutes, shake twice and brush with olive oil. Serve the mozzarella sticks immediately with marinara sauce.

Chipotle Sunflower Seeds

Serves 4 | Total Time: 20 minutes

2 cups sunflower seeds	1 garlic clove, minced
2 tsp olive oil	¼ tsp salt
½ tsp chipotle powder	1 tsp granulated sugar

Preheat air fryer to 325°F. In a bowl, mix the sunflower seeds, olive oil, chipotle powder, garlic, salt, and sugar until well coated. Place the mixture in the frying basket and Air Fry for 10 minutes, shaking once. Serve chilled.

Spiced Roasted Pepitas

Serves 4 | Total Time: 25 minutes

2 cups pumpkin seeds	½ tsp dried parsley
1 tbsp butter, melted	½ tsp garlic powder
Salt and pepper to taste	¼ tsp dried chives
½ tsp shallot powder	¼ tsp dry mustard
½ tsp smoked paprika	¼ tsp celery seed

Preheat air fryer to 325°F. Combine the pumpkin seeds, butter, and salt in a bowl. Place the seed mixture in the frying basket and Roast for 13 minutes, turning once. Transfer to a medium serving bowl. Stir in shallot powder, paprika, parsley, garlic powder, chives, dry mustard, celery seed, and black pepper. Serve right away.

Spiced Parsnip Chips

Serves 2 | Total Time: 35 minutes

½ tsp smoked paprika	⅛ tsp granulated sugar
¼ tsp chili powder	1 tsp salt
¼ tsp garlic powder	1 parsnip, cut into chips
⅛ tsp onion powder	2 tsp olive oil
⅛ tsp cayenne pepper	

Preheat air fryer to 400°F. Mix all spices in a bowl and reserve. In another bowl, combine parsnip chips, olive oil, and salt. Place parsnip chips in the lightly greased frying basket and Air Fry for 12 minutes, shaking once. Transfer the chips to a bowl, toss in seasoning mix, and let sit for 15 minutes before serving.

Nicoise Deviled Eggs

Serves 4 | Total Time: 20 minutes

4 eggs	2 tbsp goat cheese crumbles
2 tbsp mayonnaise	Salt and pepper to taste
10 chopped Nicoise olives	2 tbsp chopped parsley

Preheat air fryer to 260°F. Place the eggs in silicone muffin cups to avoid bumping around and cracking during the cooking process. Add silicone cups to the frying basket and Air Fry for 15 minutes. Remove and run the eggs under cold water. When cool, remove the shells and halve them lengthwise.

Spoon yolks into a separate medium bowl and arrange white halves on a large plate. Mash the yolks with a fork. Stir in the remaining ingredients. Spoon mixture into white halves and scatter with mint to serve.

Roasted Jalapeño Salsa Verde

Serves 4 | Total Time: 20 minutes

¾ lb fresh tomatillos, husked	½ tsp salt
1 jalapeño, stem removed	1 tsp lime juice
4 green onions, sliced	¼ tsp apple cider vinegar
3 garlic cloves, peeled	¼ cup cilantro leaves

Preheat air fryer to 400°F. Add tomatillos and jalapeño to the frying basket and Bake for 5 minutes. Put in green onions and garlic and Bake for 5 more minutes. Transfer it into a food processor along with salt, lime juice, vinegar and cilantro and blend until the sauce is finely chopped. Pour it into a small sealable container and refrigerate it until ready to use up to five days.

Cheesy Jalapeño Cauliflower Tots

Serves 4 | Total Time: 30 minutes

1 egg	2 tbsp scallions, chopped
¾ cup riced cauliflower	1/3 cup flour
2 jalapeño peppers, minced	½ tsp salt
1/3 cup grated Colby cheese	½ tsp paprika
1 oz cream cheese, softened	¼ tsp garlic powder

Preheat air fryer to 375°F. Whisk the egg with riced cauliflower, jalapeño peppers, Colby cheese, cream cheese, scallions, flour, salt, paprika, and garlic powder in a bowl. Shape the mixture into bite-sized tots. Add them to the foil-lined frying basket and Air Fry for 8-10 minutes, shaking halfway through the cooking time. Let chill for 5 minutes before serving. Enjoy!

Parmesan Eggplant Sticks

Serves 4 | Total Time: 35 minutes

2 eggs	½ cup grated Parmesan
2 tbsp heavy cream	½ tsp salt
½ cup bread crumbs	1 eggplant, cut into sticks
½ tsp Italian seasoning	½ cup tomato sauce, warm

Preheat air fryer to 400°F. In a bowl, mix the eggs and heavy cream. In another bowl, combine bread crumbs, Parmesan cheese, Italian seasoning and salt. Dip eggplant fries in egg mixture and dredge them in crumb mixture.

Place the fries in the greased frying basket and Air Fry for 12 minutes, shaking once. Transfer to a large serving plate and serve with warmed tomato sauce.

Mouth-Watering Vegetable Casserole

Serves: 3 | Total Time: 45 minutes

1 red bell pepper, chopped	2 tbsp balsamic vinegar
½ lb okra, trimmed	1 tbsp allspice
1 red onion, chopped	1 tsp ground cumin
1 (28-oz) can diced tomatoes	1 cup baby spinach

Preheat air fryer to 400°F. Combine the bell pepper, red onion, okra, tomatoes and juices, balsamic vinegar, allspice, and cumin in a baking pan and Roast for 25 minutes, stirring every 10 minutes. Stir in spinach and Roast for another 5 minutes. Serve warm.

MEATLESS RECIPES

Crunchy Rice Paper Samosas

Serves: 2 | Total Time: 20 minutes

1 boiled potato, mashed	½ tsp cayenne pepper
¼ cup green peas	½ tsp turmeric powder
1 tsp garam masala powder	Salt and pepper to taste
½ tsp ginger garlic paste	3 rice paper wrappers

Preheat air fryer to 350°F. Place the mashed potatoes in a bowl. Add the peas, garam masala powder, ginger garlic paste, cayenne pepper, turmeric powder, salt, and pepper and stir until ingredients are evenly blended.

Lay the rice paper wrappers out on a lightly floured surface. Divide the potato mixture between the wrappers and fold the top edges over to seal. Transfer the samosas to the greased frying basket and Air Fry for 12 minutes, flipping once until the samosas are crispy and flaky. Remove and leave to cool for 5 minutes. Serve and enjoy!

Two-Cheese Grilled Sandwiches

Serves: 2 | Total Time: 30 minutes

4 sourdough bread slices	1 tbsp butter
2 cheddar cheese slices	2 dill pickles, sliced
2 Swiss cheese slices	

Preheat air fryer to 360°F. Smear both sides of the sourdough bread with butter and place them in the frying basket. Toast the bread for 6 minutes, flipping once.

Divide the cheddar cheese between 2 of the bread slices. Cover the remaining 2 bread slices with Swiss cheese slices. Bake for 10 more minutes until the cheeses have melted and lightly bubbled and the bread has golden brown. Set the cheddar-covered bread slices on a serving plate, cover with pickles, and top each with the Swiss-covered slices. Serve and enjoy!

Thyme Lentil Patties

Serves: 2 | Total Time: 35 minutes

½ cup grated American cheese	
1 cup cooked lentils	Salt and pepper to taste
¼ tsp dried thyme	1 cup bread crumbs
2 eggs, beaten	

Preheat air fryer to 350°F. Put the eggs, lentils, and cheese in a bowl and mix to combine. Stir in half the bread crumbs, thyme, salt, and pepper. Form the mixture into 2 patties and coat them in the remaining bread crumbs. Transfer to the greased frying basket. Air Fry for 14-16 minutes until brown, flipping once. Serve.

Cheese & Bean Burgers

Serves: 2 | Total Time: 35 minutes

1 cup cooked black beans	Salt and pepper to taste
½ cup shredded cheddar	1 cup bread crumbs
1 egg, beaten	½ cup grated carrots

Preheat air fryer to 350°F. Mash the beans with a fork in a bowl. Mix in the cheese, salt, and pepper until evenly combined. Stir in half of the bread crumbs and egg. Shape the mixture into 2 patties. Coat each patty with the remaining bread crumbs and spray with cooking oil. Air Fry for 14-16 minutes, turning once. When ready, remove to a plate. Top with grated carrots and serve.

Fennel Tofu Bites

Serves: 4 | Total Time: 35 minutes + marinating time

1/3 cup vegetable broth	½ tsp garlic powder
2 tbsp tomato sauce	Salt and pepper to taste
2 tsp soy sauce	14 oz firm tofu, cubed
1 tbsp nutritional yeast	2/3 cup bread crumbs
1 tsp Italian seasoning	1 tsp Italian seasoning
1 tsp granulated sugar	2 tsp toasted sesame seeds
1 tsp ginger grated	1 cup marinara sauce, warm
½ tsp fennel seeds	

In a large bowl, whisk the vegetable broth, soy sauce, ginger, tomato sauce, nutritional yeast, Italian seasoning, sugar, fennel seeds, garlic powder, salt and black pepper. Toss in tofu to coat. Let marinate covered in the fridge for 30 minutes, tossing once.

Preheat air fryer to 350°F. Mix the breadcrumbs, Italian seasoning, and salt in a bowl. Strain marinade from tofu cubes and dredge them in the breadcrumb mixture. Place tofu cubes in the greased frying basket and Air Fry for 10 minutes, turning once. Serve sprinkled with sesame seeds and marinara sauce on the side.

Bell Pepper & Lentil Tacos

Serves: 2 | Total Time: 40 minutes

2 corn tortilla shells	½ green pepper, sliced
½ cup cooked lentils	½ yellow pepper, sliced
½ white onion, sliced	½ cup shredded mozzarella
½ red pepper, sliced	½ tsp Tabasco sauce

Preheat air fryer to 320°F. Sprinkle half of the mozzarella cheese over one of the tortillas, then top with lentils, Tabasco sauce, onion, and peppers. Scatter the remaining mozzarella cheese, cover with the other tortilla and place in the frying basket. Bake for 6 minutes, flipping halfway through cooking. Serve and enjoy!

Effortless Mac `n´ Cheese

Serves: 4 | Total Time: 15 minutes

1 cup heavy cream	2 tsp grated Parmesan cheese
1 cup milk	16 oz cooked elbow macaroni
½ cup mozzarella cheese	

Preheat air fryer to 400°F. Whisk the heavy cream, milk, mozzarella cheese, and Parmesan cheese until smooth in a bowl. Stir in the macaroni and pour into a baking dish. Cover with foil and Bake in the air fryer for 6 minutes. Remove foil and Bake until cooked through and bubbly, 3-5 minutes. Serve warm.

Caprese-Style Sandwiches

Serves: 2 | Total Time: 20 minutes

2 tbsp balsamic vinegar	2 tomatoes, sliced
4 sandwich bread slices	8 basil leaves
2 oz mozzarella shreds	8 baby spinach leaves
3 tbsp pesto sauce	2 tbsp olive oil

Preheat air fryer to 350°F. Drizzle balsamic vinegar on the bottom of bread slices and smear with pesto sauce. Then, layer mozzarella cheese, tomatoes, baby spinach leaves and basil leaves on top. Add top bread slices. Rub the outside top and bottom of each sandwich with olive oil. Place them in the frying basket and Bake for 5 minutes, flipping once. Serve right away.

Sicilian-Style Vegetarian Pizza

Serves: 2 | Total Time: 20 minutes

1 pizza pie crust	½ tsp dried oregano
¼ cup ricotta cheese	¼ cup Sicilian olives, sliced
½ tbsp tomato paste	¼ cup grated mozzarella
½ white onion, sliced	

Preheat air fryer to 350°F. Lay the pizza dough on a parchment paper sheet. Spread the tomato paste evenly over the pie crust, allowing at least ½ inch border. Sprinkle with oregano and scatter the ricotta cheese on top. Cover with onion and Sicilian olive slices and finish with a layer of mozzarella cheese. Bake for 10 minutes until the cheese has melted and lightly crisped, and the crust is golden brown. Serve sliced and enjoy!

Chili Tofu & Quinoa Bowls

Serves: 2 | Total Time: 30 minutes

1 cup diced peeled sweet potatoes
¼ cup chopped mixed bell peppers
1/8 cup sprouted green lentils

½ onion, sliced	½ tsp chili powder
1 tsp avocado oil	¼ tsp salt
1/8 cup chopped carrots	2 tsp lime zest
8 oz extra-firm tofu, cubed	1 cup cooked quinoa
½ tsp smoked paprika	2 lime wedges

Preheat air fryer to 350°F. Combine the onion, carrots, bell peppers, green lentils, sweet potato, and avocado oil in a bowl. In another bowl, mix the tofu, paprika, chili powder, and salt. Add veggie mixture to the frying basket and Air Fry for 8 minutes. Stir in tofu mixture and cook for 8 more minutes. Combine lime zest and quinoa. Divide into 2 serving bowls. Top each with the tofu mixture and squeeze a lime wedge over. Serve warm.

Tofu & Spinach Lasagna

Serves: 4 | Total Time: 30 minutes

8 oz cooked lasagne noodles	1 tsp onion powder
1 tbsp olive oil	Salt and pepper to taste
2 cups crumbled tofu	2 garlic cloves, minced
2 cups fresh spinach	2 cups marinara sauce
2 tbsp cornstarch	½ cup shredded mozzarella

Warm the olive oil in a large pan over medium heat. Add the tofu and spinach and stir-fry for a minute. Add the cornstarch, onion powder, salt, pepper, and garlic. Stir until the spinach wilts. Remove from heat.

Preheat air fryer to 390°F. Pour a thin layer of pasta sauce in a baking pan. Layer 2-3 lasagne noodles on top of the marinara sauce. Top with a little more sauce and some of the tofu mix. Add another 2-3 noodles on top, then another layer of sauce, then another layer of tofu. Finish with a layer of noodles and a final layer of sauce. Sprinkle with mozzarella cheese on top. Place the pan in the air fryer and Bake for 15 minutes or until the noodle edges are browned and the cheese is melted. Cut and serve.

Tex-Mex Potatoes with Avocado Dressing

Serves: 2 | Total Time: 60 minutes

¼ cup chopped parsley, dill, cilantro, chives

¼ cup yogurt	Salt and pepper to taste
½ avocado, diced	2 tsp olive oil
2 tbsp milk	2 russet potatoes, scrubbed
2 tsp lemon juice	and perforated with a fork
½ tsp lemon zest	1 cup steamed broccoli florets
1 green onion, chopped	½ cup canned white beans
2 cloves garlic, quartered	

In a food processor, blend the yogurt, avocado, milk, lemon juice, lemon zest, green onion, garlic, parsley, dill, cilantro, chives, salt, and pepper until smooth. Transfer it to a small bowl and let chill the dressing covered in the fridge until ready to use.

Preheat air fryer to 400°F. Rub olive oil over both potatoes and sprinkle with salt and pepper. Place them in the frying basket and Bake for 45 minutes, flipping at 30 minutes mark. Let cool onto a cutting board for 5 minutes until cool enough to handle. Cut each potato lengthwise into slices and pinch ends together to open up each slice. Stuff broccoli and beans into potatoes and put them back into the basket, and cook for 3 more minutes. Drizzle avocado dressing over and serve.

Farfalle with White Sauce

Serves: 4 | Total Time: 30 minutes

4 cups cauliflower florets	1 tbsp nutritional yeast
1 medium onion, chopped	2 large garlic cloves, peeled
8 oz farfalle pasta	2 tbsp fresh lemon juice
2 tbsp chives, minced	Salt and pepper to taste
½ cup cashew pieces	

Preheat air fryer to 390°F. Put the cauliflower in the fryer, spray with oil, and Bake for 8 minutes. Remove the basket, stir, and add the onion. Roast for 10 minutes or until the cauliflower is golden and the onions soft. Cook the farfalle pasta according to the package directions. Set aside. Put the roasted cauliflower and onions along with the cashews, 1 ½ of cups water, yeast, garlic, lemon, salt, and pepper in a blender. Blend until creamy. Pour a large portion of the sauce on top of the warm pasta and add the minced scallions. Serve.

Golden Breaded Mushrooms

Serves: 2 | Total Time: 20 minutes

2 cups crispy rice cereal
1 tsp nutritional yeast
2 tsp garlic powder
1tsp dried oregano
1 tsp dried basil
Salt to taste

1 tbsp Dijon mustard
1 tbsp mayonnaise
¼ cup milk
8 oz whole mushrooms
4 tbsp chili sauce
3 tbsp mayonnaise

Preheat air fryer to 350°F. Blend rice cereal, garlic powder, oregano, basil, nutritional yeast, and salt in a food processor until it gets a breadcrumb consistency. Set aside in a bowl. Mix the mustard, mayonnaise, and milk in a bowl. Dip mushrooms in the mustard mixture; shake off any excess. Then, dredge them in the breadcrumbs; shake off any excess. Place mushrooms in the greased frying basket and Air Fry for 7 minutes, shaking once. Mix the mayonnaise with chili sauce in a small bowl. Serve the mushrooms with the dipping sauce on the side.

Chili & Cilantro Grilled Pineapple Salsa

Serves: 4 | Total Time: 15 minutes

½ peeled pineapple, sliced
Salt to taste
1 tsp coconut oil, melted
1 serrano pepper, diced
6 cherry tomatoes, halved
1 avocado, diced

½ diced red onion
1 tbsp chopped cilantro
2 cloves garlic, minced
½ tsp brown sugar
½ lime, juiced and zested

Preheat air fryer to 400°F. Combine pineapple cubes, coconut oil, and salt in a bowl. Add the pineapple to the greased frying basket and Air Fry for 8 minutes, shaking once. Place cherry tomatoes, avocado, red onion, cilantro, garlic, brown sugar, lime juice, lime zest, and salt in a bowl and mix well. Add the pineapple and stir until well combined. Let chill in the fridge before using.

Spicy Bean Patties

Serves: 4 | Total Time: 20 minutes

1 cup canned black beans
1 bread slice, torn
2 tbsp spicy brown mustard
1 tbsp chili powder
1 egg white
2 tbsp grated carrots

¼ diced green bell pepper
1-2 jalapeño peppers, diced
¼ tsp ground cumin
¼ tsp smoked paprika
2 tbsp cream cheese
1 tbsp olive oil

Preheat air fryer to 350°F. Using a fork, mash beans until smooth. Stir in the remaining ingredients, except olive oil. Form mixture into 4 patties. Place bean patties in the greased frying basket and Air Fry for 6 minutes, turning once, and brush with olive oil. Serve immediately.

Golden Fried Tofu

Serves: 4 | Total Time: 20 minutes

¼ cup flour
¼ cup cornstarch
1 tsp garlic powder
¼ tsp onion powder

Salt and pepper to taste
1 (14-oz) firm tofu, cubed
2 tbsp cilantro, chopped

Preheat air fryer to 390°F. Combine the flour, cornstarch, salt, garlic, onion powder, and black pepper in a bowl. Stir well. Place the tofu cubes in the flour mix. Toss to coat. Spray the tofu with oil and place them in a single layer in the greased frying basket. Air Fry for 14-16 minutes, flipping the pieces once until golden and crunchy. Top with freshly chopped cilantro and serve immediately.

Party Giant Nachos

Serves: 2 | Total Time: 20 minutes

2 tbsp sour cream
½ tsp chili powder
Salt to taste
2 soft corn tortillas
2 tsp avocado oil
½ cup refried beans
¼ cup cheddar cheese shreds

2 tbsp Parmesan cheese
2 tbsp sliced black olives
¼ cup torn iceberg lettuce
¼ cup baby spinach
½ sliced avocado
1 tomato, diced
2 lime wedges

Preheat air fryer to 400°F. Whisk the sour cream, chili powder, and salt in a small bowl. Brush tortillas with avocado oil and season one side with salt. Place tortillas in the frying basket and Bake for 3 minutes. Set aside.

Layer the refried beans, Parmesan and cheddar cheeses in the tortillas. Place them back into the basket and Bake for 2 minutes. Divide tortillas into 2 serving plates. Top each tortilla with black olives, baby spinach, lettuce, and tomatoes. Dollop sour cream mixture on each. Serve with lime and avocado wedges on the side.

Cheddar Bean Taquitos

Serves: 4 | Total Time: 25 minutes

1 cup refried beans
2 cups cheddar shreds
½ jalapeño pepper, minced

¼ chopped white onion
1 tsp oregano
15 soft corn tortillas

Preheat air fryer to 350°F. Spread refried beans, jalapeño pepper, white onion, oregano and cheddar shreds down the center of each corn tortilla. Roll each tortilla tightly. Place tacos, seam side down, in the frying basket, and Air Fry for 4 minutes. Serve immediately.

Sweet & Spicy Vegetable Stir-Fry

Serves: 2 | Total Time: 45 minutes

½ pineapple, cut into bite-size chunks
¼ cup Tabasco sauce
¼ cup lime juice
2 tsp allspice
5 oz cauliflower florets

1 carrot, thinly sliced
1 cup frozen peas, thawed
2 scallions, chopped

Preheat air fryer to 400°F. Whisk Tabasco sauce, lime juice, and allspice in a bowl. Then toss in cauliflower, pineapple, and carrots until coated. Strain the remaining sauce; reserve it. Air Fry the veggies for 12 minutes, shake, and Air Fry for 10-12 more minutes until cooked. Once the veggies are ready, remove to a bowl. Combine peas, scallions, and reserved sauce until coated. Transfer to a pan and Air Fry them for 3 minutes. Remove them to the bowl and serve right away.

Fajita Stuffed Bell Peppers

Serves: 4 | Total Time: 75 minutes

4 green and red bell peppers, tops and insides discarded
2 russet potatoes, scrubbed and perforated with a fork
2 tsp olive oil   Salt and pepper to taste
1 cup mushrooms, chopped   ¼ cup canned corn kernels
2 tbsp milk   ½ cup mozzarella shreds
2 tbsp yogurt   2 tsp chopped parsley
1 tsp olive oil   1 cup bechamel sauce
1 tbsp fajita seasoning

Preheat air fryer to 400°F. Rub olive oil over both potatoes and sprinkle with salt and pepper. Place them in the frying basket and Bake for 45 minutes, flipping at 30 minutes mark. Let cool onto a cutting board for 5 minutes until cool enough to handle. Scoop out cooled potato into a bowl. Discard skins.

Place the mushrooms in the frying basket and Air Fry for 2 minutes. Using the back of a fork, mash cooked potatoes, yogurt, milk, olive oil, Italian seasoning, salt, and pepper until smooth. Toss in cooked mushrooms, corn, and mozzarella cheese. Stuff bell peppers with the potato mixture. Place bell peppers in the frying basket and Bake for 10 minutes. Serve immediately sprinkled with parsley and bechamel sauce on side. Enjoy!

Hearty Salad

Serves: 2 | Total Time: 15 minutes

5 oz cauliflower, cut into florets
2 grated carrots
1 tbsp olive oil   ¼ cup mayonnaise
1 tbsp lemon juice   1/8 tsp black pepper
2 tbsp raisins   1 tsp cumin
2 tbsp roasted pepitas   ½ tsp chia seeds
2 tbsp diced red onion   ½ tsp sesame seeds

Preheat air fryer to 350°F. Combine the cauliflower, cumin, olive oil, black pepper and lemon juice in a bowl, place it in the frying basket, and Bake for 5 minutes. Transfer it to a serving dish. Toss in the remaining ingredients. Let chill covered in the fridge until ready to use. Serve sprinkled with sesame and chia seeds.

Grilled Cheese Sandwich

Serves: 1 | Total Time: 15 minutes

2 sprouted bread slices   1 garlic clove, minced
1 tsp sunflower oil   2 tbsp kimchi
2 Halloumi cheese slices   1 cup Iceberg lettuce, torn
1 tsp mellow white miso

Preheat air fryer to 390°F. Brush the outside of the bread with sunflower oil. Put the sliced cheese, buttered sides facing out inside and close the sandwich. Put the sandwich in the frying basket and Air Fry for 12 minutes, flipping once until golden and crispy on the outside.

On a plate, open the sandwich and spread the miso and garlic clove over the inside of one slice. Top with kimchi and lettuce, close the sandwich, cut in half, and serve.

Eggplant Pizza Bites

Serves: 4 | Total Time: 25 minutes

3 tsp olive oil   1 eggplant, sliced
1 shallot, chopped   Salt and pepper to taste
½ tsp garlic powder   1 cup shredded mozzarella
½ tsp dried oregano   2 tbsp Parmesan cheese
½ cup diced mushrooms   ¼ cup chopped basil
½ cup marinara sauce

Warm 2 tsp of olive oil in a skillet over medium heat. Add in shallot and mushrooms and cook for 4-5 minutes until the mushrooms are tender. Stir in marinara sauce, oregano, and garlic powder. Turn the heat off.

Preheat air fryer to 380°F. Rub the remaining olive oil over both sides of the eggplant circles. Arrange the circles on the frying basket and sprinkle with salt and black pepper. Top each circle with the marinara sauce mixture and shredded mozzarella and Parmesan cheese. Place the frying basket in the air fryer and Bake for 5-6 minutes. Scatter with the basil and serve warm.

Rainbow Quinoa Patties

Serves: 4 | Total Time: 20 minutes

1 cup canned tri-bean blend, drained and rinsed
2 tbsp olive oil   ¼ cup shredded carrot
½ tsp ground cumin   2 tbsp chopped cilantro
½ tsp garlic salt   1 tsp chili powder
1 tbsp paprika   ½ tsp salt
1/3 cup uncooked quinoa 2 tbsp mascarpone cheese
2 tbsp chopped onion

Place 1/3 cup of water, 1 tbsp of olive oil, cumin, and salt in a saucepan over medium heat and bring it to a boil. Remove from the heat and stir in quinoa. Let rest covered for 5 minutes.

Preheat air fryer to 350°F. Using the back of a fork, mash beans until smooth. Toss in cooked quinoa and the remaining ingredients. Form mixture into 4 patties. Place patties in the greased frying basket and Air Fry for 6 minutes, turning once, and brush with the remaining olive oil. Serve immediately.

Black Bean Stuffed Potato Boats

Serves: 4 | Total Time: 55 minutes

4 russets potatoes   1 scallion, chopped
1 cup chipotle mayonnaise   1/3 cup chopped cilantro
1 cup canned black beans   1 poblano chile, minced
2 tomatoes, chopped   1 avocado, diced

Preheat air fryer to 390°F. Clean the potatoes, poke with a fork, and spray with oil. Put in the air fryer and Bake for 30 minutes or until softened.

Heat the beans in a pan over medium heat. Put the potatoes on a plate and cut them across the top. Open them with a fork so you can stuff them. Top each potato with chipotle mayonnaise, beans, tomatoes, scallions, cilantro, poblano chile, and avocado. Serve immediately.

Mushroom Lasagna

Serves: 4 | Total Time: 40 minutes

2 tbsp olive oil
1 zucchini, diced
½ cup diced mushrooms
¼ cup diced onion
1 cup marinara sauce
1 cup ricotta cheese
1/3 cup grated Parmesan
1 egg
2 tsp Italian seasoning
2 tbsp fresh basil, chopped
½ tsp thyme
1 tbsp red pepper flakes
½ tsp salt
5 lasagna noodle sheets
1 cup grated mozzarella

Heat the oil in a skillet over medium heat. Add zucchini, mushrooms, 1 tbsp of basil, thyme, red pepper flakes and onion and cook for 4 minutes until the veggies are tender. Toss in marinara sauce, and bring it to a bowl. Then, low the heat and simmer for 3 minutes.

Preheat air fryer to 375°F. Combine ricotta cheese, Parmesan cheese, egg, Italian seasoning, and salt in a bowl. Spoon ¼ of the veggie mixture into a cake pan. Add a layer of lasagna noodles on top, breaking apart noodles first to fit the pan. Then, top with 1/3 of ricotta mixture and ¼ of mozzarella cheese. Repeat the layer 2 more times, finishing with mozzarella cheese on top. Cover cake pan with aluminum foil.

Place the cake pan in the frying basket and Bake for 12 minutes. Remove the foil and cook for 3 more minutes. Let rest for 10 minutes before slicing. Serve immediately sprinkled with the remaining fresh basil.

Vegetarian Cottage Pie

Serves: 4 | Total Time: 40 minutes

1 russet potato, peeled and diced
1 tbsp olive oil
2 tbsp balsamic vinegar
¼ cup cheddar shreds
2 tbsp milk
Salt and pepper to taste
2 tsp avocado oil
1 cup cooked lentils
½ onion, diced
3 cloves garlic
1 carrot, diced
¼ diced green bell peppers
1 celery stalk, diced
2/3 cup tomato sauce
1 tsp chopped rosemary
1 tbsp sesame seeds
1 tsp thyme leaves
1 lemon

Add salted water to a pot over high heat and bring it to a boil. Add in diced potatoes and cook for 5 minutes until fork tender. Drain and transfer it to a bowl. Add the olive oil, cheddar shreds,, milk, salt, and pepper and mash it until smooth. Set the potato topping aside.

Preheat air fryer to 350°F. Place avocado oil, lentils, garlic, onion, carrot, bell pepper, and celery in a skillet over medium heat and cook for 4 minutes until the veggies are tender. Stir in the remaining ingredients and turn the heat off. Spoon the filling into a greased cake pan. Top with the potato topping. Using the tines of a fork, create shallow lines along the top of mashed potatoes. Place the cake pan in the frying basket and Bake for 10-12 minutes. Let rest for 10 minutes before serving, sprinkled with sesame seeds and squeezed lemon.

Brown Rice & Bean Burrito Bowls

Serves: 4 | Total Time: 10 minutes

1 cup sour cream
2 tbsp milk
1 tsp ground cumin
1 tsp chili powder
1/8 tsp cayenne pepper
1 tbsp tomato paste
1 white onion, chopped
1 garlic clove, minced
½ tsp ground turmeric
½ tsp salt
1 cup canned black beans
1 cup canned corn kernels
1 tsp olive oil
4 cups cooked brown rice
3 tomatoes, diced
1 avocado, diced

Whisk the sour cream, milk, cumin, ground turmeric, chili powder, cayenne pepper, and salt in a bowl. Let chill covered in the fridge until ready to use.

Preheat air fryer to 350°F. Combine beans, white onion, tomato paste, garlic, corn, and olive oil in a bowl. Transfer it into the frying basket and Air Fry for 5 minutes. Divide cooked rice into 4 serving bowls. Top each with bean mixture, tomatoes, and avocado and drizzle with sour cream mixture over. Serve immediately.

Fried Cauliflower Tacos

Serves: 4 | Total Time: 20 minutes

2 tomatoes, diced
½ tsp ground cumin
½ diced red onion
1 jalapeño, finely diced
½ lime, juiced and zested
¼ cup chopped cilantro
Garlic salt to taste
1 egg
2 tbsp milk
1 cup bread crumbs
½ cup flour
10 oz cauliflower florets
8 corn tortillas
1 cup coleslaw mix

In a bowl, combine the tomatoes, cumin, jalapeño, onion, lime juice, lime zest, cilantro, and garlic salt. Let chill the resulting salsa covered in the fridge until ready to use.

Preheat air fryer to 375°F. In a small bowl, beat the egg and milk. In another bowl, mix flour and breadcrumbs. Dip cauliflower florets in the egg mixture, then dredge them in the mixed flour and breadcrumbs. Place the cauliflower in the greased frying basket and Air Fry for 8-10 minutes, shaking once. Divide the fried cauliflower between the tortillas. Top with coleslaw mix and salsa.

Kale & Lentils with Crispy Onions

Serves: 4 | Total Time: 40 minutes

2 cups cooked red lentils
1 onion, cut into rings
½ cup kale, steamed
3 garlic cloves, minced
½ lemon, juiced and zested
2 tsp cornstarch
1 tsp dried oregano
Salt and pepper to taste

Preheat air fryer to 390°F. Put the onion rings in the greased frying basket; do not overlap. Spray with oil and season with salt. Air Fry for 14-16 minutes, stirring twice until crispy and crunchy. Place the kale and lentils into a pan over medium heat and stir until heated through. Remove and add the garlic, lemon juice, cornstarch, salt, zest, oregano and black pepper. Stir well and pour in bowls. Top with the crisp onion rings and serve.

Pine Nut Eggplant Dip

Serves: 4 | Total Time: 35 minutes

2 ½ tsp olive oil	1 tbsp lemon juice
1 eggplant, halved lengthwise	2 cloves garlic, minced
1/2 cup Parmesan cheese	1/8 tsp ground cumin
2 tsp pine nuts	1 tsp smoked paprika
1 tbsp chopped walnuts	Salt and pepper to taste
¼ cup tahini	1 tbsp chopped parsley

Preheat air fryer to 375°F. Rub olive oil over eggplant and pierce the eggplant flesh 3 times with a fork. Place eggplant, flat side down, in the frying basket and Bake for 25 minutes. Let cool onto a cutting board for 5 minutes until cool enough to handle. Scoop out eggplant flesh. Add pine nuts and walnuts to the basket and Air Fry for 2 minutes, shaking every 30 seconds to ensure they don´t burn. Set aside in a bowl.

In a food processor, blend eggplant flesh, tahini, lemon juice, garlic, smoked paprika, cumin, salt, and pepper until smooth. Transfer to a bowl. Scatter with the roasted pine nuts, Parmesan cheese, and parsley. Drizzle the dip with the remaining olive oil. Serve and enjoy!

Lentil Burritos with Cilantro Chutney

Serves: 4 | Total Time: 30 minutes

1 cup cilantro chutney	Salt to taste
1 lb cooked potatoes, mashed	½ tsp turmeric
2 tsp sunflower oil	¼ tsp cayenne powder
3 garlic cloves, minced	4 large flour tortillas
1 ½ tbsp fresh lime juice	1 cup cooked lentils
1 ½ tsp cumin powder	½ cup shredded cabbage
1 tsp onion powder	¼ cup minced red onions
1 tsp coriander powder	

Preheat air fryer to 390°F. Place the mashed potatoes, sunflower oil, garlic, lime, cumin, onion powder, coriander, salt, turmeric, and cayenne in a large bowl. Stir well until combined. Lay the tortillas out flat on the counter. In the middle of each, distribute the potato filling. Add some of the lentils, cabbage, and red onions on top of the potatoes. Close the wraps by folding the bottom of the tortillas up and over the filling, then folding the sides in, then roll the bottom up to form a burrito. Place the wraps in the greased frying basket, seam side down. Air Fry for 6-8 minutes, flipping once until golden and crispy. Serve topped with cilantro chutney.

Tortilla Pizza Margherita

Serves: 1 | Total Time: 15 minutes

1 flour tortilla	1/3 cup grated mozzarella
¼ cup tomato sauce	3 basil leaves

Preheat air fryer to 350°F. Put the tortilla in the greased basket and pour the sauce in the center. Spread across the whole tortilla. Sprinkle with cheese and Bake for 8-10 minutes or until crisp. Remove carefully and top with basil leaves. Serve hot.

Pinto Bean Casserole

Serves: 2 | Total Time: 15 minutes

1 (15-oz) can pinto beans	½ tsp dried oregano
¼ cup tomato sauce	½ tsp cumin
2 tbsp cornstarch	1 tsp smoked paprika
2 garlic cloves, minced	Salt and pepper to taste

Preheat air fryer to 390°F. Stir the beans, tomato sauce, cornstarch, garlic, oregano, cumin, smoked paprika, salt, and pepper in a bowl until combined. Pour the bean mix into a greased baking pan. Bake in the fryer for 4 minutes. Remove, stir, and Bake for 4 minutes or until the mix is thick and heated through. Serve hot.

Zucchini Tamale Pie

Serves: 4 | Total Time: 45 minutes

1 cup canned diced tomatoes with juice	
1 zucchini, diced	1 tsp onion powder
3 tbsp safflower oil	Salt to taste
1 cup cooked pinto beans	½ tsp red chili flakes
3 garlic cloves, minced	½ cup ground cornmeal
1 tbsp corn masa flour	1 tsp nutritional yeast
1 tsp dried oregano	2 tbsp chopped cilantro
½ tsp ground cumin	½ tsp lime zest

Warm 2 tbsp of the oil in a skillet over medium heat and sauté the zucchini for 3 minutes or until they begin to brown. Add the beans, tomatoes, garlic, flour, oregano, cumin, onion powder, salt, and chili flakes. Cook over medium heat, stirring often, about 5 minutes until the mix is thick and no liquid remains. Remove from heat. Spray a baking pan with oil and pour the mix inside. Smooth out the top and set aside.

In a pot over high heat, add the cornmeal, 1 ½ cups of water, and salt. Whisk constantly as the mix begins to boil. Once it boils, reduce the heat to low. Add the yeast and oil and continue to cook, stirring often, for 10 minutes or until the mix is thick and hard to stir. Remove. Preheat air fryer to 325°F. Add the cilantro and lime zest into the cornmeal mix and thoroughly combine. Using a rubber spatula, spread it evenly over the filling in the baking pan to form a crust topping. Put in the frying basket and Bake for 20 minutes or until the top is golden. Let it cool for 5 to 10 minutes, then cut and serve.

Mushroom Bolognese Casserole

Serves: 4 | Total Time: 20 minutes

1 cup canned diced tomatoes	¾ tsp dried oregano
2 garlic cloves, minced	1 cup chopped mushrooms
1 tsp onion powder	16 oz cooked spaghetti
¾ tsp dried basil	

Preheat air fryer to 400°F. Whisk the tomatoes and their juices, garlic, onion powder, basil, oregano, and mushrooms in a baking pan. Cover with aluminum foil and Bake for 6 minutes. Slide out the pan and add the cooked spaghetti; stir to coat. Cover with aluminum foil and Bake for 3 minutes until bubbly. Serve and enjoy!

Cheesy Eggplant Lasagna

Serves: 4 | Total Time: 40 minutes

¾ cup chickpea flour	2 cups panko bread crumbs
½ cup milk	1 eggplant, sliced
3 tbsp lemon juice	2 cups jarred tomato sauce
1 tbsp chili sauce	½ cup ricotta cheese
2 tsp allspice	1/3 cup mozzarella cheese

Preheat air fryer to 400°F. Whisk chickpea flour, milk, lemon juice, chili sauce, and allspice until smooth. Set aside. On a plate, put the breadcrumbs. Submerge each eggplant slice into the batter, shaking off any excess, and dip into the breadcrumbs until well coated. Bake for 10 minutes, turning once. Let cool slightly.

Spread 2 tbsp of tomato sauce at the bottom of a baking pan. Lay a single layer of eggplant slices, scatter with ricotta cheese and top with tomato sauce. Repeat the process until no ingredients are left. Scatter with mozzarella cheese on top and Bake at 350°F for 10 minutes until the eggplants are cooked and the cheese golden brown. Serve immediately.

Cheddar-Bean Flautas

Serves: 4 | Total Time: 15 minutes

8 corn tortillas	1 cup shredded cheddar
1 (15-oz) can refried beans	1 cup guacamole

Preheat air fryer to 390°F. Wet the tortillas with water. Spray the frying basket with oil and stack the tortillas inside. Air Fry for 1 minute. Remove to a flat surface, laying them out individually. Scoop an equal amount of beans in a line down the center of each tortilla. Top with cheddar cheese. Roll the tortilla sides over the filling and put seam-side down in the greased frying basket. Air Fry for 7 minutes or until the tortillas are golden and crispy. Serve immediately topped with guacamole.

Colorful Meatless Pizza

Serves: 4 | Total Time: 50 minutes

½ cup pizza sauce	1 yellow pepper, sliced
1 tsp dried oregano	1 green pepper, sliced
10 fresh basil leaves	16 cherry tomatoes, halved
1 pizza dough	½ cup mozzarella cheese

Preheat air fryer to 400°F. Form 4 balls with the pizza dough and roll out each into a 6-inch round pizza. Spread the pizza sauce over the bases and sprinkle with oregano. Arrange the peppers and tomatoes on top and finally cover with mozzarella cheese. Working in batches, Bake the pizzas for 10-12 minutes until golden brown and the crust is crispy. Top with basil leaves. Serve and enjoy!

Quinoa Green Pizza

Serves: 2 | Total Time: 25 minutes

¾ cup quinoa flour	½ tsp dried oregano
½ tsp dried basil	1 tbsp apple cider vinegar
1/3 cup ricotta cheese	½ tsp garlic powder
2/3 cup chopped broccoli	

Preheat air fryer to 350°F. Whisk quinoa flour, basil, oregano, apple cider vinegar, and ½ cup of water until smooth. Set aside. Cut 2 pieces of parchment paper. Place the quinoa mixture on one paper, top with another piece, and flatten to create a crust. Discard the top piece of paper. Bake for 5 minutes, turn and discard the other piece of paper. Spread the ricotta cheese over the crust, scatter with broccoli, and sprinkle with garlic. Grill at 400°F for 5 minutes until golden brown. Serve warm.

Tex-Mex Stuffed Sweet Potatoes

Serves: 2 | Total Time: 40 minutes

2 medium sweet potatoes	1 tsp taco seasoning
1 (15.5-oz) can black beans	2 tbsp lime juice
2 scallions, finely sliced	¼ cup Ranch dressing
1 tbsp hot sauce	

Preheat air fryer to 400°F. Add in sweet potatoes and Roast for 30 minutes. Toss the beans, scallions, hot sauce, taco seasoning, and lime juice. Set aside. Once the potatoes are ready, cut them lengthwise, 2/3 through. Spoon 1/4 of the bean mixture into each half and drizzle Ranch dressing before serving.

Tomato & Squash Stuffed Mushrooms

Serves: 2 | Total Time: 15 minutes

12 whole white button mushrooms	
3 tsp olive oil	¼ tsp salt
2 tbsp diced zucchini	2 tbsp tomato paste
1 tsp soy sauce	1 tbsp chopped parsley

Preheat air fryer to 350°F. Remove the stems from the mushrooms. Chop the stems finely and set in a bowl. Brush 1 tsp of olive oil around the top ridge of mushroom caps. To the bowl of the stem, add all ingredients, except for parsley, and mix. Divide and press mixture into tops of mushroom caps. Place the mushrooms in the frying basket and Air Fry for 5 minutes. Top with parsley. Serve.

Powerful Jackfruit Fritters

Serves 4 | Total Time: 30 minutes

1 (20-oz) can jackfruit, chopped	
1 egg, beaten	2 tbsp chopped nori
1 tbsp Dijon mustard	2 tbsp flour
1 tbsp mayonnaise	1 tbsp Cajun seasoning
1 tbsp prepared horseradish	¼ tsp garlic powder
2 tbsp grated yellow onion	¼ tsp salt
2 tbsp chopped parsley	2 lemon wedges

In a bowl, combine jackfruit, egg, mustard, mayonnaise, horseradish, onion, parsley, nori, flour, Cajun seasoning, garlic, and salt. Let chill in the fridge for 15 minutes. Preheat air fryer to 350°F. Divide the mixture into 12 balls. Place them in the frying basket and Air Fry for 10 minutes. Serve with lemon wedges.

Gorgeous Jalapeño Poppers

Serves: 6 | Total Time: 25 minutes

1 cup panko breadcrumbs   ¼ cup grated Gruyere cheese
6 jalapeños, halved lengthwise   2 tbsp chives, chopped
4 oz cream cheese

Scoop out the seeds and membranes of the jalapeño halves, discard. Combine cream cheese, Gruyere cheese, and chives in a bowl. Fill the jalapeño halves with the cream cheese filling using a small spoon. Sprinkle with breadcrumbs and spritz the top with cooking spray.

Preheat air fryer to 325°F. Put the stuffed peppers in a single layer on the greased frying basket and Bake until the peppers are tender, cheese is melted, and the top is brown, 11-13minutes. Serve warm and enjoy!

Vegetarian Stuffed Bell Peppers

Serves: 3 | Total Time: 40 minutes

1 cup mushrooms, chopped   2 tbsp dried parsley
1 tbsp allspice   2 tbsp hot sauce
¾ cup Alfredo sauce   Salt and pepper to taste
½ cup canned diced tomatoes   3 large bell peppers
1 cup cooked rice

Preheat air fryer to 375°F. Whisk mushrooms, allspice and 1 cup of boiling water until smooth. Stir in Alfredo sauce, tomatoes and juices, rice, parsley, hot sauce, salt, and black pepper. Set aside. Cut the top of each bell pepper, take out the core and seeds without breaking the pepper. Fill each pepper with the rice mixture and cover them with a 6-inch square of aluminum foil, folding the edges. Roast for 30 minutes until tender. Let cool completely before unwrapping. Serve immediately.

Easy Zucchini Lasagna Roll-Ups

Serves: 2 | Total Time: 40 minutes

2 medium zucchini   1 tbsp allspice
2 tbsp lemon juice   2 cups marinara sauce
1 ½ cups ricotta cheese   1/3 cup mozzarella cheese

Preheat air fryer to 400°F. Cut the ends off each zucchini, then slice into 1/4-inch thick pieces and drizzle with lemon juice. Roast for 5 minutes until slightly tender. Let cool slightly. Combine ricotta cheese and allspice in a bowl; set aside. Spread 2 tbsp of marinara sauce on the bottom of a baking pan. Spoon 1-2 tbsp of the ricotta mixture onto each slice, roll up each slice and place them spiral-side up in the pan. Scatter with the remaining ricotta mixture and drizzle with marinara sauce. Top with mozzarella cheese and Bake at 360°F for 20 minutes until the cheese is bubbly and golden brown. Serve warm.

Colorful Vegetable Medley

Serves: 4 | Total Time: 20 minutes

1 lb green beans, chopped   1 zucchini, cut into chunks
2 carrots, cubed   1 red bell pepper, sliced
Salt and pepper to taste

Preheat air fryer to 390°F. Combine green beans, carrots, salt, and pepper in a large bowl. Spray with cooking oil and transfer to the frying basket. Roast for 6 minutes.

Combine zucchini and red pepper in a bowl. Season to taste and spray with cooking oil; set aside. When the cooking time is up, add the zucchini and red pepper to the basket. Cook for another 6 minutes. Serve and enjoy.

Quick-To-Make Quesadillas

Serves: 4 | Total Time: 30 minutes

12 oz goat cheese   2 tbsp lemon juice
2 tbsp vinegar   4 flour tortillas
1 tbsp taco seasoning   ¼ cup hot sauce
1 ripe avocado, pitted   ½ cup Alfredo sauce
4 scallions, finely sliced   16 cherry tomatoes, halved

Preheat air fryer to 400°F. Slice goat cheese into 4 pieces. Set aside. In a bowl, whisk vinegar and taco seasoning until combined. Submerge each slice into the vinegar and Air Fry for 12 minutes until crisp, turning once. Let cool slightly before cutting into 1/2-inch thick strips.

Using a fork, mash the avocado in a bowl. Stir in scallions and lemon juice and set aside. Lay one tortilla on a flat surface, cut from one edge to the center, then spread ¼ of the avocado mixture on one quadrant, 1 tbsp of hot sauce on the next quadrant, and finally 2 tbsp of Alfredo sauce on the other half. Top the non-sauce half with ¼ of cherry tomatoes and ¼ of goat cheese strips.

To fold, start with the avocado quadrant, folding each over the next one until you create a stacked triangle. Repeat the process with the remaining tortillas. Air Fry for 5 minutes until crispy, turning once. Serve warm.

Stuffed Portobellos

Serves: 4 | Total Time: 45 minutes

1 cup cherry tomatoes   ¼ tsp dried thyme
2 ¼ tsp olive oil   Salt and pepper to taste
3 tbsp grated mozzarella   ¼ cup bread crumbs
1 cup chopped baby spinach   4 portobello mushrooms,
1 garlic clove, minced   stemmed and gills removed
¼ tsp dried oregano   1 tbsp chopped parsley

Preheat air fryer to 360°F. Combine tomatoes, ¼ teaspoon olive oil, and salt in a small bowl. Arrange in a single layer in the parchment-lined frying basket and Air Fry for 10 minutes. Stir and flatten the tomatoes with the back of a spoon, then Air Fry for another 6-8 minutes. Transfer the tomatoes to a medium bowl and combine with spinach, garlic, oregano, thyme, pepper, bread crumbs, and the rest of the olive oil.

Place the mushrooms on a work surface with the gills facing up. Spoon tomato mixture and mozzarella cheese equally into the mushroom caps and transfer the mushrooms to the frying basket. Air Fry for 8-10 minutes until the mushrooms have softened and the tops are golden. Garnish with chopped parsley and serve.

Chive Potato Pierogi

Serves: 4 | Total Time: 55 minutes

2 boiled potatoes, mashed	1 tbsp chopped parsley
Salt and pepper to taste	1 ¼ cups flour
1 tsp cumin powder	¼ tsp garlic powder
2 tbsp sour cream	¾ cup Greek yogurt
¼ cup grated Parmesan	1 egg
2 tbsp chopped chives	

Combine the mashed potatoes along with sour cream, cumin, parsley, chives, pepper, and salt and stir until slightly chunky. Mix the flour, salt, and garlic powder in a large bowl. Stir in yogurt until it comes together as a sticky dough. Knead in the bowl for about 2-3 minutes to make it smooth. Whisk the egg and 1 teaspoon of water in a small bowl. Roll out the dough on a lightly floured work surface to ¼-inch thickness. Cut out 12 circles with a cookie cutter.

Preheat air fryer to 350°F. Divide the potato mixture and Parmesan cheese between the dough circles. Brush the edges of them with the egg wash and fold the dough over the filling into half-moon shapes. Crimp the edges with a fork to seal. Arrange the on the greased frying basket and Air Fry for 8-10 minutes, turning the pierogies once, until the outside is golden. Serve warm.

Curried Cauliflower

Serves: 2 | Total Time: 30 minutes

1 cup canned diced tomatoes	1 tsp ground ginger
2 cups milk	½ tsp ground cumin
2 tbsp lime juice	12 oz frozen cauliflower
1 tbsp allspice	16 oz cheddar cheese, cubed
1 tbsp curry powder	¼ cup chopped cilantro

Preheat air fryer to 375°F. Combine the tomatoes and their juices, milk, lime juice, allspice, curry powder, ginger, and cumin in a baking pan. Toss in cauliflower and cheddar cheese until coated. Roast for 15 minutes, stir and Roast for another 10 minutes until bubbly. Scatter with cilantro before serving.

Bengali Samosa with Mango Chutney

Serves: 4 | Total Time: 65 minutes

¼ tsp ground fenugreek seeds

1 cup diced mango	1 potato, mashed
1 tbsp minced red onion	½ tsp garam masala
2 tsp honey	¼ tsp ground turmeric
1 tsp minced ginger	⅛ tsp chili powder
1 tsp apple cider vinegar	¼ tsp ground cumin
1 phyllo dough sheet	½ cup green peas
2 tbsp olive oil	2 scallions, chopped

Mash mango in a small bowl until chunky. Stir in onion, ginger, honey, and vinegar. Save in the fridge until ready to use. Place the mashed potato in a bowl. Add half of the olive oil, garam masala, turmeric, chili powder, ground fenugreek seeds, cumin, and salt and stir until mostly smooth. Stir in peas and scallions.

Preheat air fryer to 425°F. Lightly flour a flat work surface and transfer the phyllo dough. Cut into 8 equal portions and roll each portion into ¼-inch thick rounds. Divide the potato filling between the dough rounds. Fold in three sides and pinch at the meeting point, almost like a pyramid. Arrange the samosas in the frying basket and brush with the remaining olive oil. Bake for 10 minutes, then flip the samosas. Bake for another 4-6 minutes until the crust is crisp and golden. Serve with mango chutney.

Healthy Living Mushroom Enchiladas

Serves: 4 | Total Time: 40 minutes

2 cups sliced mushrooms	¼ tsp red pepper flakes
½ onion, thinly sliced	1 cup grated mozzarella
2 garlic cloves, minced	1 cup sour cream
1 tbsp olive oil	2 tbsp mayonnaise
10 oz spinach, chopped	Juice of 1 lime
½ tsp ground cumin	Salt and pepper to taste
1 tbsp dried oregano	8 corn tortillas
1 tsp chili powder	1 jalapeño pepper, diced
¼ cup grated feta cheese	¼ cup chopped cilantro

Preheat air fryer to 400°F. Combine mushrooms, onion, oregano, garlic, chili powder, olive oil, and salt in a small bowl until well coated. Transfer to the greased frying basket. Cook for 5 minutes, then shake the basket. Cook for another 3 to 4 minutes, then transfer to a medium bowl. Wipe out the frying basket. Take the garlic cloves from the mushroom mixture and finely mince them. Return half of the garlic to the bowl with the mushrooms. Stir in spinach, cumin, red pepper flakes, and ½ cup of mozzarella. Place the other half of the minced garlic in a small bowl along with sour cream, mayonnaise, feta, the rest of the mozzarella, lime juice, and black pepper.

To prepare the enchiladas, spoon 2 tablespoons of mushroom mixture in the center of each tortilla. Roll the tortilla and place it seam-side down in the baking dish. Repeat for the rest of the tortillas. Top with sour cream mixture and garnish with jalapenos. Place the dish in the frying basket and bake for 20 minutes until heated through and just brown on top. Top with cilantro. Serve.

Vegetarian Paella

Serves: 3 | Total Time: 50 minutes

½ cup chopped artichoke hearts	
½ sliced red bell peppers	3 tbsp hot sauce
4 mushrooms, thinly sliced	2 tbsp lemon juice
½ cup canned diced tomatoes	1 tbsp allspice
½ cup canned chickpeas	1 cup rice

Preheat air fryer to 400°F. Combine the artichokes, peppers, mushrooms, tomatoes and their juices, chickpeas, hot sauce, lemon juice, and allspice in a baking pan. Roast for 10 minutes. Pour in rice and 2 cups of boiling water, cover with aluminum foil, and Roast for 22 minutes. Discard the foil and Roast for 3 minutes until the top is crisp. Let cool slightly before stirring. Serve.

Veggie & Tofu Buddha Bowls

Serves: 2 | Total Time: 45 minutes

½ cup quinoa
1 cup pumpkin cubes
12 oz broccoli florets
¾ cup bread crumbs
¼ cup chickpea flour
¼ cup sriracha sauce

16 oz super-firm tofu, cubed
1 tsp lemon juice
2 tsp olive oil
Salt to taste
2 scallions, thinly sliced
1 tbsp sesame seeds

Preheat air fryer to 400°F. Add quinoa and 1 cup of boiling water in a baking pan, cover it with aluminum foil, and Air Fry for 10 minutes. Set aside covered. Put the pumpkin in the basket and Air Fry for 2 minutes. Add in broccoli and Air Fry for 5 more minutes. Shake up and cook for another 3 minutes. Set the veggies aside.

On a plate, put the breadcrumbs. In a bowl, whisk chickpea flour and sriracha sauce. Toss in tofu cubes until coated and dip them in the breadcrumbs. Air Fry for 10 minutes until crispy. Share quinoa and fried veggies into 2 bowls. Top with crispy tofu and drizzle with lemon juice, olive oil and salt to taste. Scatter with scallions and sesame seeds before serving. Enjoy!

Pineapple & Veggie Souvlaki

Serves: 4 | Total Time: 35 minutes

1 (15-oz) can pineapple rings in pineapple juice
1 red bell pepper, stemmed and seeded
1/3 cup butter
2 tbsp apple cider vinegar
2 tbsp hot sauce
1 tbsp allspice

1 tsp ground nutmeg
16 oz feta cheese
1 red onion, peeled
8 mushrooms, quartered

Preheat air fryer to 400°F. Whisk the butter, pineapple juice, apple vinegar, hot sauce, allspice, and nutmeg until smooth. Set aside. Slice feta cheese into 16 cubes, then the bell pepper into 16 chunks, and finally red onion into 8 wedges, separating each wedge into 2 pieces.

Cut pineapple ring into quarters. Place veggie cubes and feta into the butter bowl and toss to coat. Thread the veggies, tofu, and pineapple onto 8 skewers, alternating 16 pieces on each skewer. Grill for 15 minutes until golden brown and cooked. Serve warm.

Sushi-Style Deviled Eggs

Serves 4 | Total Time: 20 minutes

¼ cup canned artichoke hearts, chopped
4 eggs
2 tbsp mayonnaise
½ tsp soy sauce
¼ avocado, diced
¼ tsp wasabi powder

2 tbsp diced cucumber
1 sheet nori, sliced
8 jarred pickled ginger slices
1 tsp toasted sesame seeds
2 spring onions, sliced

Preheat air fryer to 260°F. Place the eggs in muffin cups to avoid bumping around and cracking during the cooking process. Add silicone cups to the frying basket and Air Fry for 15 minutes. Remove and plunge the eggs immediately into an ice bath to cool, about 5 minutes.

Carefully peel and slice them in half lengthwise. Spoon yolks into a separate medium bowl and arrange white halves on a large plate. Mash the yolks with a fork. Stir in mayonnaise, soy sauce, avocado, and wasabi powder until smooth. Mix in cucumber and spoon into white halves. Scatter eggs with artichoke hearts, nori, pickled ginger, spring onions and sesame seeds to serve.

Quinoa & Black Bean Stuffed Peppers

Serves: 4 | Total Time: 30 minutes

½ cup vegetable broth
½ cup quinoa
1 (15-oz) can black beans
½ cup diced red onion
1 garlic clove, minced
½ tsp salt
½ tsp ground cumin

¼ tsp paprika
¼ tsp ancho chili powder
4 bell peppers, any color
½ cup grated cheddar
¼ cup chopped cilantro
½ cup red enchilada sauce

Add vegetable broth and quinoa to a small saucepan over medium heat. Bring to a boil, then cover and let it simmer for 5 minutes. Turn off the heat.

Preheat air fryer to 350°F. Transfer quinoa to a medium bowl and stir in black beans, onion, red enchilada sauce, ancho chili powder, garlic, salt, cumin, and paprika. Cut the top ¼-inch off the bell peppers. Remove seeds and membranes. Scoop quinoa filling into each pepper and top with cheddar cheese. Transfer peppers to the frying basket and bake for 10 minutes until peppers are soft and filling is heated through. Garnish with cilantro. Serve warm along with salsa. Enjoy!

Rice & Bean Burritos

Serves: 4 | Total Time: 20 minutes

1 bell pepper, sliced
½ red onion, thinly sliced
2 garlic cloves, peeled
1 tbsp olive oil
1 cup cooked brown rice
1 (15-oz) can pinto beans
½ tsp salt
¼ tsp chili powder

¼ tsp ground cumin
¼ tsp smoked paprika
1 tbsp lime juice
4 tortillas
2 tsp grated Parmesan cheese
1 avocado, diced
4 tbsp salsa
2 tbsp chopped cilantro

Preheat air fryer to 400°F. Combine bell pepper, onion, garlic, and olive oil. Place in the frying basket and Roast for 5 minutes. Shake and roast for another 5 minutes.

Remove the garlic from the basket and mince finely. Add to a large bowl along with brown rice, pinto beans, salt, chili powder, cumin, paprika, and lime juice. Divide the roasted vegetable mixture between the tortillas. Top with rice mixture, Parmesan, avocado, cilantro, and salsa. Fold in the sides, then roll the tortillas over the filling. Serve.

Ajillo Mushrooms

Serves: 4 | Total Time: 30 minutes

16 garlic cloves, peeled
2 tsp olive oil
16 button mushrooms

2 tbsp fresh chives, snipped
Salt and pepper to taste
1 tbsp white wine

Preheat air fryer to 350°F. Coat the garlic with some olive oil in a baking pan, then Roast in the air fryer for 12 minutes. When done, take the pan out and stir in the mushrooms, salt, and pepper. Then add the remaining olive oil and white wine. Put the pan back into the fryer and Bake for 10-15 minutes until the mushrooms and garlic soften. Sprinkle with chives and serve warm.

Sesame Orange Tofu with Snow Peas

Serves: 4 | Total Time: 40 minutes

14 oz tofu, cubed	¼ cup vegetable broth
1 tbsp tamari	1 orange, zested
1 tsp olive oil	1 garlic clove, minced
1 tsp sesame oil	¼ tsp ground ginger
1 ½ tbsp cornstarch, divided	2 scallions, chopped
½ tsp salt	1 tbsp sesame seeds
¼ tsp garlic powder	2 cups cooked jasmine rice
1 cup snow peas	2 tbsp chopped parsley
½ cup orange juice	

Preheat air fryer to 400°F. Combine tofu, tamari, olive oil, and sesame oil in a large bowl until tofu is coated. Add in 1 tablespoon cornstarch, salt, and garlic powder and toss. Arrange the tofu on the frying basket. Air Fry for 5 minutes, then shake the basket. Add snow peas and Air Fry for 5 minutes. Place tofu mixture in a bowl.

Bring the orange juice, vegetable broth, orange zest, garlic, and ginger to a boil over medium heat in a small saucepan. Whisk the rest of the cornstarch and 1 tablespoon water in a small bowl to make a slurry. Pour the slurry into the saucepan and constantly stir for 2 minutes until the sauce has thickened. Let off the heat for 2 minutes. Pour the orange sauce, scallions, and sesame seeds in the bowl with the tofu and stir to coat. Serve with jasmine rice sprinkled with parsley. Enjoy!

Berbere Eggplant Spread

Serves 4 | Total Time: 35 minutes

1 eggplant, halved lengthwise

3 tsp olive oil	¼ tsp berbere seasoning
2 tsp pine nuts	⅛ tsp ground cumin
¼ cup tahini	Salt and pepper to taste
1 tbsp lemon juice	1 tbsp chopped parsley
2 cloves garlic, minced	

Preheat air fryer to 370°F. Brush the eggplant with some olive oil. With a fork, pierce the eggplant flesh a few times. Place them, flat sides-down, in the frying basket. Air Fry for 25 minutes. Transfer the eggplant to a cutting board and let cool for 3 minutes until easy to handle. Place pine nuts in the frying basket and Air Fry for 2 minutes, shaking every 30 seconds. Set aside in a bowl.

Scoop out the eggplant flesh and add to a food processor. Add in tahini, lemon juice, garlic, berbere seasoning, cumin, salt, and black pepper and pulse until smooth. Transfer to a serving bowl. Scatter with toasted pine nuts, parsley, and the remaining olive oil. Serve immediately.

Spring Veggie Empanadas

Serves: 4 | Total Time: 75 minutes

10 empanada pastry discs	½ cup diced carrots
1 tbsp olive oil	¼ cup diced celery
1 shallot, minced	⅛ tsp ground nutmeg
1 garlic clove, minced	1 tsp cumin powder
½ cup whole milk	1 tsp minced ginger
1 cup chopped broccoli	1 egg
½ cup chopped cauliflower	

Melt the olive oil in a pot over medium heat. Stir in shallot and garlic and cook through for 1 minute. Next, add 1 tablespoon of flour and continue stirring. Whisk in milk, then lower the heat. After that, add broccoli, cauliflower, carrots, celery, cumin powder, pepper, ginger, and nutmeg. Cook for 2 minutes, then remove from the heat. Allow to cool for 5 minutes.

Preheat air fryer to 350°F. Lightly flour a flat work surface and turn out the pastry discs. Scoop ¼ of the vegetables in the center of each circle. Whisk the egg and 1 teaspoon of water in a small bowl and brush the entire edge of the circle with the egg wash and fold the dough over the filling into a half-moon shape. Crimp the edge with a fork to seal. Arrange the patties in a single layer in the frying basket and bake for 12 minutes. Flip the patties and bake for another 10 to 12 minutes until the outside crust is golden. Serve immediately and enjoy.

Hellenic Zucchini Bites

Serves 4 | Total Time: 20 minutes

8 pitted Kalamata olives, halved

2 tsp olive oil	½ cup marinara sauce
1 zucchini, sliced	½ cup feta cheese crumbles
½ tsp salt	2 tbsp chopped dill
½ tsp Greek oregano	

Preheat air fryer to 350°F. Brush olive oil over both sides of the zucchini circles. Lay out slices on a large plate and sprinkle with salt. Then, top with marinara sauce, feta crumbles, Greek oregano and olives. Place the topped circles in the frying basket and Air Fry for 5 minutes. Garnish with chopped dill to serve.

Meatless Kimchi Bowls

Serves 4 | Total Time: 20 minutes

2 cups canned chickpeas	1 tsp rice vinegar
1 carrot, julienned	2 tsp granulated sugar
6 scallions, sliced	1 tbsp gochujang
1 zucchini, diced	¼ tsp salt
2 tbsp coconut aminos	½ cup kimchi
2 tsp sesame oil	2 tsp roasted sesame seeds

Preheat air fryer to 350°F. Combine all ingredients, except for the kimchi, 2 scallions, and sesame seeds, in a baking pan. Place the pan in the frying basket and Air Fry for 6 minutes. Toss in kimchi and cook for 2 more minutes. Divide between 2 bowls and garnish with the remaining scallions and sesame seeds. Serve immediately.

Vegan Buddha Bowls

Serves 4 | Total Time: 20 minutes

1 carrot, peeled and julienned
½ onion, sliced into half-moons
¼ cup apple cider vinegar   2 tsp fresh lime zest
½ tsp ground ginger   1 cup fresh arugula
⅛ tsp cayenne pepper   ½ cup cooked quinoa
1 parsnip, diced   2 tbsp canned kidney beans
1 tsp avocado oil   2 tbsp canned sweetcorn
4 oz extra-firm tofu, cubed   1 avocado, diced
½ tsp five-spice powder   2 tbsp pine nuts
½ tsp chili powder

Preheat air fryer to 350°F. Combine carrot, vinegar, ginger, and cayenne in a bowl. In another bowl, combine onion, parsnip, and avocado oil. In a third bowl, mix the tofu, five-spice powder, and chili powder.

Place the onion mixture in the greased basket. Air Fry for 6 minutes. Stir in tofu mixture and cook for 8 more minutes. Mix in lime zest. Divide arugula, cooked quinoa, kidney beans, sweetcorn, drained carrots, avocado, pine nuts, and tofu mixture between 2 bowls. Serve.

Easy Cheese & Spinach Lasagna

Serves: 6 | Total Time: 50 minutes

1 zucchini, cut into strips   3 tbsp grated mozzarella
1 tbsp butter   ½ cup grated cheddar
4 garlic cloves, minced   3 tsp grated Parmesan cheese
½ yellow onion, diced   ⅛ cup chopped basil
1 tsp dried oregano   2 tbsp chopped parsley
¼ tsp red pepper flakes   Salt and pepper to taste
1 (15-oz) can diced tomatoes   ¼ tsp ground nutmeg
4 oz ricotta

Preheat air fryer to 375°F. Melt butter in a medium skillet over medium heat. Stir in half of the garlic and onion and cook for 2 minutes. Stir in oregano and red pepper flakes and cook for 1 minute. Reduce the heat to medium-low and pour in crushed tomatoes and their juices. Cover the skillet and simmer for 5 minutes.

Mix ricotta, mozzarella, cheddar cheese, rest of the garlic, basil, black pepper, and nutmeg in a large bowl. Arrange a layer of zucchini strips in the baking dish. Scoop 1/3 of the cheese mixture and spread evenly over the zucchini. Spread 1/3 of the tomato sauce over the cheese. Repeat the steps two more times, then top the lasagna with Parmesan cheese. Bake in the frying basket for 25 minutes until the mixture is bubbling and the mozzarella is melted. Allow sitting for 10 minutes before cutting. Serve warm sprinkled with parsley and enjoy!

Balsamic Caprese Hasselback

Serves 4 | Total Time: 15 minutes

4 tomatoes   1 tbsp olive oil
12 fresh basil leaves   2 tsp balsamic vinegar
1 ball fresh mozzarella   1 tbsp basil, torn
Salt and pepper to taste

Preheat air fryer to 325°F. Remove the bottoms from the tomatoes to create a flat surface. Make 4 even slices on each tomato, 3/4 of the way down. Slice the mozzarella cheese, then cut the slices into 12 pieces. Stuff 1 basil leaf and a piece of mozzarella into each slice. Sprinkle with salt and pepper. Place the stuffed tomatoes in the frying basket and Air Fry for 3 minutes. Transfer to a large serving plate. Drizzle with olive oil and balsamic vinegar and scatter the basil over. Serve and enjoy!

Ricotta Veggie Potpie

Serves: 4 | Total Time: 30 minutes

1 ¼ cup flour   ¼ cup diced yellow onion
¾ cup ricotta cheese   1 garlic clove, minced
1 tbsp olive oil   1 tbsp unsalted butter
1 potato, peeled and diced   1 cup milk
¼ cup diced mushrooms   ½ tsp ground black pepper
¼ cup diced carrots   1 tsp dried thyme
¼ cup diced celery   2 tbsp dill, chopped

Preheat air fryer to 350°F. Combine 1 cup flour and ricotta cheese in a medium bowl and stir until the dough comes together. Heat oil over medium heat in a small skillet. Stir in potato, mushroom, carrots, dill, thyme, celery, onion, and garlic. Cook for 4-5 minutes, often stirring, until the onions are soft and translucent.

Add butter and melt, then stir in the rest of the flour. Slowly pour in the milk and keep stirring. Simmer for 5 minutes until the sauce has thickened, then stir in pepper and thyme. Spoon the vegetable mixture into four 6-ounce ramekins. Cut the dough into 4 equal sections and work it into rounds that fit over the size of the ramekins. Top the ramekins with the dough, then place the ramekins in the frying basket. Bake for 10 minutes until the crust is golden. Serve hot and enjoy.

Crispy Avocados with Pico de Gallo

Serves 2 | Total Time: 15 minutes

1 cup diced tomatoes   2 cloves garlic, minced
1 tbsp lime juice   1 tbsp diced white onions
1 tsp lime zest   ½ tsp salt
2 tbsp chopped cilantro   2 avocados, halved and pitted
1 serrano chiles, minced   4 tbsp cheddar shreds

Preheat air fryer to 350°F. Combine all ingredients, except for avocados and cheddar cheese, in a bowl and let chill covered in the fridge. Place avocado halves, cut sides-up, in the frying basket, scatter cheese shreds over top of avocado halves, and Air Fry for 4 minutes. Top with pico de gallo and serve.

Mini Zucchini "Pizzas"

Serves 4 | Total Time: 25 minutes

½ cup diced baby Bella mushrooms
2 tbsp olive oil   1 tsp salt
½ diced yellow onion   1 cup shredded mozzarella
½ cup pizza sauce   8 black olives, sliced
1 zucchini, cut ¼-inch slices   1 tbsp chopped basil

Warm the olive oil in a pan over medium heat. Add onion and mushrooms and stir-fry for 4-5 minutes until softened. Stir in pizza sauce. Remove the pan from the heat.

Preheat air fryer to 390°F. Season the zucchini slices with salt on both sides. Arrange the slices on the greased frying basket and top with the sauce mixture and shredded mozzarella cheese. Air Fry for 5 minutes or until the cheese is melted. Garnish with black olives and sprinkle with basil. Serve warm and enjoy!

Fried Rice with Curried Tofu

Serves 4 | Total Time: 25 minutes

8 oz extra-firm tofu, cubed	2 cups cooked rice
½ cup canned coconut milk	1 tbsp turmeric powder
2 tsp red curry paste	Salt and pepper to taste
2 cloves garlic, minced	4 lime wedges
1 tbsp avocado oil	¼ cup chopped cilantro
1 tbsp coconut oil	

Preheat air fryer to 350°F. Combine tofu, coconut milk, curry paste, garlic, and avocado oil in a bowl. Pour the mixture into a baking pan. Place the pan in the frying basket and Air Fry for 10 minutes, stirring once.

Melt the coconut oil in a skillet over medium heat. Add in rice, turmeric powder, salt, and black pepper, and cook for 2 minutes or until heated through. Divide the cooked rice between 4 medium bowls and top with tofu mixture and sauce. Top with cilantro and lime wedges to serve.

Veggie-Stuffed Bell Peppers

Serves 4 | Total Time: 40 minutes

½ cup canned fire-roasted diced tomatoes, including juice

2 red bell peppers	¼ cup tomato sauce
4 tsp olive oil	2 tsp Italian seasoning
½ yellow onion, diced	¼ tsp smoked paprika
1 zucchini, diced	Salt and pepper to taste
¾ cup chopped mushrooms	

Cut bell peppers in half from top to bottom and discard the seeds. Brush inside and tops of the bell peppers with some olive oil. Set aside. Warm the remaining olive oil in a skillet over medium heat. Stir-fry the onion, zucchini, and mushrooms for 5 minutes until the onions are tender. Combine tomatoes and their juice, tomato sauce, Italian seasoning, paprika, salt, and pepper in a bowl.

Preheat air fryer to 350°F. Divide both mixtures between bell pepper halves. Place bell pepper halves in the frying basket and Air Fry for 8 minutes. Serve immediately.

Roasted Veggie Bowls

Serves 4 | Total Time: 30 minutes

1 cup Brussels sprouts, trimmed and quartered
½ onion, cut into half-moons

½ cup green beans, chopped	1 tbsp olive oil
1 cup broccoli florets	½ tsp chili powder
1 red bell pepper, sliced	¼ tsp ground cumin
1 yellow bell pepper, sliced	¼ tsp ground coriander

Preheat air fryer to 350°F. Combine all ingredients in a bowl. Place veggie mixture in the frying basket and Air Fry for 15 minutes, tossing every 5 minutes. Divide between 4 medium bowls and serve.

Creamy Broccoli & Mushroom Casserole

Serves 4 | Total Time: 30 minutes

4 cups broccoli florets, chopped	
1 cup crushed cheddar cheese crisps	
¼ cup diced onion	1 egg
¼ tsp dried thyme	2 tbsp sour cream
¼ tsp dried marjoram	¼ cup mayonnaise
¼ tsp dried oregano	Salt and pepper to taste
½ cup diced mushrooms	

Preheat air fryer to 350°F. Combine all ingredients, except for the cheese crisps, in a bowl. Spoon mixture into a round cake pan. Place cake pan in the frying basket and Bake for 14 minutes. Let sit for 10 minutes. Distribute crushed cheddar cheese crisps over the top and serve.

Cheddar Stuffed Portobellos with Salsa

Serves: 4 | Total Time: 20 minutes

8 portobello mushrooms	½ cup shredded cheddar
1/3 cup salsa	2 tbsp cilantro, chopped

Preheat air fryer to 370°F. Remove the mushroom stems. Divide the salsa between the caps. Top with cheese and sprinkle with cilantro. Place the mushrooms in the greased frying basket and Bake for 8-10 minutes. Let cool slightly, then serve.

Crispy Apple Fries with Caramel Sauce

Serves: 4 | Total Time: 15 minutes

4 medium apples, cored	¼ tsp nutmeg
¼ tsp cinnamon	1 cup caramel sauce

Preheat air fryer to 350°F. Slice the apples to a 1/3-inch thickness for a crunchy chip. Place in a large bowl and sprinkle with cinnamon and nutmeg. Place the slices in the air fryer basket. Bake for 6 minutes. Shake the basket, then cook for another 4 minutes or until crunchy. Serve drizzled with caramel sauce and enjoy!

Fried Potatoes with Bell Peppers

Serves: 4 | Total Time: 30 minutes

3 russet potatoes, cubed	Salt and pepper to taste
1 tbsp canola oil	1 chopped shallot
1 tbsp olive oil	½ chopped red bell peppers
1 tsp paprika	½ diced yellow bell peppers

Preheat air fryer to 370°F. Whisk the canola oil, olive oil, paprika, salt, and pepper in a bowl. Toss in the potatoes to coat. Place the potatoes in the air fryer and Bake for 20 minutes, shaking the basket periodically. Top the potatoes with shallot and bell peppers and cook for an additional 3-4 minutes or until the potatoes are cooked through and the peppers are soft. Serve warm.

Brussels Sprouts with Saffron Aioli

Serves: 4 | Total Time: 20 minutes

1 lb Brussels sprouts, halved | 1 tbsp Dijon mustard
1 tsp garlic powder | 1 tsp minced garlic
Salt and pepper to taste | Salt and pepper to taste
½ cup mayonnaise | ½ tsp liquid saffron
½ tbsp olive oil

Preheat air fryer to 380°F. Combine the Brussels sprouts, garlic powder, salt, and pepper in a large bowl. Place in the fryer and spray with cooking oil. Bake for 12-14 minutes, shaking once, until just brown.

Meanwhile, in a small bowl, mix mayonnaise, olive oil, mustard, garlic, saffron, salt, and pepper. When the Brussels sprouts are slightly cool, serve with aioli. Enjoy!

Green Bean & Baby Potato Mix

Serves: 4 | Total Time: 25 minutes

1 lb baby potatoes, halved | ½ tsp hot paprika
4 garlic cloves, minced | ½ tbsp taco seasoning
2 tbsp olive oil | 1 tbsp chopped parsley
Salt and pepper to taste | ½ lb green beans, trimmed

Preheat air fryer to 375°F. Toss potatoes, garlic, olive oil, salt, pepper, hot paprika, and taco seasoning in a large bowl. Arrange the potatoes in a single layer in the air fryer basket. Air Fry for 10 minutes, then stir in green beans. Air Fry for another 10 minutes. Serve hot sprinkled with parsley.

Smoked Paprika Sweet Potato Fries

Serves: 4 | Total Time: 35 minutes

2 sweet potatoes, peeled | 1 tsp smoked paprika
1 ½ tbsp cornstarch | 1 tsp garlic powder
1 tbsp canola oil | Salt and pepper to taste
1 tbsp olive oil | 1 cup cocktail sauce

Cut the potatoes lengthwise to form French fries. Put in a resealable plastic bag and add cornstarch. Seal and shake to coat the fries. Combine the canola oil, olive oil, paprika, garlic powder, salt, and pepper fries in a large bowl. Add the sweet potato fries and mix to combine.

Preheat air fryer to 380°F. Place fries in the greased basket and fry for 20-25 minutes, shaking the basket once until crisp. Drizzle with Cocktail sauce to serve.

Fake Shepherd's Pie

Serves: 6 | Total Time: 40 minutes

½ head cauliflower, cut into florets
1 sweet potato, diced | 2 cloves garlic, minced
1 tbsp olive oil | 1 carrot, diced
¼ cup cheddar shreds | ½ cup green peas
2 tbsp milk | 1 stalk celery, diced
Salt and pepper to taste | 2/3 cup tomato sauce
2 tsp avocado oil | 1 tsp chopped rosemary
1 cup beefless grounds | 1 tsp thyme leaves
½ onion, diced

Place cauliflower and sweet potato in a pot of salted boiling water over medium heat and simmer for 7 minutes until fork tender. Strain and transfer to a bowl. Put in avocado oil, cheddar, milk, salt, and pepper. Mash until smooth.

Warm olive oil in a skillet over medium-high heat and stir in beefless grounds and vegetables and stir-fry for 4 minutes until veggies are tender. Stir in tomato sauce, rosemary, thyme, salt, and black pepper. Set aside.

Preheat air fryer to 350°F. Spoon filling into a round cake pan lightly greased with olive oil and cover with the topping. Using the tines of a fork, run shallow lines in the top of cauliflower for a decorative touch. Place cake pan in the frying basket and Air Fry for 12 minutes. Let sit for 10 minutes before serving.

Italian-Style Fried Cauliflower

Serves: 4 | Total Time: 35 minutes

2 eggs | 3 tsp grated Parmesan cheese
1/3 cup all-purpose flour | Salt and pepper to taste
½ tsp Italian seasoning | 1 head cauliflower, cut into
½ cup bread crumbs | florets
1 tsp garlic powder | ½ tsp ground coriander

Preheat air fryer to 370°F. Set out 3 small bowls. In the first, mix the flour with Italian seasoning. In the second, beat the eggs. In the third bowl, combine the crumbs, garlic, Parmesan, ground coriander, salt, and pepper.

Dip the cauliflower in the flour, then dredge in egg, and finally in the bread crumb mixture. Place a batch of cauliflower in the greased frying basket and spray with cooking oil. Bake for 10-12 minutes, shaking once until golden. Serve warm and enjoy!

Basil Green Beans

Serves: 4 | Total Time: 15 minutes

1 ½ lb green beans, trimmed | 1 tbsp fresh basil, chopped
1 tbsp olive oil | Garlic salt to taste

Preheat air fryer to 400°F. Coat the green beans with olive oil in a large bowl. Combine with fresh basil powder and garlic salt. Put the beans in the frying basket and Air Fry for 7-9 minutes, shaking once until the beans begin to brown. Serve warm and enjoy!

Garlic Roasted Okra Rounds

Serves: 4 | Total Time: 20 minutes

2 cups okra, cut into rounds | 1 tsp powdered paprika
1 ½ tbsp. melted butter | Salt and pepper to taste
1 garlic clove, minced

Preheat air fryer to 350°F. Toss okra, melted butter, paprika, garlic, salt, and pepper in a medium bowl until okra is coated. Place okra in the frying basket and Air Fry for 5 minutes. Shake the basket and Air Fry for another 5 minutes. Shake one more time and Air Fry for 2 minutes until crispy. Serve warm and enjoy.

Honey Pear Chips

Serves: 4 | Total Time: 30 minutes

2 firm pears, thinly sliced	½ tsp ground cinnamon
1 tbsp lemon juice	1 tsp honey

Preheat air fryer to 380°F. Arrange the pear slices on the parchment-lined cooking basket. Drizzle with lemon juice and honey and sprinkle with cinnamon. Air Fry for 6-8 minutes, shaking the basket once, until golden. Leave to cool. Serve immediately or save for later in an airtight container. Good for 2 days.

Cheesy Eggplant Slices

Serves: 4 | Total Time: 35 minutes

1 eggplant, peeled	Salt and pepper to taste
2 eggs	¾ cup tomato passata
½ cup all-purpose flour	½ cup shredded Parmesan
¾ cup bread crumbs	½ cup shredded mozzarella
2 tbsp grated Swiss cheese	

Preheat air fryer to 400°F. Slice the eggplant into ½-inch rounds. Set aside. Set out three small bowls. In the first bowl, add flour. In the second bowl, beat the eggs. In the third bowl, mix the crumbs, 2 tbsp of grated Swiss cheese, salt, and pepper. Dip each eggplant in the flour, then dredge in egg, then coat with bread crumb mixture. Arrange the eggplant rounds on the greased frying basket and spray with cooking oil. Bake for 7 minutes. Top each eggplant round with 1 tsp passata and ½ tbsp each of shredded Parmesan and mozzarella. Cook until the cheese melts, 2-3 minutes. Serve warm and enjoy!

Mushroom-Rice Stuffed Bell Peppers

Serves: 4 | Total Time: 30 minutes

4 red bell peppers, tops sliced	¾ cup tomato sauce
1 ½ cups cooked rice	Salt and pepper to taste
¼ cup chopped leeks	¾ cup shredded mozzarella
¼ cup sliced mushrooms	2 tbsp parsley, chopped

Fill a large pot of water and heat on high until it boils. Remove seeds and membranes from the peppers. Carefully place peppers into the boiling water for 5 minutes. Remove and set aside to cool. Mix together rice, leeks, mushrooms, tomato sauce, parsley, salt, and pepper in a large bowl. Stuff each pepper with the rice mixture. Top with mozzarella.

Preheat air fryer to 350°F. Arrange the peppers on the greased frying basket and Bake for 10 minutes. Serve.

Pesto Parmesan Pizza Bread

Serves 4 | Total Time: 25 minutes

2 eggs, beaten	½ tsp baking powder
2 tbsp flour	⅛ tsp salt
2 tbsp cassava flour	3 tsp grated Parmesan cheese
1/3 cup whipping cream	½ cup pesto
1/3 cup grated mozzarella	
2 tsp Italian seasoning	

Preheat air fryer to 300°F. Combine all ingredients, except for the Parmesan and pesto sauce, in a bowl until mixed. Pour the batter into a pizza pan. Place it in the frying basket and Bake for 20 minutes. After, sprinkle Parmesan on top and cook for 1 minute. Let chill for 5 minutes before slicing. Serve with warmed pesto sauce.

Buttered Rainbow Carrots

Serves: 4 | Total Time: 25 minutes

6 peeled rainbow carrots	2 tbsp cilantro, chopped
2 tbsp butter, melted	1 tsp sea salt flakes

Preheat air fryer to 390°F. Halve the carrots lengthwise then slice them diagonally into 1-inch pieces. Add the carrots to a baking pan and pour over butter and 2-3 tbsp of water. Mix well. Sprinkle with sea salt. Transfer the pan to the air fryer. Roast for 10-12 minutes, shaking the basket once. Sprinkle with cilantro and serve warm.

Veggie Turnovers

Serves: 6 | Total Time: 30 minutes

2 tbsp cream cheese, softened	
2 spring onions, chopped	½ tsp ground turmeric
2 garlic cloves, minced	2 tsp olive oil
½ cup mixed vegetables	6 phyllo dough sheets

Preheat air fryer to 390°F. Toss the spring onions, garlic, mixed vegetables, and some oil in a baking pan. Air Fry for 2-4 minutes until the veggies are soft. Pour into a bowl. Mix in the cream cheese and turmeric and let chill.

To make the dough, first lay a sheet of phyllo on a clean workspace and spritz with olive oil, then add a second sheet on top. Repeat with the rest of the phyllo sheets until you have 3 stacks of 2 layers. Cut the stacks into 4 lengthwise strips. Add 2 tsp of the veggie mix at the bottom of each strip, then make a triangle by lifting one corner over the filling. Continue the triangle making, like folding a flag, and seal with water. Repeat until all strips are filled and folded. Bake the samosas in the air fryer for 4-7 minutes, until golden and crisp. Serve warm.

Cheesy Veggie Frittata

Serves: 2 | Total Time: 65 minutes

4 oz Bella mushrooms, chopped	
¼ cup halved grape tomatoes	
1 cup baby spinach	1 tbsp milk
1/3 cup chopped leeks	¼ tsp garlic powder
1 baby carrot, chopped	¼ tsp dried oregano
4 eggs	Salt and pepper to taste
½ cup grated cheddar	

Preheat air fryer to 300°F. Crack the eggs into a bowl and beat them with a fork or whisk. Mix in the remaining ingredients until well combined. Pour into a greased cake pan. Put the pan into the frying basket and Bake for 20-23 minutes or until eggs are set in the center. Remove from the fryer. Cut into halves and serve.

Spiced Vegetable Galette

Serves: 4 | Total Time: 30 minutes

¼ cup cooked eggplant, chopped
¼ cup cooked zucchini, chopped

1 refrigerated pie crust	1 red chili, finely sliced
2 eggs	¼ cup tomato, chopped
¼ cup milk	½ cup shredded mozzarella
Salt and pepper to taste	cheese

Preheat air fryer to 360°F. In a baking dish, add the crust and press firmly. Trim off any excess edges. Poke a few holes. Beat the eggs in a bowl. Stir in the milk, half of the cheese, eggplant, zucchini, tomato, red chili, salt, and pepper. Mix well. Transfer the mixture to the baking dish and place in the air fryer. Bake for 15 minutes or until firm and almost crusty. Slide the basket out and top with the remaining cheese. Cook further for 5 minutes, or until golden brown. Let cool slightly and serve.

Harissa Veggie Fries

Serves: 4 | Total Time: 55 minutes

1 pound red potatoes, cut into rounds

1 onion, diced	Salt and pepper to taste
1 green bell pepper, diced	¾ tsp garlic powder
1 red bell pepper, diced	¾ tsp harissa seasoning
2 tbsp olive oil	

Combine all ingredients in a large bowl and mix until potatoes are well coated and seasoned. Preheat air fryer to 350°F. Pour all of the contents in the bowl into the frying basket. Bake for 35 minutes, shaking every 10 minutes, until golden brown and soft. Serve hot.

Sweet Corn Bread

Serves: 6 | Total Time: 35 minutes

2 eggs, beaten	¼ tsp salt
½ cup cornmeal	¼ tsp baking soda
½ cup pastry flour	½ tbsp lemon juice
1/3 cup sugar	½ cup milk
1 tsp lemon zest	¼ cup sunflower oil
½ tbsp baking powder	

Preheat air fryer to 350°F. Add the cornmeal, flour, sugar, lemon zest, baking powder, salt, and baking soda in a bowl. Stir with a whisk until combined. Add the eggs, lemon juice, milk, and oil to another bowl and stir well. Add the wet mixture to the dry mixture and stir gently until combined. Spray a baking pan with oil. Pour the batter in and Bake in the fryer for 25 minutes or until golden and a knife inserted in the center comes out clean. Cut into wedges and serve.

Zucchini Tacos

Serves: 3 | Total Time: 20 minutes

1 small zucchini, sliced	1 (15-oz) can refried beans
1 yellow onion, sliced	6 corn tortillas, warm
¼ tsp garlic powder	1 cup guacamole
Salt and pepper to taste	1 tbsp cilantro, chopped

Preheat air fryer to 390°F. Place the zucchini and onion in the greased frying basket. Spray with more oil and sprinkle with garlic, salt, and pepper to taste. Roast for 6 minutes. Remove, shake, or stir, then cook for another 6 minutes, until the veggies are golden and tender.

In a pan, heat the refried beans over low heat. Stir often. When warm enough, remove from heat and set aside. Place a corn tortilla on a plate and fill it with beans, roasted vegetables, and guacamole. Top with cilantro to serve.

Vietnamese Gingered Tofu

Serves: 4 | Total Time: 25 minutes

1 (8-oz) package extra-firm	Black pepper to taste
tofu, cubed	2 tbsp nutritional yeast
4 tsp shoyu	1 tsp dried rosemary
1 tsp onion powder	1 tsp dried dill
½ tsp garlic powder	2 tsp cornstarch
½ tsp ginger powder	2 tsp sunflower oil
½ tsp turmeric powder	

Sprinkle the tofu with shoyu and toss to coat. Add the onion, garlic, ginger, turmeric, and pepper. Gently toss to coat. Add the yeast, rosemary, dill, and cornstarch. Toss to coat. Dribble with the oil and toss again.

Preheat air fryer to 390°F. Spray the fryer basket with oil, put the tofu in the basket and Bake for 7 minutes. Remove, shake gently, and cook for another 7 minutes or until the tofu is crispy and golden. Serve warm.

Banana Vegan French Toast

Serves: 4 | Total Time: 15 minutes

1 ripe banana, mashed	2 tbsp ground flaxseed
¼ cup protein powder	4 bread slices
½ cup milk	2 tbsp agave syrup

Preheat air fryer to 370°F. Combine the banana, protein powder, milk, and flaxseed in a shallow bowl and mix well. Dip bread slices into the mixture. Place the slices on a lightly greased pan in a single layer and pour any of the remaining mixture evenly over the bread. Air Fry for 10 minutes, or until golden brown and crispy, flipping once. Serve warm, topped with agave syrup.

Shoestring Sweet Potatoes

Serves: 4 | Total Time: 25 minutes

2 large sweet potatoes, peeled and cut into matchsticks

2 tbsp olive oil	¼ tsp cayenne pepper
Salt and pepper to taste	1 tbsp pumpkin pie spice
¼ tsp garlic powder	1 tbsp chopped parsley

Preheat air fryer to 375°F. Toss sweet potato slices, olive oil, salt, pepper, garlic powder, pumpkin pie spice and cayenne pepper in a large bowl. Place the potatoes in the frying basket. Air Fry for 5-7 minutes, then shake the basket. Air Fry for another 5 minutes and shake the basket again. Air Fry for 2-5 minutes until crispy. Serve sprinkled with parsley and enjoy!

Authentic Mexican Esquites

Serves: 4 | Total Time: 25 minutes

4 ears of corn, husk and silk removed

1 tbsp ground coriander	1 tsp cayenne pepper
1 tbsp smoked paprika	3 tbsp mayonnaise
1 tsp sea salt	3 tbsp grated Cotija cheese
1 tsp garlic powder	1 tbsp butter, melted
1 tsp onion powder	1 tsp epazote seasoning
1 tsp dried lime peel	

Preheat the air fryer to 400°F. Combine coriander, paprika, salt, garlic powder, onion powder, lime peel, epazote and cayenne pepper in a bowl and mix well. Pour into a small glass jar. Put the corn in the greased frying basket. Bake for 6-8 minutes or until the corn is crispy but tender, flipping the ears halfway through cooking.

While the corn is frying, combine the mayonnaise, cheese, and melted butter in a small bowl. Spread the mixture over the cooked corn, return to the fryer, and Bake for 3-5 minutes more or until the corn has brown spots. Remove from the fryer and sprinkle each cob with about ½ tsp of the spice mix.

Home-Style Cinnamon Rolls

Serves: 4 | Total Time: 40 minutes

½ (16-oz) pizza dough	¼ cup butter, softened
1/3 cup dark brown sugar	½ tsp ground cinnamon

Preheat air fryer to 360°F. Roll out the dough into a rectangle. Using a knife, spread the brown sugar and butter, covering all the edges, and sprinkle with cinnamon. Fold the long side of the dough into a log, then cut it into 8 equal pieces, avoiding compression. Place the rolls, spiral-side up, onto a parchment-lined sheet. Let rise for 20 minutes. Grease the rolls with cooking spray and Bake for 8 minutes until golden brown. Serve right away.

Brussels Sprouts Cakes

Serves: 4 | Total Time: 25 minutes

1 lb Brussels sprouts, trimmed and shredded

1 cup grated Parmesan	2 eggs, beaten
¼ cup flour	1 cup ricotta cheese
2 green onions, chopped	1 tbsp olive oil

Preheat air fryer to 400°F. Mix the sprouts, Parmesan, and flour in a bowl. Add the green onions, eggs, and ricotta cheese and combine with your hands. Make 4 patties out of the mixture and flatten them to ½-inch thick. Grease the patties with olive oil. Air Fry in the fryer for 12-14 minutes until crispy, turning once. Serve.

Bite-Sized Blooming Onions

Serves: 4 | Total Time: 35 minutes + cooling time

1 lb cipollini onions	1 tsp cayenne pepper
1 cup flour	2 eggs
1 tsp salt	2 tbsp milk
½ tsp paprika	

Preheat the air fryer to 375°F. Carefully peel the onions and cut a ½ inch off the stem ends and trim the root ends. Place them root-side down on the cutting surface and cut the onions into quarters. Be careful not to cut all the way to the bottom. Cut each quarter into 2 sections and pull the wedges apart without breaking them.

In a shallow bowl, add the flour, salt, paprika, and cayenne, and in a separate shallow bowl, beat the eggs with the milk. Dip the onions in the flour, then dip in the egg mix, coating evenly, and then in the flour mix again. Shake off excess flour. Put the onions in the frying basket, cut-side up, and spray with cooking oil. Air Fry for 10-15 minutes until the onions are crispy on the outside, and tender on the inside. Let cool for 10 minutes, then serve.

Spinach & Brie Frittata

Serves 4 | Total Time: 25 minutes

5 eggs	1 shallot, diced
Salt and pepper to taste	4 oz brie cheese, cubed
½ cup baby spinach	1 tomato, sliced

Preheat air fryer to 320°F. Whisk all ingredients, except for the tomato slices, in a bowl. Transfer to a baking pan greased with olive oil and top with tomato slices. Place the pan in the frying basket and Bake for 14 minutes. Let cool for 5 minutes before slicing. Serve and enjoy!

Green Bean Sautée

Serves: 4 | Total Time: 25 minutes

1 ½ lb green beans, trimmed	Salt and pepper to taste
1 tbsp olive oil	4 garlic cloves, thinly sliced
½ tsp garlic powder	1 tbsp fresh basil, chopped

Preheat the air fryer to 375°F. Toss the beans with the olive oil, garlic powder, salt, and pepper in a bowl, then add to the frying basket. Air Fry for 6 minutes, shaking the basket halfway through the cooking time. Add garlic to the air fryer and cook for 3-6 minutes or until the green beans are tender and the garlic slices start to brown. Sprinkle with basil and serve warm.

Zucchini & Bell Pepper Stir-Fry

Serves: 4 | Total Time: 25 minutes

1 zucchini, cut into rounds	1 tbsp lemon juice
1 red bell pepper, sliced	2 tsp cornstarch
3 garlic cloves, sliced	1 tsp dried basil
2 tbsp olive oil	Salt and pepper to taste
1/3 cup vegetable broth	

Preheat the air fryer to 400°F. Combine the veggies, garlic, and olive oil in a bowl. Put the bowl in the frying basket and Air Fry the zucchini mixture for 5 minutes, stirring once; drain. While the veggies are cooking, whisk the broth, lemon juice, cornstarch, basil, salt, and pepper in a bowl. Pour the broth into the bowl along with the veggies and stir. Air Fry for 5-9 more minutes until the veggies are tender and the sauce is thick. Serve and enjoy!

POULTRY RECIPES

Chicken Parmigiana

Serves: 2 | Total Time: 35 minutes

2 chicken breasts	1 tbsp dried basil
1 cup breadcrumbs	1 cup passata
2 eggs, beaten	2 provolone cheese slices
Salt and pepper to taste	1 tbsp Parmesan cheese

Preheat air fryer to 350°F. Mix the breadcrumbs, basil, salt, and pepper in a mixing bowl. Coat the chicken breasts with the crumb mixture, then dip in the beaten eggs. Finally, coat again with the dry ingredients. Arrange the coated chicken breasts on the greased frying basket and Air Fry for 20 minutes. At the 10-minutes mark, turn the breasts over and cook for the remaining 10 minutes.

Pour half of the passata into a baking pan. When the chicken is ready, remove it to the passata-covered pan. Pour the remaining passata over the fried chicken and arrange the provolone cheese slices on top and sprinkle with Parmesan cheese. Bake for 5 minutes until the chicken is crisped and the cheese melted and lightly toasted. Serve.

Cajun Fried Chicken Legs

Serves: 3 | Total Time: 35 minutes

1 cup Cajun seasoning	6 chicken legs, bone-in
½ tsp mango powder	

Preheat air fryer to 360°F. Place half of the Cajun seasoning and 3/4 cup of water in a bowl and mix well to dissolve any lumps. Add the remaining Cajun seasoning and mango powder to a shallow bowl and stir to combine. Dip the chicken in the batter, then coat it in the mango seasoning. Lightly spritz the chicken with cooking spray. Place the chicken in the air fryer and Air Fry for 14-16 minutes, turning once until the chicken is cooked and the coating is brown. Serve and enjoy!

Gruyère Asparagus & Chicken Quiche

Serves: 4 | Total Time: 30 minutes

1 grilled chicken breast, diced	
½ cup shredded Gruyère cheese	
1 premade pie crust	Salt and pepper to taste
2 eggs, beaten	½ lb asparagus, sliced
¼ cup milk	1 lemon, zested

Preheat air fryer to 360°F. Carefully press the crust into a baking dish, trimming the edges. Prick the dough with a fork a few times. Add the eggs, milk, asparagus, salt, pepper, chicken, lemon zest, and half of Gruyère cheese to a mixing bowl and stir until completely blended. Pour the mixture into the pie crust. Bake in the air fryer for 15 minutes. Sprinkle the remaining Gruyère cheese on top of the quiche filling. Bake for 5 more minutes until the quiche is golden brown. Remove and allow to cool for a few minutes before cutting. Serve sliced and enjoy!

Kale & Rice Chicken Rolls

Serves: 4 | Total Time: 35 minutes

4 boneless, skinless chicken thighs	
½ tsp ground fenugreek seeds	
1 cup cooked wild rice	1 tsp salt
2 sundried tomatoes, diced	1 lemon, juiced
½ cup chopped kale	½ cup crumbled feta
2 garlic cloves, minced	1 tbsp olive oil

Preheat air fryer to 380°F. Put the chicken thighs between two pieces of plastic wrap, and using a meat mallet or a rolling pin, pound them out to about ¼-inch thick. Combine the rice, tomatoes, kale, garlic, salt, fenugreek seeds and lemon juice in a bowl and mix well.

Divide the rice mixture among the chicken thighs and sprinkle with feta. Fold the sides of the chicken thigh over the filling, and then gently place each of them seam-side down into the greased air frying basket. Drizzle the stuffed chicken thighs with olive oil. Roast the stuffed chicken thighs for 12 minutes, then turn them over and cook for an additional 10 minutes. Serve and enjoy!

Chicken Flatbread Pizza with Kale

Serves: 1 | Total Time: 15 minutes

½ cup cooked chicken breast, cubed	
¼ cup grated mozzarella	¼ tsp red pepper flakes
1 flatbread	½ cup kale
1 tbsp olive oil	¼ sliced red onion
1 garlic clove, minced	

Preheat air fryer to 380°F. Lightly brush the top of the flatbread with olive oil and top with garlic, red pepper flakes, kale, onion, chicken, and mozzarella. Put the pizza into the frying basket and Bake for 6-8 minutes. Serve.

Greek Gyros with Chicken & Rice

Serves: 4 | Total Time: 25 minutes

1 lb chicken breasts, cubed	¼ tsp ground nutmeg
¼ cup cream cheese	Salt and pepper to taste
2 tbsp olive oil	¼ tsp ground turmeric
1 tsp dried oregano	2 cups cooked rice
1 tsp ground cumin	1 cup Tzatziki sauce
1 tsp ground cinnamon	

Preheat air fryer to 380°F. Put all ingredients in a bowl and mix together until the chicken is coated well. Spread the chicken mixture in the frying basket, then Bake for 10 minutes. Stir the chicken mixture and Bake for an additional 5 minutes. Serve with rice and tzatziki sauce.

Bacon & Chicken Flatbread

Serves: 2 | Total Time: 35 minutes

1 flatbread dough	2 tsp dry rosemary
1 chicken breast, cubed	1 tsp fajita seasoning
1 cup breadcrumbs	1 tsp onion powder
2 eggs, beaten	3 bacon strips
Salt and pepper to taste	½ tbsp ranch sauce

Preheat air fryer to 360°F. Place the breadcrumbs, onion powder, rosemary, salt, and pepper in a mixing bowl. Coat the chicken with the mixture, dip into the beaten eggs, then roll again into the dry ingredients. Arrange the coated chicken pieces on one side of the greased frying basket. On the other side of the basket, lay the bacon strips. Air Fry for 6 minutes. Turn the bacon pieces over and flip the chicken and cook for another 6 minutes.

Roll the flatbread out and spread the ranch sauce all over the surface. Top with the bacon and chicken and sprinkle with fajita seasoning. Close the bread to contain the filling and place it in the air fryer. Cook for 10 minutes, flipping the flatbread once until golden brown. Let it cool for a few minutes. Then slice and serve.

Chicken Skewers

Serves: 4 | Total Time: 55 minutes + marinating time

1 lb boneless skinless chicken thighs, cut into pieces
1 sweet onion, cut into 1-inch pieces
1 zucchini, cut into 1-inch pieces
1 red bell pepper, cut into 1-inch pieces

¼ cup olive oil	½ tsp dried thyme
1 tsp garlic powder	¼ cup lemon juice
1 tsp shallot powder	1 tbsp apple cider vinegar
1 tsp ground cumin	12 grape tomatoes
½ tsp dried oregano	

Combine the olive oil, garlic powder, shallot powder, cumin, oregano, thyme, lemon juice, and vinegar in a bowl; mix well. Alternate skewering the chicken, bell pepper, onion, zucchini, and tomatoes. Once all of the skewers are prepared, place them in a greased baking dish and pour the olive oil marinade over the top. Turn to coat. Cover with plastic wrap and refrigerate.

Preheat air fryer to 380°F. Remove the skewers from the marinade and arrange them in a single layer on the frying basket. Bake for 25 minutes, rotating once. Let the skewers sit for 5 minutes. Serve and enjoy!

Country Chicken Hoagies

Serves: 2 | Total Time: 30 minutes

¼ cup button mushrooms, sliced

1 hoagie bun, halved	1 cup bell pepper strips
1 chicken breast, cubed	2 cheddar cheese slices
½ white onion, sliced	

Preheat air fryer to 320°F. Place the chicken pieces, onions, bell pepper strips, and mushroom slices on one side of the frying basket. Lay the hoagie bun halves, crusty side up and soft side down, on the other half of the air fryer. Bake for 10 minutes. Flip the hoagie buns and cover with cheddar cheese. Stir the chicken and vegetables. Cook for another 6 minutes until the cheese is melted and the chicken is juicy on the inside and crispy on the outside. Place the cheesy hoagie halves on a serving plate and cover one half with the chicken and veggies. Close with the other cheesy hoagie half. Serve.

Irresistible Cheesy Chicken Sticks

Serves: 2 | Total Time: 30 minutes

6 mozzarella sticks	¼ tsp crushed chilis
1 cup flour	¼ tsp cayenne pepper
2 eggs, beaten	½ tsp garlic powder
1 lb ground chicken	¼ tsp shallot powder
1 ½ cups breadcrumbs	½ tsp oregano

Preheat air fryer to 390°F. Combine crushed chilis, cayenne pepper, garlic powder, shallot powder, and oregano in a bowl. Add the ground chicken and mix well with your hands until evenly combined. In another mixing bowl, beat the eggs until fluffy and until the yolks and whites are fully combined, and set aside.

Pour the beaten eggs, flour, and bread crumbs into 3 separate bowls. Roll the mozzarella sticks in the flour, then dip them in the beaten eggs. With your hands, wrap the stick in a thin layer of the chicken mixture. Finally, coat the sticks in the crumbs. Place the sticks in the greased frying basket fryer and Air Fry for 18-20 minutes, turning once until crispy. Serve hot.

Chilean-Style Chicken Empanadas

Serves: 4 | Total Time: 25 minutes

4 oz chorizo sausage, casings removed and crumbled

1 tbsp olive oil	1 tsp paprika
4 oz chicken breasts, diced	¼ cup raisins
¼ cup black olives, sliced	4 empanada shells
1 tsp chili powder	

Preheat air fryer to 350°F. Warm the oil in a skillet over medium heat. Sauté the chicken and chorizo, breaking up the chorizo, 3-4 minutes. Add the raisins, chili powder, paprika, and olives and stir. Kill the heat and let the mixture cool slightly. Divide the chorizo mixture between the empanada shells and fold them over to cover the filling. Seal edges with water and press down with a fork to secure. Place the empanadas in the frying basket. Bake for 15 minutes, flipping once until golden. Serve warm.

Daadi Chicken Salad

Serves: 2 | Total Time: 30 minutes

½ cup chopped golden raisins
1 Granny Smith apple, grated

2 chicken breasts	½ sliced avocado
Salt and pepper to taste	1 scallion, minced
¾ cup mayonnaise	2 tbsp chopped pecans
1 tbsp lime juice	1 tsp poppy seeds
1 tsp curry powder	

Preheat air fryer to 350°F. Sprinkle chicken breasts with salt and pepper, place them in the greased frying basket, and Air Fry for 8-10 minutes, tossing once. Let rest for 5 minutes before cutting. In a salad bowl, combine chopped chicken, mayonnaise, lime juice, curry powder, raisins, apple, avocado, scallion, and pecans. Let sit covered in the fridge until ready to eat. Before serving, sprinkle with poppy seeds. Enjoy!

Yogurt-Marinated Chicken Legs

Serves: 4 | Total Time: 50 minutes + marinating time

1 cup Greek yogurt	1 tsp dried thyme
1 tbsp Dijon mustard	1 teaspoon ground cumin
1 tsp smoked paprika	¼ cup lemon juice
1 tbsp crushed red pepper	Salt and pepper to taste
1 tsp garlic powder	1 ½ lb chicken legs
1 tsp dried oregano	3 tbsp butter, melted

Combine all ingredients, except chicken and butter, in a bowl. Fold in chicken legs and toss until coated. Let sit covered in the fridge for 60 minutes up to overnight.

Preheat air fryer to 375°F. Shake excess marinade from chicken; place them in the greased frying basket and Air Fry for 18 minutes, brush melted butter and flip once. Let chill for 5 minutes before serving.

Buttered Chicken Thighs

Serves: 4 | Total Time: 30 minutes

4 bone-in chicken thighs, skinless

2 tbsp butter, melted	Salt and pepper to taste
1 tsp garlic powder	1 lemon, sliced
1 tsp lemon zest	

Preheat air fryer to 380°F. Rub the chicken thighs with butter, lemon zest, garlic powder, and salt. Divide the chicken thighs between 4 pieces of foil and sprinkle with black pepper, and then top with slices of lemon. Bake in the air fryer for 20-22 minutes until golden. Serve.

Crunchy Chicken Strips

Serves: 4 | Total Time: 40 minutes

1 chicken breast, sliced into strips
1 tbsp grated Parmesan cheese

1 cup breadcrumbs	2 eggs, beaten
1 tbsp chicken seasoning	Salt and pepper to taste

Preheat air fryer to 350°F. Mix the breadcrumbs, Parmesan cheese, chicken seasoning, salt, and pepper in a mixing bowl. Coat the chicken with the crumb mixture, then dip in the beaten eggs. Finally, coat again with the dry ingredients. Arrange the coated chicken pieces on the greased frying basket and Air Fry for 15 minutes. Turn over halfway through cooking and cook for another 15 minutes. Serve immediately.

Chicken Salad with White Dressing

Serves: 2 | Total Time: 20 minutes

2 chicken breasts, cut into strips
¼ cup diced peeled red onion
½ peeled English cucumber, diced
1 tbsp crushed red pepper flakes

1 cup Greek yogurt	2 cloves garlic, minced
3 tbsp light mayonnaise	Salt and pepper to taste
1 tbsp mustard	3 cups mixed greens
1 tsp chopped dill	10 Kalamata olives, halved
1 tsp chopped mint	1 tomato, diced
1 tsp lemon juice	¼ cup feta cheese crumbles

Preheat air fryer to 350°F. In a small bowl, whisk the Greek yogurt, mayonnaise, mustard, cucumber, dill, mint, salt, lemon juice, and garlic, and let chill the resulting dressing covered in the fridge until ready to use. Sprinkle the chicken strips with salt and pepper. Place them in the frying basket and Air Fry for 10 minutes, tossing once. Place the mixed greens and pepper flakes in a salad bowl. Top each with red onion, olives, tomato, feta cheese, and grilled chicken. Drizzle with the dressing and serve.

Korean-Style Chicken Bulgogi

Serves: 4 | Total Time: 30 minutes

6 boneless, skinless chicken thighs, cubed
3 scallions, sliced, whites and green separated

2 carrots, grated	1 tbsp lime juice
½ cup rice vinegar	1 tbsp soy sauce
2 tsp granulated sugar	2 cloves garlic, minced
Salt to taste	½ Asian pear
2 tbsp tamari	2 tsp minced ginger
2 tsp sesame oil	4 cups cooked white rice
1 tbsp light brown sugar	2 tsp sesame seeds

In a bowl, combine the carrots, half of the rice vinegar, sugar, and salt. Let chill covered in the fridge until ready to use. Mix the tamari, sesame oil, soy sauce, brown sugar, remaining rice vinegar, lime juice, garlic, Asian pear, ginger, and scallion whites in a bowl. Toss in chicken thighs and let marinate for 10 minutes.

Preheat air fryer to 350°F. Using a slotted spoon, transfer chicken thighs to the frying basket, reserve marinade, and Air Fry for 10-12 minutes, shaking once. Place chicken over a rice bed on serving plates and scatter with scallion greens and sesame seeds. Serve with pickled carrots.

Indian Chicken Tandoori

Serves: 2 | Total Time: 35 minutes + marinating time

2 chicken breasts, cubed	1 tsp red chili powder
½ cup hung curd	1 tsp chaat masala powder
1 tsp turmeric powder	Pinch of salt

Preheat air fryer to 350°F. Mix the hung curd, turmeric, red chili powder, chaat masala powder, and salt in a mixing bowl. Stir until the mixture is free of lumps. Coat the chicken with the mixture, cover, and refrigerate for 30 minutes to marinate. Place the marinated chicken chunks in a baking pan and drizzle with the remaining marinade. Bake for 25 minutes until the chicken is juicy and spiced. Serve warm.

Maewoon Chicken Legs

Serves: 4 | Total Time: 30 minutes + chilling time

4 scallions, sliced, whites and greens separated

¼ cup tamari	4 cloves garlic, minced
2 tbsp sesame oil	½ tsp ground ginger
1 tsp sesame seeds	Salt and pepper to taste
¼ cup honey	1 tbsp parsley
2 tbsp gochujang	1 ½ lb chicken legs
2 tbsp ketchup	

Whisk all ingredients, except chicken and scallion greens, in a bowl. Reserve ¼ cup of marinade. Toss chicken legs in the remaining marinade and chill for 30 minutes.

Preheat air fryer to 400°F. Place chicken legs in the greased frying basket and Air Fry for 10 minutes. Turn chicken. Cook for 8 more minutes. Let sit in a serving dish for 5 minutes. Coat the cooked chicken with the reserved marinade and scatter with scallion greens, sesame seeds and parsley to serve.

Chipotle Chicken Drumsticks

Serves: 4 | Total Time: 40 minutes

1 can chipotle chilies packed in adobe sauce
2 tbsp grated Mexican cheese
6 chicken drumsticks   1 tbsp corn flakes
1 egg, beaten   Salt and pepper to taste
½ cup bread crumbs

Preheat air fryer to 350°F. Place the chilies in the sauce in your blender and pulse until a fine paste is formed. Transfer to a bowl and add the beaten egg. Combine thoroughly. Mix the breadcrumbs, Mexican cheese, corn flakes, salt, and pepper in a separate bowl, and set aside.

Coat the chicken drumsticks with the crumb mixture, then dip into the bowl with wet ingredients, then dip again into the dry ingredients. Arrange the chicken drumsticks on the greased frying basket in a single flat layer. Air Fry for 14-16 minutes, turning each chicken drumstick over once. Serve warm.

Barberton Chicken Breasts

Serves: 4 | Total Time: 20 minutes

2 tbsp melted lard   ½ cup flour
4 chicken breasts   2 eggs, beaten
1 cup bread crumbs

Preheat air fryer to 350°F. Roll chicken in flour. Dip in beaten eggs, then coat in bread crumbs, pressing crumbs into chicken; gently shake off excess. Brush with melted lard and Air Fry for 14-16 minutes until golden brown.

Adobo Chicken Wings

Serves: 2 | Total Time: 40 minutes

1 lb chicken wings   2 tsp cayenne pepper
½ cup melted butter   1 tsp garlic powder
2 tbsp Tabasco sauce   1 tsp lemon zest
½ tbsp lemon juice   1 tsp adobo seasoning
1 tbsp Worcestershire sauce Salt and pepper to taste

Preheat air fryer to 350°F. Place the melted butter, Tabasco, lemon juice, Worcestershire sauce, cayenne, garlic, lemon zest, adobo seasoning, salt, and pepper in a bowl and stir to combine. Dip the chicken wings into the mixture, coating thoroughly. Lay the coated chicken wings on the foil-lined frying basket in an even layer. Air Fry for 16-18 minutes. Shake the basket several times during cooking until the chicken wings are crispy brown.

Chicken Thighs in Salsa Verde

Serves: 4 | Total Time: 35 minutes

4 boneless, skinless chicken thighs
1 cup salsa verde   1 tsp mashed garlic

Preheat air fryer to 350°F. Add chicken thighs to a cake pan and cover with salsa verde and mashed garlic. Place the cake pan in the frying basket and Bake for 30 minutes. Let rest for 5 minutes before serving.

Paprika Chicken Drumettes

Serves: 2 | Total Time: 30 minutes + marinating time

1 lb chicken drumettes   1 tsp chicken seasoning
1 cup buttermilk   ½ tsp garlic powder
3/4 cup bread crumbs   Salt and pepper to taste
½ tsp smoked paprika   3 tsp of lemon juice

Mix drumettes and buttermilk in a bowl and let sit covered in the fridge overnight. Preheat air fryer to 350°F. In a shallow bowl, combine the remaining ingredients. Shake excess buttermilk off drumettes and dip them in the breadcrumb mixture. Place breaded drumettes in the greased frying basket and Air Fry for 12 minutes. Increase air fryer temperature to 400°F, toss chicken, and cook for 8 minutes. Let rest for 5 minutes before serving.

Chicken Burgers with Blue Cheese Sauce

Serves: 4 | Total Time: 40 minutes

¼ cup crumbled blue cheese
¼ cup sour cream   1 lb ground chicken
2 tbsp mayonnaise   2 tbsp grated carrot
1 tbsp red hot sauce   2 tbsp diced celery
Salt to taste   1 egg white
3 tbsp buffalo wing sauce

Whisk the blue cheese, sour cream, mayonnaise, red hot sauce, salt, and 1 tbsp of buffalo sauce in a bowl. Let sit covered in the fridge until ready to use.

Preheat air fryer to 350°F. In another bowl, combine the remaining ingredients. Form the mixture into 4 patties, making a slight indentation in the middle of each. Place patties in the greased frying basket and Air Fry for 13 minutes until you reach your desired doneness, flipping once. Serve with the blue cheese sauce.

German Chicken Frikadellen

Serves: 6 | Total Time: 20 minutes

1 lb ground chicken   1 grated carrot
1 egg   1 tsp yellow mustard
3/4 cup bread crumbs   Salt and pepper to taste
¼ cup diced onions   ¼ cup chopped parsley

Preheat air fryer to 350°F. In a bowl, combine the ground chicken, egg, crumbs, onions, carrot, parsley, salt, and pepper. Mix well with your hands. Form mixture into meatballs. Place them in the frying basket and Air Fry for 8-10 minutes, tossing once until golden. Serve right away.

Satay Chicken Skewers

Serves: 4 | Total Time: 35 minutes

2 chicken breasts, cut into strips
1 ½ tbsp Thai red curry paste

¼ cup peanut butter	¼ tsp minced ginger
1 tbsp maple syrup	1 garlic clove, minced
1 tbsp tamari	1 cup coconut milk
1 tbsp lime juice	1 tsp fish sauce
2 tsp chopped onions	1 tbsp chopped cilantro

Mix the peanut butter, maple syrup, tamari, lime juice, ¼ tsp of sriracha, onions, ginger, garlic, and 2 tbsp of water in a bowl. Reserve 1 tbsp of the sauce. Set aside. Combine the reserved peanut sauce, fish sauce, coconut milk, Thai red curry paste, cilantro and chicken strips in a bowl and let marinate in the fridge for 15 minutes.

Preheat air fryer to 350°F. Thread chicken strips onto skewers and place them on a kebab rack. Place rack in the frying basket and Air Fry for 12 minutes. Serve with previously prepared peanut sauce on the side.

Vip´s Club Sandwiches

Serves: 4 | Total Time: 50 minutes

1 cup buttermilk	4 tbsp mayonnaise
1 egg	4 tsp yellow mustard
1 cup bread crumbs	8 dill pickle chips
1 tsp garlic powder	4 pieces iceberg lettuce
Salt and pepper to taste	½ sliced avocado
4 chicken cutlets	4 slices cooked bacon
3 tbsp butter, melted	8 vine-ripe tomato slices
4 hamburger buns	1 tsp chia seeds

Preheat air fryer to 400°F. Beat the buttermilk and egg in a bowl. In another bowl, combine breadcrumbs, garlic powder, salt, and black pepper. Dip chicken cutlets in the egg mixture, then dredge them in the breadcrumbs mixture. Brush chicken cutlets lightly with melted butter on both sides, place them in the greased frying basket, and Air Fry 18-20 minutes. Spread the mayonnaise on the top buns and mustard on the bottom buns. Add chicken onto bottom buns and top with pickles, lettuce, chia seeds, avocado, bacon, and tomato. Cover with the top buns. Serve and enjoy!

Stilton Chicken Cobb Salad

Serves: 2 | Total Time: 30 minutes

4 oz cooked bacon, crumbled	2 cups torn iceberg lettuce
¼ cup diced red onion	2 cups baby spinach
2 oz crumbled Stilton cheese	½ cup ranch dressing
Salt and pepper to taste	½ avocado, diced
1 tbsp olive oil	1 beefsteak tomato, diced
½ tsp apple cider vinegar	1 hard-boiled egg, diced
½ lb chicken breasts	2 tbsp parsley

Preheat air fryer to 350°F. Cover the chicken with plastic wraps and pound it with a meat tenderizer to ½-inch thickness. Season with salt and pepper and rub with olive oil. Place chicken breasts in the frying basket.

Air Fry for 14-16 minutes, flipping them halfway through the cooking time. Let them cool, then chop them into bite-sized pieces. Combine the lettuce, baby spinach, parsley, and half of the ranch dressing on a salad plate and toss to coat. Arrange the cooked chicken and the remaining ingredients in rows over the greens. Drizzle with the remaining ranch dressing. Serve immediately.

Cheesy Chicken-Avocado Paninis

Serves: 2 | Total Time: 25 minutes

2 tbsp mayonnaise	1 avocado, sliced
4 tsp yellow mustard	1 tomato, sliced
4 sandwich bread slices	Salt and pepper to taste
4 oz sliced deli chicken ham	1 tsp sesame seeds
2 oz sliced provolone cheese	2 tbsp butter, melted
2 oz sliced mozzarella	

Preheat air fryer to 350°F. Rub mayonnaise and mustard on the inside of each bread slice. Top 2 bread slices with chicken ham, provolone and mozzarella cheese, avocado, sesame seeds, and tomato slices. Season with salt and pepper. Then, close the sandwiches with the remaining bread slices. Brush the top and bottom of each sandwich lightly with melted butter. Place sandwiches in the frying basket and Bake for 6 minutes, flipping once. Serve.

Fantasy Sweet Chili Chicken Strips

Serves: 2 | Total Time: 20 minutes

1 lb chicken strips	½ cup bread crumbs
1 cup sweet chili sauce	½ cup cornmeal

Preheat air fryer to 350°F. Combine chicken strips and sweet chili sauce in a bowl until fully coated. In another bowl, mix the remaining ingredients. Dredge strips in the mixture. Shake off any excess. Place chicken strips in the greased frying basket and Air Fry for 10 minutes, tossing once. Serve right away.

Mustardy Chicken Bites

Serves: 4 | Total Time: 20 minutes + chilling time

2 tbsp horseradish mustard	2 chicken breasts, cubes
1 tbsp mayonnaise	1 tbsp parsley
1 tbsp olive oil	

Combine all ingredients, excluding parsley, in a bowl. Let marinate covered in the fridge for 30 minutes. Preheat air fryer to 350°F. Place chicken cubes in the greased frying basket and Air Fry for 9 minutes, tossing once. Serve immediately sprinkled with parsley.

Chicken Salad with Roasted Vegetables

Serves: 4 | Total Time: 25 minutes

4 tbsp honey-mustard salad dressing

3 chicken breasts, cubed	½ tsp dried thyme
1 red onion, sliced	½ cup mayonnaise
1 orange bell pepper, sliced	2 tbsp lemon juice
1 cup sliced zucchini	

Preheat air fryer to 400°F. Add chicken, onion, pepper, and zucchini to the fryer. Drizzle with 1 tbsp of the salad dressing and sprinkle with thyme. Toss to coat. Bake for 5-6 minutes. Shake the basket, then continue cooking for another 5-6 minutes. In a bowl, combine the rest of the dressing, mayonnaise, and lemon juice. Transfer the chicken and vegetables and toss to coat. Serve and enjoy!

Italian-Inspired Chicken Pizzadillas

Serves: 4 | Total Time: 25 minutes

2 cups cooked boneless, skinless chicken, shredded
1 cup grated provolone cheese
8 basil and menta leaves, julienned
½ tsp salt   8 flour tortillas
1 tsp garlic powder   1 cup marinara sauce
3 tbsp butter, melted   1 cup grated cheddar cheese

Preheat air fryer to 360°F. Sprinkle the chicken with salt and garlic powder. Brush one side of a tortilla lightly with melted butter. Spread ¼ cup of marinara sauce, then top with ½ cup of chicken, ¼ cup of cheddar cheese, ¼ cup of provolone, and finally, ¼ of basil and menta leaves. Top with a second tortilla and lightly brush the top with butter. Repeat with the remaining ingredients. Put the quesadillas, butter side down, in the fryer and Bake for 3 minutes. Cut them into 6 sections and serve.

Fiery Stuffed Chicken Meatballs

Serves: 4 | Total Time: 20 minutes

½ pickled jalapeño pepper, seeded and diced
1 tbsp cream cheese   ¼ tsp chili powder
3 tsp grated cheddar cheese 1 garlic clove, minced
Salt and pepper to taste   1 cup bread crumbs
1 lb ground chicken   2 tbsp olive oil

In a bowl, combine the pickled jalapeño, cream cheese, cheddar cheese, and salt. Shape the mixture into 8 balls. Also, mix the ground chicken, chili, garlic, salt, and pepper in a bowl. Divide into 8 meatballs.

Form a hole in each chicken meatball and place a cheese ball into the hole. Mold the chicken up and around to enclose the cheese balls until completely covered. Repeat the process until you run out of ingredients.

Preheat air fryer to 380°F. Mix the breadcrumbs and salt in a bowl. Roll stuffed meatballs in the mixture and brush them with some olive oil. Place the meatballs in the greased frying basket. Air Fry for 6-8 minutes. Slide out the basket, turn the balls, and brush them with the remaining olive oil. Continue cooking for another 6 minutes. Serve immediately and enjoy!

Cantonese Chicken Drumsticks

Serves: 4 | Total Time: 30 minutes

3 tbsp lime juice   3 tbsp honey
3 tbsp oyster sauce   3 tbsp brown sugar
6 chicken drumsticks   2 tbsp ketchup
1 tbsp peanut oil   ¼ cup pineapple juice

Preheat air fryer to 350°F. Drizzle some lime juice and oyster sauce on the drumsticks. Transfer to the frying basket and drizzle with peanut oil. Shake the basket to coat. Bake for 18 minutes until the drumsticks are almost done.

Meanwhile, combine the rest of the lime juice and the oyster sauce along with the honey, sugar, ketchup and pineapple juice in a 6-inch metal bowl. When the chicken is done, transfer to the bowl and coat the chicken with the sauce. Put the metal bowl in the basket and cook for 5-7 minutes, turning halfway, until golden and cooked through. Serve and enjoy!

Family Chicken Fingers

Serves: 4 | Total Time: 30 minutes

1 lb chicken breast fingers   Salt and pepper to taste
1 tbsp chicken seasoning   2 eggs
½ tsp mustard powder   1 cup bread crumbs

Preheat air fryer to 400°F. Add the chicken fingers to a large bowl along with chicken seasoning, mustard, salt, and pepper; mix well. Set up two small bowls. In one bowl, beat the eggs. In the second bowl, add the bread crumbs. Dip the chicken in the egg, then dredge in breadcrumbs. Place the nuggets in the air fryer. Lightly spray with cooking oil, then Air Fry for 8 minutes, shaking the basket once until crispy and cooked through. Serve warm.

Chicken Roulades

Serves: 4 | Total Time: 35 minutes

½ green bell pepper, cut into strips
1 carrot, cut into strips   2 tbsp adobo seasoning
4 chicken breast halves   1 spring onion, thinly sliced
½ lime, juiced

Preheat air fryer to 400°F. Place the chicken breasts between two plastic wraps and gently pound with a rolling pin to ¼-inch thickness. Drizzle with lime juice and season with adobo seasoning. Divide the carrot, green pepper, and spring onion equally between the 4 breasts. Roll up each chicken breast and secure with toothpicks. Place the roulades in the frying basket and lightly spray with cooking oil. Bake for 12 minutes, turning once. Serve warm.

Restaurant-Style Chicken Thighs

Serves: 4 | Total Time: 30 minutes

1 lb boneless, skinless chicken thighs
¼ cup barbecue sauce   2 tbsp parsley, chopped
2 cloves garlic, minced   2 tbsp lemon juice
1 tsp lemon zest

Coat the chicken with barbecue sauce, garlic, and lemon juice in a medium bowl. Leave to marinate for 10 minutes.

Preheat air fryer to 380°F. When ready to cook, remove the chicken from the bowl and shake off any drips. Arrange the chicken in the air fryer and Bake for 16-18 minutes, until golden and cooked through. Serve topped with lemon zest and parsley. Enjoy!

Cajun Chicken Livers

Serves: 2 | Total Time: 45 minutes + marinating time

1 lb chicken livers, rinsed, connective tissue discarded
1 cup whole milk   2 eggs
½ cup cornmeal   1 ½ cups bread crumbs
3/4 cup flour   1 tbsp olive oil
1 tsp salt and black pepper   2 tbsp chopped parsley
1 tsp Cajun seasoning

Pat chicken livers dry with paper towels, then transfer them to a small bowl and pour in the milk and black pepper. Let sit covered in the fridge for 2 hours.

Preheat air fryer to 375°F. In a bowl, combine cornmeal, flour, salt, and Cajun seasoning. In another bowl, beat the eggs, and in a third bowl, add bread crumbs. Dip chicken livers first in the cornmeal mixture, then in the egg, and finally in the bread crumbs. Place chicken livers in the greased frying basket, brush the tops lightly with olive oil, and Air Fry for 16 minutes, turning once. Serve right away sprinkled with parsley.

Enchilada Chicken Quesadillas

Serves: 4 | Total Time: 35 minutes

2 cups cooked chicken breasts, shredded
1 (7-oz) can diced green chilies, including juice
2 cups grated Mexican cheese blend
3/4 cup sour cream   1 tsp dried onion flakes
2 tsp chili powder   ½ tsp salt
1 tsp cumin   3 tbsp butter, melted
1 tbsp chipotle sauce   8 flour tortillas

In a small bowl, whisk the sour cream, chipotle sauce and chili powder. Let chill in the fridge until ready to use.

Preheat air fryer to 350°F. Mix the chicken, green chilies, cumin, and salt in a bowl. Set aside. Brush on one side of a tortilla lightly with melted butter. Layer with ¼ cup of chicken, onion flakes and ¼ cup of Mexican cheese. Top with a second tortilla and lightly brush with butter on top. Repeat with the remaining ingredients. Transfer the quesadillas butter side down to the frying basket and Bake for 3 minutes. Cut them into 6 sections and serve with cream sauce on the side. Enjoy!

Party Buffalo Chicken Drumettes

Serves: 6 | Total Time: 30 minutes

16 chicken drumettes   Black pepper to taste
1 tsp garlic powder   ¼ cup Buffalo wings sauce
1 tbsp chicken seasoning   2 spring onions, sliced

Preheat air fryer to 400°F. Sprinkle garlic, chicken seasoning, and black pepper on the drumettes. Place them in the fryer and spray with cooking oil. Air Fry for 10 minutes, shaking the basket once. Transfer the drumettes to a large bowl. Drizzle with Buffalo wing sauce and toss to coat. Place in the fryer and Fry for 7-8 minutes, until crispy. Allow to cool slightly. Top with spring onions and serve warm.

Spiced Chicken Breasts

Serves: 4 | Total Time: 20 minutes

½ tsp dried oregano   ¼ tsp sweet paprika
½ tsp granulated garlic   Salt and pepper to taste
½ tsp granulated onion   1 lb chicken breasts, sliced
½ tsp chili powder   2 tbsp yellow mustard

Preheat air fryer to 375°F. Mix together oregano, salt, garlic, onion, chili powder, paprika, and black pepper in a small bowl. Coat the chicken with mustard in a bowl. Sprinkle the seasoning mix over the chicken. Place the chicken in the greased frying basket and Air Fry for 7-8, flipping once until cooked through. Serve immediately.

Chicken Pasta Pie

Serves: 4 | Total Time: 40 minutes

1/3 cup green bell peppers, diced
¼ cup yellow bell peppers, diced
½ cup mozzarella cheese, grated
3/4 cup grated Parmesan cheese
2/3 cup ricotta cheese   1/3 cup diced onions
2 tbsp butter, melted   2 cloves minced garlic
1 egg   ¼ lb ground chicken
¼ tsp salt   1 cup marinara sauce
6 oz cooked spaghetti   ½ tsp dried oregano
2 tsp olive oil

Combine the ricotta cheese, 1 tbsp of Parmesan cheese, minced garlic, and salt in a bowl. Whisk the melted butter and egg in another bowl. Add the remaining Parmesan cheese and cooked spaghetti and mix well. Set aside. Warm the olive oil in a skillet over medium heat. Add in onions, green bell peppers, yellow bell peppers and cook for 3 minutes until the onions are tender. Stir in ground chicken and cook for 5 minutes until no longer pink.

Preheat air fryer to 350°F. Press spaghetti mixture into a greased baking pan, then spread ricotta mixture on top, and finally top with the topping mixture, followed by the marinara sauce. Place baking pan in the frying basket and Bake for 10 minutes. Scatter with mozzarella cheese on top and cook for 4 more minutes. Let rest for 20 minutes before releasing the sides of the baking pan. Cut into slices and serve sprinkled with oregano.

Granny Pesto Chicken Caprese

Serves: 4 | Total Time: 30 minutes

2 tbsp grated Parmesan cheese
4 oz fresh mozzarella cheese, thinly sliced
16 grape tomatoes, halved   1 large egg, beaten
4 garlic cloves, minced   ½ cup bread crumbs
1 tsp olive oil   2 tbsp Italian seasoning
Salt and pepper to taste   1 tsp balsamic vinegar
4 chicken cutlets   2 tbsp chopped fresh basil
1 tbsp prepared pesto

Preheat air fryer to 400°F. In a bowl, coat the tomatoes with garlic, olive oil, salt, and pepper. Air Fry for 5 minutes, shaking them twice. Set aside when soft.

Place the cutlets between two sheets of parchment paper. Pound the chicken to ¼-inch thickness using a meat mallet. Season on both sides with salt and pepper. Spread an even coat of pesto. Put the beaten egg in a shallow bowl. Mix the crumbs, Italian seasoning, and Parmesan in a second shallow bowl. Dip the chicken in the egg bowl and then in the crumb mix. Press the crumbs so that they stick to the chicken.

Place the chicken in the greased frying basket. Air Fry the chicken for 6-8 minutes, flipping once until golden and cooked through. Put 1 oz of mozzarella and ¼ of the tomatoes on top of each cutlet. When all of the cutlets are cooked, return them to the frying basket and melt the cheese for 2 minutes. Remove from the fryer, drizzle with balsamic vinegar, and sprinkle basil on top.

Mexican-Inspired Chicken Breasts

Serves: 4 | Total Time: 20 minutes

⅛ tsp crushed red pepper flakes
1 red pepper, deseeded and diced

Salt to taste	½ tsp Mexican oregano
4 chicken breasts	1 tomato, chopped
¾ tsp garlic powder	½ diced red onion
½ tsp onion powder	3 tbsp fresh lime juice
½ tsp ground cumin	10 ounces avocado, diced
½ tsp ancho chile powder	1 tbsp chopped cilantro
½ tsp sweet paprika	

Preheat air fryer to 380°F. Stir together salt, garlic and onion powder, cumin, ancho chili powder, paprika, Mexican oregano, and pepper flakes in a bowl. Spray the chicken with cooking oil and rub with the spice mix. Air Fry the chicken for 10 minutes, flipping once until browned and fully cooked. Repeat for all of the chicken. Mix the onion and lime juice in a bowl. Fold in the avocado, cilantro, red pepper, salt, and tomato and coat gently. To serve, top the chicken with guacamole salsa.

Jalapeño Chicken with Black Beans

Serves: 4 | Total Time: 30 minutes

1 lb chicken breasts, cubed	2 tsp olive oil
2 green onions, chopped	2/3 cup canned black beans
1 cup mixed bell pepper strips	½ cup salsa
1 jalapeño pepper, minced	2 tsp Mexican chili powder

Preheat air fryer to 400°F. Combine the chicken, green onions, bell pepper, jalapeño, and olive oil in a bowl. Transfer to a bowl to the frying basket and Air Fry for 10 minutes, stirring once during cooking. When done, stir in the black beans, salsa, and chili powder. Air Fry for 7-10 minutes or until cooked through. Serve warm.

Italian Herb Stuffed Chicken Breasts

Serves: 4 | Total Time: 30 minutes

2 tbsp olive oil	2 tbsp Italian seasoning
3 tbsp balsamic vinegar	1 tbsp chopped fresh basil
3 garlic cloves, minced	1 tsp thyme, chopped
1 tomato, diced	4 chicken breasts

Preheat air fryer to 370°F. Combine the olive oil, balsamic vinegar, garlic, thyme, tomato, half of the Italian seasoning, and basil in a medium bowl. Set aside.

Cut 4-5 slits into the chicken breasts ¾ of the way through. Season with the rest of the Italian seasoning and place the chicken with the slits facing up, in the greased frying basket. Bake for 7 minutes. Spoon the bruschetta mixture into the slits of the chicken. Cook for another 3 minutes. Allow chicken to sit and cool for a few minutes. Serve and enjoy!

Crispy Chicken Cordon Bleu

Serves: 4 | Total Time: 25 minutes

4 deli ham slices, halved lengthwise

2 tbsp grated Parmesan	2 egg whites
4 chicken breast halves	¾ cup bread crumbs
Salt and pepper to taste	1 tsp garlic powder
8 Swiss cheese slices	1 tsp onion powder
1 egg	1 tsp mustard powder

Preheat air fryer to 400°F. Season the chicken cutlets with salt and pepper. On one cutlet, put a half slice of ham and cheese on the top. Roll the chicken tightly, then set aside. Beat the eggs and egg whites in a shallow bowl. Put the crumbs, Parmesan, garlic, onion, and mustard powder, in a second bowl. Dip the cutlet in the egg bowl and then in the crumb mix. Press so that they stick to the chicken. Put the rolls of chicken seam side down in the greased frying basket and Air Fry for 12-14 minutes, flipping once until golden and cooked through. Serve.

Sticky Chicken Drumsticks

Serves: 4 | Total Time: 45 minutes

1 lb chicken drumsticks	Salt and pepper to taste
1 tbsp chicken seasoning	¼ cup honey
1 tsp dried chili flakes	1 cup barbecue sauce

Preheat air fryer to 390°F. Season drumsticks with chicken seasoning, chili flakes, salt, and pepper. Place one batch of drumsticks in the greased frying basket and Air Fry for 18-20 minutes, flipping once until golden.

While the chicken is cooking, combine honey and barbecue sauce in a small bowl. Remove the drumsticks to a serving dish. Drizzle honey-barbecue sauce over and serve.

Garlic Chicken Thighs

Serves: 4 | Total Time: 30 minutes

4 bone-in skinless chicken thighs

1 tbsp olive oil	1 tsp dried sage
1 tbsp lemon juice	Black pepper to taste
3 tbsp cornstarch	20 garlic cloves, unpeeled

Preheat air fryer to 370°F. Brush the chicken with olive oil and lemon juice, then drizzle cornstarch, sage, and pepper. Put the chicken in the frying basket and scatter the garlic cloves on top. Roast for 25 minutes or until the garlic is soft and the chicken is cooked through. Serve.

Tuscan-Style Chicken Roll-Ups

Serves: 4 | Total Time: 30 minutes

1/3 cup ricotta cheese	1 tbsp chicken seasoning
1 cup Tuscan kale, chopped	Salt and pepper to taste
4 chicken breasts	1 tsp paprika

Preheat air fryer to 370°F. Soften the ricotta cheese in a microwave-safe bowl for 15 seconds. Combine in a bowl along with Tuscan kale. Set aside. Cut 4-5 slits in the top of each chicken breast about ¾ of the way down. Season with chicken seasoning, salt, and pepper.

Place the chicken with the slits facing up in the greased frying basket. Lightly spray the chicken with oil. Bake for 6-8 minutes. Slide-out and stuff the cream cheese mixture into the chicken slits. Sprinkle ½ tsp of paprika and cook for another 3 minutes. Serve and enjoy!

Fancy Chicken Piccata Linguine

Serves: 4 | Total Time: 30 minutes

1 lb chicken breasts, cut into cutlets

Salt and pepper to taste	½ onion powder
2 eggs	¼ cup fino sherry
1 cup bread crumbs	1 lemon, juiced and zested
1 tsp Italian seasoning	1 tbsp capers
1 tbsp butter	1 lemon, sliced
½ cup chicken broth	16 oz cooked linguine

Preheat air fryer to 370°F. Place the cutlets between two sheets of parchment paper. Using a rolling pin, pound the chicken to a ¼-inch thickness and season with salt and pepper. Beat the eggs with 1 tsp of the caper liquid in a bowl. Put the bread crumbs, Parmesan cheese, onion powder, and Italian seasoning in a second bowl and stir. Dip the cutlet in the egg mixture and then in the crumb mix. Put the cutlets in the greased frying basket. Air Fry for 6 minutes, flipping once until crispy and golden.

Melt butter in a skillet over medium heat. Stir in broth, sherry, lemon juice, lemon zest, and pepper. Bring to a boil and cook for 3-4 minutes until the sauce is reduced by half. Remove from heat. Stir in capers. Divide the linguine between plates and top with chicken. Pour the sauce over and garnish with lemon slices. Serve warm.

Masala Chicken with Charred Vegetables

Serves: 4 | Total Time: 35 minutes + marinating time

8 boneless, skinless chicken thighs

¼ cup yogurt	¼ tsp red pepper flakes
3 garlic cloves, minced	1 ¼ tsp salt
1 tbsp lime juice	7 oz shishito peppers
1 tsp ginger-garlic paste	2 vine tomatoes, quartered
1 tsp garam masala	1 tbsp chopped cilantro
¼ tsp ground turmeric	1 lime, cut into wedges

Mix yogurt, garlic, lime juice, ginger paste, garam masala, turmeric, flakes, and salt in a bowl. Place the thighs in a zipper bag and pour in the marinade. Massage the chicken to coat and refrigerate for 2 hours.

Preheat air fryer to 400°F. Remove the chicken from the bag and discard the marinade. Put the chicken in the greased frying basket and Arr Fry for 13-15 minutes, flipping once until browned and thoroughly cooked. Set chicken aside and cover with foil. Lightly spray shishitos and tomatoes with cooking oil. Place in the frying basket and Bake for 8 minutes, shaking the basket once until soft and slightly charred. Sprinkle with salt. Top the chicken and veggies with cilantro and lemon wedges.

Chicken Cordon Bleu Patties

Serves: 4 | Total Time: 30 minutes

1/3 cup grated Fontina cheese	
3 tbsp milk	Salt and pepper to taste
1/3 cup bread crumbs	1 ¼ lb ground chicken
1 egg, beaten	¼ cup finely chopped ham
½ tsp dried parsley	

Preheat air fryer to 350°F. Mix milk, breadcrumbs, egg, parsley, salt, and pepper in a bowl. Using your hands, add the chicken and gently mix until just combined. Divide into 8 portions and shape into thin patties. Place on waxed paper. On 4 of the patties, top with ham and Fontina cheese, then place another patty on top of that. Gently pinch the edges together so that none of the ham or cheese is peeking out. Arrange the burgers in the greased frying basket and Air Fry until cooked through, for 14-16 minutes. Serve and enjoy!

Popcorn Chicken Tenders with Vegetables

Serves: 4 | Total Time: 30 minutes

2 tbsp cooked popcorn, ground	
Salt and pepper to taste	1 tbsp olive oil
1 lb chicken tenders	2 carrots, sliced
½ cup bread crumbs	12 baby potatoes
½ tsp dried thyme	

Preheat air fryer to 380°F. Season the chicken tenders with salt and pepper. In a shallow bowl, mix the crumbs, popcorn, thyme, and olive oil until combined. Coat the chicken with the mixture. Press firmly so the crumbs adhere. Arrange the carrots and baby potatoes in the greased frying basket and top them with the chicken tenders. Bake for 9-10 minutes. Shake the basket and continue cooking for another 9-10 minutes until the vegetables are tender. Serve and enjoy!

Za'atar Chicken Drumsticks

Serves: 4 | Total Time: 45 minutes

2 tbsp butter, melted	Salt and pepper to taste
8 chicken drumsticks	1 lemon, zested
1 ½ tbsp Za'atar seasoning	2 tbsp parsley, chopped

Preheat air fryer to 390°F. Mix the Za'atar seasoning, lemon zest, parsley, salt, and pepper in a bowl. Add the chicken drumsticks and toss to coat. Place them in the air fryer and brush them with butter. Air Fry for 18-20 minutes, flipping once until crispy. Serve and enjoy!

Favourite Fried Chicken Wings

Serves: 4 | Total Time: 30 minutes

16 chicken wings	Black pepper to taste
1 tsp garlic powder	½ cup flour
½ tsp paprika	¼ cup sour cream
1 tsp chicken seasoning	2 tsp red chili flakes

Preheat air fryer to 400°F. Put the wings in a resealable bag along with garlic powder, chicken seasoning, paprika, and pepper. Seal the bag and shake until the chicken is completely coated. Prepare a clean resealable bag and add the flour. Pour sour cream into a large bowl.

Dunk the wings into the sour cream, then transfer them to the bag of flour. Seal the bag and shake until coated. Transfer the wings to the frying basket. Lightly spray them with cooking oil and Air Fry for 20-25 minutes, shaking the basket a few times until crispy and golden brown. Remove to a plate and allow to cool slightly. Sprinkle with red chili flakes. Serve and enjoy!

Greek Chicken Wings

Serves: 4 | Total Time: 30 minutes

8 whole chicken wings	½ tsp Greek seasoning
½ lemon, juiced	Salt and pepper to taste
½ tsp garlic powder	¼ cup buttermilk
1 tsp shallot powder	½ cup all-purpose flour

Preheat air fryer to 400°F. Put the wings in a resealable bag along with lemon juice, garlic, shallot, Greek seasoning, salt, and pepper. Seal the bag and shake to coat. Set up bowls large enough to fit the wings.

In one bowl, pour the buttermilk. In the other, add flour. Using tongs, dip the wings into the buttermilk, then dredge in flour. Transfer the wings to the greased frying basket, spraying lightly with cooking oil. Air Fry for 25 minutes, shaking twice, until golden and cooked through. Allow to cool slightly, and serve.

Herb-Marinated Chicken Breasts

Serves: 4 | Total Time: 25 minutes + marinating time

4 chicken breasts	Salt and pepper to taste
2 tsp rosemary, minced	½ cup chopped cilantro
2 tsp thyme, minced	1 lime, juiced

Place chicken in a resealable bag. Add rosemary, thyme, salt, pepper, cilantro, and lime juice. Seal the bag and toss to coat, then place in the refrigerator for 2 hours.

Preheat air fryer to 400°F. Arrange the chicken in a single layer in the greased frying basket. Spray the chicken with cooking oil. Air Fry for 6-7 minutes, then flip the chicken. Cook for another 3 minutes. Serve and enjoy!

Chicken Breast Burgers

Serves: 4 | Total Time: 35 minutes + marinating time

2 chicken breasts	1 cup buttermilk
1 cup dill pickle juice	1 egg
½ cup flour	4 buns
Salt and pepper to taste	2 pickles, sliced

Cut the chicken into cutlets by cutting them in half horizontally on a cutting board. Transfer them to a large bowl along with pickle juice and ½ cup of buttermilk. Toss to coat, then marinate for 30 minutes in the fridge.

Preheat air fryer to 370°F. In a shallow bowl, beat the egg and the rest of the buttermilk to combine. In another shallow bowl, mix flour, salt, and pepper. Dip the marinated cutlet in the egg mixture, then dredge in flour. Place the cutlets in the greased frying basket and Air Fry for 12 minutes, flipping once halfway through. Remove the cutlets and pickles on buns and serve.

Asian Sweet Chili Chicken

Serves: 4 | Total Time: 30 minutes

2 chicken breasts, cut into 1-inch pieces	
1 cup cornstarch	2 eggs
1 tsp chicken seasoning	1 ½ cups sweet chili sauce
Salt and pepper to taste	

Preheat air fryer to 360°F. Mix cornstarch, chicken seasoning, salt, and pepper in a large bowl. In another bowl, beat the eggs. Dip the chicken in the cornstarch mixture to coat. Next, dip the chicken into the egg, then return to the cornstarch. Transfer chicken to the air fryer.

Lightly spray all of the chicken with cooking oil. Air Fry for 15-16 minutes, shaking the basket once or until golden. Transfer chicken to a serving dish and drizzle with sweet chili sauce. Serve immediately.

Harissa Chicken Wings

Serves: 4 | Total Time: 25 minutes

8 whole chicken wings	¼ tsp dried oregano
1 tsp garlic powder	1 tbsp harissa seasoning

Preheat air fryer to 400°F. Season the wings with garlic, harissa seasoning, and oregano. Place them in the greased frying basket and spray with cooking oil spray. Air Fry for 10 minutes, shake the basket, and cook for another 5-7 minutes until golden and crispy. Serve warm.

Cornflake Chicken Nuggets

Serves: 4 | Total Time: 25 minutes

1 egg white	1 lb chicken breast fingers
1 tbsp lemon juice	½ cup ground cornflakes
½ tsp dried basil	2 bread slices, crumbled
½ tsp ground paprika	

Preheat air fryer to 400°F. Whisk the egg white, lemon juice, basil, and paprika, then add the chicken and stir. Combine the cornflakes and breadcrumbs on a plate, then put the chicken fingers in the mix to coat. Put the nuggets in the frying basket and Air Fry for 10-13 minutes, turning halfway through, until golden, crisp and cooked through. Serve hot.

Saucy Chicken Thighs

Serves: 4 | Total Time: 35 minutes

8 boneless, skinless chicken thighs
1 tbsp Italian seasoning
Salt and pepper to taste
2 garlic cloves, minced
½ tsp apple cider vinegar
½ cup honey
¼ cup Dijon mustard

Preheat air fryer to 400°F. Season the chicken with Italian seasoning, salt, and black pepper. Place in the greased frying basket and Bake for 15 minutes, flipping once halfway through cooking.

While the chicken is cooking, add garlic, honey, vinegar, and Dijon mustard in a saucepan and stir-fry over medium heat for 4 minutes or until the sauce has thickened and warmed through. Transfer the thighs to a serving dish and drizzle with honey-mustard sauce. Serve and enjoy!

Ranch Chicken Tortillas

Serves: 4 | Total Time: 35 minutes

2 chicken breasts
1 tbsp Ranch seasoning
1 tbsp taco seasoning
1 cup flour
1 egg
½ cup bread crumbs
4 flour tortillas
1 ½ cups shredded lettuce
3 tbsp ranch dressing
2 tbsp cilantro, chopped

Preheat air fryer to 370°F. Slice the chicken breasts into cutlets by cutting them in half horizontally on a cutting board. Rub with ranch and taco seasonings. In one shallow bowl, add flour. In another shallow bowl, beat the egg. In the third shallow bowl, add bread crumbs.

Lightly spray the air fryer basket with cooking oil. First, dip the cutlet in the flour, dredge in egg, and then finish by coating with bread crumbs. Place the cutlets in the fryer and Bake for 6-8 minutes. Flip them and cook further for 4 minutes until crisp. Allow the chicken to cook for a few minutes, then cut into strips. Divide into 4 equal portions along with shredded lettuce, ranch dressing, cilantro and tortillas. Serve and enjoy!

Punjabi-Inspired Chicken

Serves: 4 | Total Time: 35 minutes + marinating time

2/3 cup plain yogurt
2 tbsp lemon juice
2 tsp curry powder
½ tsp ground cinnamon
2 garlic cloves, minced
½-inch piece ginger, grated
2 tsp olive oil
4 chicken breasts

Mix the yogurt, lemon juice, curry powder, cinnamon, garlic, ginger, and olive oil in a bowl. Slice the chicken, without cutting, all the way through by making thin slits, then toss it into the yogurt mix. Coat well and let marinate for 10 minutes.

Preheat air fryer to 360°F. Take the chicken out of the marinade, letting the extra liquid drip off. Toss the rest of the marinade away. Air Fry the chicken for 10 minutes. Turn each piece, then cook for 8-13 minutes more until cooked through and no pink meat remains. Serve warm.

Parmesan Chicken Meatloaf

Serves: 4 | Total Time: 45 minutes

1 ½ tsp evaporated cane sugar
1 lb ground chicken
4 garlic cloves, minced
2 tbsp grated Parmesan
¼ cup heavy cream
¼ cup minced onion
2 tbsp chopped basil
2 tbsp chopped parsley
Salt and pepper to taste
½ tsp onion powder
½ cup bread crumbs
¼ tsp red pepper flakes
1 egg
1 cup tomato sauce
½ tsp garlic powder
½ tsp dried thyme
½ tsp dried oregano
1 tbsp coconut aminos

Preheat air fryer to 400°F. Combine chicken, garlic, minced onion, oregano, thyme, basil, salt, pepper, onion powder, Parmesan cheese, red pepper flakes, bread crumbs, egg, and cream in a large bowl. Transfer the chicken mixture to a prepared baking dish. Stir together tomato sauce, garlic powder, coconut aminos, and sugar in a small bowl. Spread over the meatloaf. Loosely cover with foil. Place the pan in the frying basket and bake for 15 minutes. Take the foil off and bake for another 15 minutes. Allow resting for 10 minutes before slicing. Serve sprinkled with parsley.

Sunday Chicken Skewers

Serves: 4 | Total Time: 25 minutes

1 green bell pepper, cut into chunks
1 red bell pepper, cut into chunks
4 chicken breasts, cubed
1 tbsp chicken seasoning
Salt and pepper to taste
16 cherry tomatoes
8 pearl onions, peeled

Preheat air fryer to 360°F. Season the cubes with chicken seasoning, salt, and pepper. Thread metal skewers with chicken, bell pepper chunks, cherry tomatoes, and pearl onions. Put the kabobs in the greased frying basket. Bake for 14-16 minutes, flipping once until cooked through. Let cool slightly. Serve.

Buttery Chicken Legs

Serves 4 | Total Time: 50 minutes

1 tsp baking powder
1 tsp dried mustard
1 tsp smoked paprika
1 tsp garlic powder
1 tsp dried thyme
Salt and pepper to taste
1 ½ lb chicken legs
3 tbsp butter, melted

Preheat air fryer to 370°F. Combine all ingredients, except for butter, in a bowl until coated. Place the chicken legs in the greased frying basket. Air Fry for 18 minutes, flipping once and brushing with melted butter on both sides. Let chill onto a serving plate for 5 minutes before serving.

Chicken Tenders with Basil-Strawberry Glaze

Serves 4 | Total Time: 20 minutes + marinating time

1 lb chicken tenderloins
¼ cup strawberry preserves
3 tbsp chopped basil
1 tsp orange juice
½ tsp orange zest
Salt and pepper to taste

Combine all ingredients, except for 1 tbsp of basil, in a bowl. Marinade in the fridge covered for 30 minutes.

Preheat air fryer to 350°F. Place the chicken tenders in the frying basket and Air Fry for 4-6 minutes. Shake the basket gently and turn over the chicken. Cook for 5 more minutes. Top with the remaining basil to serve.

Chicken & Rice Sautée

Serves: 4 | Total Time: 25 minutes

1 (8-oz) can pineapple chunks, drained, ¼ cup juice reserved
1 cup cooked long-grain rice
1 lb chicken breasts, cubed   1 tbsp cornstarch
1 red onion, chopped   ½ tsp ground ginger
1 tbsp peanut oil   ¼ tsp chicken seasoning
1 peeled peach, cubed

Preheat air fryer to 400°F. Combine the chicken, red onion, pineapple, and peanut oil in a metal bowl, then put the bowl in the fryer. Air Fry for 8-10 minutes, remove, and stir. Toss the peach in and put the bowl back into the fryer for 3 minutes. Slide out and stir again. Mix the reserved pineapple juice, corn starch, ginger, and chicken seasoning in a bowl, then pour over the chicken mixture and stir well. Put the bowl back into the fryer and cook for 3 more minutes or until the chicken is cooked through and the sauce is thick. Serve over cooked rice.

Spring Chicken Salad

Serves: 4 | Total Time: 25 minutes

3 chicken breasts, cubed   2 tbsp ranch salad dressing
1 small red onion, sliced   2 tbsp lemon juice
1 red bell pepper, sliced   ½ tsp dried basil
1 cup green beans, sliced   10 oz spring mix

Preheat air fryer to 400°F. Put the chicken, red onion, red bell pepper, and green beans in the frying basket and Roast for 10-13 minutes until the chicken is cooked through. Shake the basket at least once while cooking. As the chicken is cooking, combine the ranch dressing, lemon juice, and basil. When the cooking is done, remove the chicken and veggies to a bowl and let cool slightly. Pour the dressing over. Stir to coat. Serve with spring mix.

Chicken Breasts Wrapped in Bacon

Serves: 4 | Total Time: 35 minutes

¼ cup mayonnaise   1 tbsp light brown sugar
¼ cup sour cream   1 lb chicken tenders
3 tbsp ketchup   1 tsp dried parsley
1 tbsp yellow mustard   8 bacon slices

Preheat the air fryer to 370°F. Combine the mayonnaise, sour cream, ketchup, mustard, and brown sugar in a bowl and mix well, then set aside. Sprinkle the chicken with the parsley and wrap each one in a slice of bacon. Put the wrapped chicken in the frying basket in a single layer and Air Fry for 18-20 minutes, flipping once until the bacon is crisp. Serve with sauce.

Creole Chicken Drumettes

Serves 4 | Total Time: 50 minutes

1 lb chicken drumettes   ½ cup bread crumbs
½ cup flour   1 tbsp Creole seasoning
½ cup heavy cream   2 tbsp melted butter
½ cup sour cream

Preheat air fryer to 370°F. Combine chicken drumettes and flour in a bowl. Shake away excess flour and set aside. Mix the heavy cream and sour cream in a bowl. In another bowl, combine bread crumbs and Creole seasoning. Dip floured drumettes in cream mixture, then dredge them in crumbs. Place the chicken drumettes in the greased frying basket and Air Fry for 20 minutes, tossing once and brushing with melted butter. Let rest for a few minutes on a plate and serve.

Mom's Chicken Wings

Serves 4 | Total Time: 35 minutes

2 lb chicken wings, split at the joint
1 tbsp water   1 tbsp tamari
1 tbsp sesame oil   1 tsp honey
2 tbsp Dijon mustard   1 tsp white wine vinegar
¼ tsp chili powder

Preheat air fryer to 400°F. Coat the wings with sesame oil. Place them in the frying basket and Air Fry for 16-18 minutes, tossing once or twice. Whisk the remaining ingredients in a bowl. Reserve. When ready, transfer the wings to a serving bowl. Pour the previously prepared sauce over and toss to coat. Serve immediately.

Pesto Chicken Cheeseburgers

Serves 4 | Total Time: 40 minutes

¼ cup shredded Pepper Jack cheese
1 lb ground chicken   1 egg white, beaten
2 tbsp onion   1 tbsp pesto
¼ cup chopped parsley   Salt and pepper to taste

Preheat air fryer to 350°F. Combine ground chicken, onion, cheese, parsley, egg white, salt, and pepper in a bowl. Make 4 patties out of the mixture. Place them in the greased frying basket and Air Fry for 12-14 minutes until golden, flipping once. Serve topped with pesto.

Chicken Meatballs with a Surprise

Serves 4 | Total Time: 35 minutes

1/3 cup cottage cheese crumbles
1 lb ground chicken   ½ cup bread crumbs
½ tsp onion powder   ½ tsp garlic powder
¼ cup chopped basil

Preheat air fryer to 350°F. Combine the ground chicken, onion, basil, cottage cheese, bread crumbs, and garlic powder in a bowl. Form into 18 meatballs, about 2 tbsp each. Place the chicken meatballs in the greased frying basket and Air Fry for 12 minutes, shaking once. Serve.

Chicken & Fruit Biryani

Serves: 4 | Total Time: 30 minutes

3 chicken breasts, cubed	1 apple, chopped
2 tsp olive oil	½ cup chicken broth
2 tbsp cornstarch	1/3 cup dried cranberries
1 tbsp curry powder	1 cooked basmati rice

Preheat air fryer to 380°F. Combine the chicken and olive oil, then add some corn starch and curry powder. Mix to coat, then add the apple and pour the mix into a baking pan. Put the pan in the air fryer and Bake for 8 minutes, stirring once. Add the chicken broth, cranberries, and 2 tbsp of water and continue baking for 10 minutes, letting the sauce thicken. The chicken should be lightly charred and cooked through. Serve warm with basmati rice.

Spicy Honey Mustard Chicken

Serves: 4 | Total Time: 30 minutes

1/3 cup tomato sauce	2 garlic cloves, minced
2 tbsp yellow mustard	1 Fresno pepper, minced
2 tbsp apple cider vinegar	1 tsp onion powder
1 tbsp honey	4 chicken breasts

Preheat air fryer to 370°F. Mix the tomato sauce, mustard, apple cider vinegar, honey, garlic, Fresno pepper, and onion powder in a bowl, then use a brush to rub the mix over the chicken breasts. Put the chicken in the air fryer and Grill for 10 minutes. Remove it, turn it, and rub with more sauce. Cook further for about 5 minutes. Remove the basket and flip the chicken. Add more sauce, return to the fryer, and cook for 3-5 more minutes or until the chicken is cooked through. Serve warm.

Cajun Chicken Kebabs

Serves: 4 | Total Time: 30 minutes

3 tbsp lemon juice	½ Cajun seasoning
2 tsp olive oil	1 lb chicken breasts, cubed
2 tbsp chopped parsley	1 cup cherry tomatoes
½ tsp dried oregano	1 zucchini, cubed

Preheat air fryer to 400°F. Combine the lemon juice, olive oil, parsley, oregano, and Cajun seasoning in a bowl. Toss in the chicken and stir, making sure all pieces are coated. Allow marinating for 10 minutes. Take 8 bamboo skewers and poke the chicken, tomatoes, and zucchini, alternating the pieces. Use a brush to put more marinade on them, then lay them in the air fryer. Air Fry the kebabs for 15 minutes, turning once, or until the chicken is cooked through, with no pink showing. Get rid of the leftover marinade. Serve and enjoy!

Hawaiian Chicken

Serves: 4 | Total Time: 25 minutes

1 (15-oz) can diced pineapple	3 garlic cloves, minced
1 kiwi, sliced	Salt and pepper to taste
2 tbsp coconut aminos	½ tsp paprika
1 tbsp honey	1 lb chicken breasts

Preheat air fryer to 360°F. Stir together pineapple, kiwi, coconut aminos, honey, garlic, salt, paprika, and pepper in a small bowl. Arrange the chicken in a single layer in a baking dish. Spread half of the pineapple mixture over the top of the chicken. Transfer the dish into the frying basket. Roast for 8 minutes, then flip the chicken. Spread the rest of the pineapple mixture over the top of the chicken and Roast for another 8-10 until the chicken is done. Allow sitting for 5 minutes. Serve and enjoy!

Moroccan-Style Chicken Strips

Serves: 4 | Total Time: 30 minutes

4 chicken breasts, cut into strips	
2 tsp olive oil	¼ cup lemon juice
2 tbsp cornstarch	1 tbsp honey
3 garlic cloves, minced	½ tsp ras el hanout
½ cup chicken broth	1 cup cooked couscous

Preheat air fryer to 400°F. Mix the chicken and olive oil in a bowl, then add the cornstarch. Stir to coat. Add the garlic and transfer to a baking pan. Put the pan in the fryer. Bake for 10 minutes. Stir at least once during cooking.

When done, pour in the chicken broth, lemon juice, honey, and ras el hanout. Bake for an additional 6-9 minutes or until the sauce is thick and the chicken cooked through with no pink showing. Serve with couscous.

Prosciutto Chicken Rolls

Serves: 4 | Total Time: 30 minutes

½ cup chopped broccoli	Salt and pepper to taste
½ cup grated cheddar cheese	½ tsp dried oregano
2 scallions, sliced	½ tsp dried basil
2 garlic cloves, minced	4 chicken breasts
4 prosciutto thin slices	2 tbsp chopped cilantro
¼ cup cream cheese	

Preheat air fryer to 375°F. Combine broccoli, scallion, garlic, cheddar cheese, cream cheese, salt, pepper, oregano, and basil in a small bowl. Prepare the chicken by placing it between two pieces of plastic wrap. Pound the chicken with a meat mallet or heavy can until it is evenly ½-inch thickness. Top each with a slice of prosciutto and spoon ¼ of the cheese mixture in the center of the chicken breast. Fold each breast over the filling and transfer to a greased baking dish. Place the dish in the frying basket and bake for 8 minutes. Flip the chicken and bake for another 8-12 minutes. Allow resting for 5 minutes. Serve warm sprinkled with cilantro and enjoy!

Fennel & Chicken Ratatouille

Serves 4 | Total Time: 30 minutes

1 lb boneless, skinless chicken thighs, cubed	
2 tbsp grated Parmesan cheese	
1 eggplant, cubed	1 tsp Italian seasoning
1 zucchini, cubed	2 tbsp olive oil
1 bell pepper, diced	1 (14-oz) can diced tomatoes
1 fennel bulb, sliced	1 tsp pasta sauce
1 tsp salt	2 tbsp basil leaves

Preheat air fryer to 400°F. Mix the chicken, eggplant, zucchini, bell pepper, fennel, salt, Italian seasoning, and oil in a bowl. Place the chicken mixture in the frying basket and Air Fry for 7 minutes. Transfer it to a cake pan. Mix in tomatoes along with juices and pasta sauce. Air Fry for 8 minutes. Scatter with Parmesan and basil. Serve and enjoy.

Farmer's Fried Chicken

Serves: 4 | Total Time: 55 minutes + marinating time

3 lb whole chicken, cut into breasts, drumsticks, and thighs

2 cups flour	2 tsp smoked paprika
4 tsp salt	1 tsp mustard powder
4 tsp dried basil	1 tsp celery salt
4 tsp dried thyme	1 cup kefir
2 tsp dried shallot powder	¼ cup honey

Preheat the air fryer to 370°F. Combine the flour, salt, basil, thyme, shallot, paprika, mustard powder, and celery salt in a bowl. Pour into a glass jar. Mix the kefir and honey in a large bowl and add the chicken; stir to coat. Marinate for 15 minutes at room temperature. Remove the chicken from the kefir mixture; discard the rest. Put 2/3 cup of the flour mix onto a plate and dip the chicken. Shake gently and put on a wire rack for 10 minutes. Line the frying basket with round parchment paper with holes punched in it. Place the chicken in a single layer and spray with cooking oil. Air Fry for 18-25 minutes, flipping once around minute 10. Serve hot.

Mumbai Chicken Nuggets

Serves: 4 | Total Time: 30 minutes

1 lb boneless, skinless chicken breasts

4 tsp curry powder	1 cup panko bread crumbs
Salt and pepper to taste	½ cup coconut yogurt
1 egg, beaten	1/3 cup mango chutney
2 tbsp sesame oil	¼ cup mayonnaise

Preheat the air fryer to 400°F. Cube the chicken into 1-inch pieces and sprinkle with 3 tsp of curry powder, salt, and pepper; toss to coat. Beat together the egg and sesame oil in a shallow bowl and scatter the panko onto a separate plate. Dip the chicken in the egg, then in the panko, and press to coat. Lay the coated nuggets on a wire rack as you work. Set the nuggets in the greased frying basket and Air Fry for 7-10 minutes, rearranging once halfway through cooking. While the nuggets are cooking, combine the yogurt, chutney, mayonnaise, and the remaining teaspoon of curry powder in a small bowl. Serve the nuggets with the dipping sauce.

Katsu Chicken Thighs

Serves: 4 | Total Time: 35 minutes

1 ½ lb boneless, skinless chicken thighs

3 tbsp tamari sauce	1 cup chicken stock
3 tbsp lemon juice	2 tbsp hoisin sauce
½ tsp ground ginger	2 tbsp light brown sugar
Black pepper to taste	2 tbsp sesame seeds
6 tbsp cornstarch	

Preheat the air fryer to 400°F. After cubing the chicken thighs, put them in a cake pan. Add a tbsp of tamari sauce, a tbsp of lemon juice, ginger, and black pepper. Mix and let marinate for 10 minutes. Remove the chicken and coat it in 4 tbsp of cornstarch; set aside. Add the rest of the marinade to the pan and add the stock, hoisin sauce, brown sugar, and the remaining tamari sauce, lemon juice, and cornstarch. Mix well. Put the pan in the frying basket and Air Fry for 5-8 minutes or until bubbling and thick, stirring once. Remove and set aside. Put the chicken in the frying basket and Fry for 15-18 minutes, shaking the basket once. Remove the chicken to the sauce in the pan and return to the fryer to reheat for 2 minutes. Sprinkle with the sesame seeds and serve.

Glazed Chicken Thighs

Serves: 4 | Total Time: 25 minutes

1 lb boneless, skinless chicken thighs

¼ cup balsamic vinegar	3 garlic cloves, minced
3 tbsp honey	Salt and pepper to taste
2 tbsp brown sugar	½ tsp smoked paprika
1 tsp whole-grain mustard	2 tbsp chopped shallots
¼ cup soy sauce	

Preheat air fryer to 375°F. Whisk vinegar, honey, sugar, soy sauce, mustard, garlic, salt, pepper, and paprika in a small bowl. Arrange the chicken in the frying basket and brush the top of each with some of the vinegar mixture. Air Fry for 7 minutes, then flip the chicken. Brush the tops with the rest of the vinegar mixture and Air Fry for another 5 to 8 minutes. Allow resting for 5 minutes before slicing. Serve warm sprinkled with shallots.

Hazelnut Chicken Salad with Strawberries

Serves 4 | Total Time: 30 minutes

2 chicken breasts, cubed	½ cup chopped hazelnuts
Salt and pepper to taste	½ cup chopped celery
¾ cup mayonnaise	½ cup diced strawberries
1 tbsp lime juice	

Preheat air fryer to 350°F. Sprinkle chicken cubes with salt and pepper. Place them in the frying basket and Air Fry for 9 minutes, shaking once. Remove to a bowl and leave it to cool. Add the mayonnaise, lime juice, hazelnuts, celery, and strawberries. Serve.

Lime Chicken Goujons

Serves 4 | Total Time: 25 minutes

2 chicken breasts, cut into strips
1 cup lightly crushed corn crackers

3 tbsp flour	½ tsp lime pepper seasoning
2 tsp olive oil	3 egg whites, beaten

Preheat air fryer to 380°F. Season the chicken strips with lime pepper seasoning, then dust them in the flour. Next, dip in the egg whites and coat in the corn crackers. Put onto the greased frying basket. Air Fry for 10-14 minutes, turning halfway through, until golden and crisp.

Curried Chicken Legs

Serves 4 | Total Time: 40 minutes

¾ cup Greek yogurt
1 tbsp tomato paste
2 tsp curry powder
½ tbsp oregano
1 tsp salt
1 ½ lb chicken legs
2 tbsp chopped fresh mint

Combine yogurt, tomato paste, curry powder, oregano and salt in a bowl. Divide the mixture in half. Cover one half and store it in the fridge. Into the other half, toss in the chicken until coated and marinate covered in the fridge for 30 minutes up to overnight.

Preheat air fryer to 370°F. Shake excess marinade from chicken. Place chicken legs in the greased frying basket and Air Fry for 18 minutes, flipping once and brushing with yogurt mixture. Serve topped with mint.

Asian-Style Orange Chicken

Serves: 4 | Total Time: 25 minutes

1 lb chicken breasts, cubed
Salt and pepper to taste
6 tbsp cornstarch
1 cup orange juice
¼ cup orange marmalade
¼ cup ketchup
½ tsp ground ginger
2 tbsp soy sauce
1 1/3 cups edamame beans

Preheat the air fryer to 375°F. Sprinkle the cubes with salt and pepper. Coat with 4 tbsp of cornstarch and set aside on a wire rack. Mix the orange juice, marmalade, ketchup, ginger, soy sauce, and the remaining cornstarch in a cake pan, then stir in the beans. Set the pan in the frying basket and Bake for 5-8 minutes, stirring once during cooking, until the sauce is thick and bubbling. Remove from the fryer and set aside. Put the chicken in the frying basket and fry for 10-12 minutes, shaking the basket once. Stir the chicken into the sauce and beans in the pan. Return to the fryer and reheat for 2 minutes.

Chicken Pinchos Morunos

Serves: 4 | Total Time: 35 minutes

1 yellow summer squash, sliced
3 chicken breasts
¼ cup plain yogurt
2 tbsp olive oil
1 tsp sweet pimentón
1 tsp dried thyme
½ tsp sea salt
½ tsp garlic powder
½ tsp ground cumin
2 red bell peppers
3 scallions
16 large green olives

Preheat the air fryer to 400°F. Combine yogurt, olive oil, pimentón, thyme, cumin, salt, and garlic in a bowl and add the chicken. Stir to coat. Cut the bell peppers and scallions into 1-inch pieces. Remove the chicken from the marinade; set aside the rest of the marinade. Thread the chicken, peppers, scallions, squash, and olives onto the soaked skewers. Brush the kebabs with marinade. Discard any remaining marinade. Lay the kebabs in the frying basket. Add a raised rack and put the rest of the kebabs on it. Bake for 18-23 minutes, flipping once around minute 10. Serve hot.

Chicken Pigs in Blankets

Serves: 4 | Total Time: 40 minutes

8 chicken drumsticks, boneless, skinless
2 tbsp light brown sugar
2 tbsp ketchup
1 tbsp grainy mustard
8 smoked bacon slices
1 tsp chopped fresh sage

Preheat the air fryer to 350°F. Mix brown sugar, sage, ketchup, and mustard in a bowl and brush the chicken with it. Wrap slices of bacon around the drumsticks and brush with the remaining mix. Line the frying basket with round parchment paper with holes. Set 4 drumsticks on the paper, add a raised rack and set the other drumsticks on it. Bake for 25-35 minutes, moving the bottom drumsticks to the top, top to the bottom, and flipping at about 14-16 minutes. Sprinkle with sage and serve.

The Ultimate Chicken Bulgogi

Serves: 4 | Total Time: 30 minutes + marinating time

1 ½ lb boneless, skinless chicken thighs, cubed
1 cucumber, thinly sliced
¼ cup apple cider vinegar
4 garlic cloves, minced
¼ tsp ground ginger
⅛ tsp red pepper flakes
2 tsp honey
⅛ tsp salt
2 tbsp tamari
2 tsp sesame oil
2 tsp granular honey
2 tbsp lemon juice
½ tsp lemon zest
3 scallions, chopped
2 cups cooked white rice
2 tsp roasted sesame seeds

In a bowl, toss the cucumber, vinegar, half of the garlic, half of the ginger, pepper flakes, honey, and salt and store in the fridge covered. Combine the tamari, sesame oil, granular honey, lemon juice, remaining garlic, remaining ginger, and chicken in a large bowl. Toss to coat and marinate in the fridge for 10 minutes.

Preheat air fryer to 350°F. Place chicken in the frying basket, do not discard excess marinade. Air Fry for 10-12 minutes, shaking once and pouring excess marinade over. Place the chicken bulgogi over the cooked rice and scatter with scallion greens, pickled cucumbers, and sesame seeds. Serve and enjoy!

Cheesy Chicken Tenders

Serves: 4 | Total Time: 25 minutes

1 cup grated Parmesan cheese
¼ cup grated cheddar cheese
1 ¼ lb chicken tenders
1 egg, beaten
2 tbsp milk
Salt and pepper to taste
½ tsp garlic powder
1 tsp dried thyme
¼ tsp shallot powder

Preheat the air fryer to 400°F. Stir the egg and milk until combined. Mix the salt, pepper, garlic, thyme, shallot, cheddar cheese, and Parmesan cheese on a plate. Dip the chicken in the egg mix, then in the cheese mix, and press to coat. Lay the tenders in the frying basket in a single layer. Add a raised rack to cook more at one time. Spray all with oil and Bake for 12-16 minutes, flipping once halfway through cooking. Serve hot.

Christmas Chicken & Roasted Grape Salad

Serves: 4 | Total Time: 40 minutes

3 chicken breasts, pat-dried	2 tbsp honey mustard
1 tsp paprika	2 tbsp fresh lemon juice
Salt and pepper to taste	1 cup chopped celery
2 cups seedless red grapes	2 scallions, chopped
½ cup mayonnaise	2 tbsp walnuts, chopped
½ cup plain yogurt	

Preheat the air fryer to 370°F. Sprinkle the chicken breasts with paprika, salt, and pepper. Transfer to the greased frying basket and Air Fry for 16-19 minutes, flipping once. Remove and set on a cutting board. Put the grapes in the fryer and spray with cooking oil. Fry for 4 minutes or until the grapes are hot and tender. Mix the mayonnaise, yogurt, honey mustard, and lemon juice in a bowl and whisk. Cube the chicken and add to the dressing along with the grapes, walnuts, celery, and scallions. Toss gently and serve.

Japanese-Inspired Glazed Chicken

Serves: 4 | Total Time: 25 minutes

4 chicken breasts	2 garlic cloves, minced
Chicken seasoning to taste	¼ cup molasses
Salt and pepper to taste	2 tbsp tamari sauce
2 tsp grated fresh ginger	

Preheat air fryer to 400°F. Season the chicken with seasoning, salt, and pepper. Place the chicken in the greased frying basket and Air Fry for 7 minutes, then flip the chicken. Cook for another 3 minutes.

While the chicken is cooking, combine ginger, garlic, molasses, and tamari sauce in a saucepan over medium heat. Cook for 4 minutes or until the sauce thickens. Transfer all of the chicken to a serving dish. Drizzle with ginger-tamari glaze and serve.

Sweet Nutty Chicken Breasts

Serves 4 | Total Time: 30 minutes

2 chicken breasts, halved lengthwise	
¼ cup honey mustard	1 tbsp olive oil
¼ cup chopped pecans	1 tbsp parsley, chopped

Preheat air fryer to 350°F. Brush chicken breasts with honey mustard and olive oil on all sides. Place the pecans in a bowl. Add and coat the chicken breasts. Place the breasts in the greased frying basket and Air Fry for 25 minutes, turning once. Let chill onto a serving plate for 5 minutes. Sprinkle with parsley and serve.

Guajillo Chile Chicken Meatballs

Serves 4 | Total Time: 30 minutes

1 lb ground chicken	2 tbsp grated onion
1 large egg	2 tbsp tomato paste
½ cup bread crumbs	1 tsp ground cumin
1 tbsp sour cream	1 tsp guajillo chile powder
2 tsp brown mustard	2 tbsp olive oil

Preheat air fryer to 350°F. Mix the ground chicken, egg, bread crumbs, sour cream, mustard, onion, tomato paste, cumin, and chili powder in a bowl. Form into 16 meatballs. Place the meatballs in the greased frying basket and Air Fry for 8-10 minutes, shaking once until browned and cooked through. Serve immediately.

Chicken Wings al Ajillo

Serves 4 | Total Time: 35 minutes

2 lb chicken wings, split at the joint	
2 tbsp melted butter	½ tbsp hot paprika
2 tbsp grated Cotija cheese	¼ tsp salt
4 cloves garlic, minced	

Preheat air fryer to 250°F. Coat the chicken wings with 1 tbsp of butter. Place them in the basket and Air Fry for 12 minutes, tossing once. In another bowl, whisk 1 tbsp of butter, Cotija cheese, garlic, hot paprika, and salt. Reserve. Increase temperature to 400°F. Air Fry wings for 10 more minutes, tossing twice. Transfer them to the bowl with the sauce, and toss to coat. Serve immediately.

Teriyaki Chicken Bites

Serves 4 | Total Time: 30 minutes

1 lb boneless, skinless chicken thighs, cubed	
1 green onion, sliced diagonally	
1 large egg	3 cloves garlic, minced
1 tbsp teriyaki sauce	2 tsp grated fresh ginger
4 tbsp flour	2 tsp chili garlic sauce
1 tsp sesame oil	2 tsp granular honey
2 tsp balsamic vinegar	Salt and pepper to taste
2 tbsp tamari	

Preheat air fryer to 400°F. Beat the egg, teriyaki sauce, and flour in a bowl. Stir in chicken pieces until fully coated. In another bowl, combine the remaining ingredients, except for the green onion. Reserve. Place chicken pieces in the frying basket lightly greased with olive oil and Air Fry for 15 minutes, tossing every 5 minutes. Remove them to the bowl with the sauce and toss to coat. Scatter with green onions to serve. Enjoy!

Lemon Herb Whole Cornish Hen

Serves: 2 | Total Time: 50 minutes

1 (1 ½-lb) Cornish hen	Salt and pepper to taste
¼ cup olive oil	1 celery stalk, chopped
2 tbsp lemon juice	½ small onion
2 tbsp sage, chopped	½ lemon, juiced and zested
2 tbsp thyme, chopped	2 tbsp chopped parsley
4 garlic cloves, chopped	

Preheat air fryer to 380°F. Whisk the olive oil, lemon juice, sage, thyme, garlic, salt, and pepper in a bowl. Rub the mixture on the tops and sides of the hen. Pour any excess inside the cavity of the bird. Add the celery, onion, and lemon juice and zest to the hen cavity. Put it breast side down in the frying basket and Roast for 40-45 minutes, turning once. Serve garnished with parsley.

Smoky Chicken Fajita Bowl

Serves 4 | Total Time: 35 minutes + chilling time

1 jalapeño, sliced and seeded
½ cup queso fresco crumbles
1 tbsp olive oil
2 tsp flour
¼ tsp chili powder
¼ tsp fajita seasoning
¼ tsp smoked paprika
¼ tsp ground cumin
½ tsp granular honey
⅛ tsp onion powder
⅛ tsp garlic powder
1 lb chicken breast strips
4 tomatoes, diced
½ diced red onion
4 tbsp sour cream
1 avocado, diced

Combine all the spices, olive oil, flour, and chicken strips in a bowl. Let chill in the fridge for 30 minutes.

Preheat air fryer to 400°F. Place the chicken strips in the frying basket and Air Fry for 8 minutes, shaking once. Divide between 4 medium bowls. Add tomatoes, jalapeño, onion, queso fresco, sour cream, and avocado to the bowls. Serve right away.

Simple Salsa Chicken Thighs

Serves 2 | Total Time: 35 minutes

1 lb boneless, skinless chicken thighs
1 cup mild chunky salsa   2 lime wedges for serving
½ tsp taco seasoning

Preheat air fryer to 350°F. Add chicken thighs into a baking pan and pour salsa and taco seasoning over. Place the pan in the frying basket and Air Fry for 30 minutes until golden brown. Serve with lime wedges.

Classic Chicken Cobb Salad

Serves 4 | Total Time: 30 minutes

4 oz cooked bacon, crumbled
2 chicken breasts, cubed
1 tbsp sesame oil
Salt and pepper to taste
4 cups torn romaine lettuce
2 tbsp olive oil
1 tbsp white wine vinegar
2 hard-boiled eggs, sliced
2 tomatoes, diced
6 radishes, finely sliced
¼ cup blue cheese crumbles
¼ cup diced red onions
1 avocado, diced

Preheat air fryer to 350°F. Combine chicken cubes, sesame oil, salt, and black pepper in a bowl. Place chicken cubes in the frying basket and Air Fry for 9 minutes, flipping once. Reserve. In a bowl, combine the lettuce, olive oil, and vinegar. Divide between 4 bowls. Add in the cooked chicken, hard-boiled egg slices, bacon, tomato cubes, radishes, blue cheese, onion, and avocado cubes. Serve.

Turkey Steaks with Green Salad

Serves 4 | Total Time: 20 minutes

1/3 cup shaved Parmesan cheese
3 tsp grated Parmesan cheese
4 turkey breast steaks
Salt and pepper to taste
1 large egg, beaten
½ cup bread crumbs
½ tsp dried thyme
5 oz baby spinach
5 oz watercress
1 tbsp olive oil
1 tbsp lemon juice
2 spring onions, chopped
1 lemon, cut into wedges

Place the steaks between two sheets of parchment paper. Pound the turkey to ¼-inch thick cutlets using a meat mallet or rolling pin. Season the cutlets with salt and pepper to taste. Put the beaten egg in a shallow bowl. Put the crumbs, thyme, and Parmesan in a second shallow bowl. Dip the cutlet in the egg bowl and then in the crumb mix. Press the crumbs so that they stick to the chicken. Preheat air fryer to 400°F. Fry the turkey in the greased frying basket for 8 minutes, flipping once until golden and cooked through. Repeat for all cutlets.

Put the spinach, spring onions, and watercress in a bowl. Toss with olive oil, lemon juice, salt, and pepper. Serve each cutlet on a plate topped with 1 ½ cups salad. Garnish with lemon wedges and shaved Parmesan cheese. Serve.

Japanese-Style Turkey Meatballs

Serves: 4 | Total Time: 25 minutes

1 1/3 lb ground turkey
¼ cup panko bread crumbs
4 chopped scallions
¼ cup chopped cilantro
1 egg
1 tbsp grated ginger
1 garlic clove, minced
3 tbsp shoyu
2 tsp toasted sesame oil
¾ tsp salt
2 tbsp oyster sauce sauce
2 tbsp fresh orange juice

Add ground turkey, panko, 3 scallions, cilantro, egg, ginger, garlic, 1 tbsp of shoyu sauce, sesame oil, and salt in a bowl. Mix with your hands until combined. Divide the mixture into 12 equal parts and roll into balls. Preheat air fryer to 380°F. Place the meatballs in the greased frying basket. Bake for about 9-11 minutes, flipping once until browned and cooked through. Repeat for all meatballs.

In a small saucepan over medium heat, add oyster sauce, orange juice and remaining shoyu sauce. Bring to a boil, then reduce the heat to low. Cook until the sauce is slightly reduced, 3 minutes. Serve the meatballs with the oyster sauce drizzled over them and topped with the remaining scallions.

Berry-Glazed Turkey Breast

Serves: 4 | Total Time: 1 Hour 25 minutes

1 (4 lb) bone-in, skin-on turkey breast
1 tbsp olive oil
Salt and pepper to taste
1 cup raspberries
1cup chopped strawberries
2 tbsp balsamic vinegar
2 tbsp butter, melted
1 tbsp honey mustard
1 tsp dried rosemary

Preheat the air fryer to 350°F. Lay the turkey breast skin-side up in the frying basket, brush with the oil, and sprinkle with salt and pepper. Bake for 55-65 minutes, flipping twice. Meanwhile, mix the berries, vinegar, melted butter, rosemary and honey mustard in a blender and blend until smooth. Turn the turkey skin-side up inside the fryer and brush with half of the berry mix. Bake for 5 more minutes. Put the remaining berry mix in a small saucepan and simmer for 3-4 minutes while the turkey cooks. When the turkey is done, let it stand for 10 minutes, then carve. Serve with the remaining glaze.

Goat Cheese Stuffed Turkey Roulade

Serves: 4 | Total Time: 55 minutes

1 (2-lb) boneless turkey breast, skinless
Salt and pepper to taste   2 garlic cloves, minced
4 oz goat cheese   2 tbsp olive oil
1 tbsp marjoram   2 tbsp chopped cilantro
1 tbsp sage

Preheat air fryer to 380°F. Butterfly the turkey breast with a sharp knife and season with salt and pepper. Mix together the goat cheese, marjoram, sage, and garlic in a bowl. Spread the cheese mixture over the turkey breast, then roll it up tightly, tucking the ends underneath.

Put the turkey breast roulade onto a piece of aluminum foil, wrap it up, and place it into the air fryer. Bake for 30 minutes. Turn the turkey breast, brush the top with oil, and then continue to cook for another 10-15 minutes. Slice and serve sprinkled with cilantro.

Sage & Paprika Turkey Cutlets

Serves: 4 | Total Time: 15 minutes

½ cup bread crumbs   ¼ tsp ground cumin
¼ tsp paprika   1 egg
Salt and pepper to taste   4 turkey breast cutlets
⅛ tsp dried sage   2 tbsp chopped chervil
⅛ tsp garlic powder

Preheat air fryer to 380°F. Combine the bread crumbs, paprika, salt, black pepper, sage, cumin, and garlic powder in a bowl and mix well. Beat the egg in another bowl until frothy. Dip the turkey cutlets into the egg mixture, then coat them in the bread crumb mixture. Put the breaded turkey cutlets in the frying basket. Bake for 4 minutes. Turn the cutlets over, then Bake for 4 more minutes. Decorate with chervil and serve.

Windsor's Chicken Salad

Serves: 4 | Total Time: 30 minutes

½ cup halved seedless red grapes
2 chicken breasts, cubed   2 tbsp chopped parsley
Salt and pepper to taste   ½ cup chopped celery
¾ cup mayonnaise   1 shallot, diced
1 tbsp lemon juice

Preheat air fryer to 350°F. Sprinkle chicken with salt and pepper. Place the chicken cubes in the frying basket and Air Fry for 9 minutes, flipping once. In a salad bowl, combine the cooked chicken, mayonnaise, lemon juice, parsley, grapes, celery, and shallot and let chill covered in the fridge for 1 hour up to overnight.

Indian-Inspired Chicken Skewers

Serves: 4 | Total Time: 40 minutes + chilling time

1 lb boneless, skinless chicken thighs, cubed
1 red onion, diced   1 cup canned coconut milk
1 tbsp grated ginger   2 tbsp tomato paste
2 tbsp lime juice   2 tbsp olive oil
1 tbsp ground cumin   ½ tsp red chili powder
1 tbsp ground coriander   ¼ tsp curry powder
1 tsp cayenne pepper   2 tsp salt
1 tsp ground turmeric   2 tbsp chopped cilantro

Toss red onion, ginger, lime juice, coconut milk, tomato paste, olive oil, cumin, coriander, cayenne pepper, turmeric, chili powder, curry powder, salt, and chicken until fully coated. Let chill in the fridge for 2 hours.

Preheat air fryer to 350°F. Thread chicken onto 8 skewers and place them on a kebab rack. Place rack in the frying basket and Air Fry for 12 minutes. Discard marinade. Garnish with cilantro to serve.

Yummy Honey-Mustard Chicken Kabobs

Serves 4 | Total Time: 35 minutes+ chilling time

1 lb boneless, skinless chicken thighs, cubed
1 green bell pepper, chopped
½ cup honey mustard   8 cherry tomatoes
½ yellow onion, chopped   2 tbsp chopped scallions

Toss chicken cubes and honey mustard in a bowl and let chill covered in the fridge for 30 minutes. Preheat air fryer to 350°F. Thread chicken cubes, onion, cherry tomatoes, and bell peppers, alternating, onto 8 skewers. Place them on a kebab rack. Place rack in the frying basket and Air Fry for 12 minutes. Top with scallions to serve.

Honey-Glazed Cornish Hen

Serves 2 | Total Time: 40 minutes

2 tbsp butter, melted   ½ tsp honey
2 tbsp Dijon mustard   1 tbsp olive oil
Salt and pepper to taste   1 (1¼-lb) Cornish game hen
⅛ tsp ground nutmeg   1 tangerine, quartered

Preheat air fryer to 350°F. Whisk the butter, mustard, salt, black pepper, nutmeg, and honey in a bowl. Brush olive oil over and inside of cornish hen and scatter with the honey mixture. Stuff tangerine into the hen's cavity.

Place hen in the frying basket and Air Fry for 28-32 minutes, flipping twice. Transfer it to a cutting board and let rest for 5 minutes until easy to handle. Split in half by cutting down the spine and serve right away.

Easy Turkey Meatballs

Serves: 4 | Total Time: 20 minutes

1 lb ground turkey   Salt and pepper to taste
½ celery stalk, chopped   ½ tsp garlic powder
1 egg   ½ tsp onion powder
¼ tsp red pepper flakes   ½ tsp cayenne pepper
¼ cup bread crumbs

Preheat air fryer to 360°F. Add all of the ingredients to a bowl and mix well. Shape the mixture into 12 balls and arrange them on the greased frying basket. Air Fry for 10-12 minutes or until the meatballs are cooked through and browned. Serve and enjoy!

Crispy Chicken Tenders

Serves: 4 | Total Time: 20 minutes

1 egg
¼ cup almond milk
¼ cup almond flour
¼ cup bread crumbs
Salt and pepper to taste
½ tsp dried thyme
½ tsp dried sage
½ tsp garlic powder
½ tsp chili powder
1 lb chicken tenderloins
1 lemon, quartered

Preheat air fryer to 360°F. Whisk together the egg and almond milk in a bowl until frothy. Mix the flour, bread crumbs, salt, pepper, thyme, sage, chili powder and garlic powder in a separate bowl. Dip each chicken tenderloin into the egg mixture, then coat with the bread crumb mixture. Put the breaded chicken tenderloins into the frying basket in a single layer. Air Fry for 12 minutes, turning once. Serve with lemon slices.

Mexican Turkey Meatloaves

Serves: 4 | Total Time: 30 minutes

¼ cup jarred chunky mild salsa
1 lb ground turkey
1/3 cup bread crumbs
1/3 cup canned black beans
1/3 cup frozen corn
¼ cup minced onion
¼ cup chopped scallions
2 tbsp chopped cilantro
1 egg, beaten
1 tbsp tomato puree
1 tsp salt
½ tsp ground cumin
1 tsp Mulato chile powder
½ tsp ground aniseed
¼ tsp ground cloves
2 tbsp ketchup
2 tbsp jarred mild salsa

In a bowl, use your hands to mix the turkey, bread crumbs, beans, corn, salsa, onion, scallions, cilantro, egg, tomato puree, salt, chile powder, aniseed, cloves, and cumin. Shape into 4 patties about 1-inch in thickness.

Preheat air fryer to 350°F. Put the meatloaves in the greased frying basket and Bake for about 18-20 minutes, flipping once until cooked through. Stir together the ketchup and salsa in a small bowl. When all loaves are cooked, brush them with the glaze and return to the fryer to heat up for 2 minutes. Serve immediately.

Spinach & Turkey Meatballs

Serves: 4 | Total Time: 45 minutes

¼ cup grated Parmesan cheese
2 scallions, chopped
1 garlic clove, minced
1 egg, beaten
1 cup baby spinach
¼ cup bread crumbs
1 tsp dried oregano
Salt and pepper to taste
1 ¼ lb ground turkey

Preheat the air fryer to 400°F and preheat the oven to 250°F. Combine the scallions, garlic, egg, baby spinach, breadcrumbs, Parmesan, oregano, salt, and pepper in a bowl and mix well. Add the turkey and mix, then form into 1½-inch balls. Add as many meatballs as will fit in a single layer in the frying basket and Air Fry for 10-15 minutes, shaking once around minute 7. Put the cooked meatballs on a tray in the oven and cover with foil to keep warm. Repeat with the remaining balls.

Mushroom & Turkey Bread Pizza

Serves: 4 | Total Time: 35 minutes

10 cooked turkey sausages, sliced
1 cup shredded mozzarella cheese
1 cup shredded Cheddar cheese
1 French loaf bread
2 tbsp butter, softened
1 tsp garlic powder
1 1/3 cups marinara sauce
1 tsp Italian seasoning
2 scallions, chopped
1 cup mushrooms, sliced

Preheat the air fryer to 370°F. Cut the bread in half crosswise, then split each half horizontally. Combine butter and garlic powder, then spread on the cut sides of the bread. Bake the halves in the fryer for 3-5 minutes or until the leaves start to brown. Set the toasted bread on a work surface and spread marinara sauce over the top. Sprinkle the Italian seasoning, then top with sausages, scallions, mushrooms, and cheeses. Set the pizzas in the air fryer and Bake for 8-12 minutes or until the cheese is melted and starting to brown. Serve hot.

Gingery Turkey Meatballs

Serves: 4 | Total Time: 25 minutes

¼ cup water chestnuts, chopped
¼ cup panko bread crumbs
1 lb ground turkey
½ tsp ground ginger
2 tbsp fish sauce
1 tbsp sesame oil
1 small onion, minced
1 egg, beaten

Preheat air fryer to 400°F. Place the ground turkey, water chestnuts, ground ginger, fish sauce, onion, egg, and bread crumbs in a bowl and stir to combine. Form the turkey mixture into 1-inch meatballs. Arrange the meatballs in the baking pan. Drizzle with sesame oil. Bake until the meatballs are cooked through, 10-12 minutes, flipping once. Serve and enjoy!

Turkey Scotch Eggs

Serves: 4 | Total Time: 30 minutes

1 ½ lb ground turkey
1 tbsp ground cumin
1 tsp ground coriander
2 garlic cloves, minced
3 raw eggs
1 ½ cups bread crumbs
6 hard-cooked eggs, peeled
½ cup flour

Preheat air fryer to 370°F. Place the ground turkey, cumin, coriander, garlic, one egg, and ½ cup of bread crumbs in a large bowl and mix until well incorporated.

Divide into 6 equal portions, then flatten each into long ovals. Set aside. In a shallow bowl, beat the remaining raw eggs. In another shallow bowl, add flour. Do the same with another plate for bread crumbs. Roll each cooked egg in flour, then wrap with one oval of chicken sausage until completely covered.

Roll again in flour, then coat in the beaten egg before rolling in bread crumbs. Arrange the eggs in the greased frying basket. Air Fry for 12-14 minutes, flipping once until the sausage is cooked and the eggs are brown. Serve.

Cal-Mex Turkey Patties

Serves: 4 | Total Time: 30 minutes

1/3 cup crushed corn tortilla chips
1/3 cup grated American cheese
1 egg, beaten   1 lb ground turkey
¼ cup salsa   1 tbsp olive oil
Salt and pepper to taste   1 tsp chili powder

Preheat air fryer to 330°F. Mix together egg, tortilla chips, salsa, cheese, salt, and pepper in a bowl. Using your hands, add the ground turkey and mix gently until just combined. Divide the meat into 4 equal portions and shape into patties about ½ inch thick. Brush the patties with olive oil and sprinkle with chili powder. Air Fry the patties for 14-16 minutes, flipping once until cooked through and golden. Serve and enjoy!

Chicago-Style Turkey Meatballs

Serves: 6 | Total Time: 15 minutes

1 lb ground turkey   1 tsp cumin powder
1 tbsp orange juice   ¼ red bell pepper, diced
Salt and pepper to taste   1 diced jalapeño pepper
½ tsp smoked paprika   2 garlic cloves, minced
½ tsp chili powder

Preheat air fryer to 400°F. Combine all of the ingredients in a large bowl. Shape into meatballs. Transfer the meatballs into the greased frying basket. Air Fry for 4 minutes, then flip the meatballs. Air Fry for another 3 minutes until cooked through. Serve immediately.

Delicious Turkey Burgers

Serves: 4 | Total Time: 30 minutes

2 tbsp finely grated Emmental
1/3 cup minced onions   1 tsp dried marjoram
¼ cup grated carrots   1 egg
2 garlic cloves, minced   1 lb ground turkey
2 tsp olive oil

Preheat air fryer to 400°F. Mix the onions, carrots, garlic, olive oil, marjoram, Emmental, and egg in a bowl, then add the ground turkey. Use your hands to mix the ingredients together. Form the mixture into 4 patties. Set them in the air fryer and Air Fry for 18-20 minutes, flipping once until cooked through and golden. Serve.

Turkey & Rice Frittata

Serves: 4 | Total Time: 30 minutes

6 large eggs   ½ cup fresh baby spinach
½ tsp dried thyme   1 red bell pepper, chopped
½ cup rice, cooked   2 tsp Parmesan cheese, grated
½ cup pulled turkey, cooked

Preheat air fryer to 320°F. Put the rice, turkey, spinach, and red bell pepper in a greased pan. Whisk the eggs, and thyme, then pour over the rice mix. Top with Parmesan cheese and Bake for 15 minutes, until the frittata is puffy and golden. Serve hot and enjoy!

Buttered Turkey Breasts

Serves: 6 | Total Time: 65 minutes

½ cup butter, melted   ½ tsp dried rosemary
6 garlic cloves, minced   Salt and pepper to taste
1 tsp dried oregano   4 lb bone-in turkey breast
½ tsp dried thyme   1 tbsp chopped cilantro

Preheat air fryer to 350°F. Combine butter, garlic, oregano, salt, and pepper in a small bowl. Place the turkey breast on a plate and coat the entire turkey with the butter mixture. Put the turkey breast-side down in the frying basket and scatter with thyme and rosemary. Bake for 20 minutes. Flip the turkey so that the breast side is up, then bake for another 20-30 minutes until it has an internal temperature of 165°F. Allow resting for 10 minutes before carving. Serve sprinkled with cilantro.

Pulled Turkey Quesadillas

Serves: 4 | Total Time: 15 minutes

¾ cup pulled cooked turkey breast
6 tortilla wraps   1 small red onion, sliced
1/3 cup grated Swiss cheese   2 tbsp Mexican chili sauce

Preheat air fryer to 400°F. Lay 3 tortilla wraps on a clean workspace, then spoon equal amounts of Swiss cheese, turkey, Mexican chili sauce, and red onion on the tortillas. Spritz the exterior of the tortillas with cooking spray. Air Fry the quesadillas, one at a time, for 5-8 minutes. The cheese should be melted and the outside crispy. Serve.

Super-Simple Herby Turkey

Serves: 4 | Total Time: 35 minutes

2 turkey tenderloins   2 tbsp minced rosemary
2 tbsp olive oil   1 tbsp minced thyme
Salt and pepper to taste   1 tbsp minced sage

Preheat the air fryer to 350°F. Brush the tenderloins with olive oil and sprinkle with salt and pepper. Mix rosemary, thyme, and sage, then rub the seasoning onto the meat. Put the tenderloins in the frying basket and Bake for 22-27 minutes, flipping once until cooked through. Lay the turkey on a serving plate, cover with foil, and let stand for 5 minutes. Slice before serving.

Turkey Tenderloin with a Lemon Touch

Serves: 4 | Total Time: 45 minutes

1 lb boneless, skinless turkey breast tenderloin
Salt and pepper to taste   ½ tsp dried thyme
½ tsp garlic powder   1 lemon, juiced
½ tsp chili powder   1 tbsp chopped cilantro

Preheat air fryer to 350°F. Dry the turkey completely with a paper towel, then season with salt, pepper, garlic powder, chili powder, and thyme. Place the turkey in the frying basket. Squeeze the lemon juice over the turkey and bake for 10 minutes. Turn the turkey and bake for another 10 to 15 minutes. Allow resting for 10 minutes before slicing. Serve sprinkled with cilantro and enjoy.

FISH & SEAFOOD

Tuscan Salmon

Serves: 4 | Total Time: 15 minutes

2 tbsp olive oil	1 tsp chopped dill
4 salmon fillets	2 tomatoes, diced
½ tsp salt	¼ cup sliced black olives
¼ tsp red pepper flakes	4 lemon slices

Preheat air fryer to 380°F. Lightly brush the olive oil on both sides of the salmon fillets and season them with salt, red flakes, and dill. Put the fillets in a single layer in the frying basket, then layer the tomatoes and black olives over the top. Top each fillet with a lemon slice. Bake for 8 minutes. Serve and enjoy!

Rich Salmon Burgers with Broccoli Slaw

Serves: 4 | Total Time: 25 minutes

1 lb salmon fillets	1 tsp fish sauce
1 egg	4 buns
¼ cup dill, chopped	3 cups chopped broccoli
1 cup bread crumbs	½ cup shredded carrots
Salt to taste	¼ cup sunflower seeds
½ tsp cayenne pepper	2 garlic cloves, minced
1 lime, zested	1 cup Greek yogurt

Preheat air fryer to 360°F. Blitz the salmon fillets in your food processor until they are finely chopped. Remove to a large bowl and add egg, dill, bread crumbs, salt, and cayenne. Stir to combine. Form the mixture into 4 patties. Put them into the frying basket and Bake for 10 minutes, flipping once. Combine broccoli, carrots, sunflower seeds, garlic, salt, lime, fish sauce, and Greek yogurt in a bowl. Serve the salmon burgers onto buns with broccoli slaw. Enjoy!

Teriyaki Salmon

Serves: 4 | Total Time: 20 minutes

¼ cup raw honey	½ tsp soy sauce
4 garlic cloves, minced	¼ tsp blackening seasoning
1 tbsp olive oil	4 salmon fillets
½ tsp salt	

Preheat air fryer to 380°F. Combine together the honey, garlic, olive oil, soy sauce, blackening seasoning and salt in a bowl. Put the salmon in a single layer on the greased frying basket. Brush the top of each fillet with the honey-garlic mixture. Roast for 10-12 minutes. Serve and enjoy!

Peanut-Crusted Salmon

Serves: 4 | Total Time: 30 minutes

4 salmon fillets	1 tsp celery salt
2 eggs, beaten	1 tbsp parsley, chopped
3 oz melted butter	1 tsp dill, chopped
1 garlic clove, minced	½ cup peanuts, crushed
1 tsp lemon zest	
1 lemon	

Preheat air fryer to 350°F. Put the beaten eggs, melted butter, lemon juice, lemon zest, garlic, parsley, celery salt, and dill in a bowl and stir thoroughly. Dip in the salmon fillets, then roll them in the crushed peanuts, coating completely. Place the coated salmon fillets in the frying basket. Air Fry for 14-16 minutes, flipping over halfway through cooking, until the salmon is cooked through and the crust is toasted and crispy. Serve.

Salmon Patties with Lemon-Dill Sauce

Serves: 4 | Total Time: 40 minutes

2 tbsp diced red bell peppers	2 tsp lime juice
¼ cup sour cream	1 tsp honey
6 tbsp mayonnaise	1 (14.5-oz) can salmon
2 cloves garlic, minced	1 egg
2 tbsp cup onion	½ cup bread crumbs
2 tbsp chopped dill	Salt and pepper to taste

Mix the sour cream, 2 tbsp of mayonnaise, honey, onion, garlic, dill, lime juice, salt, and pepper in a bowl. Let chill the resulting dill sauce in the fridge until ready to use.

Preheat air fryer to 400°F. Combine the salmon, remaining mayonnaise, egg, bell peppers, breadcrumbs, and salt in a bowl. Form mixture into patties. Place salmon cakes in the greased frying basket and Air Fry for 10 minutes, flipping once. Let rest for 5 minutes before serving with dill sauce on the side.

Herb-Rubbed Salmon with Avocado

Serves: 4 | Total Time: 30 minutes

1 tbsp sweet paprika	Salt and pepper to taste
½ tsp cayenne pepper	4 wild salmon fillets
1 tsp garlic powder	2 tbsp chopped red onion
1 tsp dried oregano	1 ½ tbsp fresh lemon juice
½ tsp dried coriander	1 tsp olive oil
1 tsp dried thyme	2 tbsp cilantro, chopped
½ tsp dried dill	1 avocado, diced

Mix paprika, cayenne, garlic powder, oregano, thyme, dill, coriander, salt, and pepper in a small bowl. Spray and rub cooking oil on both sides of the fish, then cover with the spices. Add red onion, lemon juice, olive oil, cilantro, salt, and pepper in a bowl. Set aside for 5 minutes, then carefully add avocado.

Preheat air fryer to 400°F. Place the salmon skin-side down in the greased frying basket and Bake for 5-7 minutes or until the fish flakes easily with a fork. Transfer to a plate and top with the avocado salsa.

Southeast Asian-Style Tuna Steaks

Serves: 4 | Total Time: 20 minutes

1 stalk lemongrass, bent in half	
4 tuna steaks	⅛ tsp pepper
2 tbsp soy sauce	3 tbsp lemon juice
2 tsp sesame oil	2 tbsp chopped cilantro
2 tsp rice wine vinegar	1 sliced red chili
1 tsp grated fresh ginger	

Preheat air fryer to 390°F. Place the tuna steak on a shallow plate. Mix together soy sauce, sesame oil, rice wine vinegar, and ginger in a small bowl. Pour over the tuna, rubbing the marinade gently into both sides of the fish. Marinate for about 10 minutes. Then sprinkle with pepper. Place the lemongrass in the frying basket and top with tuna steaks. Add the remaining lemon juice and 1 tablespoon of water to the pan below the basket. Bake until the tuna is cooked through, 8-10 minutes. Discard the lemongrass before topping with cilantro and red chili. Serve and enjoy!

Mediterranean Cod Croquettes

Serves: 4 | Total Time: 30 minutes + marinating time

½ cup instant mashed potatoes

12 oz raw cod fillet, flaked	1 cup bread crumbs
2 large eggs, beaten	1 tsp lemon juice
¼ cup sour cream	Salt and pepper to taste
2 tsp olive oil	½ tsp dried basil
1/3 cup chopped thyme	5 tbsp Greek yogurt
1 shallot, minced	½ tsp harissa paste
1 garlic clove, minced	1 tbsp chopped dill

In a bowl, combine the fish, 1 egg, sour cream, instant mashed potatoes, olive oil, thyme, shallot, garlic, 2 tbsp of the bread crumbs, salt, dill, lemon juice, and pepper; mix well. Refrigerate for 30 minutes. Mix yogurt, harissa paste, and basil in a bowl until blended. Set aside.

Preheat air fryer to 350°F. Take the fish mixture out of the refrigerator. Knead and shape the mixture into 12 longs. In a bowl, place the remaining egg. In a second bowl, add the remaining bread crumbs. Dip the croquettes into the egg and shake off the excess drips. Then roll the logs into the breadcrumbs. Place the croquettes in the greased frying basket. Air Fry for 10 minutes, flipping once until golden. Serve with the yogurt sauce.

Potato Chip-Crusted Cod

Serves: 2 | Total Time: 20 minutes

½ cup crushed potato chips	¼ cup buttermilk
1 tsp chopped tarragon	1 tsp lemon juice
1/8 tsp salt	1 tbsp butter, melted
1 tsp cayenne powder	2 cod fillets
1 tbsp Dijon mustard	

Preheat air fryer to 350°F. Mix all ingredients in a bowl. Press potato chip mixture evenly across tops of cod. Place cod fillets in the greased frying basket and Air Fry for 10 minutes until the fish is opaque and flakes easily with a fork. Serve immediately.

Collard Green & Cod Packets

Serves: 4 | Total Time: 20 minutes

2 cups collard greens, chopped

1 tsp salt	4 cod fillets
½ tsp dried rosemary	1 shallot, thinly sliced
½ tsp dried thyme	¼ cup olive oil
½ tsp garlic powder	1 lemon, juiced

Preheat air fryer to 380°F. Mix together the salt, rosemary, thyme, and garlic powder in a small bowl. Rub the spice mixture onto the cod fillets. Divide the fish fillets among 4 sheets of foil. Top with shallot slices and collard greens. Drizzle with olive oil and lemon juice. Fold and seal the sides of the foil packets and then place them into the frying basket. Steam in the fryer for 11-13 minutes until the cod is cooked through. Serve and enjoy!

Peppery Tilapia Roulade

Serves: 4 | Total Time: 25 minutes

4 jarred roasted red pepper slices	
1 egg	2 tbsp butter, melted
½ cup breadcrumbs	4 lime wedges
Salt and pepper to taste	1 tsp dill
4 tilapia fillets	

Preheat air fryer to 350°F. Beat the egg and 2 tbsp of water in a bowl. In another bowl, mix the breadcrumbs, salt, and pepper. Place a red pepper slice and sprinkle with dill on each fish fillet. Tightly roll tilapia fillets from one short end to the other. Secure with toothpicks. Roll each fillet in the egg mixture, then dredge them in the breadcrumbs. Place the fish rolls in the greased frying basket and drizzle the tops with melted butter. Roast for 6 minutes. Let rest in a serving dish for 5 minutes before removing the toothpicks. Serve with lime wedges. Enjoy!

Cilantro Sea Bass

Serves: 2 | Total Time: 15 minutes

Salt and pepper to taste	2 tsp chopped cilantro
1 tsp olive oil	1 tsp dried thyme
2 sea bass fillets	½ tsp garlic powder
½ tsp berbere seasoning	4 lemon quarters

Preheat air fryer to 375°F. Rub sea bass fillets with olive oil, thyme, garlic powder, salt and black pepper. Season with berbere seasoning. Place fillets in the greased frying basket and Air Fry for 6-8 minutes. Let rest for 5 minutes on a serving plate. Scatter with cilantro and serve with lemon quarters on the side.

Creole Tilapia with Garlic Mayo

Serves: 4 | Total Time: 20 minutes

4 tilapia fillets	½ tsp chili powder
2 tbsp olive oil	2 garlic cloves, minced
1 tsp paprika	1 tbsp mayonnaise
1 tsp garlic powder	1 tsp olive oil
1 tsp dried basil	½ lemon, juiced
½ tsp Creole seasoning	Salt and pepper to taste

Preheat air fryer to 400°F. Coat the tilapia with some olive oil, then season with paprika, garlic powder, basil, and Creole seasoning. Bake in the greased frying basket for 15 minutes, flipping once during cooking.

While the fish is cooking, whisk together garlic, mayonnaise, olive oil, lemon juice, chili powder, salt, and pepper in a bowl. Serve the cooked fish with the aioli.

Asian-Style Salmon Fillets

Serves: 4 | Total Time: 15 minutes

1 tbsp sesame oil	½ tsp garlic powder
2 tbsp miso paste	½ tsp ginger powder
2 tbsp tamari	4 salmon fillets
2 tbsp soy sauce	4 cups cooked brown rice
2 tbsp dark brown sugar	4 lemon slices

Preheat air fryer to 375°F. In a bowl, combine all ingredients, except for salmon and cooked rice. Add 1/3 of the marinade to a shallow dish, submerge salmon fillets and let marinate covered in the fridge for 10 minutes. Reserve the remaining marinade. Place salmon fillets, skin side up, in the greased frying basket and Air Fry for 6-8 minutes, turning once, and brush with the reserved marinade. Divide cooked rice into serving dishes and top each with a salmon fillet. Pour the remaining marinade on top and serve with lemon slices on the side.

Yummy Salmon Burgers with Salsa Rosa

Serves: 4 | Total Time: 35 minutes + chilling time

¼ cup minced red onion	1 garlic clove, minced
¼ cup slivered onions	1 large egg, lightly beaten
½ cup mayonnaise	1 tbsp Dijon mustard
2 tsp ketchup	1 tsp fresh lemon juice
1 tsp brandy	1 tbsp chopped parsley
2 tsp orange juice	Salt to taste
1 lb salmon fillets	4 buns
5 tbsp panko bread crumbs	8 Boston lettuce leaves

Mix the mayonnaise, ketchup, brandy, and orange juice in a bowl until blended. Set aside the resulting salsa rosa until ready to serve. Cut a 4-oz section of salmon and place it in a food processor. Pulse until it turns into a paste. Chop the remaining salmon into cubes and transfer to a bowl along with the salmon paste. Add the panko, minced onion, garlic, egg, mustard, lemon juice, parsley, and salt. Toss to combine. Divide into 5 patties about ¾-inch thick. Refrigerate for 30 minutes.

Preheat air fryer to 400°F. Place the patties in the greased frying basket. Air Fry for 12-14 minutes, flipping once until golden. Serve each patty on a bun, 2 lettuce leaves, 2 tbsp of salsa rosa, and slivered onions. Enjoy!

Mexican-Style Salmon Stir-Fry

Serves: 4 | Total Time: 30 minutes

12 oz salmon fillets, cubed	2 tbsp tomato juice
1 red bell pepper, chopped	2 tsp peanut oil
1 red onion, chopped	1 tsp chili powder
1 jalapeño pepper, minced	2 tbsp cilantro, chopped
¼ cup salsa	

Preheat air fryer to 360°F. Mix salmon, bell pepper, onion, jalapeño, salsa, tomato juice, peanut oil, and chili powder in a bowl and put it into the air fryer. Air Fry for 12-14 minutes until the salmon is firm and the veggies are crispy and soft, stirring once. Serve topped with cilantro.

Lemon & Herb Crusted Salmon

Serves: 4 | Total Time: 20 minutes

1/3 cup crushed potato chips	½ tsp dried thyme
4 skinless salmon fillets	½ tsp dried basil
3 tbsp honey mustard	¼ cup panko bread crumbs
½ tsp lemon zest	2 tbsp olive oil

Preheat air fryer to 320°F. Place the salmon on a work surface. Mix together mustard, lemon zest, thyme, and basil in a small bowl. Spread on top of the salmon evenly. In a separate small bowl, mix together bread crumbs and potato chips before drizzling with olive oil. Place the salmon in the frying basket. Bake until the salmon is cooked through and the topping is crispy and brown, about 10 minutes. Serve hot and enjoy!

Spiced Salmon Croquettes

Serves: 6 | Total Time: 20 minutes

1 (14.75-oz) can Alaskan pink salmon, bones removed	
1 lime, zested	½ cup bread crumbs
1 red chili, minced	2 scallions, diced
2 tbsp cilantro, chopped	1 tsp garlic powder
1 egg, beaten	Salt and pepper to taste

Preheat air fryer to 400°F. Mix salmon, beaten egg, bread crumbs and scallions in a large bowl. Add garlic, lime, red chili, cilantro, salt, and pepper. Divide into 6 even portions and shape into patties. Place them in the greased frying basket and Air Fry for 7 minutes. Flip them and cook for 4 minutes or until golden. Serve.

Almond Topped Trout

Serves: 4 | Total Time: 20 minutes

4 trout fillets	2 garlic cloves, sliced
2 tbsp olive oil	1 lemon, sliced
Salt and pepper to taste	1 tbsp flaked almonds

Preheat air fryer to 380°F. Lightly brush each fillet with olive oil on both sides and season with salt and pepper. Put the fillets in a single layer in the frying basket. Put the sliced garlic over the tops of the trout fillets, then top with lemon slices and cook for 12-15 minutes. Serve topped with flaked almonds and enjoy!

French Grouper Nicoise

Serves: 4 | Total Time: 20 minutes

4 grouper fillets	¼ cup sliced Nicoise olives
Salt to taste	¼ cup dill, chopped
½ tsp ground cumin	1 lemon, juiced
3 garlic cloves, minced	¼ cup olive oil
1 tomato, sliced	

Preheat air fryer to 380°F. Sprinkle the grouper fillets with salt and cumin. Arrange them on the greased frying basket and top with garlic, tomato slices, olives, and fresh dill. Drizzle with lemon juice and olive oil. Bake for 10-12 minutes. Serve and enjoy!

Easy Asian-Style Tuna

Serves: 4 | Total Time: 25 minutes

1 jalapeño pepper, minced	2 garlic cloves, grated
½ tsp Chinese five-spice	1 tbsp grated fresh ginger
4 tuna steaks	Black pepper to taste
½ tsp toasted sesame oil	2 tbsp lemon juice

Preheat air fryer to 380°F. Pour sesame oil over the tuna steaks and let them sit while you make the marinade. Combine the jalapeño, garlic, ginger, five-spice powder, black pepper, and lemon juice in a bowl, then brush the mix on the fish. Let it sit for 10 minutes. Air Fry the tuna in the fryer for 6-11 minutes until it is cooked through and flakes easily when pressed with a fork. Serve warm.

Smoked Paprika Cod Goujons

Serves: 2 | Total Time: 30 minutes

1 cod fillet, cut into chunks	1 lemon, juiced
2 eggs, beaten	½ tbsp garlic powder
¼ cup breadcrumbs	1 tsp smoked paprika
¼ cup rice flour	Salt and pepper to taste

Preheat air fryer to 350°F. In a bowl, stir the beaten eggs and lemon juice thoroughly. Dip the cod chunks in the mixture. In another bowl, mix the bread crumbs, rice flour, garlic powder, smoked paprika, salt, and pepper.

Coat the cod with the crumb mixture. Transfer the coated cod to the greased frying basket. Air Fry for 14-16 minutes until the fish goujons are cooked through and their crust is golden, brown, and delicious. Toss the basket two or three times during the cooking time. Serve.

Herb-Crusted Sole

Serves: 4 | Total Time: 20 minutes

½ lemon, juiced and zested	½ tsp dried parsley
4 sole fillets	Black pepper to taste
½ tsp dried thyme	1 bread slice, crumbled
½ tsp dried marjoram	2 tsp olive oil

Preheat air fryer to 320°F. In a bowl, combine the lemon zest, thyme, marjoram, parsley, pepper, breadcrumbs, and olive oil and stir. Arrange the sole fillets on a lined baking pan, skin-side down. Pour the lemon juice over the fillets, then press them firmly into the breadcrumb mixture to coat. Air Fry for 8-11 minutes, until the breadcrumbs are crisp and golden brown. Serve warm.

Mediterranean Salmon Burgers

Serves: 4 | Total Time: 30 minutes

1 lb salmon fillets	1 lemon, sliced
1 scallion, diced	1 tbsp chopped dill
4 tbsp mayonnaise	¼ cup bread crumbs
1 egg	4 buns, toasted
1 tsp capers, drained	4 tsp whole-grain mustard
Salt and pepper to taste	4 lettuce leaves
¼ tsp paprika	1 small tomato, sliced
1 lemon, zested	

Preheat air fryer to 400°F. Divide salmon in half. Cut one of the halves into chunks and transfer the chunks to the food processor. Also, add scallion, 2 tablespoons mayonnaise, egg, capers, dill, salt, pepper, paprika, and lemon zest. Pulse to puree. Dice the rest of the salmon into ¼-inch chunks. Combine chunks and puree along with bread crumbs in a large bowl. Shape the fish into 4 patties and transfer to the frying basket. Air Fry for 5 minutes, then flip the patties. Air Fry for another 5 to 7 minutes. Place the patties each on a bun along with 1 teaspoon mustard, mayonnaise, lettuce, lemon slices, and a slice of tomato. Serve and enjoy.

Sea Bass with Fruit Salsa

Serves: 4 | Total Time: 30 minutes

3 halved nectarines, pitted	1 cup red grapes
4 sea bass fillets	1 tbsp lemon juice
2 tsp olive oil	1 tbsp honey
3 plums, halved and pitted	½ tsp dried thyme

Preheat air fryer to 390°F. Lay the sea bass fillets in the frying basket, then spritz olive oil over the top. Air Fry for 4 minutes. Take the basket out of the fryer and add the nectarines and plums. Pour the grapes over, spritz with lemon juice and honey, then add a pinch of thyme. Put the basket back into the fryer and Bake for 5-9 minutes. The fish should flake when finished, and the fruits should be soft. Serve hot.

Quick Tuna Tacos

Serves: 4 | Total Time: 20 minutes

2 cups torn romaine lettuce	½ tsp toasted sesame oil
1 lb fresh tuna steak, cubed	4 tortillas
1 tbsp grated fresh ginger	¼ cup mild salsa
2 garlic cloves, minced	1 red bell pepper, sliced

Preheat air fryer to 390°F. Combine the tuna, ginger, garlic, and sesame oil in a bowl and allow to marinate for 10 minutes. Lay the marinated tuna in the fryer and Grill for 4-7 minutes. Serve right away with tortillas, mild salsa, lettuce, and bell pepper for delicious tacos.

Sweet & Spicy Swordfish Kebabs

Serves: 4 | Total Time: 30 minutes

½ cup canned pineapple chunks, drained, juice reserved	
1 lb swordfish steaks, cubed	2 tsp grated fresh ginger
½ cup large red grapes	1 tsp olive oil
1 tbsp honey	Pinch cayenne pepper

Preheat air fryer to 370°F. Poke 8 bamboo skewers through the swordfish, pineapple, and grapes. Mix the honey, 1 tbsp of pineapple juice, ginger, olive oil, and cayenne in a bowl, then use a brush to rub the mix on the kebabs. Allow the marinate to sit on the kebab for 10 minutes. Grill the kebabs for 8-12 minutes until the fish is cooked through and the fruit is soft and glazed. Brush the kebabs again with the mix, then toss the rest of the marinade. Serve warm and enjoy!

Asparagus & Salmon Spring Rolls

Serves: 4 | Total Time: 30 minutes

½ lb salmon fillets	4 asparagus, thinly sliced
1 tsp toasted sesame oil	1 carrot, shredded
1 onion, sliced	1/3 cup chopped parsley
8 rice paper wrappers	¼ cup chopped fresh basil

Preheat air fryer to 370°F. Lay the salmon in the frying basket and pour some sesame oil over, then toss in the onion. Air Fry for 8-10 minutes. The salmon should flake when poked with a fork and the onion should be soft. Pour warm water into a shallow bowl, then one at a time, wet the rice paper wrappers and put them on a clean workspace. Put an eighth of salmon/onion mix on each wrapper as well as asparagus, carrot, parsley, and basil. Fold the wrappers and roll up, sealing the ingredients inside. Air Fry in the fryer for 7-9 minutes until crispy and golden. Serve hot.

Halibut with Coleslaw

Serves: 4 | Total Time: 30 minutes

1 (12-oz) bag coleslaw mix	½ cup buttermilk
¼ cup mayonnaise	1 tsp grated onion
1 tsp lemon zest	4 (6-oz) halibut fillets
1 tbsp lemon juice	Salt and pepper to taste
1 shredded carrot	

Combine coleslaw mix, mayonnaise, carrot, buttermilk, onion, lemon zest, lemon juice, and salt in a bowl. Let chill the coleslaw covered in the fridge until ready to use. Preheat air fryer to 350°F. Sprinkle halibut with salt and pepper. Place them in the greased frying basket and Air Fry for 10 minutes until the fillets are opaque and flake easily with a fork. Serve with chilled coleslaw.

Garlicky Sea Bass with Root Veggies

Serves: 4 | Total Time: 25 minutes

1 carrot, diced	4 sea bass fillets
1 parsnip, diced	Celery salt to taste
½ rutabaga, diced	½ tsp onion powder
½ turnip, diced	2 garlic cloves, minced
¼ cup olive oil	1 lemon, sliced

Preheat air fryer to 380°F. Coat the carrot, parsnip, turnip and rutabaga with olive oil and salt in a small bowl. Lightly season the sea bass with celery salt and onion powder, then place into the frying basket. Spread the garlic over the top of the fillets, then cover with lemon slices. Pour the prepared vegetables into the basket around and on top of the fish. Roast for 15 minutes. Serve and enjoy!

Dilly Red Snapper

Serves: 4 | Total Time: 40 minutes

Salt and pepper to taste	2 tbsp butter
½ tsp ground cumin	2 garlic cloves, minced
¼ tsp cayenne	¼ cup dill
¼ teaspoon paprika	4 lemon wedges
1 (1½-lb) whole red snapper	

Preheat air fryer to 360°F. Combine salt, pepper, cumin, paprika and cayenne in a bowl. Brush the fish with butter, then rub with the seasoning mix. Stuff the minced garlic and dill inside the cavity of the fish. Put the snapper into the basket of the air fryer and Roast for 20 minutes. Flip the snapper over and Roast for 15 more minutes. Serve with lemon wedges and enjoy!

Aromatic Ahi Tuna Steaks

Serves: 4 | Total Time: 15 minutes

1 tsp garlic powder	¼ tsp cayenne pepper
½ tsp salt	4 ahi tuna steaks
¼ tsp dried thyme	2 tbsp olive oil
¼ tsp dried oregano	1 lemon, cut into wedges

Preheat air fryer to 380°F. Stir together the garlic powder, salt, thyme, cayenne pepper and oregano in a bowl to combine. Coat the tuna steaks with olive oil. Season both sides of each steak with the seasoning mix. Put the steaks in the frying basket. Air Fry for 5 minutes, then flip and cook for an additional 3-4 minutes. Serve warm with lemon wedges on the side.

Mom's Tuna Melt Toastie

Serves: 4 | Total Time: 30 minutes

4 white bread slices	½ red onion, finely sliced
2 oz canned tuna	1 red tomato, sliced
2 tbsp mayonnaise	4 cheddar cheese slices
½ lemon, zested and juiced	2 tbsp butter, melted
Salt and pepper to taste	

Preheat air fryer to 360°F. Put the butter-greased bread slices in the frying basket. Toast for 6 minutes. Meanwhile, mix the tuna, lemon juice and zest, salt, pepper, and mayonnaise in a small bowl. When the time is over, slide the frying basket out, flip the bread slices, and spread the tuna mixture evenly all over them. Cover with tomato slices, red onion, and cheddar cheese. Toast for 10 minutes or until the cheese is melted and lightly bubbling. Serve and enjoy!

Lemony Tuna Steaks

Serves: 4 | Total Time: 20 minutes + marinating time

½ tbsp olive oil	1 tbsp chopped cilantro
1 garlic clove, minced	½ tbsp chopped dill
Salt to taste	4 tuna steaks
¼ tsp jalapeno powder	1 lemon, thinly sliced
1 tbsp lemon juice	

Stir olive oil, garlic, salt, jalapeno powder, lemon juice, and cilantro in a wide bowl. Coat the tuna on all sides in the mixture. Cover and marinate for at least 20 minutes

Preheat air fryer to 380°F. Arrange the tuna on a single layer in the greased frying basket and throw out the excess marinade. Bake for 6-8 minutes. Remove the basket and let the tuna rest in it for 5 minutes. Transfer to plates and garnish with lemon slices. Serve sprinkled with dill.

Lemon-Dill Salmon with Green Beans

Serves: 4 | Total Time: 20 minutes

20 halved cherry tomatoes
4 tbsp butter
4 garlic cloves, minced
¼ cup chopped dill
Salt and pepper to taste

4 wild-caught salmon fillets
¼ cup white wine
1 lemon, thinly sliced
1 lb green beans, trimmed
2 tbsp chopped parsley

Preheat air fryer to 390°F. Combine butter, garlic, dill, wine, salt, and pepper in a small bowl. Spread the seasoned butter over the top of the salmon. Arrange the fish in a single layer in the frying basket. Top with ½ of the lemon slices and surround the fish with green beans and tomatoes. Bake for 12-15 minutes until salmon is cooked and vegetables are tender. Top with parsley and serve with lemon slices on the side.

Halibut Quesadillas

Serves: 2 | Total Time: 30 minutes

¼ cup shredded cheddar
¼ cup shredded mozzarella
1 tsp olive oil
2 tortilla shells
1 halibut fillet

½ peeled avocado, sliced
1 garlic clove, minced
Salt and pepper to taste
½ tsp lemon juice

Preheat air fryer to 350°F. Brush the halibut fillet with olive oil and sprinkle with salt and pepper. Bake in the air fryer for 12-14 minutes, flipping once until cooked through. Combine the avocado, garlic, salt, pepper, and lemon juice in a bowl and, using a fork, mash lightly until the avocado is slightly chunky. Add and spread the resulting guacamole on one tortilla. Top with the cooked fish and cheeses, and cover with the second tortilla. Bake in the air fryer 6-8, flipping once until the cheese is melted. Serve immediately.

Buttered Swordfish Steaks

Serves: 4 | Total Time: 30 minutes

4 swordfish steaks
2 eggs, beaten
3 oz melted butter
½ cup breadcrumbs

Black pepper to taste
1 tsp dried rosemary
1 tsp dried marjoram
1 lemon, cut into wedges

Preheat air fryer to 350°F. Place the eggs and melted butter in a bowl and stir thoroughly. Combine the breadcrumbs, rosemary, marjoram, and black pepper in a separate bowl. Dip the swordfish steaks in the beaten eggs, then coat with the crumb mixture. Place the coated fish in the frying basket. Air Fry for 12-14 minutes, turning once until the fish is cooked through and the crust is toasted and crispy. Serve with lemon wedges.

Mahi Mahi with Cilantro-Chili Butter

Serves: 4 | Total Time: 20 minutes

Salt and pepper to taste
4 mahi-mahi fillets
2 tbsp butter, melted

2 garlic cloves, minced
¼ tsp chili powder
¼ tsp lemon zest

1 tsp ginger, minced
1 tsp Worcestershire sauce

1 tbsp lemon juice
1 tbsp chopped cilantro

Preheat air fryer to 375°F. Combine butter, Worcestershire sauce, garlic, salt, lemon juice, ginger, pepper, lemon zest, and chili powder in a small bowl. Place the mahi-mahi on a large plate, then spread the seasoned butter on the top of each. Arrange the fish in a single layer in the parchment-lined frying basket. Bake for 6 minutes, then carefully flip the fish. Bake for another 6-7 minutes until the fish is flaky and cooked through. Serve immediately sprinkled with cilantro and enjoy.

Kid's Flounder Fingers

Serves: 4 | Total Time: 45 minutes

1 lb catfish flounder fillets, cut into 1-inch chunks
½ cup seasoned fish fry breading mix

Preheat air fryer to 400°F. In a resealable bag, add flounder and breading mix. Seal bag and shake until the fish is coated. Place the nuggets in the greased frying basket and Air Fry for 18-20 minutes, shaking the basket once until crisp. Serve warm and enjoy!

Californian Tilapia

Serves: 4 | Total Time: 15 minutes

Salt and pepper to taste
¼ tsp garlic powder
¼ tsp chili powder
¼ tsp dried oregano
¼ tsp smoked paprika

1 tbsp butter, melted
4 tilapia fillets
2 tbsp lime juice
1 lemon, sliced

Preheat air fryer to 400°F. Combine salt, pepper, oregano, garlic powder, chili powder, and paprika in a small bowl. Place tilapia in a pie pan, then pour lime juice and butter over the fish. Season both sides of the fish with the spice blend. Arrange the tilapia in a single layer of the parchment-lined frying basket without touching each other. Air Fry for 4 minutes, then carefully flip the fish. Air Fry for another 4 to 5 minutes until the fish is cooked and the outside is crispy. Serve immediately with lemon slices on the side and enjoy.

Horseradish Tuna Croquettes

Serves 4 | Total Time: 40 minutes

1 (12-oz) can tuna in water, drained
1/3 cup mayonnaise
1 tbsp minced celery
1 green onion, sliced
2 tsp dried dill

1 tsp lime juice
1 cup bread crumbs
1 egg
1 tsp prepared horseradish

Preheat air fryer to 370°F. Add the tuna, mayonnaise, celery, green onion, dill, lime juice, ¼ cup bread crumbs, egg, and horseradish in a bowl and mix to combine. Mold the mixture into 12 rectangular mound shapes. Roll each croquette in a shallow dish with 3/4 cup of bread crumbs. Place croquettes in the lightly greased frying basket and Air Fry for 12 minutes on all sides. Serve.

Cheesy Tuna Tower

Serves 2 | Total Time: 15 minutes

½ cup grated mozzarella	1 tbsp minced celery
1 (6-oz) can tuna in water	1 tbsp minced green onion
¼ cup mayonnaise	Salt and pepper to taste
2 tsp yellow mustard	4 tomato slices
1 tbsp minced dill pickle	8 avocado slices

Preheat air fryer to 350°F. In a bowl, combine tuna, mayonnaise, mustard, pickle, celery, green onion, salt, and pepper. Cut a piece of parchment paper to fit the bottom of the frying basket. Place tomato slices on paper in a single layer and top with 2 avocado slices. Share tuna salad over avocado slices and top with mozzarella cheese. Place the towers in the frying basket and Bake for 4 minutes until the cheese starts to brown. Serve warm.

Cheesy Salmon-Stuffed Avocados

Serves 2 | Total Time: 20 minutes

¼ cup apple cider vinegar	2 halved avocados, pitted
1 tsp granular sugar	4 oz smoked salmon
¼ cup sliced red onions	¼ tsp dried dill
2 oz cream cheese, softened	2 cherry tomatoes, halved
1 tbsp capers	1 tbsp cilantro, chopped

Warm apple vinegar and sugar in a saucepan over medium heat and simmer for 4 minutes until boiling. Add in onion and turn the heat off. Let sit until ready to use. Drain before using. In a small bowl, combine cream cheese and capers. Let chill in the fridge until ready to use.

Preheat air fryer to 350°F. Place avocado halves, cut sides-up, in the frying basket, and Air Fry for 4 minutes. Transfer avocado halves to 2 plates. Top with cream cheese mixture, smoked salmon, dill, red onions, tomato halves and cilantro. Serve immediately.

Lime Halibut Parcels

Serves: 4 | Total Time: 45 minutes

1 lime, sliced	1 shredded carrot
4 halibut fillets	1 red bell pepper, sliced
1 tsp dried thyme	½ cup sliced celery
Salt and pepper to taste	2 tbsp butter

Preheat the air fryer to 400°F. Tear off four 14-inch lengths of parchment paper and fold each piece in half crosswise. Put the lime slices in the center of half of each piece of paper, then top with halibut. Sprinkle each fillet with thyme, salt, and pepper, then top each with ¼ of the carrots, bell pepper, and celery. Add a dab of butter. Fold the parchment paper in half and crimp the edges all around to enclose the halibut and vegetables. Put one parchment bundle in the basket, add a raised rack, and add another bundle. Bake for 12-14 minutes or until the bundle puff up. The fish should flake with a fork; put the bundles in the oven to keep warm. Repeat for the second batch of parchment bundles. Hot steam will be released when the bundles are opened.

Mediterranean Salmon Cakes

Serves 4 | Total Time: 30 minutes

¼ cup heavy cream	2 tsp lemon zest
5 tbsp mayonnaise	1 egg
2 cloves garlic, minced	¼ minced red bell peppers
¼ tsp caper juice	½ cup flour
2 tsp lemon juice	⅛ tsp salt
1 tbsp capers	2 tbsp sliced green olives
1 (14.75-oz) can salmon	

Combine heavy cream, 2 tbsp of mayonnaise, garlic, caper juices, capers, and lemon juice in a bowl. Place the resulting caper sauce in the fridge until ready to use.

Preheat air fryer to 400°F. Combine canned salmon, lemon zest, egg, remaining mayo, bell peppers, flour, and salt in a bowl. Form into 8 patties. Place the patties in the greased frying basket and Air Fry for 10 minutes, turning once. Let rest for 5 minutes before drizzling with lemon sauce. Garnish with green olives to serve.

Crunchy Flounder Gratin

Serves: 4 | Total Time: 20 minutes

¼ cup grated Parmesan	Salt and pepper to taste
4 flounder fillets	½ tsp dried oregano
4 tbsp butter, melted	½ tsp dried basil
¼ cup panko bread crumbs	1 tsp dried thyme
½ tsp paprika	1 lemon, quartered
1 egg	1 tbsp chopped parsley

Preheat air fryer to 375°F. In a bowl, whisk together egg until smooth. Brush the fillets on both sides with some of the butter. Combine the rest of the butter, bread crumbs, Parmesan cheese, salt, paprika, thyme, oregano, basil, and pepper in a small bowl until crumbly. Dip the fish into the egg and then into the bread crumb mixture and coat completely. Transfer the fish to the frying basket and bake for 5 minutes. Carefully flip the fillets and bake for another 6 minutes until crispy and golden on the outside. Garnish with lemon wedges and parsley. Serve and enjoy.

Sriracha Salmon Melt Sandwiches

Serves: 4 | Total Time: 20 minutes

2 tbsp butter, softened	1 tbsp fresh lemon juice
2 (5-oz) cans pink salmon	1/3 cup chopped celery
2 English muffins	½ tsp sriracha sauce
1/3 cup mayonnaise	4 tomato slices
2 tbsp Dijon mustard	4 Swiss cheese slices

Preheat the air fryer to 370°F. Split the English muffins with a fork and spread butter on the 4 halves. Put the halves in the basket and Bake for 3-5 minutes, or until toasted. Remove and set aside. Combine the salmon, mayonnaise, mustard, lemon juice, celery, and sriracha in a bowl. Divide among the English muffin halves. Top each sandwich with tomato and cheese and put it in the frying basket. Bake for 4-6 minutes or until the cheese is melted and starts to brown. Serve hot.

Tilapia al Pesto

Serves 4 | Total Time: 25 minutes

4 tilapia fillets	Salt and pepper to taste
1 egg	4 tsp pesto
2 tbsp buttermilk	2 tbsp butter, melted
1 cup crushed cornflakes	4 lemon wedges

Preheat air fryer to 350°F. Whisk egg and buttermilk in a bowl. In another bowl, combine cornflakes, salt, and pepper. Spread 1 tsp of pesto on each tilapia fillet, then tightly roll the fillet from one short end to the other. Secure with a toothpick. Dip each fillet in the egg mixture and dredge in the cornflake mixture. Place fillets in the greased frying basket, drizzle with melted butter, and Air Fry for 6 minutes. Let rest on a serving dish for 5 minutes before removing the toothpicks. Serve with lemon wedges.

Breaded Parmesan Perch

Serves: 5 | Total Time: 15 minutes

¼ cup grated Parmesan	2 tsp Dijon mustard
½ tsp salt	2 tbsp bread crumbs
¼ tsp paprika	4 ocean perch fillets
1 tbsp chopped dill	1 lemon, quartered
1 tsp dried thyme	2 tbsp chopped cilantro

Preheat air fryer to 400°F. Combine salt, paprika, pepper, dill, mustard, thyme, Parmesan, and bread crumbs in a wide bowl. Coat all sides of the fillets in the breading, then transfer to the greased frying basket. Air Fry for 8 minutes until the outside is golden and the inside is cooked through. Garnish with lemon wedges and sprinkle with cilantro. Serve and enjoy!

Caribbean Jerk Cod Fillets

Serves 2 | Total Time: 20 minutes

¼ cup chopped cooked shrimp	
¼ cup diced mango	2 tsp lime juice
1 tomato, diced	Salt and pepper to taste
2 tbsp diced red onion	2 (6-oz) cod fillets
1 tbsp chopped parsley	2 tsp Jerk seasoning
¼ tsp ginger powder	

In a bowl, combine the shrimp, mango, tomato, red onion, parsley, ginger powder, lime juice, salt, and black pepper. Let chill the salsa in the fridge until ready to use.

Preheat air fryer to 350°F. Sprinkle cod fillets with Jerk seasoning. Place them in the greased frying basket and Air Fry for 10 minutes or until the cod is opaque and flakes easily with a fork. Divide between 2 medium plates. Serve topped with the Caribbean salsa.

Panko-Breaded Cod Fillets

Serves 2 | Total Time: 20 minutes

1 lemon wedge, juiced and zested	
½ cup panko bread crumbs	1 tbsp butter, melted
Salt to taste	2 cod fillets
1 tbsp Dijon mustard	

Preheat air fryer to 350°F. Combine all ingredients, except for the fish, in a bowl. Press mixture evenly across tops of cod fillets. Place fillets in the greased frying basket and Air Fry for 10 minutes until the cod is opaque and flakes easily with a fork. Serve immediately.

Sinaloa Fish Fajitas

Serves: 4 | Total Time: 30 minutes

1 lemon, thinly sliced	1 carrot, shredded
16 oz red snapper fillets	2 tbsp orange juice
1 tbsp olive oil	½ cup salsa
1 tbsp cayenne pepper	4 flour tortillas
½ tsp salt	½ cup sour cream
2 cups shredded coleslaw	2 avocados, sliced

Preheat the air fryer to 350°F. Lay the lemon slices at the bottom of the basket. Drizzle the fillets with olive oil and sprinkle with cayenne pepper and salt. Lay the fillets on top of the lemons and Bake for 6-9 minutes or until the fish easily flakes. While the fish cooks, toss the coleslaw, carrot, orange juice, and salsa in a bowl. When the fish is done, remove it and cover. Toss the lemons. Air Fry the tortillas for 2-3 minutes to warm up. Add the fish to the tortillas and top with a cabbage mix, sour cream, and avocados. Serve and enjoy!

Fish Nuggets with Broccoli Dip

Serves: 4 | Total Time: 40 minutes

1 lb cod fillets, cut into chunks	
1 ½ cups broccoli florets	2 tbsp olive oil
¼ cup grated Parmesan	2 egg whites
3 garlic cloves, peeled	1 cup panko bread crumbs
3 tbsp sour cream	1 tsp dried dill
2 tbsp lemon juice	Salt and pepper to taste

Preheat the air fryer to 400°F. Put the broccoli and garlic in the greased frying basket and Air Fry for 5-7 minutes or until tender. Remove to a blender and add sour cream, lemon juice, olive oil, and ½ tsp of salt and process until smooth. Set the sauce aside. Beat the egg whites until frothy in a shallow bowl. On a plate, combine the panko, Parmesan, dill, pepper, and the remaining ½ tsp of salt. Dip the cod fillets in the egg whites, then the breadcrumbs, pressing to coat. Put half the cubes in the frying basket and spray with cooking oil. Air Fry for 6-8 minutes or until the fish is cooked through. Serve the fish with the sauce and enjoy!

Lime Flaming Halibut

Serves 2 | Total Time: 20 minutes

2 tbsp butter, melted	½ cup bread crumbs
½ tsp chili powder	2 halibut fillets

Preheat air fryer to 350°F. In a bowl, mix the butter, chili powder and bread crumbs. Press mixture onto tops of halibut fillets. Place halibut in the greased frying basket and Air Fry for 10 minutes or until the fish is opaque and flakes easily with a fork. Serve right away.

Mojo Sea Bass

Serves 2 | Total Time: 15 minutes

1 tbsp butter, melted
1/4 tsp chili powder
2 cloves garlic, minced
1 tbsp lemon juice
1/4 tsp salt
2 sea bass fillets
2 tsp chopped cilantro

Preheat air fryer to 370°F. Whisk the butter, chili powder, garlic, lemon juice, and salt in a bowl. Rub mixture over the tops of each fillet. Place the fillets in the frying basket and Air Fry for 7 minutes. Let rest for 5 minutes. Divide between 2 plates and garnish with cilantro to serve.

Catalan Sardines with Romesco Sauce

Serves 2 | Total Time: 15 minutes

2 (3.75-oz) cans skinless, boneless sardines in oil, drained
1/2 cup warmed romesco sauce
1/2 cup bread crumbs

Preheat air fryer to 350°F. In a shallow dish, add bread crumbs. Roll in sardines to coat. Place sardines in the greased frying basket and Air Fry for 6 minutes, turning once. Serve with romesco sauce.

Sardinas Fritas

Serves: 2 | Total Time: 15 minutes

2 (3.75-oz) cans boneless, skinless sardines in mustard sauce
Salt and pepper to taste
1/2 cup bread crumbs
2 lemon wedges
1 tsp chopped parsley

Preheat air fryer to 350°F. Add breadcrumbs, salt and black pepper to a bowl. Roll sardines in the breadcrumbs to coat. Place them in the greased frying basket and Air Fry for 6 minutes, flipping once. Transfer them to a serving dish. Serve topped with parsley and lemon wedges.

Family Fish Nuggets with Tartar Sauce

Serves 4 | Total Time: 30 minutes

1/2 cup mayonnaise
1 tbsp yellow mustard
1/2 cup diced dill pickles
Salt and pepper to taste
1 egg, beaten
1/4 cup cornstarch
1/4 cup flour
1 lb cod, cut into sticks

In a bowl, whisk the mayonnaise, mustard, pickles, salt, and pepper. Set aside the resulting tarter sauce.

Preheat air fryer to 350°F. Add the beaten egg to a bowl. In another bowl, combine cornstarch, flour, salt, and pepper. Dip fish nuggets in the egg and roll them in the flour mixture. Place fish nuggets in the lightly greased frying basket and Air Fry for 10 minutes, flipping once. Serve with the sauce on the side.

Old Bay Fish `n´ Chips

Serves 4 | Total Time: 40 minutes

2 russet potatoes, peeled
2 tbsp olive oil
4 tilapia fillets
1/4 cup flour

Salt and pepper to taste
1 tsp Old Bay seasoning
1 lemon, zested
1 egg, beaten
1 cup panko bread crumbs
3 tbsp tartar sauce

Preheat the air fryer to 400°F. Slice the potatoes into 1/2-inch-thick chips and drizzle with olive oil. Sprinkle with salt. Add the fries to the frying basket and Air Fry for 12-16 minutes, shaking once. Remove the potatoes to a plate. Cover loosely with foil to keep warm. Sprinkle the fish with salt and season with black pepper, lemon zest, and Old Bay seasoning, then lay on a plate. Put the egg in a shallow bowl and spread the panko on a separate plate. Dip the fish in the flour, then the egg, then the panko. Press to coat completely. Add half the fish to the frying basket and spray with cooking oil. Set a raised rack on the frying basket, top with the other half of the fish, and spray with cooking oil. Air Fry for 8-10 minutes until the fish flakes. Serve the fish and chips with tartar sauce.

Authentic Greek Fish Pitas

Serves: 4 | Total Time: 25 minutes

1 lb pollock, cut into 1-inch pieces
1/4 cup olive oil
1 tsp salt
1/2 tsp dried oregano
1/2 tsp dried thyme
1/2 tsp garlic powder
1/4 tsp chili powder
4 pitas
1 cup grated lettuce
4 Kalamata olives, chopped
2 tomatoes, diced
1 cup Greek yogurt

Preheat air fryer to 380°F. Coat the pollock with olive oil, salt, oregano, thyme, garlic powder, and chili powder in a bowl. Put the pollock into the frying basket and Air Fry for 15 minutes. Serve inside pitas with lettuce, tomato, olives, and Greek yogurt. Enjoy!

Home-Style Fish Sticks

Serves: 4 | Total Time: 30 minutes

1 lb cod fillets, cut into sticks
1 cup flour
1 egg
1/4 cup cornmeal
Salt and pepper to taste
1/4 tsp smoked paprika
1 lemon

Preheat air fryer to 350°F. In a bowl, add 1/2 cup of flour. In another bowl, beat the egg and in a third bowl, combine the remaining flour, cornmeal, salt, black pepper and paprika. Roll the sticks in the flour and shake off excess flour. Then, dip them in the egg. Lastly, dredge them in the cornmeal mixture. Place fish fingers in the greased frying basket and Air Fry for 10 minutes, flipping once. Serve with squeezed lemon.

Fish Piccata with Crispy Potatoes

Serves: 4 | Total Time: 30 minutes

4 cod fillets
1 tbsp butter
2 tsp capers
1 garlic clove, minced
2 tbsp lemon juice
1/2 lb asparagus, trimmed
2 large potatoes, cubed
1 tbsp olive oil
Salt and pepper to taste
1/4 tsp garlic powder

1 tsp dried rosemary
1 tsp dried parsley

1 tsp chopped dill

Preheat air fryer to 380°F. Place each fillet on a large piece of foil. Top each fillet with butter, capers, dill, garlic, and lemon juice. Fold the foil over the fish and seal the edges to make a pouch. Mix asparagus, parsley, potatoes, olive oil, salt, rosemary, garlic powder, and pepper in a large bowl. Place asparagus in the frying basket. Roast for 4 minutes, then shake the basket. Top vegetable with foil packets and Roast for another 8 minutes. Turn off the air fryer and let it stand for 5 minutes. Serve and enjoy.

Fish Goujons with Tartar Sauce

Serves: 4 | Total Time: 20 minutes

¼ cup flour
Salt and pepper to taste
¼ tsp smoked paprika
¼ tsp dried oregano
1 tsp dried thyme

1 egg
4 haddock fillets
1 lemon, thinly sliced
½ cup tartar sauce

Preheat air fryer to 400°F. Combine flour, salt, pepper, paprika, thyme, and oregano in a wide bowl. Whisk egg and 1 teaspoon water in another wide bowl. Slice each fillet into 4 strips. Dip the strips in the egg mixture. Then roll them in the flour mixture and coat completely. Arrange the fish strips on the greased frying basket. Air Fry for 4 minutes. Flip the fish and Air Fry for another 4 to 5 minutes until crisp. Serve warm with lemon slices and tartar sauce on the side and enjoy.

Fish Tortillas with Coleslaw

Serves: 4 | Total Time: 30 minutes

1 tbsp olive oil
1 lb cod fillets
3 tbsp lemon juice
2 cups chopped red cabbage

½ cup salsa
1/3 cup sour cream
6 taco shells, warm
1 avocado, chopped

Preheat air fryer to 400°F. Brush oil on the cod and sprinkle with some lemon juice. Place in the frying basket and Air Fry until the fish flakes with a fork, 9-12 minutes.

Meanwhile, mix together the remaining lemon juice, red cabbage, salsa, and sour cream in a medium bowl. Put the cooked fish in a bowl, breaking it into large pieces. Then add the cabbage mixture, avocados, and warmed tortilla shells, ready for assembly. Enjoy!

Crispy Fish Sandwiches

Serves: 4 | Total Time: 25 minutes

½ cup torn iceberg lettuce
½ cup mayonnaise
1 tbsp Dijon mustard
½ cup diced dill pickles
1 tsp capers
1 tsp tarragon
1 tsp dill
Salt and pepper to taste
1/3 cup flour

2 tbsp cornstarch
1 tsp smoked paprika
¼ cup milk
1 egg
½ cup bread crumbs
4 cod fillets, cut in half
1 vine-ripe tomato, sliced
4 hamburger buns

Mix the mayonnaise, mustard, pickles, capers, tarragon, dill, salt, and pepper in a bowl and let the resulting tartare sauce chill covered in the fridge until ready to use. Preheat air fryer to 375°F. In a bowl, mix the flour, cornstarch, paprika, and salt. In another bowl, beat the milk and egg and in a third bowl, add the breadcrumbs. Roll the cod in the flour mixture, shake off excess flour. Then, dip in the egg, shaking off the excess. Lastly, dredge in the breadcrumbs mixture. Place fish pieces in the greased frying basket and Air Fry for 6 minutes, flipping once. Add cooked fish, lettuce, tomato slices, and tartar sauce to each bottom bun and top with the top bun. Serve.

Chinese Fish Noodle Bowls

Serves: 4 | Total Time: 40 minutes

1 (8-oz) can crushed pineapple, drained
1 shallot, minced
2 tbsp chopped cilantro
2 ½ tsp lime juice
1 tbsp honey
Salt and pepper to taste
1 ½ cups grated red cabbage
¼ chopped green beans
2 grated baby carrots

½ tsp granulated sugar
2 tbsp mayonnaise
1 garlic clove, minced
8 oz cooked rice noodles
2 tsp sesame oil
1 tsp sesame seeds
4 cod fillets
1 tsp Chinese five-spice

Preheat air fryer to 350°F. Combine the pineapple, shallot, honey, 2 tsp of lime juice, salt, and black pepper in a bowl. Let chill the salsa covered in the fridge until ready to use. Mix the cabbage, green beans, carrots, sugar, remaining lime juice, mayonnaise, garlic, salt, and pepper in a bowl. Let chill covered in the fridge until ready to use. In a bowl, toss cooked noodles and sesame oil, stirring occasionally to avoid sticking.

Sprinkle cod fillets with salt and five-spice. Place them in the greased frying basket and Air Fry for 10 minutes until the fish is opaque and flakes easily with a fork. Divide noodles into 4 bowls and top each with salsa, slaw, and fish. Serve right away, sprinkled with cilantro and sesame seeds.

Masala Fish & Chips

Serves: 4 | Total Time: 40 minutes

1 ½ lb russet potatoes, peeled and cut into wedges
4 pollock fillets
Salt and pepper to taste
1 tsp garam masala

1 egg white
¾ cup bread crumbs
2 tbsp olive oil

Preheat air fryer to 400°F. In a bowl, toss the potato wedges with olive oil, salt, and pepper. Place them in the frying basket and Air Fry for 18-20 minutes, shaking once. Remove them and cover with foil to keep warm. Coat the pollock fillets with salt, pepper, and garam masala. In a bowl, whisk the egg white until frothy. Add the bread crumbs to a separate bowl. Dip the fillets into the egg white, then coat with bread crumbs. Arrange the fish fillets on the frying basket and cook them for 8-10 minutes, flipping once. Add the chops back to the basket and cook until heated through, 2 minutes. Serve warm.

Fish Tacos with Hot Coleslaw

Serves: 4 | Total Time: 25 minutes

2 cups shredded green cabbage
½ red onion, thinly sliced   1 tbsp apple cider vinegar
1 jalapeño, thinly sliced   Salt to taste
1 tsp lemon juice   1 large egg, beaten
1 tbsp chives, chopped   1 cup crushed tortilla chips
3 tbsp mayonnaise   1 lb cod fillets, cubed
1 tbsp hot sauce   8 corn tortillas
2 tbsp chopped cilantro

Mix the lemon juice, chives, mayonnaise, and hot sauce in a bowl until blended. Add the cabbage to a large bowl. Then add onion, jalapeño, cilantro, vinegar and salt. Toss until well mixed. Put in the fridge until ready to serve.

Preheat air fryer to 360°F. In one shallow bowl, add the beaten egg. In another shallow bowl, add the crushed tortilla chips. Salt the cod, then dip into the egg mixture. Allow excess to drip off. Next, dip into the crumbs, gently pressing into the crumbs. Place the fish in the greased frying basket and Air Fry for 6 minutes, flipping once until crispy and completely cooked. Place 2 warm tortillas on each plate. Top with cod cubes, ¼ cup of slaw, and drizzle with spicy mayo. Serve and enjoy!

British Fish & Chips

Serves: 4 | Total Time: 40 minutes

2 peeled russet potatoes, thinly sliced
1 egg white   2 bread slices, crumbled
1 tbsp lemon juice   ½ tsp dried basil
1/3 cup ground almonds   4 haddock fillets

Preheat air fryer to 390°F. Lay the potato slices in the frying basket and Air Fry for 11-15 minutes. Turn the fries a couple of times while cooking. While the fries are cooking, whisk the egg white and lemon juice together in a bowl. On a plate, combine the almonds, breadcrumbs, and basil. First, one at a time, dip the fillets into the egg mix and then coat in the almond/breadcrumb mix. Lay the fillets on a wire rack until the fries are done. Preheat the oven to 350°F. After the fries are done, move them to a pan and place in the oven to keep warm. Put the fish in the frying basket and Air Fry for 10-14 minutes or until cooked through, golden, and crispy. Serve with the fries.

Korean-Style Fried Calamari

Serves 4 | Total Time: 25 minutes

2 tbsp tomato paste   1 tsp smoked paprika
1 tbsp gochujang   ½ tsp salt
1 tbsp lime juice   1 cup bread crumbs
1 tsp lime zest   1/3 lb calamari rings

Preheat air fryer to 400°F. Whisk tomato paste, gochujang, lime juice and zest, paprika, and salt in a bowl. Add the bread crumbs to another bowl. Dredge calamari rings in the tomato mixture, shake off excess, then roll through the crumbs. Place calamari rings in the greased frying basket and Air Fry for 4-5 minutes, flipping once. Serve.

Parmesan Fish Bites

Serves: 2 | Total Time: 30 minutes

1 haddock fillet, cut into bite-sized pieces
1 tbsp shredded cheddar   ½ cup breadcrumbs
2 tbsp shredded Parmesan   Salt and pepper to taste
2 eggs, beaten   ½ cup mayoracha sauce

Preheat air fryer to 350°F. Dip the strips in the beaten eggs. Place the bread crumbs, Parmesan, cheddar, salt, and pepper in a bowl and mix well. Coat the fish strips in the dry mixture and place them on the foil-lined frying basket. Air Fry for 14-16 minutes. Halfway through the cooking time, shake the basket. When the cooking time is over, the fish will be cooked through and crust golden brown. Serve with mayoracha sauce (mixed mayo with sriracha) for dipping and enjoy!

Hazelnut-Crusted Fish

Serves: 4 | Total Time: 30 minutes

½ cup hazelnuts, ground   Salt and pepper to taste
1 scallion, finely chopped   3 skinless sea bass fillets
1 lemon, juiced and zested   1 tsp Dijon mustard
½ tbsp olive oil

Place the hazelnuts in a small bowl along with scallion, lemon zest, olive oil, salt, and pepper. Mix everything until combined. Spray only the top of the fish with cooking oil, then squeeze lemon juice onto the fish. Coat the top of the fish with mustard. Spread with hazelnuts and press gently so that it stays on the fish.

Preheat air fryer to 375°F. Air Fry the fish in the greased frying basket for 7-8 minutes until the fish is cooked through. Serve hot.

Mojito Fish Tacos

Serves: 4 | Total Time: 30 minutes

1 ½ cups chopped red cabbage
1 lb cod fillets   1 tbsp white rum
2 tsp olive oil   ½ cup salsa
3 tbsp lemon juice   1/3 cup Greek yogurt
1 large carrot, grated   4 soft tortillas

Preheat air fryer to 390°F. Rub the fish with olive oil, then a splash with a tablespoon of lemon juice. Place in the fryer and Air Fry for 9-12 minutes. The fish should flake when done. Mix the remaining lemon juice, red cabbage, carrots, salsa, rum, and yogurt in a bowl. Take the fish out of the fryer and tear it into large pieces. Serve with tortillas and cabbage mixture. Enjoy!

The Best Oysters Rockefeller

Serves: 2 | Total Time: 30 minutes

4 tsp grated Parmesan   ⅛ tsp Tabasco hot sauce
2 tbsp butter   ½ tsp lemon juice
1 sweet onion, minced   ½ tsp lemon zest
1 garlic clove, minced   ¼ cup bread crumbs
1 cup baby spinach   12 oysters, on the half shell

Melt butter in a skillet over medium heat. Stir in onion, garlic, and spinach and stir-fry for 3 minutes until the onion is translucent. Mix in Parmesan cheese, hot sauce, lemon juice, lemon zest, and bread crumbs. Divide this mixture between the tops of oysters.

Preheat air fryer to 400°F. Place oysters in the frying basket and Air Fry for 6 minutes. Serve immediately.

Crab Stuffed Tomatoes

Serves 4 | Total Time: 25 minutes

4 medium tomatoes, top removed
1 cup lump crabmeat, shells discarded
1 tsp lemon juice   2 tbsp butter, melted
Salt and pepper to taste   ¼ cup chopped dill
2 tbsp bread crumbs   2 tbsp grated Parmesan

Preheat air fryer to 350°F. Scoop out the pulp of the tomatoes. Chop the pulp and place it in a bowl. Add the crabmeat, lemon juice, dill, salt, and pepper and mix well. Fill the tomatoes with crab stuffing, scatter bread crumbs over and drizzle melted butter over the crumbs. Place the stuffed tomatoes in the frying basket. Sprinkle with Parmesan cheese and Bake for 10-15 minutes. Serve.

Garlic-Lemon Steamer Clams

Serves 2 | Total Time: 30 minutes

25 Manila clams, scrubbed   1 garlic clove, minced
2 tbsp butter, melted   2 lemon wedges

Add the clams to a large bowl filled with water and let sit for 10 minutes. Drain. Pour more water and let sit for 10 more minutes. Drain. Preheat air fryer to 350°F. Place clams in the basket and Air Fry for 7 minutes. Discard any clams that don´t open. Remove clams from shells and place them into a large serving dish. Drizzle with melted butter and garlic and squeeze lemon on top. Serve.

Lime Bay Scallops

Serves 4 | Total Time: 10 minutes

2 tbsp butter, melted   1 lb bay scallops
1 lime, juiced   2 tbsp chopped cilantro
¼ tsp salt

Preheat air fryer to 350°F. Combine all ingredients in a bowl, except for the cilantro. Place scallops in the frying basket and Air Fry for 5 minutes, tossing once. Serve immediately topped with cilantro.

Stuffed Shrimp Wrapped in Bacon

Serves 4 | Total Time: 30 minutes

1 lb shrimp, deveined and shelled
3 tbsp crumbled goat cheese
2 tbsp panko bread crumbs   2 tsp mayonnaise
¼ tsp soy sauce   Black pepper to taste
½ tsp prepared horseradish   5 slices bacon, quartered
¼ tsp garlic powder   ¼ cup chopped parsley
½ tsp chili powder

Preheat air fryer to 400°F. Butterfly shrimp by cutting down the spine of each shrimp without going all the way through. Combine the goat cheese, bread crumbs, soy sauce, horseradish, garlic powder, chili powder, mayonnaise, and black pepper in a bowl. Evenly press goat cheese mixture into shrimp. Wrap a piece of bacon around each piece of shrimp to hold in the cheese mixture. Place them in the frying basket and Air Fry for 8-10 minutes, flipping once. Top with parsley to serve.

Basil Crab Cakes with Fresh Salad

Serves 2 | Total Time: 25 minutes

8 oz lump crabmeat   1 tbsp basil, minced
2 tbsp mayonnaise   1 tbsp olive oil
½ tsp Dijon mustard   2 tsp white wine vinegar
½ tsp lemon juice   Salt and pepper to taste
½ tsp lemon zest   4 oz arugula
2 tsp minced yellow onion   ½ cup blackberries
¼ tsp prepared horseradish   ¼ cup pine nuts
¼ cup flour   2 lemon wedges
1 egg white, beaten

Preheat air fryer to 400°F. Combine the crabmeat, mayonnaise, mustard, lemon juice and zest, onion, horseradish, flour, egg white, and basil in a bowl. Form mixture into 4 patties. Place the patties in the lightly greased frying basket and Air Fry for 10 minutes, flipping once. Combine olive oil, vinegar, salt, and pepper in a bowl. Toss in the arugula and share into 2 medium bowls. Add 2 crab cakes to each bowl and scatter with blackberries, pine nuts, and lemon wedges. Serve warm.

Garlic-Butter Lobster Tails

Serves 2 | Total Time: 20 minutes

2 lobster tails   ½ tsp garlic powder
1 tbsp butter, melted   1 tbsp chopped parsley
½ tsp Old Bay Seasoning   2 lemon wedges

Preheat air fryer to 400°F. Using kitchen shears, cut down the middle of each lobster tail on the softer side. Carefully run your finger between the lobster meat and the shell to loosen the meat. Place lobster tails in the frying basket, cut sides up, and Air Fry for 4 minutes. Rub with butter, garlic powder and Old Bay seasoning and cook for 4 more minutes. Garnish with parsley and lemon wedges. Serve and enjoy!

Timeless Garlic-Lemon Scallops

Serves 2 | Total Time: 15 minutes

2 tbsp butter, melted   1 tbsp lemon juice
1 garlic clove, minced   1 lb jumbo sea scallops

Preheat air fryer to 400°F. Whisk butter, garlic, and lemon juice in a bowl. Roll scallops in the mixture to coat all sides. Place scallops in the frying basket and Air Fry for 4 minutes, flipping once. Brush the tops of each scallop with butter mixture and cook for 4 more minutes, flipping once. Serve and enjoy!

Easy-Peasy Prawns

Serves 2 | Total Time: 15 minutes

1 lb tail-on prawns, deveined	1 lemon wedge
2 tbsp butter, melted	½ red chili, thinly sliced

Preheat air fryer to 360°F. Combine shrimp and butter in a bowl. Place shrimp in the greased frying basket and Air Fry for 6 minutes, flipping once. Squeeze lemon juice over and top with chili slices. Serve warm and enjoy!

Holliday Lobster Salad

Serves 2 | Total Time: 20 minutes

2 lobster tails	2 tsp chopped tarragon
¼ cup mayonnaise	Salt and pepper to taste
2 tsp lemon juice	2 tomato slices
1 stalk celery, sliced	4 cucumber slices
2 tsp chopped chives	1 avocado, diced

Preheat air fryer to 400°F. Using kitchen shears, cut down the middle of each lobster tail on the softer side. Carefully run your finger between the lobster meat and the shell to loosen meat. Place lobster tails, cut sides up, in the frying basket, and Air Fry for 8 minutes. Transfer to a large plate and let cool for 3 minutes until easy to handle, then pull lobster meat from the shell and roughly chop it. Combine chopped lobster, mayonnaise, lemon juice, celery, chives, tarragon, salt, and pepper in a bowl. Divide between 2 medium plates and top with tomato slices, cucumber, and avocado. Serve immediately.

Shrimp al Pesto

Serves: 4 | Total Time: 10 minutes

1 lb peeled shrimp, deveined	1 lime, sliced
¼ cup pesto sauce	2 cups cooked farro

Preheat air fryer to 360°F. Coat the shrimp with the pesto sauce in a bowl. Put the shrimp in a single layer in the frying basket. Put the lime slices over the shrimp and Roast for 5 minutes. Remove lime and discard. Serve the shrimp over a bed of farro pilaf. Enjoy!

Feta & Shrimp Pita

Serves: 4 | Total Time: 15 minutes

1 lb peeled shrimp, deveined	Salt and pepper to taste
2 tbsp olive oil	4 whole-wheat pitas
1 tsp dried oregano	4 oz feta cheese, crumbled
½ tsp dried thyme	1 cup grated lettuce
½ tsp garlic powder	1 tomato, diced
¼ tsp shallot powder	¼ cup black olives, sliced
¼ tsp tarragon powder	1 lemon

Preheat the oven to 380°F. Mix the shrimp with olive oil, oregano, thyme, garlic powder, shallot powder, tarragon powder salt, and pepper in a bowl. Pour shrimp in a single layer in the frying basket and Bake for 6-8 minutes or until no longer pink and cooked through. Divide the shrimp into warmed pitas with feta, lettuce, tomato, olives, and a squeeze of lemon. Serve and enjoy!

Black Olive & Shrimp Salad

Serves: 4 | Total Time: 15 minutes

1 lb cleaned shrimp, deveined	¼ tsp dried basil
½ cup olive oil	¼ tsp salt
4 garlic cloves, minced	¼ tsp onion powder
1 tbsp balsamic vinegar	1 tomato, diced
¼ tsp cayenne pepper	¼ cup black olives

Preheat air fryer to 380°F. Place the olive oil, garlic, balsamic, cayenne, basil, onion powder and salt in a bowl and stir to combine. Divide the tomatoes and black olives between 4 small ramekins. Top with shrimp and pour a quarter of the oil mixture over the shrimp. Bake for 6-8 minutes until the shrimp are cooked through. Serve.

Basil Mushroom & Shrimp Spaghetti

Serves: 6 | Total Time: 20 minutes

8 oz baby Bella mushrooms, sliced	
½ cup grated Parmesan	¼ tsp cayenne
1 lb peeled shrimp, deveined	1 lb cooked pasta spaghetti
3 tbsp olive oil	5 garlic cloves, minced
¼ tsp garlic powder	Salt and pepper to taste
¼ tsp shallot powder	½ cup dill

Preheat air fryer to 380°F. Toss the shrimp, 1 tbsp of olive oil, garlic powder, shallot powder and cayenne in a bowl. Put the shrimp into the frying basket and Roast for 5 minutes. Remove and set aside.

Warm the remaining olive oil in a large skillet over medium heat. Add the garlic and mushrooms and cook for 5 minutes. Pour in the pasta, ½ cup of water, Parmesan, salt, pepper, and dill and stir to coat the pasta. Stir in the shrimp. Remove from heat, then let the mixture rest for 5 minutes. Serve and enjoy!

Restaurant-Style Breaded Shrimp

Serves: 2 | Total Time: 35 minutes

½ lb fresh shrimp, peeled	½ tsp garlic powder
2 eggs, beaten	½ tsp turmeric
½ cup breadcrumbs	½ tsp red chili powder
½ onion, finely chopped	Salt and pepper to taste
½ tsp ground ginger	½ tsp amchur powder

Preheat air fryer to 350°F. Place the beaten eggs in a bowl and dip in the shrimp. Blend the bread crumbs with all the dry ingredients in another bowl. Add in the shrimp and toss to coat. Place the coated shrimp in the greased frying basket. Air Fry for 12-14 minutes until the breaded crust of the shrimp is golden brown. Toss the basket two or three times during the cooking time. Serve.

Coconut Shrimp with Plum Sauce

Serves: 2 | Total Time: 30 minutes

½ lb raw shrimp, peeled	2 tbsp dried coconut flakes
2 eggs	Salt and pepper to taste
½ cup breadcrumbs	½ cup plum sauce
1 tsp red chili powder	

Preheat air fryer to 350°F. Whisk the eggs with salt and pepper in a bowl. Dip in the shrimp, fully submerging. Combine the bread crumbs, coconut flakes, chili powder, salt, and pepper in another bowl until evenly blended. Coat the shrimp in the crumb mixture and place them in the foil-lined frying basket. Air Fry for 14-16 minutes. Halfway through the cooking time, shake the basket. Serve with plum sauce for dipping and enjoy!

Southern Shrimp with Cocktail Sauce

Serves: 2 | Total Time: 20 minutes

½ lb raw shrimp, tail on, deveined and shelled
1 cup ketchup   2 tbsp cornstarch
2 tbsp prepared horseradish   ¼ cup milk
1 tbsp lemon juice   1 egg
½ tsp Worcestershire sauce   ½ cup bread crumbs
1/8 tsp chili powder   1 tbsp Cajun seasoning
Salt and pepper to taste   1 lemon, cut into pieces
1/3 cup flour

In a small bowl, whisk the ketchup, horseradish, lemon juice, Worcestershire sauce, chili powder, salt, and pepper. Let chill covered in the fridge until ready to use. Preheat air fryer to 375°F. In a bowl, mix the flour, cornstarch, and salt. In another bowl, beat the milk and egg and in a third bowl, combine breadcrumbs and Cajun seasoning.

Roll the shrimp in the flour mixture, shaking off the excess. Then, dip in the egg. Lastly, dredge in the breadcrumbs mixture. Place shrimp in the greased frying basket and Air Fry for 8 minutes, flipping once. Serve with cocktail sauce and lemon slices.

Hot Shrimp Wrapped in Prosciutto

Serves: 4 | Total Time: 30 minutes

1 lb shelled tail-on shrimp, deveined, sliced down the spine
2 poblano peppers, diced   1 tbsp aioli
2 tbsp grated cheddar cheese   ¼ tsp ground black pepper
3 tbsp cream cheese   20 prosciutto slices
¼ tsp smoked paprika   ¼ cup chopped parsley
1 tbsp chives, chopped   1 lemon

Preheat air fryer to 400°F. Combine the cream and cheddar cheeses, poblano peppers, paprika, aioli, chives, and black pepper in a bowl. Press cheese mixture into shrimp. Wrap 1 piece of prosciutto around each shrimp to hold in the cheese mixture. Place wrapped shrimp in the frying basket and Air Fry for 8-10 minutes, flipping once. To serve, scatter with parsley and squeeze lemon.

Cheese & Crab Stuffed Mushrooms

Serves: 2 | Total Time: 30 minutes

6 oz lump crabmeat, shells discarded
6 oz mascarpone cheese, softened
2 jalapeño peppers, minced   ½ tsp prepared horseradish
¼ cup diced red onions   ¼ tsp Worcestershire sauce
2 tsp grated Parmesan cheese   ¼ tsp smoked paprika
2 portobello mushroom caps   Salt and pepper to taste
2 tbsp butter, divided   ¼ cup bread crumbs

Melt 1 tbsp of butter in a skillet over heat for 30 seconds. Add in onion and cook for 3 minutes until tender. Stir in mascarpone cheese, Parmesan cheese, horseradish, jalapeños, Worcestershire sauce, paprika, salt, and pepper and cook for 2 minutes until smooth. Fold in crabmeat. Spoon the mixture into the mushroom caps. Set aside.

Preheat air fryer to 350°F. Microwave the remaining butter until melted. Stir in breadcrumbs. Scatter over stuffed mushrooms. Place mushrooms in the greased frying basket and Bake for 8 minutes. Serve immediately.

BBQ Fried Oysters

Serves: 2 | Total Time: 30 minutes

½ cup all-purpose flour   ½ lb shelled raw oysters
½ cup barbecue sauce   1 lemon
1 cup bread crumbs   1 tbsp chopped parsley

Preheat air fryer to 400°F. In a bowl, add flour. In another bowl, pour barbecue sauce and in a third bowl, add breadcrumbs. Roll the oysters in the flour shake off excess flour. Then, dip them into the sauce, shaking off the excess. Finally, dredge them in the breadcrumbs. Place oysters in the greased frying basket and Air Fry for 8 minutes, flipping once. Sprinkle with parsley and squeeze lemon to serve.

Cajun-Seasoned Shrimp

Serves: 2 | Total Time: 15 minutes

1 lb shelled tail-on shrimp, deveined
2 tsp grated Parmesan cheese   1 tsp garlic powder
2 tbsp butter, melted   2 tsp Cajun seasoning
1 tsp cayenne pepper   1 tbsp lemon juice

Preheat air fryer to 350°F. Toss the shrimp, melted butter, cayenne pepper, garlic powder and cajun seasoning in a bowl, place them in the greased frying basket, and Air Fry for 6 minutes, flipping once. Transfer it to a plate. Squeeze lemon juice over shrimp and stir in Parmesan cheese. Serve immediately.

Crab Cakes with Eggs Mornay

Serves: 4 | Total Time: 35 minutes

½ lb lump crabmeat, shells discarded
2 tbsp mayonnaise   Salt and pepper to taste
½ tsp yellow mustard   4 poached eggs
½ tsp lemon juice   ½ cup bechamel sauce
½ tbsp minced shallot   2 tsp grated cheddar cheese
¼ cup bread crumbs   2 tsp chopped chives
1 egg   1 lemon, cut into wedges

Preheat air fryer to 400°F. Combine all ingredients, except eggs, sauce, cheese, and chives, in a bowl. Form mixture into 4 patties. Place crab cakes in the greased frying basket and Air Fry for 10 minutes, flipping once. Transfer them to a serving dish. Top each crab cake with 1 poached egg, drizzle with Bechamel sauce and scatter with cheese, chives, and lemon wedges. Serve and enjoy!

Mediterranean Sea Scallops

Serves: 2 | Total Time: 20 minutes

1 tbsp olive oil
1 shallot, minced
2 tbsp capers
2 cloves garlic, minced
½ cup heavy cream
3 tbsp butter
1 tbsp lemon juice

Salt and pepper to taste
¼ tbsp cumin powder
¼ tbsp curry powder
1 lb jumbo sea scallops
2 tbsp chopped parsley
1 tbsp chopped cilantro

Warm the olive oil in a saucepan over medium heat. Add shallot and stir-fry for 2 minutes until translucent. Stir in capers, cumin, curry, garlic, heavy cream, 1 tbsp of butter, lemon juice, salt, and pepper and cook for 2 minutes and bring to a boil. Low the heat and simmer for 3 minutes until the caper sauce thickens. Turn the heat off.

Preheat air fryer to 400°F. Add the remaining butter and scallops to a bowl and toss to coat on all sides. Place scallops in the greased frying basket and Air Fry for 8 minutes, flipping once. Drizzle caper sauce over and scatter with parsley and cilantro. Serve and enjoy!

Old Bay Lobster Tails

Serves: 2 | Total Time: 20 minutes

¼ cup green onions, sliced
2 uncooked lobster tails
1 tbsp butter, melted
½ tsp Old Bay Seasoning
1 tbsp chopped parsley

1 tsp dried sage
1 tsp dried thyme
1 garlic clove, chopped
1 tbsp basil paste
2 lemon wedges

Preheat air fryer to 400°F. Using kitchen shears, cut down the middle of each lobster tail on the softer side. Carefully run your finger between lobster meat and shell to loosen the meat. Place lobster tails, cut side-up, in the frying basket and Air Fry for 4 minutes. Brush the tail meat with butter and season with old bay seasoning, sage, thyme, garlic, green onions, and basil paste and cook for another 4 minutes. Scatter with parsley and serve with lemon wedges. Enjoy!

Chinese Firecracker Shrimp

Serves: 4 | Total Time: 20 minutes

1 lb peeled shrimp, deveined
2 green onions, chopped
2 tbsp sesame seeds
Salt and pepper to taste
1 egg

½ cup all-purpose flour
¾ cup panko bread crumbs
1/3 cup sour cream
2 tbsp Sriracha sauce
¼ cup sweet chili sauce

Preheat air fryer to 400°F. Set out three small bowls. In the first, add flour. In the second, beat the egg. In the third, add the crumbs. Season the shrimp with salt and pepper. Dip the shrimp in the flour, then dredge in the egg, and finally in the bread crumbs. Place the shrimp in the greased frying basket and Air Fry for 8 minutes, flipping once until crispy. Combine the sour cream, Sriracha sauce, and sweet chili sauce in a bowl. Top the shrimp with sesame seeds and green onions and serve with the chili sauce.

Hot Calamari Rings

Serves: 4 | Total Time: 25 minutes

½ cup all-purpose flour
2 tsp hot chili powder
2 eggs
1 tbsp milk
1 cup bread crumbs

Salt and pepper to taste
1 lb calamari rings
1 lime, quartered
½ cup aioli sauce

Preheat air fryer to 400°F. In a shallow bowl, add flour and hot chili powder. In another bowl, mix the eggs and milk. In a third bowl, mix the breadcrumbs, salt, and pepper. Dip calamari rings in flour mix first, then in eggs mix and shake off excess. Roll the calamari ring through bread crumb mixture. Place calamari rings in the greased frying basket and Air Fry for 4 minutes, tossing once. Squeeze lime quarters over calamari. Serve with aioli sauce.

Malaysian Shrimp with Sambal Mayo

Serves: 4 | Total Time: 30 minutes

24 jumbo shrimp, peeled and deveined
2/3 cup panko bread crumbs
3 tbsp mayonnaise
1 tbsp sambal oelek paste
2/3 cup shredded coconut
1 lime, zested

½ tsp ground coriander
Salt to taste
2 tbsp flour
2 eggs

Mix together mayonnaise and sambal oelek in a bowl. Set aside. In another bowl, stir together coconut, lime, coriander, panko bread crumbs, and salt. In a shallow bowl, add flour. In another shallow bowl, whisk eggs until blended. Season shrimp with salt. First, dip the shrimp into the flour, shake, and dip into the egg mix. Dip again in the coconut mix. Gently press the coconut and panko to the shrimp. Preheat air fryer to 360°F. Put the shrimp in the greased frying basket and Air Fry for 8 minutes, flipping once until the crust is golden and the shrimp is cooked. Serve alongside the sweet chili mayo.

Piña Colada Shrimp

Serves: 4 | Total Time: 25 minutes

1 lb large shrimp, deveined and shelled
1 (8-oz) can crushed pineapple
½ cup sour cream
¼ cup pineapple preserves
2 egg whites
1 tbsp dark rum

2/3 cup cornstarch
2/3 cup sweetened coconut
1 cup panko bread crumbs

Preheat air fryer to 400°F. Drain the crushed pineapple and reserve the juice. Next, transfer the pineapple to a small bowl and mix with sour cream and preserves. Set aside. In a shallow bowl, beat egg whites with 1 tbsp of the reserved pineapple juice and rum. Add the cornstarch to a plate. Stir together coconut and bread crumbs on another plate. Coat the shrimp with cornstarch. Then, dip the shrimp into the egg white mixture. Shake off drips and then coat with the coconut mixture. Place the shrimp in the greased frying basket. Air Fry until crispy and golden, 7 minutes. Serve warm.

Spiced Shrimp Empanadas

Serves: 5 | Total Time: 30 minutes

½ lb peeled and deveined shrimp, chopped
2 tbsp diced red bell peppers | ¼ tsp sweet paprika
1 shallot, minced | ⅛ tsp salt
1 scallion, chopped | ⅛ tsp red pepper flakes
2 garlic cloves, minced | ¼ tsp ground nutmeg
2 tbsp chopped cilantro | 1 large egg, beaten
½ tbsp lemon juice | 10 empanada discs

Combine all ingredients, except the egg and empanada discs, in a bowl. Toss to coat. Beat the 1 egg with 1 tsp of water in a small bowl until blended. Set aside.

On your work board, place one empanada disc. Add 2 tbsp of shrimp mixture in the middle. Brush the edges of the disc with the egg mixture. Fold the disc in half and seal the edges. Crimp with a fork by pressing around the edges. Brush the tops with the egg mixture. Preheat air fryer to 380°F. Put the empanadas in the greased frying basket and Air Fry for 9 minutes, flipping once until golden and crispy. Serve hot.

Old Bay Crab Cake Burgers

Serves: 4 | Total Time: 30 minutes

½ cup panko bread crumbs | ⅛ tsp sweet paprika
1 egg, beaten | Salt and pepper to taste
1 tbsp hummus | 10 oz lump crabmeat
1 tsp Dijon mustard | ¼ cup mayonnaise
¼ cup minced parsley | 2 tbsp minced dill pickle
2 spring onions, chopped | 1 tsp fresh lemon juice
½ tsp red chili powder | ¾ tsp Cajun seasoning
1 tbsp lemon juice | 4 Boston lettuce leaves
½ tsp Old Bay seasoning | 4 buns, split

Mix the crumbs, egg, hummus, mustard, parsley, lemon juice, red chili, spring onions, Old Bay seasoning, paprika, salt, and pepper in a large bowl. Fold in crabmeat until just coated without overmixing. Divide into 4 equal parts, about ½ cup each, and shape into patties, about ¾-inch thick. Preheat air fryer to 400°F.

Place the cakes in the greased frying basket and Air Fry for 10 minutes, flipping them once until the edges are golden. Meanwhile, mix mayonnaise, lemon juice and Cajun seasoning in a small bowl until well blended. Set aside. When you are ready to serve, start with the bottom of the bun. Add a lettuce leaf, then a crab cake. Top with a heaping tbsp of Cajun mayo, minced pickles, and top with the bun and enjoy.

Caribbean Skewers

Serves: 4 | Total Time: 25 minutes

1 ½ lb large shrimp, peeled and deveined
1 (8-oz) can pineapple chunks, drained, liquid reserved
1 red bell pepper, chopped | ½ tsp jerk seasoning
3 scallions, chopped | ⅛ tsp cayenne pepper
1 tbsp lemon juice | 2 tbsp cilantro, chopped
1 tbsp olive oil

Preheat the air fryer to 370°F. Thread the shrimp, pineapple, bell pepper, and scallions onto 8 bamboo skewers. Mix 3 tbsp of pineapple juice with lemon juice, olive oil, jerk seasoning, and cayenne pepper. Brush every bit of the mix over the skewers. Place 4 kebabs in the frying basket, add a rack, and put the rest of the skewers on top. Bake for 6-9 minutes and rearrange at about 4-5 minutes. Cook until the shrimp curl and pinken. Sprinkle with freshly chopped cilantro and serve.

Herby Prawn & Zucchini Bake

Serves: 4 | Total Time: 30 minutes

1 ¼ lb prawns, peeled and deveined
2 zucchini, sliced | ⅛ tsp red pepper flakes
2 tbsp butter, melted | ½ lemon, juiced
½ tsp garlic salt | 1 tbsp chopped mint
1 ½ tsp dried oregano | 1 tbsp chopped dill

Preheat air fryer to 350°F. Combine the prawns, zucchini, butter, garlic salt, oregano, and pepper flakes in a large bowl. Toss to coat. Put the prawns and zucchini in the greased frying basket and Air Fry for about 6-8 minutes, shaking the basket once until the zucchini is golden and the shrimp are cooked. Remove the shrimp to a serving plate and cover with foil. Serve hot topped with lemon juice, mint, and dill. Enjoy!

Dijon Shrimp Cakes

Serves: 4 | Total Time: 30 minutes

1 cup cooked shrimp, minced | 1 egg, beaten
¾ cup saltine cracker crumbs | ¼ cup mayonnaise
1 cup lump crabmeat | 2 tbsp Dijon mustard
3 green onions, chopped | 1 tbsp lemon juice

Preheat the air fryer to 375°F. Combine the crabmeat, shrimp, green onions, egg, mayonnaise, mustard, ¼ cup of cracker crumbs, and the lemon juice in a bowl and mix gently. Make 4 patties, sprinkle with the rest of the cracker crumbs on both sides, and spray with cooking oil. Line the frying basket with a round parchment paper with holes poked in it. Coat the paper with cooking spray and lay the patties on it. Bake for 10-14 minutes or until the patties are golden brown. Serve warm.

Speedy Shrimp Paella

Serves: 4 | Total Time: 20 minutes

2 cups cooked rice | ½ tsp dried thyme
1 red bell pepper, chopped | 1 cup cooked small shrimp
¼ cup vegetable broth | ½ cup baby peas
½ tsp turmeric | 1 tomato, diced

Preheat air fryer to 340°F. Gently combine rice, red bell pepper, broth, turmeric, and thyme in a baking pan. Bake in the air fryer until the rice is hot, about 9 minutes. Remove the pan from the air fryer and gently stir in shrimp, peas, and tomato. Return to the air fryer and cook until bubbling and all ingredients are hot, 5-8 minutes. Serve and enjoy!

Catalan-Style Crab Samfaina

Serves: 4 | Total Time: 30 minutes

1 peeled eggplant, cubed	1 tbsp olive oil
1 zucchini, cubed	½ tsp dried thyme
1 onion, chopped	½ tsp dried basil
1 red bell pepper, chopped	Salt and pepper to taste
2 large tomatoes, chopped	1 ½ cups cooked crab meat

Preheat air fryer to 400°F. In a pan, mix together all ingredients, except the crabmeat. Place the pan in the air fryer and Bake for 9 minutes. Remove the bowl and stir in the crabmeat. Return to the air fryer and Roast for another 2-5 minutes until the vegetables are tender and the ratatouille is bubbling. Serve hot.

Chili Blackened Shrimp

Serves: 4 | Total Time: 15 minutes

1 lb peeled shrimp, deveined	½ tsp red chili flakes
1 tsp paprika	½ lemon, juiced
½ tsp dried dill	Salt and pepper to taste

Preheat air fryer to 400°F. To a resealable bag, add shrimp, paprika, dill, red chili flakes, lemon juice, salt, and pepper. Seal and shake well. Place the shrimp in the greased frying basket and Air Fry for 7-8 minutes, shaking the basket once until blackened. Let cool slightly and serve.

Classic Shrimp Po'Boy Sandwiches

Serves: 4 | Total Time: 20 minutes

1 lb peeled shrimp, deveined	1 tsp minced garlic
1 egg	2 tbsp sweet pickle relish
½ cup flour	1 tsp Louisiana hot sauce
¾ cup cornmeal	½ tsp Creole seasoning
Salt and pepper to taste	4 rolls
½ cup mayonnaise	2 cups shredded lettuce
1 tsp Creole mustard	8 tomato slices
1 tsp Worcestershire sauce	

Preheat air fryer to 400°F. Set up three small bowls. In the first, add flour. In the second, beat the egg. In the third, mix cornmeal with salt and pepper. First, dip the shrimp in the flour, then dredge in the egg, then dip in the cornmeal. Place in the greased frying basket. Air Fry for 8 minutes, flipping once until crisp. Let cool slightly.

While the shrimp is cooking, mix mayonnaise, mustard, Worcestershire, garlic, pickle relish juice, hot sauce, and Creole seasoning in a small bowl. Set aside. To assemble the po'boys, split rolls along the crease and spread the inside with remoulade. Layer ¼ of the shrimp, ½ cup shredded lettuce, and 2 slices of tomato. Serve and enjoy!

King Prawns al Ajillo

Serves: 4 | Total Time: 15 minutes

1 ¼ lb peeled king prawns, deveined	
½ cup grated Parmesan	½ tsp garlic powder
1 tbsp olive oil	2 garlic cloves, minced
1 tbsp lemon juice	

Preheat the air fryer to 350°F. In a large bowl, add the prawns and sprinkle with olive oil, lemon juice, and garlic powder. Toss in the minced garlic and Parmesan, then toss to coat. Put the prawns in the frying basket and Air Fry for 10-15 minutes or until the prawns cook through. Shake the basket once while cooking. Serve immediately.

Summer Sea Scallops

Serves: 4 | Total Time: 30 minutes

1 cup asparagus	2 tsp olive oil
1 cup peas	½ tsp dried oregano
1 cup chopped broccoli	12 oz sea scallops

Preheat air fryer to 400°F. Add the asparagus, peas, and broccoli to a bowl and mix with olive oil. Put the bowl in the fryer and Air Fry for 4-6 minutes until crispy and soft. Take the veggies out and add the herbs; let sit. Add the scallops to the fryer and Air Fry for 4-5 minutes until the scallops are springy to the touch. Serve immediately with the vegetables. Enjoy!

Saucy Shrimp

Serves: 4 | Total Time: 30 minutes

1 lb peeled shrimp, deveined	½ tsp rice vinegar
½ cup grated coconut	1 tbsp hot sauce
¼ cup bread crumbs	⅛ tsp red pepper flakes
¼ cup flour	¼ cup orange juice
¼ tsp smoked paprika	1 tsp cornstarch
Salt and pepper to taste	½ cup banana ketchup
1 egg	1 lemon, sliced
2 tbsp maple syrup	

Preheat air fryer to 360°F. Combine the grated coconut, bread crumbs, flour, smoked paprika, salt, and black pepper in a medium bowl. In a separate bowl, whisk egg and 1 teaspoon water. Dip one shrimp into the egg bowl and shake off excess drips. Dip the shrimp in the bread crumb mixture and coat it completely. Continue the process for all of the shrimp. Arrange the shrimp on the greased frying basket. Air Fry for 5 minutes, then flip the shrimp. Cook for another 2-3 minutes.

To make the sauce, add maple syrup, banana ketchup, hot sauce, vinegar, and red pepper flakes in a small saucepan over medium heat. Make a slurry in a small bowl with orange juice and cornstarch. Stir in slurry and continue stirring. Bring the sauce to a boil and cook for 5 minutes. When the sauce begins to thicken, remove from heat and allow to sit for 5 minutes. Serve shrimp warm along with sauce and lemon slices on the side.

Holiday Shrimp Scampi

Serves: 4 | Total Time: 25 minutes

1 ½ lb peeled shrimp, deveined	
¼ tsp lemon pepper seasoning	
6 garlic cloves, minced	3 tbsp sunflower oil
1 tsp salt	3 tbsp butter
½ tsp grated lemon zest	2 tsp fresh thyme leaves
3 tbsp fresh lemon juice	1 lemon, cut into wedges

Preheat the air fryer to 400°F. Combine the shrimp and garlic in a cake pan, then sprinkle with salt and lemon pepper seasoning. Toss to coat, then add the lemon zest, lemon juice, oil, and butter. Place the cake pan in the frying basket and Bake for 10-13 minutes, stirring once, until no longer pink. Sprinkle with thyme leaves. Serve hot with lemon wedges on the side.

Oyster Shrimp with Fried Rice

Serves: 4 | Total Time: 40 minutes

1 lb peeled shrimp, deveined	2 eggs, beaten
1 shallot, chopped	2 cups cooked rice
2 garlic cloves, minced	1 cup baby peas
1 tbsp olive oil	2 tbsp fish sauce
1 tbsp butter	1 tbsp oyster sauce

Preheat the air fryer to 370°F. Combine the shrimp, shallot, garlic, and olive oil in a cake pan. Put the cake pan in the air fryer and Bake the shrimp for 5-7 minutes, stirring once, until shrimp are no pinker. Remove into a bowl, and set aside. Put the butter in the hot cake pan to melt. Add the eggs and return to the fryer. Bake for 4-6 minutes, stirring once, until the eggs are set. Remove the eggs from the pan and set aside.

Add the rice, peas, oyster sauce, and fish sauce to the pan and return it to the fryer. Bake for 12-15 minutes, stirring once halfway through. Pour in the shrimp and eggs and stir. Cook for 2-3 more minutes until everything is hot.

Corn & Shrimp Boil

Serves: 4 | Total Time: 40 minutes

8 frozen "mini" corn on the cob

1 tbsp smoked paprika	1 tsp cayenne pepper
2 tsp dried thyme	1 lb baby potatoes, halved
1 tsp dried marjoram	1 tbsp olive oil
1 tsp sea salt	1 lb peeled shrimp, deveined
1 tsp garlic powder	1 avocado, sliced
1 tsp onion powder	

Preheat the air fryer to 370°F. Combine the paprika, thyme, marjoram, salt, garlic, onion, and cayenne and mix well. Pour into a small glass jar. Add the potatoes, corn, and olive oil to the frying basket and sprinkle with 2 tsp of the spice mix and toss. Air Fry for 15 minutes, shaking the basket once until tender. Remove and set aside. Put the shrimp in the frying basket and sprinkle with 2 tsp of the spice mix. Air Fry for 5-8 minutes, shaking once until shrimp are tender and pink. Combine all the ingredients in the frying basket and sprinkle with 2 tsp of the spice mix. Toss to coat and cook for 1-2 more minutes or until hot. Serve topped with avocado.

Salty German-Style Shrimp Pancakes

Serves: 4 | Total Time: 15 minutes

1 tbsp butter	⅛ tsp salt
3 eggs, beaten	1 cup salsa
½ cup flour	1 cup cooked shrimp, minced
½ cup milk	2 tbsp cilantro, chopped

Preheat air fryer to 390°F. Mix the eggs, flour, milk, and salt in a bowl until frothy. Pour the batter into a greased baking pan and place it in the air fryer. Bake for 15 minutes or until the pancake is puffed and golden. Flip the pancake onto a plate. Mix the salsa, shrimp, and cilantro. Top the pancake with the mixture and serve.

The Best Shrimp Risotto

Serves: 4 | Total Time: 50 minutes + 5 minutes to sit

1/3 cup grated Parmesan	Salt and pepper to taste
2 tbsp olive oil	1 cup Carnaroli rice
1 lb peeled shrimp, deveined	2 1/3 cups vegetable stock
1 onion, chopped	2 tbsp butter
1 red bell pepper, chopped	1 tbsp heavy cream

Preheat the air fryer to 380°F. Add a tbsp of olive oil to a cake pan, then toss in the shrimp. Put the pan in the frying basket and cook the shrimp for 4-7 minutes or until they curl and pinken. Remove the shrimp and set aside. Add the other tbsp of olive oil to the cake pan, then add the onion, bell pepper, salt, and pepper and Air Fry for 3 minutes. Add the rice to the cake pan, stir, and cook for 2 minutes. Add the stock, stir again, and cover the pan with foil. Bake for another 18-22 minutes, stirring twice until the rice is tender. Remove the foil. Return the shrimp to the pan along with butter, heavy cream, and Parmesan, then cook for another minute. Stir and serve.

Seared Scallops in Beurre Blanc

Serves: 4 | Total Time: 15 minutes

1 lb sea scallops	1 lemon, zested and juiced
Salt and pepper to taste	2 tbsp dry white wine
2 tbsp butter, melted	

Preheat the air fryer to 400°F. Sprinkle the scallops with salt and pepper, then set in a bowl. Combine the butter, lemon zest, lemon juice, and white wine in another bowl; mix well. Put the scallops in a baking pan and drizzle over them the mixture. Air Fry for 8-11 minutes, flipping over at about 5 minutes until opaque. Serve and enjoy!

Shrimp Taquitos

Serves: 4 | Total Time: 30 minutes

1 shallot, chopped	2 tbsp minced fresh parsley
2 garlic cloves, minced	Salt to taste
2 tbsp avocado oil	8 corn tortillas, warm
1 tomato, diced	4 tsp grated pepper jack cheese
1 lb peeled shrimp, chopped	1 cup guacamole

Warm the avocado oil in a skillet over medium heat. Sauté shallot and garlic for 3 minutes until soft. Add tomato and cook for 4 minutes until thickened. Stir in shrimp, parsley, and salt for 1 minute.

Preheat air fryer to 400°F. Divide the mixture between the tortillas and top with cheese; roll them around the filling. Place the taquitos in the greased frying basket and Air Fry for 7-10 minutes or until the tortillas are golden and slightly crisp. Serve taquitos with guacamole.

MEAT RECIPES

Golden Pork Quesadillas

Serves: 2 | Total Time: 50 minutes

¼ cup shredded Monterey jack cheese
2 tortilla wraps
4 oz pork shoulder, sliced
1 tsp taco seasoning
½ white onion, sliced
½ red bell pepper, sliced
½ green bell pepper, sliced
½ yellow bell pepper, sliced
1 tsp chopped cilantro

Preheat air fryer to 350°F. Place the pork, onion, bell peppers, and taco seasoning in the greased frying basket. Air Fry for 20 minutes, stirring twice; remove.

Sprinkle half the shredded Monterey jack cheese over one of the tortilla wraps, cover with the pork mixture, and scatter with the remaining cheese and cilantro. Top with the second tortilla wrap. Place in the frying basket. Bake for 12 minutes, flipping once halfway through cooking until the tortillas are browned and crisp. Let cool for a few minutes before slicing. Serve and enjoy!

Egg Stuffed Pork Meatballs

Serves: 2 | Total Time: 40 minutes

3 soft boiled eggs, peeled
8 oz ground pork
2 tsp dried tarragon
½ tsp hot paprika
2 tsp garlic powder
Salt and pepper to taste

Preheat air fryer to 350°F. Combine the pork, tarragon, hot paprika, garlic powder, salt, and pepper in a bowl and stir until all spices are evenly spread throughout the meat. Divide the meat mixture into three equal portions in the mixing bowl, and shape each into balls.

Flatten one of the meatballs on top to make a wide, flat meat circle. Place an egg in the middle. Use your hands to mold the mixture up and around to enclose the egg. Repeat with the remaining eggs. Place the stuffed balls in the air fryer. Air Fry for 18-20 minutes, shaking the basket once until the meat is crispy and golden brown. Serve.

Cajun Pork Loin Chops

Serves: 4 | Total Time: 25 minutes

8 thin boneless pork loin chops
¾ tsp sea salt
1 egg, beaten
1 tsp Cajun seasoning
½ cup bread crumbs
1 cucumber, sliced
1 tomato, sliced

Place the chops between two sheets of parchment paper. Pound the pork to ¼-inch thickness using a meat mallet or rolling pin. Season with sea salt. In a shallow bowl, beat the egg with 1 tsp of water and Cajun seasoning. In a second bowl, add the breadcrumbs. Dip the chops into the egg mixture, shake, and dip into the crumbs.

Preheat air fryer to 400°F. Place the chops in the greased frying basket and Air Fry for 6-8 minutes, flipping once until golden and cooked through. Serve immediately with cucumber and tomato.

Grilled Pork & Bell Pepper Salad

Serves: 4 | Total Time: 25 minutes

1 cup sautéed button mushrooms, sliced
2 lb pork tenderloin, sliced
1 tsp olive oil
1 tsp dried marjoram
6 tomato wedges
6 green olives
6 cups mixed salad greens
1 red bell pepper, sliced
1/3 cup vinaigrette dressing

Preheat air fryer to 400°F. Combine the pork and olive oil, making sure the pork is well-coated. Season with marjoram. Lay the pork in the air fryer. Grill for 4-6 minutes, turning once until the pork is cooked through.

While the pork is cooking, toss the salad greens, red bell pepper, tomatoes, olives, and mushrooms into a bowl. Lay the pork slices on top of the salad, season with vinaigrette, and toss. Serve while the pork is still warm.

Wasabi Pork Medallions

Serves: 4 | Total Time: 20 minutes + marinate time

1 lb pork medallions
1 cup soy sauce
1 tbsp mirin
½ cup olive oil
3 cloves garlic, crushed
1 tsp fresh grated ginger
1 tsp wasabi paste
1 tbsp brown sugar

Place all ingredients, except for the pork, in a resealable bag and shake to combine. Add the pork medallions to the bag, shake again, and place in the fridge to marinate for 2 hours. Preheat air fryer to 360°F. Remove pork medallions from the marinade and place them in the frying basket in rows. Air Fry for 14-16 minutes or until the medallions are cooked through and juicy. Serve.

Mushroom & Quinoa-Stuffed Pork Loins

Serves: 3 | Total Time: 25 minutes

3 boneless center-cut pork loins, pocket cut in each loin
½ cup diced white mushrooms
1 tsp vegetable oil
3 bacon slices, diced
½ onion, peeled and diced
1 cup baby spinach
Salt and pepper to taste
½ cup cooked quinoa
½ cup mozzarella cheese

Warm the oil in a skillet over medium heat. Add the bacon and cook for 3 minutes until the fat is rendered but not crispy. Add onion and mushrooms and stir-fry for 3 minutes until the onions are translucent. Stir in spinach, salt, and pepper and cook for 1 minute until the spinach wilts. Set aside and toss in quinoa.

Preheat air fryer to 350°F. Stuff quinoa mixture into each pork loin and sprinkle with mozzarella cheese. Place them in the frying basket and Air Fry for 10-12 minutes. Let rest on a cutting board for 5 minutes before serving.

Horseradish Mustard Pork Chops

Serves 2 | Total Time: 20 minutes

½ cup grated Pecorino cheese
1 egg white
1 tbsp horseradish mustard
¼ tsp black pepper
2 pork chops
¼ cup chopped cilantro

Preheat air fryer to 350°F. Whisk egg white and horseradish mustard in a bowl. In another bowl, combine Pecorino cheese and black pepper. Dip pork chops in the mustard mixture, then dredge them in the Parmesan mixture. Place pork chops in the frying basket lightly greased with olive oil and Air Fry for 12-14 minutes until cooked through and tender, flipping twice. Transfer the chops to a cutting board and let sit for 5 minutes. Scatter with cilantro to serve.

Kochukaru Pork Lettuce Cups

Serves: 4 | Total Time: 25 minutes + marinating time

1 tsp kochukaru (chili pepper flakes)
12 baby romaine lettuce leaves
1 lb pork tenderloin, sliced   ½ tbsp honey
Salt and pepper to taste   1 tbsp grated fresh ginger
3 scallions, chopped   2 tbsp rice vinegar
3 garlic cloves, crushed   1 tsp toasted sesame oil
¼ cup soy sauce   2 ¼ cups cooked brown rice
2 tbsp gochujang   ½ tbsp sesame seeds
½ tbsp light brown sugar   2 spring onions, sliced

Mix the scallions, garlic, soy sauce, kochukaru, honey, brown sugar, and ginger in a small bowl. Mix well. Place the pork in a large bowl. Season with salt and pepper. Pour the marinade over the pork, tossing the meat in the marinade until coated. Cover the bowl with plastic wrap and allow to marinate overnight. When ready to cook,

Preheat air fryer to 400°F. Remove the pork from the bowl and discard the marinade. Place the pork in the greased frying basket and Air Fry for 10 minutes, flipping once until browned and cooked through. To prepare the gochujang sauce, whisk the gochujang, rice vinegar, and sesame oil until smooth in a bowl. Divide the brown rice between the lettuce leaves. Place a slice of pork on top of each leaf, drizzle with gochujang sauce and sprinkle with sesame seeds and spring onions. Wrap the lettuce over the mixture, similar to a burrito. Serve warm.

Chinese-Style Lamb Chops

Serves: 4 | Total Time: 25 minutes + marinating time

8 lamb chops, trimmed   ¼ cup dark soy sauce
2 tbsp scallions, sliced   2 tsp orange juice
¼ tsp Chinese five-spice   3 tbsp honey
3 garlic cloves, crushed   ½ tbsp light brown sugar
½ tsp ginger powder   ¼ tsp red pepper flakes

Season the chops with garlic, ginger, soy sauce, five-spice powder, orange juice, and honey in a bowl. Toss to coat. Cover the bowl with plastic wrap and marinate for 2 hours and up to overnight.

Preheat air fryer to 400°F. Remove the chops from the bowl but reserve the marinade. Place the chops in the greased frying basket and Bake for 5 minutes. Using tongs, flip the chops. Brush the lamb with the reserved marinade, then sprinkle with brown sugar and pepper flakes. Cook for another 4 minutes until brown and caramelized medium-rare. Serve with scallions on top.

Sriracha Pork Strips with Rice

Serves: 4 | Total Time: 30 minutes + chilling time

½ cup lemon juice   1 tsp yellow mustard
2 tbsp lemon marmalade   1 lb pork shoulder strips
1 tbsp avocado oil   4 cups cooked white rice
1 tbsp tamari   ¼ cup chopped cilantro
2 tsp sriracha   1 tsp black pepper

Whisk the lemon juice, lemon marmalade, avocado oil, tamari, sriracha, and mustard in a bowl. Reserve half of the marinade. Toss pork strips with half of the marinade and let marinate covered in the fridge for 30 minutes.

Preheat air fryer to 350°F. Place pork strips in the frying basket and Air Fry for 17 minutes, tossing twice. Transfer them to a bowl and stir in the remaining marinade. Serve over cooked rice and scatter with cilantro and pepper.

Lemon Pork Escalopes

Serves: 4 | Total Time: 45 minutes

4 pork loin chops   ½ tbsp thyme, chopped
1 cup breadcrumbs   ½ tsp smoked paprika
2 eggs, beaten   ½ tsp ground cumin
Salt and pepper to taste   1 lemon, zested

Preheat air fryer to 350°F. Mix the breadcrumbs, thyme, smoked paprika, cumin, lemon zest, salt, and pepper in a bowl. Add the pork chops and toss to coat. Dip in the beaten eggs, then dip again into the dry ingredients. Place the coated chops in the greased frying basket and Air Fry for 16-18 minutes, turning once. Serve and enjoy!

Kawaii Pork Roast

Serves: 6 | Total Time: 50 minutes

Salt and white pepper to taste   ¼ tsp ground ginger
2 tbsp soy sauce   1 tsp oregano
2 tbsp honey   2 cloves garlic, minced
1 tbsp sesame oil   1 (2-lb) boneless pork loin

Preheat air fryer to 350°F. Mix all ingredients in a bowl. Massage the mixture into all sides of the pork loin. Place pork loin in the greased frying basket and Roast for 40 minutes, flipping once. Let rest on a cutting board for 5 minutes before slicing. Serve right away.

Greek Pork Chops

Serves: 4 | Total Time: 30 minutes

3 tbsp grated Halloumi cheese
4 pork chops   ¼ cup all-purpose flour
1 tsp Greek seasoning   2 tbsp bread crumbs
Salt and pepper to taste

Preheat air fryer to 380°F. Season the pork chops with Greek seasoning, salt, and pepper. In a shallow bowl, add flour. In another shallow bowl, combine the crumbs and Halloumi. Dip the chops in the flour, then in the bread crumbs. Place them in the fryer and spray with cooking oil. Bake for 12-14 minutes, flipping once. Serve warm.

Traditional Moo Shu Pork Lettuce Wraps

Serves: 4 | Total Time: 40 minutes

½ cup sliced shiitake mushrooms
1 lb boneless pork loin, cubed ¼ tsp ground ginger
3 tbsp cornstarch   1 egg
2 tbsp rice vinegar   2 tbsp flour
3 tbsp hoisin sauce   1 (14-oz) bag coleslaw mix
1 tsp oyster sauce   1 cup chopped baby spinach
3 tsp sesame oil   3 green onions, sliced
1 tsp sesame seeds   8 iceberg lettuce leaves

Preheat air fryer to 350°F. Make a slurry by whisking 1 tbsp of cornstarch and 1 tbsp of water in a bowl. Set aside. Warm a saucepan over heat, add rice vinegar, hoisin sauce, oyster sauce, 1 tsp of sesame oil, and ginger, and cook for 3 minutes, stirring often. Add in cornstarch slurry and cook for 1 minute. Set aside and let the mixture thicken. Beat the egg, flour, and the remaining cornstarch in a bowl. Set aside.

Dredge pork cubes in the egg mixture. Shake off any excess. Place them in the greased frying basket and Air Fry for 8 minutes, shaking once. Warm the remaining sesame oil in a skillet over medium heat. Add in coleslaw mix, baby spinach, green onions, and mushrooms and cook for 5 minutes until the coleslaw wilts. Turn the heat off. Add in cooked pork, pour in oyster sauce mixture, and toss until coated. Divide mixture between lettuce leaves, sprinkle with sesame seed, roll them up, and serve.

Suwon Pork Meatballs

Serves: 4 | Total Time: 30 minutes

1 lb ground pork   ¼ tsp ground ginger
1 egg   ¼ cup bread crumbs
1 tsp cumin   1 scallion, sliced
1 tbsp gochujang   4 tbsp plum jam
1 tsp tamari   1 tsp toasted sesame seeds

Preheat air fryer to 350°F. In a bowl, combine all ingredients, except scallion greens, sesame seeds and plum jam. Form mixture into meatballs. Place meatballs in the greased frying basket and Air Fry for 8 minutes, flipping once. Garnish with scallion greens, plum jam and toasted sesame seeds to serve.

Blossom BBQ Pork Chops

Serves: 2 | Total Time: 20 minutes

2 tbsp cherry preserves   1 tbsp lime juice
1 tbsp honey   1 tbsp olive oil
1 tbsp Dijon mustard   2 cloves garlic, minced
2 tsp light brown sugar   1 tbsp chopped parsley
1 tsp Worcestershire sauce 2 pork chops

Mix all ingredients in a bowl. Toss in pork chops. Let marinate covered in the fridge for 30 minutes.

Preheat air fryer to 350°F. Place pork chops in the greased frying basket and Air Fry for 12 minutes, turning once. Let rest on a cutting board for 5 minutes. Serve.

Sticky Teriyaki Pork Ribs

Serves: 4 | Total Time: 50 minutes

3 lb rack ribs, cut into individual bones
3 tbsp Teriyaki sauce   Black pepper to taste
2 tbsp honey   1 tsp ginger powder
3 tbsp ketchup   1 tbsp sesame seeds

Preheat air fryer to 380°F. Toss the ribs with all the ingredients, except for the sesame seeds, in a baking pan that fit in the fryer to coat. Air Fry for 40 minutes, flipping every 10 minutes. Top with sesame seeds and serve.

Italian Stuffed Bell Peppers

Serves: 4 | Total Time: 35 minutes

1 link sweet Italian pork sausage
12 turkey pepperoni slices, halved
1½ cups shredded mozzarella 1 cup passata sauce
4 red bell peppers   2 tbsp fresh basil, picked

Preheat air fryer to 370°F. Bake sausage in the frying basket for 10 minutes, flipping once until cooked. Remove and let cool. Chop into small pieces. Cut the peppers in half lengthwise. Remove the seeds and membranes. Reduce the air fryer temperature to 350°F. Put the peppers in the greased frying basket and Bake for 6-8, flipping once until just softened.

Divide the passata between the pepper halves. Top with mozzarella cheese, sausage pieces, and pepperoni halves. Sprinkle with basil. Place the stuffed peppers in the greased frying basket and Bake until the cheese has melted and the passata is warmed through, 7 minutes. Serve warm.

Crispy Pork Pork Escalopes

Serves: 4 | Total Time: 20 minutes

4 pork loin steaks   ¼ cup flour
Salt and pepper to taste 2 tbsp bread crumbs

Preheat air fryer to 380°F. Season pork with salt and pepper. In one shallow bowl, add flour. In another, add bread crumbs. Dip the steaks first in the flour, then in the crumbs. Place them in the fryer and spray with oil. Bake for 12-14 minutes, flipping once until crisp. Serve.

Aromatic Pork Tenderloin

Serves: 6 | Total Time: 65 minutes

1 (3-lb) pork tenderloin 1 tsp dried marjoram
2 tbsp olive oil   1 tsp dried thyme
2 garlic cloves, minced   1 tsp paprika
1 tsp dried sage   Salt and pepper to taste

Preheat air fryer to 360°F. Drizzle oil over the tenderloin, then rub the garlic, sage, marjoram, thyme, paprika, salt, and pepper all over. Place the tenderloin in the greased frying basket and Bake for 45 minutes. Flip the pork and cook for another 15 minutes. Check the temperature for doneness. Let the cooked tenderloin rest for 10 minutes before slicing. Serve and enjoy!

Pork Chops with Cereal Crust

Serves: 2 | Total Time: 20 minutes

¼ cup grated Parmesan	¼ tsp cumin powder
1 egg	¼ tsp nutmeg
1 tbsp Dijon mustard	1 tsp horseradish powder
¼ cup crushed bran cereal	2 pork chops
¼ tsp black pepper	

Preheat air fryer to 350°F. Whisk egg and mustard in a bowl. In another bowl, combine Parmesan cheese, cumin powder, nutmeg, horseradish powder, bran cereal, and black pepper. Dip pork chops in the egg mixture, then dredge them in the cheese mixture. Place pork chops in the frying basket and Air Fry for 12 minutes, tossing once. Let rest on a cutting board for 5 minutes. Serve.

Country-Style Pork Ribs

Serves: 4 | Total Time: 30 minutes

2 tbsp cornstarch	½ tsp garlic powder
2 tbsp olive oil	1 tsp paprika
1 tsp mustard powder	Salt and pepper to taste
½ tsp thyme	12 country-style pork ribs

Preheat air fryer to 400°F. Mix together cornstarch, olive oil, mustard powder, thyme, garlic powder, paprika, salt, and pepper in a bowl. Rub the seasoned mixture onto the ribs. Put the ribs into the frying basket. Bake for 14-16 minutes, flipping once until the ribs are crisp. Serve.

Italian Sausage Bake

Serves: 4 | Total Time: 25 minutes

1 cup red bell pepper, strips	1/3 cup ketchup
¾ lb Italian sausage, sliced	2 tbsp mustard
½ cup minced onions	2 tbsp apple cider vinegar
3 tbsp brown sugar	½ cup chicken broth

Preheat air fryer to 350°F. Combine the Italian sausage, bell pepper, and minced onion into a bowl. Stir well. Mix together brown sugar, ketchup, mustard, apple cider vinegar, and chicken broth in a small bowl. Pour over the sausage. Place the bowl in the air fryer, and Bake until the sausage is hot, the vegetables are tender, and the sauce is bubbling and thickened, 10-15 minutes. Serve and enjoy!

Pork Tenderloin with Apples & Celery

Serves: 4 | Total Time: 30 minutes

1 lb pork tenderloin, cut into 4 pieces	
2 Granny Smith apples, sliced	
1 tbsp butter, melted	1 onion, sliced
2 tsp olive oil	2 tsp dried thyme
3 celery stalks, sliced	1/3 cup apple juice

Preheat air fryer to 400°F. Brush olive oil and butter all over the pork, then toss the pork, apples, celery, onion, thyme, and apple juice in a bowl and mix well. Put the bowl in the air fryer and Roast for 15-19 minutes until the pork is cooked through and the apples and veggies are soft, stirring once during cooking. Serve warm.

Exotic Pork Skewers

Serves: 4 | Total Time: 30 minutes

1/3 cup apricot jam	1 lb pork tenderloin, cubed
2 tbsp lemon juice	4 pitted cherries, halved
2 tsp olive oil	4 pitted apricots, halved
½ tsp dried tarragon	

Preheat air fryer to 380°F. Toss the jam, lemon juice, olive oil, and tarragon in a big bowl and mix well. Place the pork in the bowl, then stir well to coat. Allow marinating for 10 minutes. Poke 4 metal skewers through the pork, cherries, and apricots, alternating ingredients. Use a cooking brush to rub the marinade on the skewers, then place them in the air fryer. Toss the rest of the marinade. Air Fry the kebabs for 4-6 minutes on each side until the pork is cooked through and the fruit is soft. Serve!

French-Style Pork Medallions

Serves: 4 | Total Time: 25 minutes

1 lb pork medallions	1 shallot, diced
Salt and pepper to taste	1cup chicken stock
½ tsp dried marjoram	2 tbsp Dijon mustard
2 tbsp butter	2 tbsp grainy mustard
1 tbsp olive oil	1/3 cup heavy cream
1 tsp garlic powder	

Preheat the air fryer to 350°F. Pound the pork medallions with a rolling pin to about ¼ inch thickness. Rub them with salt, pepper, garlic, and marjoram. Place into the greased frying basket and Bake for 7 minutes or until almost done. Remove and wipe the basket clean. Combine the butter, olive oil, shallot, and stock in a baking pan, and set it in the frying basket. Bake for 5 minutes or until the shallot is crispy and tender. Add the mustard and heavy cream and cook for 4 more minutes or until the mix starts to thicken. Then add the pork to the sauce and cook for 5 more minutes, or until the sauce simmers. Remove and serve warm.

Indonesian Pork Satay

Serves: 4 | Total Time: 30 minutes + marinating time

1 lb pork tenderloin, cubed	2 tbsp coconut milk
¼ cup minced onion	½ tbsp ground coriander
2 garlic cloves, minced	½ tsp ground cumin
1 jalapeño pepper, minced	2 tbsp peanut butter
2 tbsp lime juice	2 tsp curry powder

Combine the pork, onion, garlic, jalapeño, lime juice, coconut milk, peanut butter, ground coriander, cumin, and curry powder in a bowl. Stir well and allow to marinate for 10 minutes.

Preheat air fryer to 380°F. Use a holey spoon and take the pork out of the marinade and set the marinade aside. Poke 8 bamboo skewers through the meat, then place the skewers in the air fryer. Use a cooking brush to rub the marinade on each skewer, then Grill for 10-14 minutes, adding more marinade if necessary. The pork should be golden and cooked when finished. Serve warm.

Italian Sausage Rolls

Serves: 4 | Total Time: 20 minutes

1 red bell pepper, cut into strips
4 Italian sausages
1 zucchini, cut into strips
½ onion, cut into strips

1 tsp dried oregano
½ tsp garlic powder
5 Italian rolls

Preheat air fryer to 360°F. Place all sausages in the air fryer. Bake for 10 minutes. While the sausages are cooking, season the bell pepper, zucchini and onion with oregano and garlic powder. When the time is up, flip the sausages, then add the peppers and onions. Cook for another 5 minutes or until the vegetables are soft and the sausages are cooked through. Put the sausage on Italian rolls, then top with peppers and onions. Serve.

Sriracha Short Ribs

Serves: 4 | Total Time: 15 minutes + marinating time

2 tsp sesame seeds
8 pork short ribs
½ cup soy sauce
¼ cup rice wine vinegar
½ cup chopped onion

2 garlic cloves, minced
1 tbsp sesame oil
1 tsp sriracha sauce
4 scallions, thinly sliced
Salt and pepper to taste

Put short ribs in a resealable bag. Add the soy sauce, rice wine vinegar, onion, garlic, sesame oil, sriracha sauce, half of the scallions, salt, and pepper. Seal the bag and toss to coat. Refrigerate for one hour.

Preheat air fryer to 380°F. Place the short ribs in the air fryer. Bake for 8-10 minutes, flipping once until crisp. When the ribs are done, garnish with remaining scallions and sesame seeds. Serve and enjoy!

Tarragon Pork Tenderloin

Serves: 4 | Total Time: 25 minutes

½ tsp dried tarragon
1 lb pork tenderloin, sliced
Salt and pepper to taste
2 tbsp Dijon mustard

1 garlic clove, minced
1 cup bread crumbs
2 tbsp olive oil

Preheat air fryer to 390°F. Using a rolling pin, pound the pork slices until they are about ¾ inch thick. Season both sides with salt and pepper. Coat the pork with mustard and season with garlic and tarragon. In a shallow bowl, mix bread crumbs and olive oil. Dredge the pork with the bread crumbs, pressing firmly so that it adheres. Put the pork in the frying basket and Air Fry until the pork outside is brown and crisp, 12-14 minutes. Serve warm.

Tamari-Seasoned Pork Strips

Serves 4 | Total Time: 40 minutes + marinating time

3 tbsp olive oil
2 tbsp tamari
2 tsp red chili paste
2 tsp yellow mustard
2 tsp granulated sugar
1 lb pork shoulder strips

1 cup white rice, cooked
6 scallions, chopped
½ tsp garlic powder
1 tbsp lemon juice
1 tsp lemon zest
½ tsp salt

Add 2 tbsp of olive oil, tamari, chili paste, mustard, and sugar to a bowl and whisk until everything is well mixed. Set aside half of the marinade. Toss pork strips in the remaining marinade and put in the fridge for 30 minutes. Preheat air fryer to 350°F. Place the pork strips in the frying basket and Air Fry for 16-18 minutes, tossing once. Transfer cooked pork to the bowl along with the remaining marinade and toss to coat. Set aside. In a medium bowl, stir in the cooked rice, garlic, lemon juice, lemon zest, and salt and cover. Spread on a serving plate. Arrange the pork strips over and top with scallions. Serve.

Chorizo & Veggie Bake

Serves: 4 | Total Time: 40 minutes

1 cup halved Brussels sprouts
1 lb baby potatoes, halved
1 cup baby carrots
1 onion, sliced
2 garlic cloves, sliced

2 tbsp olive oil
Salt and pepper to taste
1 lb chorizo sausages, sliced
2 tbsp Dijon mustard

Preheat the air fryer to 370°F. Put the potatoes, Brussels sprouts, baby carrots, garlic, and onion in the frying basket and drizzle with olive oil. Sprinkle with salt and pepper; toss to coat. Bake for 15 minutes or until the veggies are crisp but tender, shaking once during cooking. Add the chorizo sausages to the fryer and cook for 8-12 minutes, shaking once until the sausages are hot and the veggies tender. Drizzle with the mustard to serve.

Texas-Style Pork Ribs

Serves 4 | Total Time: 45 minutes + marinating time

2 lb country-style pork ribs
3 tsp garlic powder
3 tsp onion powder
Salt and pepper to taste

1 ½ tsp lemon pepper
2 tsp smoked paprika
1 tsp cayenne pepper
1 cup BBQ sauce

Combine garlic powder, onion powder, salt, pepper, lemon pepper, smoked paprika, and cayenne in a bowl. Add the ribs and toss to coat. Refrigerate for at least 1 hour. Preheat air fryer to 390°F. Brush the ribs with some BBQ sauce. Air Fry for 30-35 minutes, flipping and brushing them with the remaining BBQ sauce every 10 minutes.

Oktoberfest Bratwursts

Serves 4 | Total Time: 35 minutes

½ onion, cut into half-moons
1 lb pork bratwurst links
2 cups beef broth

1 cup beer
2 cups drained sauerkraut
2 tbsp German mustard

Pierce each bratwurst with a fork twice. Place them along with beef broth, beer, 1 cup of water, and onion in a saucepan over high heat and bring to a boil. Lower the heat and simmer for 15 minutes. Drain.

Preheat air fryer to 400°F. Place bratwursts and onion in the frying basket and Air Fry for 3 minutes. Flip bratwursts, add the sauerkraut and cook for 3 more minutes. Serve warm with mustard on the side.

Coffee-Rubbed Pork Tenderloin

Serves: 4 | Total Time: 30 minutes

1 tbsp packed brown sugar	1 tbsp honey
2 tsp espresso powder	½ tbsp lemon juice
1 tsp bell pepper powder	2 tsp olive oil
½ tsp dried parsley	1 pound pork tenderloin

Preheat air fryer to 400°F. Toss the brown sugar, espresso powder, bell pepper powder, and parsley in a bowl and mix together. Add the honey, lemon juice, and olive oil, then stir well. Smear the pork with the mix, then marinate for 10 minutes. before putting it in the air fryer. Roast for 9-11 minutes until the pork is cooked through. Slice before serving. Enjoy!

Hungarian Pork Burgers

Serves: 4 | Total Time: 30 minutes

8 sandwich buns, halved	¼ cup grated carrots
½ cup mayonnaise	1 lb ground pork
2 tbsp mustard	½ tsp Hungarian paprika
1 tbsp lemon juice	1 cup lettuce, torn
¼ cup sliced red cabbage	2 tomatoes, sliced

Mix the mayonnaise, 1 tbsp of mustard, lemon juice, cabbage, and carrots in a bowl. Refrigerate for 10 minutes.

Preheat air fryer to 400°F. Toss the pork, remaining mustard, and paprika in a bowl, mix, then make 8 patties. Place them in the air fryer and Air Fry for 7-9 minutes, flipping once until cooked through. Put some lettuce on one bottom bun, then top with a tomato slice, one burger, and some cabbage mix. Put another bun on top and serve. Repeat for all burgers. Serve and enjoy!

Sage Pork with Potatoes

Serves: 4 | Total Time: 30 minutes

2 cups potatoes	2 garlic cloves, minced
2 tsp olive oil	½ tsp dried sage
1 lb pork tenderloin, cubed	½ tsp fennel seeds, crushed
1 onion, chopped	2 tbsp chicken broth
1 red bell pepper, chopped	

Preheat air fryer to 370°F. Add the potatoes and olive oil to a bowl and toss to coat. Transfer them to the frying basket and Air Fry for 15 minutes. Remove the bowl. Add the pork, onion, red bell pepper, garlic, sage, and fennel seeds, to the potatoes, add chicken broth and stir gently. Return the bowl to the frying basket and cook for 10 minutes. Be sure to shake the basket at least once. The pork should be cooked through and the potatoes soft and crispy. Serve immediately.

Peachy Pork Chops

Serves: 2 | Total Time: 20 minutes

2 tbsp peach preserves	1 tbsp lime juice
2 tbsp tomato paste	1 tbsp olive oil
1 tbsp Dijon mustard	2 cloves garlic, minced
1 tsp BBQ sauce	2 pork chops

Whisk all ingredients in a bowl until well mixed and let chill covered in the fridge for 30 minutes. Preheat air fryer to 350°F. Place pork chops in the frying basket and Air Fry for 12 minutes or until cooked through and tender. Transfer the chops to a cutting board and let sit for 5 minutes before serving.

Pork Kabobs with Pineapple

Serves: 4 | Total Time: 30 minutes

2 (8-oz) cans juice-packed pineapple chunks, juice reserved	
1 green bell pepper, cut into ½-inch chunks	
1 red bell pepper, cut into ½-inch chunks	
1 lb pork tenderloin, cubed	½ tsp ground ginger
Salt and pepper to taste	½ tsp ground coriander
1 tbsp honey	1 red chili, minced

Preheat the air fryer to 375°F. Mix the coriander, chili, salt, and pepper in a bowl. Add the pork and toss to coat. Then, thread the pork pieces, pineapple chunks, and bell peppers onto skewers. Combine the pineapple juice, honey, and ginger and mix well. Use all the mixture as you brush it on the kebabs. Put the kebabs in the greased frying basket and Air Fry for 10-14 minutes or until cooked through. Serve and enjoy!

Kentucky-Style Pork Tenderloin

Serves 2 | Total Time: 30 minutes

1 lb pork tenderloin, halved crosswise	
1 tbsp smoked paprika	Salt and pepper to taste
2 tsp ground cumin	1 tsp Italian seasoning
1 tsp garlic powder	2 tbsp butter, melted
1 tsp shallot powder	1 tsp Worcestershire sauce
¼ tsp chili pepper	

Preheat air fryer to 350°F. In a shallow bowl, combine all spices. Set aside. In another bowl, whisk butter and Worcestershire sauce and brush over pork tenderloin. Sprinkle with the seasoning mix. Place pork in the lightly greased frying basket and Air Fry for 16 minutes, flipping once. Let sit onto a cutting board for 5 minutes before slicing. Serve immediately.

Cheesy Mushroom-Stuffed Pork Loins

Serves: 3 | Total Time: 30 minutes

¾ cup diced mushrooms	Salt and pepper to taste
2 tsp olive oil	3 center-cut pork loins
1 shallot, diced	6 Gruyère cheese slices

Warm the olive oil in a skillet over medium heat. Add in shallot and mushrooms and stir-fry for 3 minutes. Sprinkle with salt and pepper and cook for 1 minute.

Preheat air fryer to 350°F. Cut a pocket into each pork loin and set aside. Stuff an even amount of mushroom mixture into each chop pocket and top with 2 Gruyere cheese slices into each pocket. Place the pork in the lightly greased frying basket and Air Fry for 10-12 minutes until the pork is cooked through and the cheese has melted. Let sit onto a cutting board for 5 minutes before serving.

Citrus Pork Lettuce Wraps

Serves 4 | Total Time: 35 minutes

Salt and white pepper to taste	2 tsp olive oil
1 tbsp cornstarch	¼ tsp chili pepper
1 tbsp red wine vinegar	¼ tsp ground ginger
2 tbsp orange marmalade	1 lb pork loin, cubed
1 tsp pulp-free orange juice	8 iceberg lettuce leaves

Create a slurry by whisking cornstarch and 1 tbsp of water in a bowl. Set aside. Place a small saucepan over medium heat. Add the red wine vinegar, orange marmalade, orange juice, olive oil, chili pepper, and ginger and cook for 3 minutes, stirring continuously. Mix in the slurry and simmer for 1 more minute. Turn the heat off and let it thicken, about3 minutes.

Preheat air fryer to 350°F. Sprinkle the pork with salt and white pepper. Place them in the greased frying basket and Air Fry for 8-10 minutes until cooked through and browned, turning once. Transfer pork cubes to a bowl with the sauce and toss to coat. Serve in lettuce leaves.

Taco Pie with Meatballs

Serves: 4 | Total Time: 40 minutes + cooling time

1 cup shredded quesadilla cheese	
1 cup shredded Colby cheese	
10 cooked meatballs, halved	2 tsp chipotle powder
1 cup salsa	½ tsp ground cumin
1 cup canned refried beans	4 corn tortillas

Preheat the air fryer to 375°F. Combine the meatball halves, salsa, refried beans, chipotle powder, and cumin in a bowl. In a baking pan, add a tortilla and top with one-quarter of the meatball mixture. Sprinkle one-quarter of the cheeses on top and repeat the layers three more times, ending with cheese. Put the pan in the fryer. Bake for 15-20 minutes until the pie is bubbling and the cheese has melted. Let cool on a wire rack for 10 minutes. Run a knife around the edges of the pan and remove the sides of the pan, then cut into wedges to serve.

Homemade Pork Gyoza

Serves: 4 | Total Time: 50 minutes

8 wonton wrappers	1 tbsp vegetable oil
4 oz ground pork, browned	½ tbsp oyster sauce
1 green apple	1 tbsp soy sauce
1 tsp rice vinegar	A pinch of white pepper

Preheat air fryer to 350°F. Combine the oyster sauce, soy sauce, rice vinegar, and white pepper in a small bowl. Add in the pork and stir thoroughly. Peel and core the apple, and slice it into small cubes. Add the apples to the meat mixture, and combine thoroughly. Divide the filling between the wonton wrappers. Wrap the wontons into triangles and seal with a bit of water. Brush the wrappers with vegetable oil. Place them in the greased frying basket. Bake for 25 minutes until crispy golden brown on the outside and juicy and delicious on the inside. Serve.

Authentic Sausage Kartoffel Salad

Serves: 4 | Total Time: 25 minutes

½ lb cooked andouille smoked sausage, sliced	
2 cooked potatoes, cubed	1 tbsp light brown sugar
1 cup chicken broth	2 tbsp cornstarch
2 tbsp olive oil	¼ cup sour cream
1 onion, chopped	1 tsp yellow mustard
2 garlic cloves, minced	2 tbsp chopped chives
¼ cup apple cider vinegar	

Preheat the air fryer to 380°F. Combine the olive oil, onion, garlic, and sausage in a baking pan and put it in the air basket. Bake for 5-7 minutes or until the onions are crispy but tender and the sausages are hot. Slide out the pan and add the broth, vinegar, brown sugar, and cornstarch. Stir to combine and return the pan to the air fryer. Bake for 5 more minutes until hot. Stir the sour cream and yellow mustard into the sauce, add the potatoes, and stir to coat. Cook for another 2-3 minutes or until hot. Serve topped with freshly chopped chives.

Chipotle Pork Meatballs

Serves 4 | Total Time: 35 minutes

1 lb ground pork	¼ cup chopped parsley
1 egg	¼ cup chopped cilantro
¼ cup chipotle sauce	¼ cup flour
¼ cup grated celery	¼ tsp salt

Preheat air fryer to 350°F. In a large bowl, combine the ground pork, egg, chipotle sauce, celery, parsley, cilantro, flour, and salt. Form mixture into 16 meatballs. Place the meatballs in the lightly greased frying basket and Air Fry for 8-10 minutes, flipping once. Serve immediately

Greek-Style Pork Stuffed Jalapeño Poppers

Serves 6 | Total Time: 30 minutes

6 jalapeños, halved lengthwise	2 tbsp feta cheese
3 tbsp diced Kalamata olives	1 oz cream cheese, softened
3 tbsp olive oil	½ tsp dried mint
¼ lb ground pork	½ cup Greek yogurt

Warm 2 tbsp of olive oil in a skillet over medium heat. Stir in ground pork and cook for 6 minutes until no longer pink. Preheat air fryer to 350°F. Mix the cooked pork, olives, feta cheese, and cream cheese in a bowl. Divide the pork mixture between the peppers. Place them in the frying basket and Air Fry for 6 minutes. Mix the Greek yogurt with the remaining olive oil and mint in a small bowl. Serve with the poppers.

Basil Cheese & Ham Stromboli

Serves: 6 | Total Time: 30 minutes

1 (13-oz) can refrigerated pizza dough	
½ cup shredded mozzarella	½ tsp dried basil
½ red bell pepper, sliced	1 tsp garlic powder
2 tsp all-purpose flour	½ tsp oregano
6 Havarti cheese slices	Black pepper to taste
12 deli ham slices	

Preheat air fryer to 400°F. Flour a flat work surface and roll out the pizza dough. Use a knife to cut into 6 equal-sized rectangles. On each rectangle, add 1 slice of Havarti, 1 tbsp of mozzarella, 2 slices of ham, and some red pepper slices. Season with basil, garlic, oregano, and black pepper. Fold one side of the dough over the filling to the opposite side. Press the edges with the back of a fork to seal them. Place one batch of stromboli in the fryer and lightly spray with cooking oil. Air Fry for 10 minutes. Serve and enjoy!

Delicious Juicy Pork Meatballs

Serves 4 | Total Time: 35 minutes

¼ cup grated cheddar cheese
1 lb ground pork
1 egg
1 tbsp Greek yogurt
½ tsp onion powder

¼ cup chopped parsley
2 tbsp bread crumbs
¼ tsp garlic powder
Salt and pepper to taste

Preheat air fryer to 350°F. In a bowl, combine the ground pork, egg, yogurt, onion, parsley, cheddar cheese, bread crumbs, garlic, salt, and black pepper. Form mixture into 16 meatballs. Place meatballs in the lightly greased frying basket and Air Fry for 8-10 minutes, flipping once. Serve.

Pepperoni Bagel Pizzas

Serves: 4 | Total Time: 20 minutes

2 bagels, halved horizontally
2 cups shredded mozzarella
¼ cup grated Parmesan
1 cup passata

1/3 cup sliced pepperoni
2 scallions, chopped
2 tbsp minced fresh chives
1tsp red chili flakes

Preheat the air fryer to 375°F. Put the bagel halves, cut side up, in the frying basket. Bake for 2-3 minutes until golden. Remove and top them with passata, pepperoni, scallions, and cheeses. Put the bagels topping-side up to the frying basket and cook for 8-12 more minutes or until the bagels are hot and the cheese has melted and is bubbling. Top with the chives and chili flakes and serve.

Honey Mustard Pork Roast

Serves 4 | Total Time: 50 minutes

1 (2-lb) boneless pork loin roast
2 tbsp Dijon mustard
2 tsp olive oil
1 tsp honey

1 garlic clove, minced
Salt and pepper to taste
1 tsp dried rosemary

Preheat air fryer to 350°F. Whisk all ingredients in a bowl. Massage into loin on all sides. Place the loin in the frying basket and Roast for 40 minutes, turning once. Let sit onto a cutting board for 5 minutes before slicing. Serve.

Honey Pork Links

Serves 4 | Total Time: 20 minutes

12 oz ground mild pork sausage, removed from casings
1 tsp rubbed sage
2 tbsp honey
⅛ tsp cayenne pepper

⅛ tsp paprika
Salt and pepper to taste

Preheat air fryer to 400°F. Remove the sausage from the casings. Transfer to a bowl and add the remaining ingredients. Mix well. Make 8 links out of the mixture. Add the links to the frying basket and Air Fry for 8-10 minutes, flipping once. Serve right away.

German-Style Pork Patties

Serves: 6 | Total Time: 35 minutes

1 lb ground pork
¼ cup diced fresh pear
1 tbsp minced sage leaves

1 garlic clove, minced
2 tbsp chopped chives
Salt and pepper to taste

Preheat the air fryer to 375°F. Combine the pork, pear, sage, chives, garlic, salt, and pepper in a bowl and mix gently but thoroughly with your hands; then make 8 patties about ½ inch thick. Lay the patties in the frying basket in a single layer and Air Fry for 15-20 minutes, flipping once halfway through. Remove and drain on paper towels, then serve. Serve and enjoy!

Spanish Meatloaf with Manzanilla Olives

Serves: 6 | Total Time: 35 minutes

2 oz Manchego cheese, grated
1 lb lean ground beef
2 eggs
2 tomatoes, diced
½ white onion, diced
½ cup bread crumbs
1 tsp garlic powder

1 tsp dried oregano
1 tsp dried thyme
Salt and pepper to taste
4 Manzanilla olives, minced
1 tbsp olive oil
2 tbsp chopped parsley

Preheat the oven to 380°F. Combine the ground beef, eggs, tomatoes, onion, bread crumbs, garlic powder, oregano, thyme, salt, pepper, olives and cheese in a bowl and mix well. Form into a loaf, flattening to 1-inch thick. Lightly brush the top with olive oil, then place the meatloaf into the frying basket. Bake for 25 minutes. Allow resting for 5 minutes. Top with parsley and slice. Serve warm.

Stuffed Cabbage Rolls

Serves: 4 | Total Time: 50 minutes

½ cup long-grain brown rice
12 green cabbage leaves
1 lb ground beef
4 garlic cloves, minced
Salt and pepper to taste
1 tsp ground cinnamon

½ tsp ground cumin
2 tbsp chopped mint
1 lemon, juiced and zested
½ cup beef broth
1 tbsp olive oil
2 tbsp parsley, chopped

Place a large pot of salted water over medium heat and bring to a boil. Add the cabbage leaves and boil them for 3 minutes. Remove from the water and set aside. Combine the ground beef, rice, garlic, salt, pepper, cinnamon, cumin, mint, lemon juice and zest in a bowl.

Preheat air fryer to 360°F. Divide the beef mixture between the cabbage leaves and roll them up. Place the finished rolls into a greased baking dish. Pour the beef broth over the cabbage rolls and then brush the tops with olive oil. Put the casserole dish into the frying basket and Bake for 30 minutes. Top with parsley and enjoy!

Seedy Rib Eye Steak Bites

Serves: 4 | Total Time: 20 minutes

1 lb rib eye steak, cubed
2 garlic cloves, minced
2 tbsp olive oil
1 tbsp thyme, chopped
1 tsp ground fennel seeds
Salt and pepper to taste
1 onion, thinly sliced

Preheat air fryer to 380°F. Place the steak, garlic, olive oil, thyme, fennel seeds, salt, pepper, and onion in a bowl. Mix until all of the beef and onion are well coated. Put the seasoned steak mixture into the frying basket. Roast for 10 minutes, stirring once. Let sit for 5 minutes. Serve.

Thyme Steak Finger Strips

Serves: 2 | Total Time: 25 minutes

½ lb top sirloin strips
1 cup breadcrumbs
½ tsp garlic powder
½ tsp steak seasoning
2 eggs, beaten
Salt and pepper to taste
½ tbsp dried thyme

Preheat air fryer to 350°F. Put the breadcrumbs, garlic powder, steak seasoning, thyme, salt, and pepper in a bowl and stir to combine. Add in the sirloin steak strips and toss to coat all sides. Dip into the beaten eggs, then dip again into the dry ingredients. Lay the coated steak pieces on the greased frying basket in an even layer. Air Fry for 16-18 minutes, turning once. Serve and enjoy!

Stress-Free Beef Patties

Serves: 2 | Total Time: 30 minutes

½ lb ground beef
1 ½ tbsp ketchup
1 ½ tbsp tamari
½ tsp jalapeño powder
½ tsp mustard powder
Salt and pepper to taste

Preheat air fryer to 350°F. Add the beef, ketchup, tamari, jalapeño, mustard salt, and pepper to a bowl and mix until evenly combined. Shape into 2 patties, then place them on the greased frying basket. Air Fry for 18-20 minutes, turning once. Serve and enjoy!

Spiced Beef Empanadas

Serves: 4 | Total Time: 35 minutes

2 tbsp olive oil
6 oz ground beef
1 shallot, diced
½ tsp ground cumin
½ tsp nutmeg
½ tsp ground cloves
1 pinch of brown sugar
2 tsp red chili powder
4 empanada dough shells

Preheat air fryer to 350°F. Warm the olive oil in a saucepan over medium heat. Crumble and cook the ground beef for 4-5 minutes. Add in the shallot, cumin, nutmeg, chili powder, and clove and stir-fry for 3 minutes. Kill the heat and let the mixture cool slightly. Divide the beef mixture between the empanada shells. Fold the empanada shells over and use a fork to seal the edges. Sprinkle brown sugar over. Place the empanadas in the foil-lined frying basket and Bake for 15 minutes. Halfway through, flip the empanadas. Cook them until golden. Serve and enjoy!

Sirloin Steak Flatbread

Serves: 2 | Total Time: 40 minutes

1 premade flatbread dough
1 sirloin steak, cubed
2 cups breadcrumbs
2 eggs, beaten
Salt and pepper to taste
2 tsp onion powder
1 tsp garlic powder
1 tsp dried thyme
½ onion, sliced
2 Swiss cheese slices

Preheat air fryer to 360°F. Place the breadcrumbs, onion powder, garlic powder, thyme, salt, and pepper in a bowl and stir to combine. Add in the steak cubes, coating all sides. Dip into the beaten eggs, then dip again into the crumbs. Lay the coated steak pieces on half of the greased fryer basket. Place the onion slices on the other half of the basket. Air Fry 6 minutes. Turn the onions over and flip the steak pieces. Continue cooking for another 6 minutes. Roll the flatbread out and pierce it several times with a fork. Cover with Swiss cheese slices.

When the steak and onions are ready, remove them to the cheese-covered flatbread dough. Fold the flatbread over. Arrange the folded flatbread on the frying basket. Bake for 10 minutes, flipping once until golden brown. Serve.

Crispy Steak Subs

Serves: 2 | Total Time: 30 minutes

1 hoagie bun baguette, halved
6 oz flank steak, sliced
½ white onion, sliced
½ red pepper, sliced
2 mozzarella cheese slices

Preheat air fryer to 320°F. Place the flank steak slices, onion, and red pepper on one side of the frying basket. Add the hoagie bun halves, crusty side up, to the other half of the air fryer. Bake for 10 minutes. Flip the hoagie buns. Cover both sides with one slice of mozzarella cheese. Gently stir the steak, onions, and peppers. Cook for 6 more minutes until the cheese is melted and the steak is juicy on the inside and crispy on the outside.

Remove the cheesy hoagie halves to a serving plate. Cover one side with the steak, and top with the onions and peppers. Close with the other cheesy hoagie half, slice into two pieces, and enjoy!

Beef Fajitas

Serves 2 | Total Time: 15 minutes

8 oz sliced mushrooms
½ onion, cut into half-moons
1 tbsp olive oil
Salt and pepper to taste
1 strip steak
½ tsp smoked paprika
½ tsp fajita seasoning
2 tbsp corn

Preheat air fryer to 400°F. Combine the olive oil, onion, and salt in a bowl. Add the mushrooms and toss to coat. Spread in the frying basket. Sprinkle steak with salt, paprika, fajita seasoning and black pepper. Place steak on top of the mushroom mixture and Air Fry for 9 minutes, flipping steak once. Let rest on a cutting board for 5 minutes before cutting in half. Divide steak, mushrooms, corn, and onions between 2 plates and serve.

Lemon-Garlic Strip Steak

Serves: 2 | Total Time: 15 minutes

3 cloves garlic, minced	1 tbsp chopped parsley
1 tbsp lemon juice	½ tsp chopped rosemary
1 tbsp olive oil	½ tsp chopped sage
Salt and pepper to taste	1 strip steak

In a small bowl, whisk all ingredients. Brush mixture over strip steak and let marinate covered in the fridge for 30 minutes. Preheat air fryer to 400°F. Place strip steak in the greased frying basket and Bake for 8 minutes until rare, turning once. Let rest on a cutting board for 5 minutes before serving.

Balsamic Short Ribs

Serves: 2 | Total Time: 30 minutes

1/8 tsp Worcestershire sauce	1 tbsp honey
¼ cup olive oil	¼ cup chopped fresh sage
¼ cup balsamic vinegar	3 cloves garlic, quartered
¼ cup chopped basil leaves	½ tsp salt
¼ cup chopped oregano	1 lb beef short ribs

Add all ingredients, except for the short ribs, to a plastic resealable bag and shake to combine. Reserve 2 tbsp of balsamic mixture in a small bowl. Place short ribs in the plastic bag and massage into ribs. Seal the bag and let marinate in the fridge for 30 minutes up to overnight.

Preheat air fryer to 325°F. Place short ribs in the frying basket and Bake for 16 minutes, turning them once and brushing with extra sauce. Serve warm.

Flank Steak with Chimichurri Sauce

Serves: 4 | Total Time: 25 minutes + chilling time

FOR MARINADE

2/3 cup olive oil	1/3 cup tamari sauce
1 tbsp Dijon mustard	2 tbsp red wine vinegar
1 orange, juiced and zested	4 cloves garlic, minced
1 lime, juiced and zested	1 (1-lb) flank steak

FOR CHIMICHURRI SAUCE

2 red jalapeños, minced	4 cloves garlic, minced
1 cup Italian parsley leaves	2 tbsp lime juice
¼ cup cilantro leaves	2 tsp lime zest
¼ cup oregano leaves	2 tbsp red wine vinegar
¼ cup olive oil	½ tsp ground cumin
½ onion, diced	½ tsp salt

Whisk all the marinade ingredients in a large bowl. Toss in flank steak and let marinate covered for at least 1 hour. In a food processor, blend parsley, cilantro, oregano, red jalapeños, olive oil, onion, garlic, lime juice, lime zest, vinegar, cumin, and salt until you reach your desired consistency. Let chill in the fridge until ready to use.

Preheat air fryer to 325°F. Place flank steak in the greased frying basket and Bake for 18-20 minutes until rare, turning once. Let rest on a cutting board for 5 minutes before slicing thinly against the grain. Serve with chimichurri sauce on the side.

Cheeseburger Sliders with Pickle Sauce

Serves: 4 | Total Time: 20 minutes

4 iceberg lettuce leaves, each halved lengthwise	
2 red onion slices, rings separated	
¼ cup shredded Swiss cheese	½ tsp mustard powder
1 lb ground beef	½ tsp dill pickle juice
1 tbsp Dijon mustard	⅛ tsp onion powder
Salt and pepper to taste	⅛ tsp garlic powder
¼ tsp shallot powder	⅛ tsp sweet paprika
2 tbsp mayonnaise	8 tomato slices
2 tsp ketchup	½ cucumber, thinly sliced

In a large bowl, use your hands to mix beef, Swiss cheese, mustard, salt, shallot, and black pepper. Do not overmix. Form 8 patties ½-inch thick. Mix together mayonnaise, ketchup, mustard powder, pickle juice, onion and garlic powder, and paprika in a medium bowl. Stir until smooth.

Preheat air fryer to 400°F. Place the sliders in the greased frying basket and Air Fry for about 8-10 minutes, flipping once until preferred doneness. Serve on top of lettuce halves with a slice of tomato, a slider, onion, a smear of special sauce, and cucumber.

Creamy Horseradish Roast Beef

Serves: 6 | Total Time: 65 minutes + chilling time

1 topside roast, tied	1 garlic clove, minced
Salt to taste	2/3 cup buttermilk
1 tsp butter, melted	2 tsp red wine
2 tbsp Dijon mustard	1 tbsp minced chives
3 tbsp prepared horseradish	Salt and pepper to taste

Preheat air fryer to 320°F. Mix salt, butter, half of the mustard, 1 tsp of horseradish, and garlic until blended. Rub all over the roast. Bake the roast in the air fryer for 30-35 minutes, flipping once until browned. Transfer to a cutting board and cover with foil. Let rest for 15 minutes.

In a bowl, mix buttermilk, horseradish, remaining mustard, chives, wine, salt, and pepper until smooth. Refrigerate. When ready to serve, carve the roast into thin slices and serve with horseradish cream on the side.

Traditional Italian Beef Meatballs

Serves 4 | Total Time: 35 minutes

1/3 cup grated Parmesan	3 cloves garlic, minced
1 lb ground beef	¼ cup grated yellow onion
1 egg, beaten	Salt and pepper to taste
2 tbsp tomato paste	¼ cup almond flour
½ tsp Italian seasonings	¼ cup chopped basil
¼ cup ricotta cheese	2 cups marinara sauce

Preheat air fryer to 400°F. In a large bowl, combine ground beef, egg, tomato paste, Italian seasoning, ricotta cheese, Parmesan cheese, garlic, onion, salt, pepper, flour, and basil. Form mixture into 4 meatballs. Add them to the greased frying basket and Air Fry for 20 minutes. Warm the marinara sauce in a skillet over medium heat for 3 minutes. Add in cooked meatballs and roll them around in sauce for 2 minutes. Serve with sauce over the top.

Argentinian Steak Asado Salad

Serves: 2 | Total Time: 35 minutes

1 jalapeño pepper, sliced thin
¼ cup shredded pepper Jack cheese
1 avocado, peeled and pitted 1 garlic clove, minced
¼ cup diced tomatoes 1 tsp ground cumin
½ diced shallot Salt and pepper to taste
2 tsp chopped cilantro ¼ lime
2 tsp lime juice 3 cups mesclun mix
½ lb flank steak ½ cup pico de gallo

Mash the avocado in a small bowl. Add tomatoes, shallot, cilantro, lime juice, salt, and pepper. Set aside. Season the steak with garlic, salt, pepper, and cumin.

Preheat air fryer to 400°F. Put the steak into the greased frying basket. Bake 8-10 minutes, flipping once until your desired doneness. Remove and let rest. Squeeze the lime over the steak and cut into thin slices. For one serving, plate half of mesclun, 2 tbsp of cheese, and ¼ cup guacamole. Place half of the steak slices on top t, then add ¼ cup pico de gallo and jalapeño if desired.

Fusion Tender Flank Steak

Serves: 4 Total Time: 25 Minutes + marinating time

2 tbsp cilantro, chopped 2 tbsp sesame oil
2 tbsp chives, chopped 5 tbsp tamari sauce
¼ tsp red pepper flakes 3 tsp honey
1 jalapeño pepper, minced 1 tbsp grated fresh ginger
1 lime, juiced 2 green onions, minced
3 tbsp olive oil 2 garlic cloves, minced
Salt and pepper to taste 1 ¼ pounds flank steak

Combine the jalapeño pepper, cilantro, chives, lime juice, olive oil, salt, and pepper in a bowl. Set aside. Mix the sesame oil, tamari sauce, honey, ginger, green onions, garlic, and pepper flakes in another bowl. Stir until the honey is dissolved. Put the steak into the bowl and massage the marinade onto the meat. Marinate for 2 hours in the fridge. Preheat air fryer to 390 F.

Remove the steak from the marinade and place it in the greased frying basket. Air Fry for about 6 minutes, flip, and continue cooking for 6-8 more minutes. Allow to rest for a few minutes, slice thinly against the grain and top with the prepared dressing. Serve and enjoy!

Easy-Peasy Beef Sliders

Serves 4 | Total Time: 25 minutes

1 lb ground beef 1/3 cup grated yellow onion
¼ tsp cumin ½ tsp smoked paprika
¼ tsp mustard power Salt and pepper to taste

Preheat air fryer to 350°F. Combine the ground beef, cumin, mustard, onion, paprika, salt, and black pepper in a bowl. Form mixture into 8 patties and make a slight indentation in the middle of each. Place beef patties in the greased frying basket and Air Fry for 8-10 minutes, flipping once. Serve right away and enjoy!

Cowboy Rib Eye Steak

Serves 2 | Total Time: 20 minutes

¼ cup barbecue sauce ¼ tsp sweet paprika
1 garlic clove, minced ¼ tsp cumin
⅛ tsp chili pepper 1 rib-eye steak

Preheat air fryer to 400°F. In a bowl, whisk the barbecue sauce, garlic, chili pepper, paprika, and cumin. Divide in half and brush the steak with half of the sauce. Add steak to the lightly greased frying basket and Air Fry for 10 minutes until you reach your desired doneness, turning once and brushing with the remaining sauce. Let rest for 5 minutes onto a cutting board before slicing. Serve warm.

Beef & Sauerkraut Spring Rolls

Serves: 4 | Total Time: 20 minutes

5 Colby cheese slices, cut into strips
2 tbsp Thousand Island Dressing for dipping
10 spring roll wrappers ½ tsp ground nutmeg
1/3 lb corned beef 1 egg, beaten
2 cups sauerkraut 1 tsp corn starch
1 tsp ground cumin

Preheat air fryer to 360°F. Mix the egg and cornstarch in a bowl to thicken. Lay out the spring roll wrappers on a clean surface. Place a few strips of the cut-up corned beef in the middle of the wraps. Sprinkle with Colby cheese, cumin, and nutmeg and top with 1-2 tablespoons of sauerkraut. Roll up and seal the seams with the egg and cornstarch mixture. Place the rolls in the greased frying basket. Bake for 7 minutes, shaking the basket several times until the spring rolls are golden brown. Serve warm with Thousand Island for dipping.

Chili con Carne Galette

Serves: 4 | Total Time: 30 minutes

1 (16-oz) can chili beans in chili sauce
½ cup canned fire-roasted diced tomatoes, drained
½ cup grated Mexican cheese blend
2 tsp olive oil ½ tsp ground cumin
½ lb ground beef ½ tsp chili powder
½ cup dark beer ¼ tsp salt
½ onion, diced 1 cup corn chips
1 carrot, peeled and diced 3 tbsp beef broth
1 celery stalk, diced 2 tsp corn masa

Warm the olive oil in a skillet over -high heat for 30 seconds. Add in ground beef, onion, carrot, and celery and cook for 5 minutes until the beef is no longer pink. Drain the fat. Mix 3 tbsp beef broth and 2 tsp corn mass until smooth and then toss it in beans, chili sauce, dark beer, tomatoes, cumin, chili powder, and salt. Cook until thickened. Turn the heat off.

Preheat air fryer to 350°F. Spoon beef mixture into a cake pan, then top with corn chips, followed by cheese blend. Place cake pan in the frying basket and Bake for 6 minutes. Let rest for 10 minutes before serving.

Canadian-Style Rib Eye Steak

Serves: 2 | Total Time: 15 minutes

2 tsp Montreal steak seasoning
1 (12-oz) ribeye steak   1 tsp chopped parsley
1 tbsp butter, halved   ½ tsp fresh rosemary

Preheat air fryer to 400°F. Sprinkle ribeye with steak seasoning and rosemary on both sides. Place it in the basket and Bake for 10 minutes, turning once. Remove it to a cutting board and top with butter halves. Let rest for 5 minutes and scatter with parsley. Serve immediately.

Jerk Meatballs

Serves: 6 | Total Time: 30 minutes

1 tsp minced habanero   2 tbsp diced onion
1 tsp Jamaican jerk seasoning 1 tsp smoked paprika
1 sandwich bread slice, torn   1 tsp black pepper
2 tbsp whole milk   1 tbsp chopped parsley
1 lb ground beef   ½ lime
1 egg

Preheat air fryer to 360°F. In a bowl, combine bread pieces with milk. Add in ground beef, egg, onion, smoked paprika, pepper, habanero, and jerk seasoning, and using your hands, squeeze ingredients together until combined.

Form mixture into meatballs. Place meatballs in the greased frying basket and Air Fry for 8 minutes, flipping once. Squeeze lime and sprinkle the parsley over.

French-Style Steak Salad

Serves: 4 | Total Time: 25 minutes

1 cup sliced strawberries   2 tbsp lemon juice
4 tbsp crumbled blue cheese   8 cups baby arugula
¼ cup olive oil   ½ red onion, sliced
Salt and pepper to taste   4 tbsp pecan pieces
1 (1-lb) flank steak   4 tbsp sunflower seeds
¼ cup balsamic vinaigrette   1 sliced kiwi
1 tbsp Dijon mustard   1 sliced orange

In a bowl, whisk olive oil, salt, lemon juice and pepper. Toss in flank steak and let marinate covered in the fridge for 30 minutes up to overnight. Preheat air fryer to 325°F. Place flank steak in the greased frying basket and Bake for 18-20 minutes until rare, flipping once. Let rest for 5 minutes before slicing thinly against the grain.

In a salad bowl, whisk balsamic vinaigrette and mustard. Stir in arugula, salt, and pepper. Top with blue cheese, onion, pecan, sunflower seeds, strawberries, kiwi, orange and sliced steak. Serve immediately.

Rosemary T-Bone Steak

Serves 2 | Total Time: 20 minutes

2 tbsp butter, softened   1 beef T-bone steak
¼ tsp lemon juice   Salt and pepper to taste
2 cloves garlic, minced   ¼ tsp onion powder
1 tsp minced fresh rosemary

In a small bowl, whisk butter, lemon juice, onion powder, garlic, and rosemary. Transfer the butter mixture onto parchment paper. Roll into a log and spin ends to tighten. Let chill in the fridge for 2 hours. Remove the steak from the fridge 30 minutes before cooking. Season.

Preheat air fryer to 400°F. Add the steak to the greased frying basket and Air Fry for 10 minutes, flipping once. Transfer steak to a cutting board and let sit for 5 minutes. Cut butter mixture into slices and top the steak. Let the butter melts over before serving. Enjoy!

Beefy Quesadillas

Serves: 4 | Total Time: 45 minutes

2 cups grated cheddar   2 tsp olive oil
1 tsp chili powder   1 red bell pepper, diced
½ tsp smoked paprika   1 grated carrot
½ tsp ground cumin   1 green bell pepper, diced
½ tsp nutmeg   ½ red onion, sliced
¼ tsp garlic powder   1 cup corn kernels
Salt and pepper to taste   3 tbsp butter, melted
1 (12-oz) ribeye steak   8 tortillas

Mix the chili powder, nutmeg, paprika, cumin, garlic powder, salt, and pepper in a bowl. Toss in ribeye until fully coated and let marinate covered in the fridge for 30 minutes. Preheat air fryer to 400°F. Place ribeye in the greased frying basket and Bake for 6 minutes until rare, flipping once. Let rest on a cutting board for 5 minutes before slicing thinly against the grain.

Warm the olive oil in a skillet over high heat. Add in bell peppers, carrot and onion and cook for 6-8 minutes until the peppers are tender. Stir in corn. Set aside. Preheat air fryer to 350°F. Brush on one side of a tortilla lightly with melted butter. Layer ¼ beef strips, ¼ bell pepper mixture, and finally, ¼ of the grated cheese. Top with a second tortilla and lightly brush with butter on top. Repeat with the remaining ingredients. Place quesadillas in the frying basket and Bake for 3 minutes. Cut them into 6 sections and serve.

Paprika Fried Beef

Serves: 4 | Total Time: 30 minutes

Celery salt to taste   2 tsp paprika
4 beef cube steaks   1 egg
½ cup milk   1 cup bread crumbs
1 cup flour   2 tbsp olive oil

Preheat air fryer to 350°F. Place the cube steaks in a zipper sealed bag or between two sheets of cling wrap. Gently pound the steaks until they are slightly thinner. Set aside. In a bowl, mix together milk, flour, paprika, celery salt, and egg until just combined. In a separate bowl, mix together the crumbs and olive oil. Take the steaks and dip them into the buttermilk batter, shake off the excess, and return to a plate for 5 minutes. Next, dip the steaks in the bread crumbs, patting the crumbs on both sides. Air Fry the steaks until the crust is crispy and brown, 12-16 minutes. Serve warm.

Beef Tacos Norteños

Serves: 4 | Total Time: 25 minutes + marinating time

1 thinly sliced red onion	½ tsp ground cumin
5 radishes, julienned	1 (1-lb) flank steak
2 tbsp white wine vinegar	10 mini flour tortillas
½ tsp honey	1 cup shredded red cabbage
Salt and pepper to taste	½ cup cucumber slices
¼ cup olive oil	½ cup fresh radish slices

Combine the onion, vinegar, honey, and salt in a bowl. Let sit covered in the fridge until ready to use. Whisk the olive oil, salt, pepper and cumin in a bowl. Toss in flank steak and let marinate in the fridge for 30 minutes.

Preheat air fryer to 325°F. Place flank steak in the frying basket and Bake for 18-20 minutes, tossing once. Let rest on a cutting board for 5 minutes before slicing thinly against the grain. Add steak slices to flour tortillas along with red cabbage, chopped purple onions, cucumber slices, radish slices and fresh radish slices. Serve warm.

Santorini Steak Bowls

Serves 2 | Total Time: 15 minutes

5 pitted Kalamata olives, halved

1 cucumber, diced	½ tsp dried dill
2 tomatoes, diced	¼ tsp garlic powder
1 tbsp apple cider vinegar	⅛ tsp ground nutmeg
2 tsp olive oil	Salt and pepper to taste
¼ cup feta cheese crumbles	1 (¾-lb) strip steak
½ tsp Greek oregano	

In a bowl, combine cucumber, tomatoes, vinegar, olive oil, olives, and feta cheese. Let chill covered in the fridge until ready to use. Preheat air fryer to 400°F. Combine all spices in a bowl, then coat the strip steak with this mixture. Add the steak to the lightly greased frying basket and Air Fry for 10 minutes or until you reach your desired doneness, flipping once. Let sit onto a cutting board for 5 minutes. Thinly slice against the grain and divide between two bowls. Top with the cucumber mixture. Serve.

Tasty Filet Mignon

Serves 2 | Total Time: 30 minutes

2 filet mignon steaks	Salt and pepper to taste
¼ tsp garlic powder	1 tbsp butter, melted

Preheat air fryer to 370°F. Sprinkle the steaks with salt, garlic and pepper on both sides. Place them in the greased frying basket and Air Fry for 12 minutes to yield a medium-rare steak, turning twice. Transfer steaks to a cutting board, brush them with butter and let rest 5 minutes before serving.

Skirt Steak with Horseradish Cream

Serves 2 | Total Time: 20 minutes

1 cup heavy cream	1 (12-oz) skirt steak, halved
3 tbsp horseradish sauce	2 tbsp olive oil
1 lemon, zested	Salt and pepper to taste

Mix together the heavy cream, horseradish sauce, and lemon zest in a small bowl. Let chill in the fridge.

Preheat air fryer to 400°F. Brush steak halves with olive oil and sprinkle with salt and pepper. Place steaks in the frying basket and Air Fry for 10 minutes or until you reach your desired doneness, flipping once. Let sit onto a cutting board for 5 minutes. Use a sharp knife to slice against the grain into thin slices. Arrange on two plates. Drizzle the horseradish sauce over. Serve and enjoy!

Tender Steak with Salsa Verde

Serves 4 | Total Time: 20 minutes + marinating time

1 (2-lb) flank steak, halved	½ tsp black pepper
1 ½ cups salsa verde	

Toss steak and 1 cup of salsa verde in a bowl and refrigerate covered for 2 hours. Preheat air fryer to 400°F. Add steaks to the lightly greased frying basket and Air Fry for 10-12 minutes or until you reach your desired doneness, flipping once. Let sit onto a cutting board for 5 minutes. Cut against the grain into thin slices and divide among four plates. Spoon over the remaining salsa verde and serve sprinkled with black pepper. Enjoy!

Premium Steakhouse Salad

Serves 2 | Total Time: 20 minutes

1 head iceberg lettuce, cut into thin strips

2 tbsp olive oil	Salt and pepper to taste
1 tbsp white wine vinegar	2 tbsp chopped walnuts
1 tbsp Greek yogurt	¼ cup blue cheese crumbles
1 tsp Dijon mustard	4 cherry tomatoes, halved
1 (¾-lb) strip steak	4 fig wedges

In a bowl, whisk the olive oil, vinegar, Greek yogurt, and mustard. Let chill covered in the fridge until ready to use. Preheat air fryer to 400°F. Sprinkle the steak with salt and pepper. Place it in the greased frying basket and Air Fry for 9 minutes or until you reach your desired doneness, flipping once. Let sit onto a cutting board for 5 minutes.

Combine lettuce and mustard dressing in a large bowl, then divide between 2 medium bowls. Thinly slice steak and add to salads. Scatter with walnuts, blue cheese, cherry tomatoes, and fig wedges. Serve immediately.

Friday Night Cheeseburgers

Serves: 4 | Total Time: 20 minutes

1 lb ground beef	Salt and pepper to taste
1 tsp Worcestershire sauce	4 cheddar cheese slices
1 tbsp allspice	4 buns

Preheat air fryer to 360°F. Combine beef, Worcestershire sauce, allspice, salt, and pepper in a large bowl. Divide into 4 equal portions and shape into patties. Place the burgers in the greased frying basket and Air Fry for 8 minutes. Flip and cook for another 3-4 minutes. Top each burger with cheddar cheese and cook for another minute until the cheese melts. Transfer to a bun and serve.

Berbere Beef Steaks

Serves: 4 | Total Time: 45 minutes + marinating time

1 chipotle pepper in adobo sauce, minced
1 lb skirt steak   ¼ tsp Berbere seasoning
2 tbsp chipotle sauce   Salt and pepper to taste

Cut the steak into 4 equal pieces, then place them on a plate. Mix together chipotle pepper, adobo sauce, salt, pepper, and Berbere seasoning in a bowl. Spread the mixture on both sides of the steak. Chill for 2 hours.

Preheat air fryer to 390°F. Place the steaks in the frying basket and Bake for 5 minutes on each side for well-done meat. Allow the steaks to rest for 5 more minutes. To serve, slice against the grain.

Cal-Mex Chimichangas

Serves: 4 | Total Time: 30 minutes

1 (15-oz) can diced tomatoes with chiles
1 cup shredded cheddar   2 tbsp taco seasoning
½ cup chopped onions   Salt and pepper to taste
2 garlic cloves, minced   4 flour tortillas
1 lb ground beef   ½ cup Pico de Gallo

Warm the olive oil in a skillet over medium heat and stir-fry the onion and garlic for 3 minutes or until fragrant. Add ground beef, taco seasoning, salt, and pepper. Stir and break up the beef with a spoon. Cook for 3-4 minutes or until it is browned. Stir in diced tomatoes with chiles. Scoop ½ cup of beef onto each tortilla. Form chimichangas by folding the sides of the tortilla into the middle, then roll up from the bottom. Use a toothpick to secure the chimichanga.

Preheat air fryer to 400°F. Lightly spray the chimichangas with cooking oil. Place the first batch in the fryer and Bake for 8 minutes. Transfer to a serving dish and top with shredded cheese and pico de gallo.

Cheesy Beef & Chorizo Empanadas

Serves: 6 | Total Time: 40 minutes

1 cup shredded Pepper Jack cheese
2 tbsp olive oil   4 oz chorizo ground sausage
½ chopped green bell pepper   1 tsp allspice
1 cup grated mozzarella   ½ tsp chili powder
2 garlic cloves, chopped   Salt and pepper to taste
½ small onion, chopped   12 empanada wrappers
4 oz ground beef   1 tbsp butter

Warm the olive oil in a skillet over medium heat. Stir-fry the garlic, green pepper, and onion for 2 minutes or until aromatic. Add beef, chorizo, allspice, chili powder, salt, and pepper. Use a spoon to break up the beef. Cook until brown. Drain the excess fat. On a clean work surface, glaze each empanada wrapper edge with water using a basting brush to soften the crust. Mound 2-3 tbsp of meat onto each wrapper. Top with mozzarella and pepper Jack cheese. Fold one side of the wrapper to the opposite side. Press the edges with the back of a fork to seal.

Preheat air fryer to 400°F. Place the empanadas in the air fryer and spray with cooking oil. Bake for 8 minutes, then flip the empanadas. Cook for another 4 minutes. Melt butter in a microwave-safe bowl for 20 seconds. Brush melted butter over the top of each empanada. Serve warm.

Balsamic London Broil

Serves: 4 | Total Time: 25 minutes + marinating time

2 ½ lb top round London broil steak
¼ cup coconut aminos   2 garlic cloves, minced
1 tbsp balsamic vinegar   1 tsp dried oregano
1 tbsp olive oil   Salt and pepper to taste
1 tbsp mustard   ¼ tsp smoked paprika
2 tsp maple syrup   2 tbsp red onions, chopped

Whisk coconut aminos, mustard, vinegar, olive oil, maple oregano, syrup, oregano garlic, red onions, salt, pepper, and paprika in a small bowl. Put the steak in a shallow container and pour the marinade over the steak. Cover and let sit for 20 minutes.

Preheat air fryer to 400°F. Transfer the steak to the frying basket and bake for 5 minutes. Flip the steak and bake for another 4 to 6 minutes. Allow sitting for 5 minutes before slicing. Serve warm and enjoy.

Classic Beef Meatballs

Serves: 4 | Total Time: 30 minutes

3 tbsp buttermilk   ½ tsp dried marjoram
1/3 cup bread crumbs   Salt and pepper to taste
1 tbsp ketchup   1 lb ground beef
1 egg   20 Swiss cheese cubes

Preheat air fryer to 390°F. Mix buttermilk, crumbs, ketchup, egg, marjoram, salt, and pepper in a bowl. Using your hands, mix in ground beef until just combined. Shape into 20 meatballs. Take one meatball and shape it around a Swiss cheese cube. Repeat this for the remaining meatballs. Lightly spray the meatballs with oil and place them into the frying basket. Bake the meatballs for 10-13 minutes, turning once until they are cooked through. Serve and enjoy!

Beef & Barley Stuffed Bell Peppers

Serves: 4 | Total Time: 30 minutes

1 cup pulled cooked roast beef   2 tsp olive oil
4 bell peppers, tops removed   2 tomatoes, chopped
1 onion, chopped   1 cup cooked barley
½ cup grated carrot   1 tsp dried marjoram

Preheat air fryer to 400°F. Cut the tops of the bell peppers, then remove the stems. Put the onion, carrots, and olive oil in a baking pan and cook for 2-4 minutes. The veggies should be crispy but soft. Put the veggies in a bowl, toss in the tomatoes, barley, roast beef, and marjoram, and stir to combine. Spoon the veggie mix into the cleaned bell peppers and put them in the frying basket. Bake for 12-16 minutes or until the peppers are tender. Serve warm.

Ground Beef Calzones

Serves: 6 | Total Time: 30 minutes

1 refrigerated pizza dough	1 lb ground beef
1 cup shredded mozzarella	1 tbsp pizza seasoning
½ cup chopped onion	Salt and pepper to taste
2 garlic cloves, minced	1 ½ cups marinara sauce
¼ cup chopped mushrooms	1 tsp flour

Warm 1 tbsp of oil in a skillet over medium heat. Stir-fry onion, garlic and mushrooms for 2-3 minutes or until aromatic. Add beef, pizza seasoning, salt, and pepper. Use a large spoon to break up the beef. Cook for 3 minutes or until brown. Stir in marinara sauce and set aside.

On a floured work surface, roll out pizza dough and cut into 6 equal-sized rectangles. On each rectangle, add ½ cup of beef and top with 1 tbsp of shredded cheese. Fold one side of the dough over the filling to the opposite side. Press the edges using the back of a fork to seal them. Preheat air fryer to 400°F. Place the first batch of calzones in the air fryer and spray with cooking oil. Bake for 10 minutes. Let cool slightly and serve warm.

Steak Fajitas

Serves: 4 | Total Time: 20 minutes

1 lb beef flank steak, cut into strips	
1 red bell pepper, cut into strips	
1 green bell pepper, cut into strips	
½ cup sweet corn	Salt and pepper to taste
1 shallot, cut into strips	2 tbsp olive oil
2 tbsp fajita seasoning	8 flour tortillas

Preheat air fryer to 380°F. Combine beef, bell peppers, corn, shallot, fajita seasoning, salt, pepper, and olive oil in a large bowl until well mixed.

Pour the beef and vegetable mixture into the air fryer. Air Fry for 9-11 minutes, shaking the basket a couple of times. Spoon a portion of the beef and vegetables in each of the tortillas and top with favorite toppings. Serve.

Provençal Grilled Rib-Eye

Serves: 4 | Total Time: 25 minutes

4 (8-oz) ribeye steaks	Salt and pepper to taste
1 tbsp herbs de Provence	

Preheat air fryer to 360°F. Season the steaks with herbs, salt, and pepper. Place them in the greased frying basket and cook for 8-12 minutes, flipping once. Use a thermometer to check for doneness and adjust time as needed. Let the steak rest for a few minutes and serve.

Original Köttbullar

Serves: 4 | Total Time: 30 minutes

1 lb ground beef	Salt and pepper to taste
1 small onion, chopped	1 cup beef broth
1 garlic clove, minced	1/3 cup heavy cream
1/3 cup bread crumbs	2 tbsp flour
1 egg, beaten	

Preheat air fryer to 370°F. Combine beef, onion, garlic, crumbs, egg, salt, and pepper in a bowl. Scoop 2 tbsp of mixture and form meatballs with your hands. Place the meatballs in the greased frying basket. Bake for 14 minutes.

Meanwhile, stir-fry beef broth and heavy cream in a saucepan over medium heat for 2 minutes; stir in flour. Cover and simmer for 4 minutes or until the sauce thickens. Transfer meatballs to a serving dish and drizzle with sauce. Serve and enjoy!

Tender St. Louis Ribs with Pineapple

Serves: 4 | Total Time: 35 minutes + marinating time

4 lb St. Louis pork spareribs	1 tsp ancho chili powder
1 tsp onion powder	1 tsp mustard powder
1 tsp garlic powder	Salt and pepper to taste
1 tsp brown sugar	½ cup barbecue sauce
1 tsp olive oil	½ pineapple, sliced

Mix the onion powder, garlic powder, brown sugar, salt, mustard, ancho chili, and pepper in a bowl. Rub the seasoning all over the meat of the ribs. Cover the ribs in plastic wrap or foil. Let them sit for 30 minutes.

Preheat air fryer to 360°F. Place the ribs in the air fryer. Bake them for 15 minutes, then flip them. Cover the ribs with pineapple silces and drizzle with olive oil; cook for another 15 minutes. Serve, drizzled with barbecue sauce.

Balsamic Beef & Veggie Skewers

Serves: 4 | Total Time: 25 minutes

2 tbsp balsamic vinegar	¾ lb round steak, cubed
2 tsp olive oil	1 red bell pepper, sliced
½ tsp dried oregano	1 yellow bell pepper, sliced
Salt and pepper to taste	1 cup cherry tomatoes

Preheat air fryer to 390°F. Put the balsamic vinegar, olive oil, oregano, salt, and black pepper in a bowl and stir. Toss the steak in and allow to marinate for 10 minutes. Poke 8 metal skewers through the beef, bell peppers, and cherry tomatoes, alternating ingredients as you go. Place the skewers in the air fryer and Air Fry for 5-7 minutes, turning once until the beef is golden and cooked through and the veggies are tender. Serve and enjoy!

Beef & Spinach Sautée

Serves: 4 | Total Time: 30 minutes

2 tomatoes, chopped	2 garlic cloves, minced
2 tbsp crumbled Goat cheese	2 cups baby spinach
½ lb ground beef	2 tbsp lemon juice
1 shallot, chopped	1/3 cup beef broth

Preheat air fryer to 370°F. Crumble the beef in a baking pan and place it in the air fryer. Air Fry for 3-7 minutes, stirring once. Drain the meat and make sure it's browned. Toss in the tomatoes, shallot, and garlic and Air Fry for an additional 4-8 minutes until soft. Toss in the spinach, lemon juice, and beef broth and cook for 2-4 minutes until the spinach wilts. Top with goat cheese and serve.

Beef Meatballs with Herbs

Serves: 6 | Total Time: 30 minutes

1 medium onion, minced	3 tbsp milk
2 garlic cloves, minced	1 tsp dried sage
1 tsp olive oil	1 tsp dried thyme
1 bread slice, crumbled	1 lb ground beef

Preheat air fryer to 380°F. Toss the onion, garlic, and olive oil in a baking pan, place it in the air fryer, and Air Fry for 2-4 minutes. The veggies should be crispy but tender. Transfer the veggies to a bowl and add in the breadcrumbs, milk, thyme, and sage, then toss gently to combine. Add in the ground beef and mix with your hands. Shape the mixture into 24 meatballs. Put them in the frying basket and Air Fry for 12-16 minutes or until the meatballs are browned on all sides. Serve and enjoy!

Broccoli & Mushroom Beef

Serves: 4 | Total Time: 30 minutes

1 lb sirloin strip steak, cubed
1 cup sliced cremini mushrooms

2 tbsp potato starch	1 onion, chopped
½ cup beef broth	1 tbsp grated fresh ginger
1 tsp soy sauce	1 cup cooked quinoa
2 ½ cups broccoli florets	

Add potato starch, broth, and soy sauce to a bowl and mix, then add in the beef and coat thoroughly. Marinate for 5 minutes. Preheat air fryer to 400°F. Set aside the broth and move the beef to a bowl. Add broccoli, onion, mushrooms, and ginger and transfer the bowl to the air fryer. Bake for 12-15 minutes until the beef is golden brown and the veggies soft. Pour the reserved broth over the beef and cook for 2-3 more minutes until the sauce is bubbling. Serve warm over cooked quinoa.

Leftover Roast Beef Risotto

Serves: 4 | Total Time: 30 minutes

½ chopped red bell pepper	1 shallot, finely chopped
½ chopped cooked roast beef	3 garlic cloves, minced
3 tbsp grated Parmesan	¾ cup short-grain rice
2 tsp butter, melted	1¼ cups beef broth

Preheat air fryer to 390°F. Add the melted butter, shallot, garlic, and red bell pepper to a baking pan and stir to combine. Air Fry for 2 minutes, or until the vegetables are crisp-tender. Remove from the air fryer and stir in the rice, broth, and roast beef. Put the cooking pan back into the fryer and Bake for 18-22 minutes, stirring once during cooking until the rice is al dente and the beef is cooked through. Sprinkle with Parmesan and serve.

Sirloin Steak Bites with Gravy

Serves: 4 | Total Time: 20 minutes

1 ½ lb sirloin steak, cubed	2 tbsp soy sauce
1 tbsp olive oil	2 tbsp Worcestershire sauce
2 tbsp cornstarch, divided	2 garlic cloves, minced

Salt and pepper to taste	½ cup sliced mushrooms
½ tsp smoked paprika	1 cup beef broth
½ cup sliced red onion	1 tbsp butter
2 fresh thyme sprigs	

Preheat air fryer to 400°F. Combine beef, olive oil, 1 tablespoon of cornstarch, garlic, pepper, Worcestershire sauce, soy sauce, thyme, salt, and paprika. Arrange the beef on the greased baking dish, then top with onions and mushrooms. Place the dish in the frying basket and bake for 4 minutes. While the beef is baking, whisk beef broth and the rest of the cornstarch in a small bowl. When the beef is ready, add butter and beef broth to the baking dish. Bake for another 5 minutes. Allow resting for 5 minutes. Serve and enjoy.

Classic Salisbury Steak Burgers

Serves: 4 | Total Time: 35 minutes

¼ cup bread crumbs	½ tsp onion powder
2 tbsp beef broth	½ tsp garlic powder
1 tbsp cooking sherry	1 lb ground beef
1 tbsp ketchup	1 cup sliced mushrooms
1tbsp Dijon mustard	1 tbsp butter
2 tsp Worcestershire sauce	4 buns, split and toasted

Preheat the air fryer to 375°F. Combine the bread crumbs, broth, cooking sherry, ketchup, mustard, Worcestershire sauce, garlic and onion powder and mix well. Add the beef and mix with your hands, then form into 4 patties and refrigerate while preparing the mushrooms. Mix the mushrooms and butter in a 6-inch pan. Place the pan in the air fryer and Bake for 8-10 minutes, stirring once, until the mushrooms are brown and tender. Remove and set aside. Line the frying basket with round parchment paper and punch holes in it. Lay the burgers in a single layer and cook for 11-14 minutes or until cooked through. Put the burgers on the bun bottoms, top with the mushrooms, then the bun tops.

Double Cheese & Beef Burgers

Serves: 4 | Total Time: 30 minutes

4 toasted onion buns, split	2 tsp cayenne pepper
¼ cup breadcrumbs	2 tbsp grated Cotija cheese
2 tbsp milk	1 ¼ lb ground beef
1 tp smoked paprika	4 Colby Jack cheese slices
6 tbsp salsa	¼ cup sour cream

Preheat the air fryer to 375°F. Combine the breadcrumbs, milk, paprika, 2 tbsp of salsa, cayenne, and Cotija cheese in a bowl and mix. Let stand for 5 minutes. Add the ground beef and mix with your hands. Form into 4 patties and lay them on wax paper. Place the patties into the greased frying basket and Air Fry for 11-14 minutes, flipping once during cooking until golden and crunchy on the outside. Put a slice of Colby jack on top of each and cook for another minute until the cheese melts. Combine the remaining salsa with sour cream. Spread the mix on the bun bottoms, lay the patties on top, and spoon the rest of the mix over. Add the top buns and serve.

Asian-Style Flank Steak

Serves: 4 | Total Time: 25 minutes

1 lb flank steak, cut into strips	2/3 cup beef stock
4 tbsp cornstarch	2 tbsp soy sauce
Black pepper to taste	2 tbsp light brown sugar
1 tbsp grated ginger	2 scallions, chopped
3 garlic cloves, minced	1 tbsp sesame seeds

Preheat the air fryer to 400°F. Sprinkle the beef with 3 tbsp of cornstarch and pepper, then toss to coat. Line the frying basket with round parchment paper with holes poked in it. Add the steak and spray with cooking oil. Bake for 8-12 minutes, shaking after 5 minutes until the beef is browned. Remove from the fryer and set aside. Combine the remaining cornstarch, ginger, garlic, beef stock, soy sauce, sugar, and scallions in a bowl and put it in the frying basket. Bake for 5-8 minutes, stirring after 3 minutes, until the sauce is thick and glossy. Plate the beef, pour the sauce over, toss, and sprinkle with sesame seeds to serve.

Lazy Mexican Meat Pizza

Serves: 4 | Total Time: 35 minutes

1 ¼ cups canned refried beans	
2 cups shredded cheddar	1 sliced jalapeño
½ cup chopped cilantro	1 pizza crust
2/3 cup salsa	16 meatballs, halved
1 red bell pepper, chopped	

Preheat the air fryer to 375°F. Combine the refried beans, salsa, jalapeño, and bell pepper in a bowl and spread on the pizza crust. Top with meatball halves and sprinkle with cheddar cheese. Put the pizza in the greased frying basket and Bake for 7-10 minutes until hot, and the cheese is brown. Sprinkle with fresh cilantro and serve.

Garlic-Buttered Rib Eye Steak

Serves: 2 | Total Time: 25 minutes

1 lb rib eye steak	1 tbsp chopped rosemary
Salt and pepper to taste	2 garlic cloves, minced
1 tbsp butter	2 tbsp chopped parsley
1 tsp paprika	1 tbsp chopped mint

Preheat air fryer to 400°F. Sprinkle salt and pepper on both sides of the rib eye. Transfer the rib eye to the greased frying basket, then top with butter, mint, paprika, rosemary, and garlic. Bake for 6 minutes, then flip the steak. Bake for another 6 minutes. For medium-rare, the steak needs to reach an internal temperature of 140°F. Allow resting for 5 minutes before slicing. Serve sprinkled with parsley and enjoy!

Mini Meatloaves with Pancetta

Serves: 4 | Total Time: 40 minutes

¼ cup grated Parmesan	1 egg
1/3 cup quick-cooking oats	1 tsp dried oregano
2 tbsp milk	Salt and pepper to taste
3 tbsp ketchup	1 lb lean ground beef
3 tbsp Dijon mustard	4 pancetta slices, uncooked

Preheat the air fryer to 375°F. Combine the oats, milk, 1 tbsp of ketchup, 1 tbsp of mustard, the egg, oregano, Parmesan cheese, salt, and pepper, and mix. Add the beef and mix with your hands, then form 4 mini loaves. Wrap each mini loaf with pancetta, covering the meat.

Combine the remaining ketchup and mustard and set aside. Line the frying basket with foil and poke holes in it, then set the loaves in the basket. Brush with the ketchup/mustard mix. Bake for 17-22 minutes or until cooked and golden. Serve and enjoy!

BBQ Back Ribs

Serves: 4 | Total Time: 40 minutes

2 tbsp light brown sugar	1 tsp dried marjoram
Salt and pepper to taste	½ tsp smoked paprika
2 tsp onion powder	1 tsp cayenne pepper
1 tsp garlic powder	1 ½ pounds baby back ribs
1 tsp mustard powder	2 tbsp barbecue sauce

Preheat the air fryer to 375°F. Combine the brown sugar, salt, pepper, onion and garlic powder, mustard, paprika, cayenne, and marjoram in a bowl and mix. Pour into a small glass jar. Brush the ribs with barbecue sauce and sprinkle 1 tbsp of the seasoning mix. Rub the seasoning all over the meat. Set the ribs in the greased frying basket. Bake for 25 minutes until nicely browned, flipping them once halfway through cooking. Serve hot.

Rib Eye Bites with Mushrooms

Serves: 4 | Total Time: 30 minutes

1 ¼ lb boneless rib-eye or sirloin steak, cubed	
8 oz button mushrooms, halved	
4 tbsp rapeseed oil	2 tsp lime juice
1 onion, chopped	1 tsp dried marjoram
2 garlic cloves, minced	2 tbsp chopped parsley
Salt and pepper to taste	

Preheat the air fryer to 400°F. Combine the rapeseed oil, onion, mushrooms, garlic, steak cubes, salt, pepper, lime juice, marjoram, and parsley in a baking pan. Put it in the frying basket and Bake for 12-15 minutes, stirring once or twice to ensure an even cooking, and until golden brown. The veggies should be tender. Serve hot.

Tex-Mex Beef Carnitas

Serves: 4 | Total Time: 30 minutes

1 ¼ lb flank steak, cut into strips	
1 ½ cups grated Colby cheese	1 red bell pepper, sliced
Salt and pepper to taste	1 yellow bell pepper, sliced
2 tbsp lime juice	1 tbsp chili oil
4 garlic cloves, minced	½ cup salsa
2 tsp chipotle powder	8 corn tortillas

Preheat the air fryer to 400°F. Lay the strips in a bowl and sprinkle with salt, pepper, lime juice, garlic, and chipotle powder. Toss well and let marinate. In the frying basket, combine the bell peppers and chili oil and toss.

Air Fry for 6 minutes or until crispy but tender. Drain the steak and discard the liquid. Lay the steak in the basket on top of the peppers and fry for 7-9 minutes more until browned. Divide the strips among tortillas and top with pepper strips, salsa, and cheese. Fold and serve.

Effortless Beef & Rice

Serves: 4 | Total Time: 35 minutes

½ lb ground beef	3 tbsp tomato paste
1 onion, chopped	2/3 cup beef broth
1 celery stalk, chopped	1 tsp smoked paprika
3 garlic cloves, minced	½ tsp dried oregano
2 cups cooked rice	½ tsp ground nutmeg
1 tomato, chopped	Salt and pepper to taste

Preheat the air fryer to 370°F. Combine the ground beef, onion, celery, and garlic in a baking pan; break up the ground beef with a fork. Put in the greased frying basket and Air Fry for 5-7 minutes until the beef browns. Add the rice, tomato, tomato paste, broth, paprika, oregano, nutmeg, salt, and pepper to the pan and stir. Then return it into the fryer and cook for 10-13 minutes, stirring once, until blended and hot. Serve and enjoy!

Lamb Chops in Currant Sauce

Serves: 4 | Total Time: 30 minutes

½ cup chicken broth	½ tsp dried thyme
2 tbsp red currant jelly	½ tsp dried mint
2 tbsp Dijon mustard	8 lamb chops
1 tbsp lemon juice	Salt and pepper to taste

Preheat the air fryer to 375°F. Combine the broth, jelly, mustard, lemon juice, mint, and thyme and mix with a whisk until smooth. Sprinkle the chops with salt and pepper and brush with some of the broth mixture.

Set 4 chops in the frying basket in a single layer, then add a raised rack and lay the rest of the chops on top. Bake for 15-20 minutes. Then, lay them in a cake pan and add the chicken broth mix. Put in the fryer and Bake for 3-5 more minutes or until the sauce is bubbling and the chops are tender.

Easter Lamb Chops with Couscous

Serves: 4 | Total Time: 30 minutes

8 lamb chops	½ tsp za'atar seasoning
2 tsp olive oil	2 garlic cloves, minced
1 tsp ground coriander	Salt and pepper to taste
1 lemon, zested	1 cup couscous

Place the couscous in a bowl and cover with 1 ½ cups of salted boiling water. Let sit until the water is absorbed.

Preheat air fryer to 390°F. Coat the lamb chops with olive oil. Mix the mint leaves, coriander, lemon zest, za'atar, garlic, salt, and pepper in a bowl. Rub the seasoning onto the chops. Place them in the greased frying basket and Air Fry for 14-16 minutes, flipping once. Let the lamb chops rest for a few minutes. Serve with the couscous.

Tandoori Lamb Samosas

Serves: 2 | Total Time: 20 minutes

6 oz ground lamb, sautéed	½ tsp red chili powder
¼ cup spinach, torn	½ tsp turmeric powder
½ onion, minced	Salt and pepper to taste
1 tsp tandoori masala	3 puff dough sheets
½ tsp ginger-garlic paste	

Preheat air fryer to 350°F. Put the ground lamb, tandoori masala, ginger garlic paste, red chili powder, turmeric powder, salt, and pepper in a bowl and stir to combine. Add in the spinach and onion and stir until the ingredients are evenly blended. Divide the mixture into three equal segments.

Lay the pastry dough sheets out on a lightly floured surface. Fill each sheet of dough with one of the three portions of lamb mix, then fold the pastry into a triangle, sealing the edges with a bit of water. Transfer the samosas to the greased frying basket and Air Fry for 12 minutes, flipping once until the samosas are crispy and flaky. Remove and leave to cool for 5 minutes. Serve.

Moroccan-Style Lamb Chops

Serves: 2 | Total Time: 25 minutes

3 lamb chops	½ tbsp mint, chopped
1 cup breadcrumbs	½ tsp garlic powder
2 eggs, beaten	½ tsp ground rosemary
Salt and pepper to taste	½ tsp cayenne powder
½ tbsp thyme	½ tsp ras el hanout

Preheat air fryer to 320°F. Mix the breadcrumbs, thyme, mint, garlic, rosemary, cayenne, ras el hanout, salt, and pepper in a bowl. Dip the lamb chops in the beaten eggs, then coat with the crumb mixture. Air Fry for 14-16 minutes, turning once. Serve and enjoy!

Baharat Lamb Kebab with Mint Sauce

Serves: 6 | Total Time 50 minutes

1 lb ground lamb	¼ tsp chili powder
¼ cup parsley, chopped	¼ tsp ground ginger
3 garlic cloves, minced	3 tbsp olive oil
1 shallot, diced	1 cup Greek yogurt
Salt and pepper to taste	½ cup mint, chopped
1 tsp ground cumin	2 tbsp lemon juice
¼ tsp ground cinnamon	¼ tsp hot paprika
¼ tsp baharat seasoning	

Preheat air fryer to 360°F. Mix the ground lamb, parsley, 2 garlic cloves, shallot, 2 tbsp olive oil, salt, black pepper, cumin, cinnamon, baharat seasoning, chili powder, and ginger in a bowl. Divide the mixture into 4 equal quantities, and roll each into a long oval. Drizzle with the remaining olive oil, place them in a single layer in the frying basket and Air Fry for 10 minutes. While the kofta is cooking, mix together the Greek yogurt, mint, remaining garlic, lemon juice, hot paprika, salt, and pepper in a bowl. Serve the kofta with mint sauce.

VEGETABLES & SIDES

Crunchy Fried Mushrooms

Serves: 4 | Total Time: 30 minutes

1 cup panko bread crumbs
1 cup white mushrooms
1 cup flour
1 egg, beaten

½ tsp smoked paprika
3 garlic cloves, minced
Salt and pepper to taste
1 cup arrabbiata sauce

Preheat the air fryer to 400°F. Put the flour on a plate. Mix the egg, garlic, and salt in a shallow bowl. Mix the panko bread crumbs, smoked paprika, salt, and pepper on a separate plate. Cut the mushrooms through the stems into quarters. Dip the mushrooms in flour, then the egg, then in the panko mix. Press to coat, then put on a wire rack and set aside. Add the mushrooms to the frying basket in a single layer and spray with cooking oil. Air Fry for 6-8 minutes, flipping them once until crisp. Serve warm with arrabbiata sauce for dipping.

Sage Hasselback Potatoes

Serves: 4 | Total Time: 45 minutes

1 lb fingerling potatoes
1 tbsp olive oil
1 tbsp butter

1tsp dried sage
Salt and pepper to taste

Preheat the air fryer to 400°F. Rinse the potatoes dry, then set them on a work surface and put two chopsticks lengthwise on either side of each so you won't cut all the way through. Make vertical, crosswise cuts in the potato, about ⅛ inch apart. Repeat with the remaining potatoes. Combine the olive oil and butter in a bowl and microwave for 30 seconds or until melted. Stir in the sage, salt, and pepper. Put the potatoes in a large bowl and drizzle with the olive oil mixture. Toss to coat, then put the potatoes in the fryer and Air Fry for 22-27 minutes, rearranging them after 10-12 minutes. Cook until the potatoes are tender. Serve hot and enjoy!

Mom's Potatoes au Gratin

Serves: 4 | Total Time: 50 minutes

4 Yukon Gold potatoes, peeled
1cup shredded cheddar cheese
2 tbsp grated Parmesan cheese
2 garlic cloves, minced
1/3 cup heavy cream
1/3 cup whole milk

½ tsp dried marjoram
Salt and pepper to taste

Preheat the air fryer to 350°F. Spray a 7-inch round pan thoroughly with cooking oil. Cut the potatoes into ⅛-inch-thick slices and layer the potatoes inside the pan along with cheddar cheese and garlic. Mix the cream, milk, marjoram, salt, and pepper in a bowl, then slowly pour the mix over the potatoes. Sprinkle with Parmesan and put the pan in the fryer. Bake for 25-35 minutes or until the potatoes are tender, the sauce is bubbling, and the top is golden. Serve warm.

Garlicky Brussels Sprouts

Serves: 4 | Total Time: 35 minutes

1 lb Brussels sprouts, halved lengthwise
1 tbsp olive oil
1 tbsp lemon juice
½ tsp sea salt
⅛ tsp garlic powder

4 garlic cloves, sliced
2 tbsp parsley, chopped
½ tsp red chili flakes

Preheat the air fryer to 375°F. Combine the olive oil, lemon juice, salt, and garlic powder in a bowl and mix well. Add the Brussels sprouts and toss to coat. Put the Brussels sprouts in the frying basket. Air Fry for 15-20 minutes, shaking the basket once until golden and crisp. Sprinkle with garlic slices, parsley, and chili flakes. Toss and cook for 2-4 minutes more until the garlic browns slightly.

Broccoli in Adobo

Serves: 4 | Total Time: 25 minutes

1 chipotle pepper in adobo sauce, minced
1 lb broccoli
2 tbsp chili oil
1 tbsp adobo sauce

2 tsp chili powder
Salt and pepper to taste

Preheat the air fryer to 375°F. Rinse the broccoli and shake dry, then cut into about 2-inch-wide florets. Combine the chili oil, chipotle pepper, adobo sauce, chili powder, salt, and pepper in a bowl and mix well. Add the broccoli and toss to coat evenly. Put the broccoli in the frying basket and Air Fry for 13-18 minutes, shaking the basket once halfway through until the broccoli is crispy.

Smoky Roasted Veggie Chips

Serves: 4 | Total Time: 40 minutes

2 tbsp butter
2 tsp smoked paprika
1 tsp dried dill
Salt and pepper to taste

2 carrots, cut into rounds
1 parsnip, cut into rounds
1 tbsp chopped fresh dill

Preheat the air fryer to 375°F. Combine the butter, paprika, dried dill, salt, and pepper in a small pan, over low heat until the butter melts. Put the carrots and parsnip in the frying basket, top with the butter mix, and toss. Air Fry for 20-25 minutes or until the veggies are tender and golden around the edges. Toss with fresh dill and serve.

Honey-Mustard Asparagus Puffs

Serves: 4 | Total Time: 35 minutes

8 asparagus spears
½ sheet puff pastry

2 tbsp honey mustard
1 egg, lightly beaten

Preheat the air fryer to 375°F. Spread the pastry with honey mustard and cut it into 8 strips. Wrap the pastry, honey mustard–side in, around the asparagus. Put a rack in the frying basket and lay the asparagus spears on the rack. Brush all over pastries with beaten egg and Air Fry for 12-17 minutes or until the pastry is golden. Serve.

Horseradish Potato Mash

Serves: 4 | Total Time: 50 minutes

1 lb baby potatoes	3 tbsp butter
1 tbsp horseradish sauce	2 garlic cloves, minced
½ cup vegetable broth	2 tsp chili powder
½ tsp sea salt	

Preheat the air fryer to 400°F. Combine the potatoes, broth, and salt in a cake pan, then cover with foil and put it in the frying basket. Bake for 20 minutes, stirring once, until they are almost tender. Drain and place them on a baking sheet. With the bottom of a glass, smash the potatoes, but don't break them apart. Put a small saucepan on the stove and mix butter, garlic, chili powder, and horseradish sauce. Melt the butter over low heat, then brush over the potatoes. Put as many as will fit in the basket in a single layer, butter-side down. Brush the tops with more of the butter mix, and Bake for 12-17 minutes, turning once until they're crisp. Keep the cooked potatoes warm in the oven at 250°F while air frying the rest of the potatoes.

Herby Roasted Cherry Tomatoes

Serves: 4 | Total Time: 20 minutes

1 tbsp dried oregano	1 tsp salt
1 tbsp dried basil	2 tbsp balsamic vinegar
2 tsp dried marjoram	20 cherry tomatoes
1 tsp dried thyme	1 tbsp olive oil

Preheat the air fryer to 400°F. Combine the oregano, basil, marjoram, thyme, and salt in a small bowl and mix well. Pout into a small glass jar. Poke each cherry tomato with a toothpick to prevent bursting. Put the tomatoes, balsamic vinegar and olive oil on a piece of aluminum foil and sprinkle with 1½ tsp of the herb mix; toss. Wrap the foil around the tomatoes, leaving air space in the packet, and seal loosely. Put the packet in the air fryer and Bake for 8-10 minutes or until the tomatoes are tender.

Honey-Mustard Roasted Cabbage

Serves: 4 | Total Time: 35 minutes

4 cups chopped green cabbage
1/3 cup honey mustard dressing

1 shallot, chopped	1 tbsp lemon juice
2 garlic cloves, minced	1 tbsp cornstarch
2 tbsp olive oil	½ tsp fennel seeds

Preheat the air fryer to 370°F. Toss the cabbage, shallot, olive oil and garlic in a cake pan. Bake for 10 minutes or until the cabbage is wilted, then drain the excess liquid. While the cabbage is cooking, combine the salad dressing, lemon juice, cornstarch, and fennel seeds in a bowl. Take cake pan out of the fryer and pour out any excess liquid. Pour the dressing mix over the drained cabbage and mix well. Return the pan to the fryer and Bake for 7-11 minutes more, stirring twice during cooking until the cabbage is tender and the sauce has thickened. Serve warm.

Sweet Roasted Pumpkin Rounds

Serves: 4 | Total Time: 35 minutes

1 (2-lb) pumpkin	¼ tsp cardamom
1 tbsp honey	¼ tsp sea salt
1 tbsp melted butter	

Preheat the air fryer to 370°F. Cut the pumpkin in half lengthwise and remove the seeds. Slice each half crosswise into 1-inch-wide half-circles, then cut each half-circle in half again to make quarter rounds. Combine the honey, butter, cardamom, and salt in a bowl and mix well. Toss the pumpkin in the mixture until coated, then put it into the frying basket. Bake for 15-20 minutes, shaking once during cooking, until the edges start to brown and the squash is tender.

Stunning Apples & Onions

Serves: 4 | Total Time: 30 minutes

2 peeled McIntosh apples, sliced

1 shallot, sliced	1 tbsp honey
2 tsp canola oil	1 tbsp butter, melted
2 tbsp brown sugar	½ tsp sea salt

Preheat the air fryer to 325°F. Toss the shallot slices with oil in a bowl until coated. Put the bowl in the fryer and Bake for 5 minutes. Remove the bowl and add the apples, brown sugar, honey, melted butter, and sea salt and stir. Put the bowl back into the fryer and Bake for 10-12 more minutes or until the onions and apples are tender. Stir again and serve.

Za'atar Bell Peppers

Serves: 4 | Total Time: 40 minutes

1 red bell pepper	2 tsp Za'atar seasoning
1 orange bell pepper	1 tbsp lemon zest
1 yellow bell pepper	½ tsp salt

Preheat the air fryer to 370°F. Pierce the peppers with a fork a few times. Put them in the greased frying basket and Air Fry for 12-15 minutes, shaking once until slightly charred. Remove them to a small and let them sit covered for 10 minutes to steam. Slice the pepper and sprinkle with Za'atar seasoning, lemon zest, and salt. Serve and enjoy!

Sesame Carrots

Serves: 4 | Total Time: 25 minutes

1 lb baby carrots	1 tsp smoked paprika
1 tbsp sesame oil	3 tbsp sesame seeds
Garlic salt to taste	1 tbsp green onions

Preheat air fryer to 380°F. In a bowl, add baby carrots, sesame oil, garlic salt, and smoked paprika. Toss to coat. Transfer the carrots to the frying basket. Roast for about 4 minutes. Shake the basket and continue roasting for another 4 minutes or until the garlic and carrots are slightly brown. Pour into a serving bowl and top with sesame seeds and green onions. Enjoy!

Simple Green Vegetable Bake

Serves: 4 | Total Time: 15 minutes

1 cup asparagus, chopped	1 cup green peas
2 cups broccoli florets	2 tbsp honey mustard
1 tbsp olive oil	Salt and pepper to taste
1 tbsp lemon juice	

Preheat air fryer to 330°F. Add asparagus and broccoli to the frying basket. Drizzle with olive oil and lemon juice and toss. Bake for 6 minutes. Remove the basket and add peas. Steam for another 3 minutes or until the vegetables are hot and tender. Pour the vegetables into a serving dish. Drizzle with honey mustard and season with salt and pepper. Toss and serve warm.

Garlicky Bell Pepper Mix

Serves: 4 | Total Time: 30 minutes

2 tbsp vegetable oil	1 orange bell pepper
½ tsp dried cilantro	1 green bell pepper
1 red bell pepper	Salt and pepper to taste
1 yellow bell pepper	1 head garlic

Preheat air fryer to 330°F. Slice the peppers into 1-inch strips. Transfer them to a large bowl along with 1 tbsp of vegetable oil. Toss to coat. Season with cilantro, salt, and pepper. Cut the top of a garlic head and place it cut-side up on an oiled square of aluminium foil. Drizzle with vegetable oil and wrap completely in the foil.

Roast the wrapped garlic in the air fryer for 15 minutes. Next, add the pepper strips and roast until the peppers are tender and the garlic is soft, 6-8 minutes. Transfer the peppers to a serving dish. Remove the garlic and unwrap the foil carefully. Once cooled, squeeze the cloves out of the garlic head and mix into the peppers' dish. Serve.

Buttered Brussels Sprouts

Serves: 4 | Total Time: 30 minutes

¼ cup grated Parmesan	1 lb Brussels sprouts
2 tbsp butter, melted	Salt and pepper to taste

Preheat air fryer to 330°F. Trim the bottoms of the sprouts and remove any discolored leaves. Place the sprouts in a medium bowl along with butter, salt, and pepper. Toss to coat, then place them in the frying basket. Roast for 20 minutes, shaking the basket twice. When done, the sprouts should be crisp with golden-brown color. Plate the sprouts in a serving dish and toss with Parmesan cheese.

Cheese & Rice Stuffed Bell Peppers

Serves: 4 | Total Time: 30 minutes

2 red bell peppers, halved and seeds and stem removed	
1 cup cooked brown rice	3 tbsp basil, chopped
2 tomatoes, diced	3 tbsp oregano, chopped
1 garlic clove, minced	1 tbsp parsley, chopped
Salt and pepper to taste	¼ cup grated Parmesan
4 oz goat cheese	

Preheat air fryer to 360°F. Place the brown rice, tomatoes, garlic, salt, and pepper in a bowl and stir. Divide the rice filling evenly among the bell pepper halves. Combine the goat cheese, basil, parsley and oregano in a small bowl. Sprinkle each bell pepper with the herbed cheese. Arrange the bell peppers on the air fryer and Bake for 20 minutes. Serve topped with grated Parmesan and parsley.

Teriyaki Tofu with Spicy Mayo

Serves: 2 | Total Time: 35 minutes + 1 Hour To Marinate

1 scallion, chopped	1 garlic clove, grated
7 oz extra-firm tofu, sliced	½ tsp grated ginger
2 tbsp soy sauce	1/3 cup sesame seeds
1 tsp toasted sesame oil	1 egg
1 red chili, thinly sliced	4 tsp mayonnaise
1 tsp mirin	1 tbsp lime juice
1 tsp light brown sugar	1 tsp hot chili powder

Squeeze most of the water from the tofu by lightly pressing the slices between two towels. Place the tofu in a baking dish. Use a whisk to mix soy sauce, sesame oil, red chili, mirin, brown sugar, garlic and ginger. Pour half of the marinade over the tofu. Using a spatula, carefully flip the tofu down and pour the other half of the marinade over. Refrigerate for 1 hour.

Preheat air fryer to 400°F. In a shallow plate, add sesame seeds. In another shallow plate, beat the egg. Remove the tofu from the refrigerator. Let any excess marinade drip off. Dip each piece in the egg mixture and then in the sesame seeds. Transfer to greased frying basket. Air Fry for 10 minutes, flipping once until toasted and crispy. Mix the mayonnaise, lime juice, and hot chili powder in a small bowl. Top with a dollop of hot chili mayo and some scallions. Serve and enjoy!

Cumin Sweet Potato Wedges

Serves: 4 | Total Time: 30 minutes

2 peeled sweet potatoes, cubed	
¼ cup grated Parmesan	½ tsp dried thyme
1 tbsp olive oil	½ tsp ground cumin
Salt and pepper to taste	

Preheat air fryer to 330°F. Add sweet potato cubes to the frying basket, then drizzle with oil. Toss to gently coat. Season with salt, pepper, thyme, and cumin. Roast the potatoes for about 10 minutes. Shake the basket and continue roasting for another 10 minutes. Shake the basket again, this time adding Parmesan cheese. Shake and return to the air fryer. Roast until the potatoes are tender, 4-6 minutes. Serve and enjoy!

Rosemary Potato Salad

Serves: 4 | Total Time: 30 minutes

3 tbsp olive oil	2 green onions, chopped
2 lb red potatoes, halved	1/3 cup lemon juice
Salt and pepper to taste	3 tbsp Dijon mustard
1 red bell pepper, chopped	1 tbsp rosemary, chopped

Preheat air fryer to 350°F. Add potatoes to the frying basket and drizzle with 1 tablespoon olive oil. Season with salt and pepper. Roast the potatoes for 25 minutes, shaking twice. Potatoes will be tender and lightly golden.

While the potatoes are roasting, add peppers and green onions in a bowl. In a separate bowl, whisk olive oil, lemon juice, and mustard. When the potatoes are done, transfer them to a large bowl. Pour the mustard dressing over and toss to coat. Serve sprinkled with rosemary.

Broccoli Au Gratin

Serves: 2 | Total Time: 25 minutes

2 cups broccoli florets, chopped
6 tbsp grated Gruyère cheese | 1/3 cup milk
1 tbsp grated Pecorino cheese | ½ tsp ground coriander
½ tbsp olive oil | Salt and black pepper
1 tbsp flour | 2 tbsp panko bread crumbs

Whisk the olive oil, flour, milk, coriander, salt, and pepper in a bowl. Incorporate broccoli, Gruyere cheese, panko bread crumbs, and Pecorino cheese until well combined. Pour in a greased baking dish.

Preheat air fryer to 330°F. Put the baking dish into the frying basket. Bake until the broccoli is crisp-tender and the top is golden, or about 12-15 minutes. Serve warm.

Tasty Brussels Sprouts with Guanciale

Serves: 4 | Total Time: 50 minutes

3 guanciale slices, halved | ¼ tsp salt
1 lb Brussels sprouts, halved | ¼ tsp dried thyme
2 tbsp olive oil

Preheat air fryer to 350°F. Air Fry Lay the guanciale in the air fryer until crispy, 10 minutes. Remove and drain on a paper towel. Give the guanciale a rough chop and Set aside. Coat Brussels sprouts with olive oil in a large bowl. Add salt and thyme, then toss. Place the sprouts in the frying basket. Air Fry for about 12-15 minutes, shake the basket once until the sprouts are golden and tender. Top with guanciale and serve.

Breaded Artichoke Hearts

Serves: 2 | Total Time: 25 minutes

1 (15-oz) can artichoke hearts in water, drained
1 egg | ¼ tsp hot paprika
¼ cup bread crumbs | ½ lemon
¼ tsp salt | ¼ cup garlic aioli

Preheat air fryer to 380°F. Whisk together the egg and 1 tbsp of water in a bowl until frothy. Mix together the bread crumbs, salt, and hot paprika in a separate bowl. Dip the artichoke hearts into the egg mixture, then coat in the bread crumb mixture. Put the artichoke hearts in a single layer in the frying basket. Air Fry for 15 minutes.

Remove the artichokes from the air fryer, and squeeze fresh lemon juice over the top. Serve with garlic aioli.

Corn Au Gratin

Serves: 4 | Total Time: 20 minutes

½ cup grated cheddar | ¼ cup milk
3 tbsp flour | ½ cup heavy cream
2 cups yellow corn | Salt and pepper to taste
1 egg, beaten | 2 tbsp butter, cubed

Preheat air fryer to 320°F. Mix flour, corn, egg, milk, and heavy cream in a medium bowl. Stir in cheddar cheese, salt, and pepper. Pour into the prepared baking pan. Top with butter. Bake for 15 minutes. Serve warm.

Herb Roasted Jicama

Serves: 6 | Total Time: 25 minutes

1 lb jicama, cut into fries | 1 garlic clove, minced
¼ cup olive oil | 4 thyme sprigs
Salt and pepper to taste

Preheat air fryer to 360°F. Coat the jicamas with olive oil, salt, pepper, and garlic in a bowl. Pour the jicama fries into the frying basket and top with the thyme sprigs. Roast for 20 minutes, stirring twice. Remove the rosemary sprigs. Serve and enjoy!

Sea Salt Radishes

Serves: 4 | Total Time: 25 minutes

1 lb radishes | ½ tsp sea salt
2 tbsp olive oil | ½ tsp garlic powder

Preheat air fryer to 360°F. Toss the radishes with olive oil, garlic powder, and salt in a bowl. Pour them into the air fryer. Air Fry for 18 minutes, turning once. Serve.

Vegetable Roast

Serves: 6 | Total Time: 20 minutes

2 tbsp dill, chopped | 2 tbsp olive oil
2 zucchini, cubed | ½ tsp salt
1 red bell pepper, diced | ½ tsp red pepper flakes
2 garlic cloves, sliced

Preheat air fryer to 380°F. Combine the zucchini, bell pepper, red pepper flakes, dill and garlic with olive oil and salt in a bowl. Pour the mixture into the frying basket and Roast for 14-16 minutes, shaking once. Serve warm.

Sage & Thyme Potatoes

Serves: 4 | Total Time: 30 minutes

2 red potatoes, peeled and cubed
¼ cup olive oil | ½ tsp salt
1 tsp dried sage | 2 tbsp grated Parmesan
½ tsp dried thyme

Preheat air fryer to 360°F. Coat the red potatoes with olive oil, sage, thyme and salt in a bowl. Pour the potatoes into the air frying basket and Roast for 10 minutes. Stir the potatoes and sprinkle the Parmesan over the top. Continue roasting for 8 more minutes. Serve hot.

Citrusy Brussels Sprouts

Serves: 4 | Total Time: 15 minutes

1 lb Brussels sprouts, quartered
1 clementine, cut into rings
2 garlic cloves, minced   1 tbsp butter, melted
1 tbsp olive oil   ½ tsp salt

Preheat air fryer to 360°F. Add the quartered Brussels sprouts with the garlic, olive oil, butter and salt in a bowl and toss until well coated. Pour the Brussels sprouts into the air fryer, top with the clementine slices, and Roast for 10 minutes. Remove from the air fryer and set the clementines aside. Toss the Brussels sprouts and serve.

Lemony Green Bean Sautée

Serves: 6 | Total Time: 15 minutes

1 tbsp cilantro, chopped   Salt and pepper to taste
1 lb green beans, trimmed   1 tbsp grapefruit juice
½ red onion, sliced   6 lemon wedges
2 tbsp olive oil

Preheat air fryer to 360°F. Coat the green beans, red onion, olive oil, salt, pepper, cilantro and grapefruit juice in a bowl. Pour the mixture into the air fryer and Bake for 5 minutes. Stir well and cook for 5 minutes more. Serve with lemon wedges. Enjoy!

Roasted Baby Carrots

Serves: 6 | Total Time: 20 minutes

1 lb baby carrots   ¼ tsp ground cinnamon
2 tbsp olive oil   ¼ tsp ground nutmeg
¼ cup raw honey   ¼ cup pecans, chopped

Preheat air fryer to 360°F. Place the baby carrots with olive oil, honey, nutmeg and cinnamon in a bowl and toss to coat. Pour into the air fryer and Roast for 6 minutes. Shake the basket, sprinkle the pecans on top, and cook for 6 minutes more. Serve and enjoy!

Asparagus & Cherry Tomato Roast

Serves: 6 | Total Time: 20 minutes

2 tbsp dill, chopped   2 tbsp olive oil
2 cups cherry tomatoes   3 garlic cloves, minced
1 ½ lb asparagus, trimmed   ½ tsp salt

Preheat air fryer to 380°F. Add all ingredients to a bowl, except for dill, and toss until the vegetables are well coated with the oil. Pour the vegetable mixture into the frying basket and Roast for 11-13 minutes, shaking once. Serve topped with fresh dill.

Greek-Inspired Ratatouille

Serves: 6 | Total Time: 55 minutes

1 cup cherry tomatoes   1 eggplant, cubed
½ bulb fennel, finely sliced   1 zucchini, cubed
2 russet potatoes, cubed   1 red onion, chopped
½ cup tomatoes, cubed   1 red bell pepper, chopped
2 garlic cloves, minced   ¼ tsp red pepper flakes
1 tsp dried mint   1/3 cup olive oil
1 tsp dried parsley   1 (8-oz) can tomato paste
1 tsp Greek dried oregano   ¼ cup vegetable broth
Salt and pepper to taste

Preheat air fryer to 320°F. Mix the potatoes, tomatoes, fennel, eggplant, zucchini, onion, bell pepper, garlic, mint, parsley, oregano, salt, black pepper, and red pepper flakes in a bowl. Whisk the olive oil, tomato paste, broth, and ¼ cup of water in a small bowl. Toss the mixture with the vegetables.

Pour the coated vegetables into the air frying basket in a single layer and Roast for 20 minutes. Stir well and spread out again. Roast for an additional 10 minutes, then repeat the process and cook for another 10 minutes. Serve and enjoy!

Spiced Pumpkin Wedges

Serves: 4 | Total Time: 35 minutes

2 ½ cups pumpkin, cubed   ¼ tsp pumpkin pie spice
2 tbsp olive oil   1 tbsp thyme
Salt and pepper to taste   ¼ cup grated Parmesan

Preheat air fryer to 360°F. Put the cubed pumpkin with olive oil, salt, pumpkin pie spice, black pepper, and thyme in a bowl and stir until the pumpkin is well coated. Pour this mixture into the frying basket and Roast for 18-20 minutes, stirring once. Sprinkle the pumpkin with grated Parmesan. Serve and enjoy!

Italian Breaded Eggplant Rounds

Serves: 4 | Total Time: 30 minutes

1 eggplant, sliced into rounds ½ tsp Italian seasoning
1 egg   ½ tsp garlic salt
½ cup bread crumbs   ½ tsp paprika
1 tsp onion powder   1 tbsp olive oil

Preheat air fryer to 360°F. Whisk the egg and 1 tbsp of water in a bowl until frothy. Mix the bread crumbs, onion powder, Italian seasoning, salt, and paprika separately. Dip the eggplant slices into the egg mixture, then coat them into the bread crumb mixture. Put the slices in a single layer in the frying basket. Drizzle with olive oil. Air Fry for 23-25 minutes, turning once. Serve warm.

Cinnamon Roasted Pumpkin

Serves: 2 | Total Time: 25 minutes

1 lb pumpkin, halved crosswise and seeded
1 tsp coconut oil   ½ tsp ground nutmeg
1 tsp sugar   1 tsp ground cinnamon

Prepare the pumpkin by rubbing coconut oil on the cut sides. In a small bowl, combine sugar, nutmeg and cinnamon. Sprinkle over the pumpkin. Preheat air fryer to 325°F. Put the pumpkin in the greased frying basket, cut sides up. Bake until the squash is soft in the center, 15 minutes. Test with a knife to ensure softness. Serve.

Goat Cheese Stuffed Portobellos

Serves: 4 | Total Time: 35 minutes

1 cup baby spinach	1 garlic clove, minced
¾ cup crumbled goat cheese	¼ cup chopped parsley
2 tsp grated Parmesan cheese	2 tbsp panko bread crumbs
4 portobello caps, cleaned	1 tbsp chopped oregano
Salt and pepper to taste	1 tbsp olive oil
2 tomatoes, chopped	Balsamic glaze for drizzling
1 leek, chopped	

Brush the mushrooms with olive oil and sprinkle with salt. Mix the remaining ingredients, excluding the balsamic glaze, in a bowl. Fill each mushroom cap with the mixture. Preheat air fryer to 370°F. Place the mushroom caps in the greased frying basket and Bake for 10-12 minutes or until the top is golden and the mushrooms are tender. Carefully transfer them to a serving dish. Drizzle with balsamic glaze and serve warm. Enjoy!

Truffle Vegetable Croquettes

Serves: 4 | Total Time: 40 minutes

2 cooked potatoes, mashed	2 tbsp melted butter
1 cooked carrot, mashed	1 tbsp truffle oil
1 tbsp onion, minced	½ tbsp flour
2 eggs, beaten	Salt and pepper to taste

Preheat air fryer to 350°F. Sift the flour, salt, and pepper in a bowl and stir to combine. Add the potatoes, carrot, onion, butter, and truffle oil to a separate bowl and mix well. Shape the potato mixture into small bite-sized patties. Dip the potato patties into the beaten eggs, coating thoroughly, then roll in the flour mixture to cover all sides. Arrange the croquettes in the greased frying basket and Air Fry for 14-16 minutes. Halfway through cooking, shake the basket. The croquettes should be crispy and golden. Serve hot and enjoy!

Balsamic Beet Chips

Serves: 4 | Total Time: 40 minutes

½ tsp balsamic vinegar	2 tbsp chopped mint
4 beets, peeled and sliced	Salt and pepper to taste
1 garlic clove, minced	3 tbsp olive oil

Preheat air fryer to 380°F. Coat all ingredients in a bowl, except balsamic vinegar. Pour the beet mixture into the frying basket and Roast for 25-30 minutes, stirring once. Serve, drizzled with vinegar and enjoy!

Roasted Bell Peppers with Garlic & Dill

Serves: 4 | Total Time: 30 minutes

4 bell peppers, seeded and cut into fourths	
1 tsp olive oil	½ tsp dried dill
4 garlic cloves, minced	

Preheat air fryer to 350°F. Add the peppers to the frying basket, spritz with olive oil, shake, and Roast for 15 minutes. Season with garlic and dill, then cook for an additional 3-5 minutes. The veggies should be soft. Serve.

Sticky Broccoli Florets

Serves: 4 | Total Time: 20 minutes

4 cups broccoli florets	½ cup grapefruit juice
2 tbsp olive oil	1 tbsp raw honey
½ tsp salt	4-6 grapefruit wedges

Preheat air fryer to 360°F. Add the broccoli, olive oil, salt, grapefruit juice, and honey to a bowl. Toss the broccoli in the liquid until well coated. Pour the broccoli mixture into the frying basket and Roast for 12 minutes, stirring once. Serve with grapefruit wedges.

Cheesy Cauliflower Tart

Serves: 4 | Total Time: 40 minutes

½ cup cooked cauliflower, chopped	
¼ cup grated Swiss cheese	¼ cup milk
¼ cup shredded cheddar	6 black olives, chopped
1 pie crust	Salt and pepper to taste
2 eggs	

Preheat air fryer to 360°F. Grease and line a tart tin with the pie crust. Trim the edges and prick lightly with a fork. Whisk the eggs in a bowl until fluffy. Add the milk, cauliflower, salt, pepper, black olives, and half the cheddar and Swiss cheeses; stir to combine. Carefully spoon the mixture into the pie crust and spread it level. Bake in the air fryer for 15 minutes. Slide the basket out and sprinkle the rest of the cheeses on top. Cook for another 5 minutes or until golden on the top and cooked through. Leave to cool before serving.

Sriracha Green Beans

Serves: 4 | Total Time: 30 minutes

½ tbsp toasted sesame seeds	4 tsp canola oil
1 tbsp tamari	12 oz trimmed green beans
½ tbsp Sriracha sauce	1 tbsp cilantro, chopped

Mix the tamari, sriracha, and 1 tsp of canola oil in a small bowl. In a large bowl, toss green beans with the remaining oil. Preheat air fryer to 375°F. Place the green beans in the frying basket and Air Fry for 8 minutes, shaking the basket once until the beans are charred and tender. Toss the beans with sauce, cilantro, and sesame seeds. Serve.

Layered Mixed Vegetables

Serves: 4 | Total Time: 30 minutes

1 Yukon Gold potato, sliced	3 garlic cloves, minced
1 eggplant, sliced	¾ cup milk
1 carrot, thinly sliced	2 tbsp cornstarch
¼ cup minced onions	½ tsp dried thyme

Preheat air fryer to 380°F. In layers, add the potato, eggplant, carrot, onion, and garlic to a baking pan. Combine the milk, cornstarch, and thyme in a bowl, then pour this mix over the veggies. Put the pan in the air fryer and Bake for 15 minutes. The casserole should be golden on top with softened veggies. Serve immediately.

Asparagus Wrapped in Pancetta

Serves: 4 | Total Time: 30 minutes

20 asparagus trimmed	4 pancetta slices
Salt and pepper pepper	1 tbsp fresh sage, chopped

Sprinkle the asparagus with fresh sage, salt, and pepper. Toss to coat. Make 4 bundles of 5 spears by wrapping the center of the bunch with one slice of pancetta.

Preheat air fryer to 400°F. Put the bundles in the greased frying basket and Air Fry for 8-10 minutes or until the pancetta is brown and the asparagus are starting to char on the edges. Serve immediately.

Simple Baked Potatoes with Dill Yogurt

Serves: 4 | Total Time: 45 minutes

4 Yukon gold potatoes	½ cup Greek yogurt
Salt and black pepper	¼ cup minced dill

Pierce the potatoes with a fork. Lightly coat them with sprays of cooking oil, then season with salt. Preheat air fryer to 400°F. Air Fry the potatoes in the greased frying basket for 30-35 minutes, flipping once halfway through cooking until completely cooked and slightly crispy. A knife will cut into the center of the potato with ease. Remove them to a serving dish. Add toppings of yogurt, dill, salt, and pepper to taste.

Mexican-Style Frittata

Serves: 4 | Total Time: 35 minutes

½ cup shredded Cotija cheese	
½ cup cooked black beans	3 eggs, beaten
1 cooked potato, sliced	Salt and pepper to taste

Preheat air fryer to 350°F. Mix the eggs, beans, half of Cotija cheese, salt, and pepper in a bowl. Pour the mixture into a greased baking dish. Top with potato slices. Place the baking dish in the frying basket and Air Fry for 10 minutes. Slide the basket out and sprinkle the remaining Cotija cheese over the dish. Cook for 10 more minutes or until golden and bubbling. Slice into wedges to serve.

Smooth & Silky Cauliflower Purée

Serves: 4 | Total Time: 25 minutes

1 head cauliflower, cut into florets	
1 rutabaga, diced	2 oz cream cheese, softened
4 tbsp butter, divided	½ cup milk
Salt and pepper to taste	1 tsp dried thyme
3 cloves garlic, peeled	

Preheat air fryer to 350°F. Combine cauliflower, rutabaga, 2 tbsp of butter, and salt to taste in a bowl. Add veggie mixture to the frying basket and Air Fry for 10 minutes, tossing once. Put in garlic and Air Fry for 5 more minutes. Let them cool a bit, then transfer them to a blender. Blend them along with 2 tbsp of butter, salt, black pepper, cream cheese, thyme and milk until smooth. Serve immediately.

Dijon Roasted Purple Potatoes

Serves: 4 | Total Time: 25 minutes

1 lb purple potatoes, scrubbed and halved	
1 tbsp olive oil	Salt and pepper to taste
1 tsp Dijon mustard	2 tbsp butter, melted
1 tsp lemon juice	1 tbsp chopped cilantro
2 cloves garlic, minced	1 tsp fresh rosemary

Mix the olive oil, mustard, garlic, lemon juice, pepper, salt and rosemary in a bowl. Let chill covered in the fridge until ready to use.

Preheat air fryer to 350°F. Toss the potatoes, salt, pepper, and butter in a bowl, place the potatoes in the frying basket, and Roast for 18-20 minutes, tossing once. Transfer them into a bowl. Drizzle potatoes with the dressing and toss to coat. Garnish with cilantro to serve.

Cheese Sage Cauliflower

Serves 4 | Total Time: 25 minutes

1 head cauliflower, cut into florets	
3 tbsp butter, melted	½ tsp garlic powder
2 tbsp grated asiago cheese	¼ tsp salt
2 tsp dried sage	

Preheat air fryer to 350°F. Mix all ingredients in a bowl. Add cauliflower mixture to the frying basket and Air Fry for 6 minutes, shaking once. Serve immediately.

Speedy Baked Caprese with Avocado

Serves 4 | Total Time: 15 minutes

4 oz fresh mozzarella	2 halved avocados, pitted
8 cherry tomatoes	¼ tsp salt
2 tsp olive oil	2 tbsp basil, torn

Preheat air fryer to 375°F. In a bowl, combine tomatoes and olive oil. Set aside. Add avocado halves, cut sides up, in the frying basket, scatter tomatoes around halves, and Bake for 7 minutes. Divide avocado halves between 4 small plates, top each with 2 tomatoes and sprinkle with salt. Cut mozzarella cheese and evenly distribute over tomatoes. Scatter with the basil to serve.

Southwestern Sweet Potato Wedges

Serves: 4 | Total Time: 30 minutes

2 sweet potatoes, peeled and cut into ½-inch wedges	
2 tsp olive oil	¼ tsp ground allspice
2 tbsp cornstarch	¼ tsp paprika
1 tsp garlic powder	⅛ tsp cayenne pepper

Preheat air fryer to 400°F. Place the sweet potatoes in a bowl. Add some olive oil and toss to coat, then transfer to the frying basket. Roast for 8 minutes. Sprinkle the potatoes with cornstarch, garlic powder, allspice, paprika, and cayenne, then toss. Put the potatoes back into the fryer and Roast for 12-17 more minutes. Shake the basket a couple of times while cooking. The potatoes should be golden and crispy. Serve warm.

Farmers' Market Veggie Medley

Serves: 4 | Total Time: 45 minutes

3 tsp grated Parmesan cheese
½ lb carrots, sliced
½ lb asparagus, sliced
½ lb zucchini, sliced

3 tbsp olive oil
Salt and pepper to taste
½ tsp garlic powder
1 tbsp thyme, chopped

Preheat air fryer to 390°F. Coat the carrots with some olive oil in a bowl. Air fry the carrots for 5 minutes. Meanwhile, mix the asparagus and zucchini together and drizzle with the remaining olive oil. Season with salt, pepper, and garlic powder.

When the time is over, slide the basket out and spread the zucchini-squash mixture on top of the carrots. Bake for 10-15 more minutes, stirring the vegetables several times during cooking. Sprinkle with Parmesan cheese and thyme. Serve and enjoy!

Hot Okra Wedges

Serves: 2 | Total Time: 35 minutes

1 cup okra, sliced
1 cup breadcrumbs
2 eggs, beaten

A pinch of black pepper
1 tsp crushed red peppers
2 tsp hot Tabasco sauce

Preheat air fryer to 350°F. Place the eggs and Tabasco sauce in a bowl and stir thoroughly; set aside. In a separate mixing bowl, combine the breadcrumbs, crushed red peppers, and pepper. Dip the okra into the beaten eggs, then coat in the crumb mixture. Lay the okra pieces on the greased frying basket. Air Fry for 14-16 minutes, shaking the basket several times during cooking. When ready, the okra will be crispy and golden brown. Serve.

Quick Air Fried Potatoes

Serves: 3 | Total Time: 55 minutes

3 whole potatoes
2 tsp olive oil
1 tbsp salt

1 tbsp minced garlic
1 tsp parsley, chopped
4 oz grated Swiss cheese

Preheat air fryer to 390°F. Prick the potatoes all over using a fork. Drizzle with olive oil all over the skins and rub them with minced garlic, salt, and parsley. Place the potatoes in the frying basket and Bake for 20-25 minutes or until tender. Remove the potatoes from the basket and serve them along with grated Swiss cheese. Serve.

Mouth-Watering Provençal Mushrooms

Serves: 4 | Total Time: 35 minutes

2 lb mushrooms, quartered
2-3 tbsp olive oil
½ tsp garlic powder

2 tsp herbs de Provence
2 tbsp dry white wine

Preheat air fryer to 320°F. Beat together the olive oil, garlic powder, herbs de Provence, and white wine in a bowl. Add the mushrooms and toss gently to coat. Spoon the mixture onto the frying basket and Bake for 16-18 minutes, stirring twice. Serve hot and enjoy!

Dauphinoise (Potatoes au Gratin)

Serves: 4 | Total Time: 30 minutes

½ cup grated cheddar cheese
3 peeled potatoes, sliced
½ cup milk
½ cup heavy cream

Salt and pepper to taste
1 tsp ground nutmeg

Preheat air fryer to 350°F. Place the milk, heavy cream, salt, pepper, and nutmeg in a bowl and mix well. Dip in the potato slices and arrange on a baking dish. Spoon the remaining mixture over the potatoes. Scatter the grated cheddar cheese on top. Place the baking dish in the air fryer and Bake for 20 minutes. Serve warm and enjoy!

Chili-Oiled Brussels Sprouts

Serves: 4 | Total Time: 30 minutes

1 cup Brussels sprouts, quartered
1 tsp olive oil
1 tsp chili oil

Salt and pepper to taste

Preheat air fryer to 350°F. Coat the Brussels sprouts with olive oil, chili oil, salt, and black pepper in a bowl. Transfer to the frying basket. Bake for 20 minutes, shaking the basket several times throughout cooking until the sprouts are crispy, browned on the outside, and juicy inside. Serve and enjoy!

Herbed Zucchini Poppers

Serves: 4 | Total Time: 30 minutes

1 tbsp grated Parmesan cheese
2 zucchini, sliced
1 cup breadcrumbs
2 eggs, beaten

Salt and pepper to taste
1 tsp dry tarragon
1 tsp dry dill

Preheat air fryer to 390°F. Place the breadcrumbs, Parmesan, tarragon, dill, salt, and pepper in a bowl and stir to combine. Dip the zucchini into the beaten eggs, then coat with Parmesan-crumb mixture. Lay the zucchini slices on the greased frying basket in an even layer. Air Fry for 14-16 minutes, shaking the basket several times during cooking. When ready, the zucchini will be crispy and golden brown. Serve hot and enjoy!

Mediterranean Roasted Vegetables

Serves: 4 | Total Time: 30 minutes

1 red bell pepper, cut into chunks
1 cup sliced mushrooms
1 cup green beans, diced
1 zucchini, sliced
1/3 cup diced red onion

3 garlic cloves, sliced
2 tbsp olive oil
1 tsp rosemary
½ tsp flaked sea salt

Preheat air fryer to 350°F. Add the bell pepper, mushrooms, green beans, red onion, zucchini, rosemary, and garlic to a bowl and mix, then spritz with olive oil. Stir until well-coated. Put the veggies in the frying basket and Air Fry for 14-18 minutes. The veggies should be soft and crispy. Serve sprinkled with flaked sea salt.

Best-Ever Brussels Sprouts

Serves: 4 | Total Time: 30 minutes

1 lb Brussels sprouts, halved lengthwise
2 tbsp olive oil   1 tbsp lemon juice
3 tsp chili powder

Preheat air fryer to 390°F. Add the sprouts in a bowl, drizzle with olive oil and 2 tsp of chili powder, and toss to coat. Set them in the frying basket and Air Fry for 12 minutes. Shake at least once. Season with the remaining chili powder and lemon juice, shake once again, and cook for 3-5 minutes until golden and crispy. Serve warm.

Pancetta Mushroom & Onion Sautée

Serves 4 | Total Time: 20 minutes

16 oz white button mushrooms, stems trimmed, halved
1 onion, cut into half-moons   1 garlic clove, minced
4 pancetta slices, diced

Preheat air fryer to 350°F. Add all ingredients, except for the garlic, to the frying basket and stir well. Air Fry for 8 minutes, tossing once. Mix in the garlic and cook for 1 more minute. Serve right away.

Roasted Thyme Asparagus

Serves: 4 | Total Time: 20 minutes

1 lb asparagus, trimmed   2 tbsp balsamic vinegar
2 tsp olive oil   ½ tsp dried thyme
3 garlic cloves, minced   ½ red chili, finely sliced

Preheat air fryer to 380°F. Put the asparagus and olive oil in a bowl and stir to coat, then put them in the frying basket. Toss some garlic over the asparagus and Roast for 4-8 minutes until crisp-tender. Spritz with balsamic vinegar and toss in some thyme leaves. Top with red chili slices and serve.

Sicilian Arancini

Serves: 4 | Total Time: 20 minutes

1/3 minced red bell pepper   3 tbsp plain flour
4 tsp grated Parmesan cheese 1/3 cup finely grated carrots
1 ¼ cup cooked rice   2 tbsp minced fresh parsley
1 egg   2 tsp olive oil

Preheat air fryer to 380°F. Add the rice, egg, and flour to a bowl and mix well. Add the carrots, bell peppers, parsley, and Parmesan cheese and mix again. Shape into 8 fritters. Brush with olive oil and place the fritters in the frying basket. Air Fry for 8-10 minutes, turning once, until golden. Serve hot and enjoy!

Roast Sweet Potatoes with Parmesan

Serves: 4 | Total Time: 30 minutes

2 peeled sweet potatoes, sliced
¼ cup grated Parmesan   1 tbsp balsamic vinegar
1 tsp olive oil   1 tsp dried rosemary

Preheat air fryer to 400°F. Place the sweet potatoes and some olive oil in a bowl and shake to coat. Spritz with balsamic vinegar and rosemary, then shake again. Put the potatoes in the frying basket and Roast for 18-25 minutes, shaking at least once until the potatoes are soft. Sprinkle with Parmesan cheese and serve warm.

Patatas Bravas

Serves: 4 | Total Time: 35 minutes

1 lb baby potatoes   2 tsp olive oil
1 onion, chopped   2 tsp Chile de Árbol, ground
4 garlic cloves, minced   ½ tsp ground cumin
2 jalapeño peppers, minced   ½ tsp dried oregano

Preheat air fryer to 370°F. Put the baby potatoes, onion, garlic, and jalapeños in a bowl, stir, then pour in the olive oil and stir again to coat. Season with ground chile de Árbol, cumin, and oregano, and stir once again. Put the bowl in the air fryer and Air Fry for 22-28 minutes, shaking the bowl once. Serve hot.

Pecorino Dill Muffins

Serves 4 | Total Time: 25 minutes

¼ cup grated Pecorino cheese
1 cup flour   2 tsp baking powder
1 tsp dried dill   1 egg
⅛ tsp salt   ¼ cup Greek yogurt
¼ tsp onion powder

Preheat air fryer to 350°F. In a bowl, combine the dry ingredients. Set aside. In another bowl, whisk the wet ingredients. Add the wet ingredients to the dry ingredients and combine until blended.

Transfer the batter to 6 silicone muffin cups lightly greased with olive oil. Place muffin cups in the frying basket and Bake for 12 minutes. Serve right away.

Gorgonzola Stuffed Mushrooms

Serves 2 | Total Time: 15 minutes

12 white button mushroom caps
2 tbsp diced white button mushroom stems
¼ cup Gorgonzola cheese, crumbled
1 tsp olive oil   2 tbsp bread crumbs
1 green onion, chopped

Preheat air fryer to 350°F. Rub around the top of each mushroom cap with olive oil. Mix the mushroom stems, green onion, and Gorgonzola cheese in a bowl. Distribute and press the mixture into the cups of mushrooms, then sprinkle bread crumbs on top. Place stuffed mushrooms in the frying basket and Bake for 5-7 minutes. Serve right away.

Succulent Roasted Peppers

Serves 2 | Total Time: 35 minutes

2 red bell peppers   Salt to taste
2 tbsp olive oil   1 tsp dill, chopped

Preheat air fryer to 400°F. Remove the tops and bottoms of the peppers. Cut along rib sections and discard the seeds. Combine the bell peppers and olive oil in a bowl. Place bell peppers in the frying basket. Roast for 24 minutes, flipping once. Transfer the roasted peppers to a small bowl and cover for 15 minutes. Then, peel and discard the skins. Sprinkle with salt and dill and serve.

Buttery Radish Wedges

Serves 2 | Total Time: 20 minutes

2 tbsp butter, melted	20 radishes, quartered
2 cloves garlic, minced	2 tbsp feta cheese crumbles
¼ tsp salt	1 tbsp chopped parsley

Preheat air fryer to 370°F. Mix the butter, garlic, and salt in a bowl. Stir in radishes. Place the radish wedges in the frying basket and Roast for 10 minutes, shaking once. Transfer to a large serving dish and stir in feta cheese. Scatter with parsley and serve.

Lemony Fried Fennel Slices

Serves 2 | Total Time: 15 minutes

1 tbsp minced fennel fronds	¼ tsp salt
1 fennel bulb	2 lemon wedges
2 tsp olive oil	1 tsp fennel seeds

Preheat air fryer to 350°F. Remove the fronds from the fennel bulb and reserve them. Cut the fennel into thin slices. Rub fennel chips with olive oil on both sides and sprinkle with salt and fennel seeds. Place fennel slices in the frying basket and Bake for 8 minutes. Squeeze lemon on top and scatter with chopped fronds. Serve.

Dijon Artichoke Hearts

Serves 4 | Total Time: 25 minutes

1 (14.75-oz) jar artichoke hearts in water, drained	
1 egg	¼ cup flour
1 tbsp Dijon mustard	6 basil leaves
½ cup bread crumbs	

Preheat air fryer to 350°F. Beat egg and mustard in a bowl. In another bowl, combine bread crumbs and flour. Dip artichoke hearts in egg mixture, then dredge in crumb mixture. Place artichoke hearts in the greased frying basket and Air Fry for 7-10 minutes until crispy. Serve topped with basil. Enjoy!

Dilly Sesame Roasted Asparagus

Serves 6 | Total Time: 15 minutes

1 lb asparagus, trimmed	1 garlic clove, minced
1 tbsp butter, melted	2 tsp chopped dill
¼ tsp salt	3 tbsp sesame seeds

Preheat air fryer to 370°F. Combine asparagus and butter in a bowl. Place asparagus mixture in the frying basket and Roast for 9 minutes, tossing once. Transfer it to a serving dish and stir in salt, garlic, sesame seeds and dill until coated. Serve immediately.

Southern Okra Chips

Serves: 2 | Total Time: 20 minutes

2 eggs	Salt and pepper to taste
¼ cup whole milk	⅛ tsp chili pepper
¼ cup bread crumbs	½ lb okra, sliced
¼ cup cornmeal	1 tbsp butter, melted
1 tbsp Cajun seasoning	

Preheat air fryer to 400°F. Beat the eggs and milk in a bowl. In another bowl, combine the remaining ingredients, except okra and butter. Dip okra chips in the egg mixture, then dredge them in the breadcrumbs mixture. Place okra chips in the greased frying basket and Roast for 7 minutes, shake once and brush with melted butter. Serve right away.

Almond Green Beans

Serves: 4 | Total Time: 20 minutes

2 cups green beans, trimmed	Salt and pepper to taste
¼ cup slivered almonds	2 tsp lemon juice
2 tbsp butter, melted	Lemon zest and slices

Preheat air fryer to 375°F. Add almonds to the frying basket and Air Fry for 2 minutes, tossing once. Set aside in a small bowl. Combine the remaining ingredients, except 1 tbsp of butter, in a bowl.

Place green beans in the frying basket and Air Fry for 10 minutes, tossing once. Then, transfer them to a large serving dish. Scatter with the melted butter, lemon juice and roasted almonds and toss. Serve immediately garnished with lemon zest and lemon slices.

Buttered Garlic Broccolini

Serves: 2 | Total Time: 20 minutes

1 bunch broccolini	2 minced cloves garlic
2 tbsp butter, cubed	2 tsp lemon juice
¼ tsp salt	

Preheat air fryer to 350°F. Place salted water in a saucepan over high heat and bring it to a boil. Then, add in broccolini and boil for 3 minutes. Drain it and transfer it into a bowl. Mix in butter, garlic, and salt. Place the broccolini in the frying basket and Air Fry for 6 minutes. Serve immediately garnished with lemon juice.

Grilled Lime Scallions

Serves: 6 | Total Time: 15 minutes

2 bunches of scallions	Salt and pepper to taste
1 tbsp olive oil	¼ tsp Italian seasoning
2 tsp lime juice	2 tsp lime zest

Preheat air fryer to 370°F. Trim the scallions and cut them in half lengthwise. Place them in a bowl and add olive oil and lime juice. Toss to coat. Place the mix in the frying basket and Air Fry for 7 minutes, tossing once. Transfer to a serving dish and stir in salt, pepper, Italian seasoning and lime zest. Serve immediately.

Simple Zucchini Ribbons

Serves 4 | Total Time: 15 minutes

2 zucchini
2 tsp butter, melted
¼ tsp garlic powder

¼ tsp chili flakes
8 cherry tomatoes, halved
Salt and pepper to taste

Preheat air fryer to 275°F. Cut the zucchini into ribbons with a vegetable peeler. Mix them with butter, garlic, chili flakes, salt, and pepper in a bowl. Transfer to the frying basket and Air Fry for 2 minutes. Toss and add the cherry tomatoes. Cook for another 2 minutes. Serve.

Savory Brussels Sprouts

Serves: 4 | Total Time: 15 minutes

1 lb Brussels sprouts, quartered
2 tbsp balsamic vinegar
1 tbsp olive oil
1 tbsp honey

Salt and pepper to taste
1 ½ tbsp lime juice
Parsley for sprinkling

Preheat air fryer to 350°F. Combine all ingredients in a bowl. Transfer them to the frying basket. Air Fry for 10 minutes, tossing once. Top with lime juice and parsley.

Charred Cherry Tomatoes

Serves: 2 | Total Time: 15 minutes

10 cherry tomatoes, halved
1 tsp olive oil

Salt to taste
2 tsp balsamic vinegar

Preheat air fryer to 380°F. Combine all ingredients in a bowl. Arrange the cherry tomatoes on the frying basket and Bake for 8 minutes until the tomatoes are blistered, shaking once. Serve drizzled with balsamic vinegar.

Carrots & Parsnips with Tahini Sauce

Serves 4 | Total Time: 20 minutes

2 parsnips, cut into half-moons
2 tsp olive oil
½ tsp salt
1 carrot, cut into sticks
1 tbsp tahini

1 tbsp lemon juice
1 garlic clove, minced
1 tbsp chopped parsley

Preheat air fryer to 375°F. Coat the parsnips and carrots with some olive oil and salt. Place them in the frying basket and Air Fry for 10 minutes, tossing once. In a bowl, whisk tahini, lemon juice, 1 tsp of water, and garlic. Pour the sauce over the cooked veggies. Scatter with parsley and serve.

Basic Corn on the Cob

Serves: 4 | Total Time: 15 minutes

3 ears of corn, shucked and halved
2 tbsp butter, melted
Salt and pepper to taste

1 tsp minced garlic
1 tsp paprika

Preheat air fryer to 400°F. Toss all ingredients in a bowl. Place corn in the frying basket and Bake for 7 minutes, turning once. Serve immediately.

Double Cheese-Broccoli Tots

Serves 4 | Total Time: 30 minutes

1/3 cup grated sharp cheddar cheese
1 cup riced broccoli
1 egg
1 oz herbed Boursin cheese
1 tbsp grated onion

1/3 cup bread crumbs
½ tsp salt
¼ tsp garlic powder

Preheat air fryer to 375°F. Mix the riced broccoli, egg, cheddar cheese, Boursin cheese, onion, bread crumbs, salt, and garlic powder in a bowl. Form into 12 rectangular mounds. Cut a piece of parchment paper to fit the bottom of the frying basket, place the tots, and Air Fry for 9 minutes. Let chill for 5 minutes before serving.

Almond-Crusted Zucchini Fries

Serves 2 | Total Time: 30 minutes

½ cup grated Pecorino cheese
1 zucchini, cut into fries
1 tsp salt
1 egg

1 tbsp almond milk
½ cup almond flour

Preheat air fryer to 370°F. Distribute zucchini fries evenly over a paper towel, sprinkle with salt, and let sit for 10 minutes to pull out moisture. Pat them dry with paper towels. In a bowl, beat egg and almond milk. In another bowl, combine almond flour and Pecorino cheese. Dip fries in egg mixture and then dredge them in flour mixture. Place zucchini fries in the lightly greased frying basket and Air Fry for 10 minutes, flipping once. Serve.

Spiced Roasted Acorn Squash

Serves: 2 | Total Time: 45 minutes

½ acorn squash half
1 tsp butter, melted
2 tsp light brown sugar

1/8 tsp ground cinnamon
2 tbsp hot sauce
¼ cup maple syrup

Preheat air fryer to 400°F. Slice off about ¼-inch from the side of the squash half to sit flat like a bowl. In a bowl, combine all ingredients. Brush over the top of the squash and pour any remaining mixture in the middle of the squash. Place squash in the frying basket and Roast for 35 minutes. Remove and cut it in half, then divide between 2 serving plates. Serve.

Easy Parmesan Asparagus

Serves: 4 | Total Time: 15 minutes

3 tsp grated Parmesan cheese
1 lb asparagus, trimmed
2 tsp olive oil

Salt to taste
1 garlic clove, minced
½ lemon

Preheat air fryer to 375°F. Toss the asparagus and olive oil in a bowl, place them in the frying basket, and Air Fry for 8-10 minutes, tossing once. Transfer them into a large serving dish. Sprinkle with salt, garlic, and Parmesan cheese and toss until coated. Serve immediately with a squeeze of lemon. Enjoy!

Spicy Bean Stuffed Potatoes

Serves: 4 | Total Time: 60 minutes

1 lb russet potatoes, scrubbed and perforated with a fork
1 (4-oz) can diced green chilies, including juice
1/3 cup grated Mexican cheese blend

1 green bell pepper, diced	2-3 jalapeños, sliced
1 yellow bell pepper, diced	1 red bell pepper, chopped
¼ cup torn iceberg lettuce	Salt and pepper to taste
2 tsp olive oil	1/3 cup canned black beans
2 tbsp sour cream	4 grape tomatoes, sliced
½ tsp chili powder	¼ cup chopped parsley

Preheat air fryer to 400°F. Brush olive oil over potatoes. Place them in the frying basket and Bake for 45 minutes, turning at 30 minutes mark. Let cool on a cutting board for 10 minutes until cool enough to handle. Slice each potato lengthwise and scoop out all but a ¼" layer of potato to form 4 boats.

Mash potato flesh, sour cream, green chilies, cheese, chili powder, jalapeños, green, yellow, and red peppers, salt, and pepper in a bowl until smooth. Fold in black beans. Divide between potato skin boats. Place potato boats in the frying basket and Bake for 2 minutes. Remove them to a serving plate. Top each boat with lettuce, tomatoes, and parsley. Sprinkle tops with salt and serve.

Rich Baked Sweet Potatoes

Serves: 2 | Total Time: 55 minutes

1 lb sweet potatoes, scrubbed and perforated with a fork

2 tsp olive oil	2 tbsp butter
Salt and pepper to taste	3 tbsp honey

Preheat air fryer to 400°F. Mix olive oil, salt, black pepper, and honey. Brush with the prepared mix over both sweet potatoes. Place them in the frying basket and Bake for 45 minutes, turning at 30 minutes mark. Let cool on a cutting board for 10 minutes until cool enough to handle. Slice each potato lengthwise. Press the ends of one potato together to open up the slices. Top with butter to serve.

Smoked Avocado Wedges

Serves 4 | Total Time: 15 minutes

½ tsp smoked paprika	8 peeled avocado wedges
2 tsp olive oil	1 tsp chipotle powder
½ lime, juiced	¼ tsp salt

Preheat air fryer to 400°F. Drizzle the avocado wedges with olive oil and lime juice. In a bowl, combine chipotle powder, smoked paprika, and salt. Sprinkle over the avocado wedges. Place them in the frying basket and Air Fry for 7 minutes. Serve immediately.

Blistered Shishito Peppers

Serves 2 | Total Time: 15 minutes + marinating time

½ lb shishito peppers	2 garlic cloves, minced
2 tsp olive oil	Salt to taste
1 tsp white wine vinegar	1 tsp parsley, chopped

Preheat air fryer to 375°F. Arrange the peppers on the greased frying basket and Air Fry for 8 minutes or until blistered and softened, turning the peppers once. Whisk the oil, vinegar, salt, garlic, and parsley in a bowl. Stir in the blistered peppers and let them sit for 1 hour. Serve.

Quick & Easy Zucchini Fritters

Serves: 4 | Total Time: 35 minutes

¼ cup crumbled feta cheese	1 tbsp butter, melted
1 large grated zucchini	1 egg
¼ cup Parmesan cheese	2 tsp chopped dill
1 minced green onion	2 tsp chopped parsley
1 tbs powder garlic	Salt and pepper to taste
1 tbsp flour	1 cup bread crumbs
1 tbsp cornmeal	

Preheat air fryer to 360°F. Place the grated zucchini into a clean kitchen towel and squeeze out as much liquid as possible. In a bowl, combine all ingredients except for the breadcrumbs. Shape 12 equal-sized patties out of the mixture. Coat the fritters with breadcrumbs and arrange them on a baking pan. Place it in the frying basket and Air Fry for 10-12 minutes, flipping once. Serve immediately.

Yukon Gold Potato Purée

Serves: 4 | Total Time: 25 minutes

1 lb Yukon Gold potatoes, scrubbed and cubed

2 tbsp butter, melted	¼ cup cream cheese
Salt and pepper to taste	1 tbsp butter, softened
1/8 cup whole milk	¼ cup chopped dill

Preheat air fryer to 350°F. Toss the potatoes and melted butter in a bowl, place them in the frying basket, and Air Fry for 13-15 minutes, tossing once. Transfer them into a bowl. Using a fork, mash the potatoes. Stir in salt, pepper, half of the milk, cream cheese, and 1 tbsp of butter until you reach your desired consistency. Garnish with dill to serve.

Baked Four-Cheese Macaroni

Serves: 4 | Total Time: 35 minutes

¼ cup shredded sharp cheddar cheese

¼ cup grated Swiss cheese	2 tsp red chili
¼ cup grated Parmesan	1 tbsp flour
½ lb cooked elbow macaroni	4 oz mascarpone cheese
3 tbsp butter, divided	¼ cup whole milk
1 sweet onion, diced	¼ cup bread crumbs

Melt 2 tbsp of butter in a skillet over medium heat. Add in onions and red chili and stir-fry for 3 minutes until tender. Stir in flour until the sauce thickens, 2-3 minutes. Add in all cheeses and milk, then mix in macaroni. Spoon macaroni mixture into a greased cake pan. Preheat air fryer to 380°F. Mix the breadcrumbs and the remaining butter in a bowl. Scatter over the pasta mixture. Place cake pan in the frying basket and Bake for 15 minutes. Let sit for 10 minutes before serving.

Cilantro Potato Gratin

Serves: 4 | Total Time: 35 minutes

2 russet potatoes, sliced	Salt and pepper to taste
½ cup grated Gruyère cheese	1 tsp smoked paprika
2 tbsp Parmesan cheese	1 cup diced cooked ham
½ cup half-and-half	1 tbsp butter, melted
2 eggs	1 tbsp bread crumbs
1 tbsp flour	1 tbsp cilantro, chopped
1 garlic clove minced	

Combine the half-and-half, eggs, flour, salt, garlic, pepper, and paprika in a bowl Toss in potatoes until all sides of potato slices are coated. Preheat air fryer to 375°F. Add half of the potato slices to a greased baking pan and pour half of the egg mixture. Top with ham and Gruyère cheese; then repeat the process with the remaining ingredients. Whisk the butter, Parmesan cheese, breadcrumbs, and cilantro in a bowl. Pour over casserole and cover with aluminum foil. Place baking pan in the fryer. Bake for 15 minutes. Uncover and cook for 5 more minutes. Let rest for 10 minutes before serving.

Herbed Baby Red Potato Hasselback

Serves: 4 | Total Time: 35 minutes

6 baby red potatoes, scrubbed	
3 tsp shredded cheddar cheese	
1 tbsp olive oil	Salt and pepper to taste
2 tbsp butter, melted	3 tsp sour cream
1 tbsp chopped thyme	¼ cup chopped parsley

Preheat air fryer to 350°F. Make slices in the width of each potato about ¼-inch apart without cutting through. Rub potato slices with olive oil, both outside and in between slices. Place potatoes in the frying basket and Air Fry for 20 minutes, tossing once, brush with melted butter, and scatter with thyme. Remove them to a large serving dish. Sprinkle with salt and black pepper. Top with a dollop of sour cream. Scatter with cheddar cheese and parsley. Serve.

Best Ever Macaroni & Cheese

Serves: 4 | Total Time: 40 minutes

1 ½ cups grated cheddar cheese	
16 oz elbow macaroni	½ tsp mustard powder
3 egg, beaten	Salt to taste
½ cup sour cream	1 cup milk
4 tbsp butter	½ cup grated Parmesan

Preheat air fryer to 350°F. Bring a pot of salted water to a boil and cook the macaroni following the packet instructions. Drain and place in a bowl.

Add cheddar cheese and butter to the hot macaroni and stir to melt. Mix the beaten eggs, milk, sour cream, mustard powder, and salt in a bowl and add the mixture to the macaroni; mix gently. Spoon the macaroni mixture into a greased baking dish and transfer the dish to the air fryer. Bake for 15 minutes. Slide the dish out and sprinkle with Parmesan cheese. Cook for 5-8 more minutes until the top is bubbling and golden. Serve and enjoy!

Toasted Choco-Nuts

Serves: 2 | Total Time: 10 minutes

2 cups almonds	2 tbsp cacao powder
2 tsp maple syrup	

Preheat air fryer to 350°F. Distribute the almonds in a single layer in the frying basket and Bake for 3 minutes. Shake the basket and Bake for another 1 minute until golden brown. Remove them to a bowl. Drizzle with maple syrup and toss. Sprinkle with cacao powder and toss until well coated. Let cool completely. Store in a container at room temperature for up to 2 weeks or in the fridge for up to a month.

Healthy Caprese Salad

Serves: 2 | Total Time: 20 minutes

1 (8-oz) ball mozzarella cheese, sliced	
16 grape tomatoes	1 tbsp balsamic vinegar
2 tsp olive oil	1 tsp mix of seeds
Salt and pepper to taste	1 tbsp chopped basil

Preheat air fryer to 350°F. Toss tomatoes with 1 tsp of olive oil and salt in a bowl. Place them in the frying basket and Air Fry for 15 minutes, shaking twice. Divide mozzarella slices between 2 serving plates, top with blistered tomatoes, and drizzle with balsamic vinegar and the remaining olive oil. Sprinkle with basil, black pepper and the mixed seeds and serve.

Summer Watermelon and Cucumber Salad

Serves: 4 | Total Time: 15 minutes

½ red onion, sliced into half-moons	
2 tbsp crumbled goat cheese	Salt and pepper to taste
10 chopped basil leaves	3 cups arugula
4 cups watermelon cubes	1 tsp balsamic vinegar
½ cucumber, sliced	1 tsp honey
4 tsp olive oil	1 tbsp chopped mint

Preheat air fryer to 375°F. Toss watermelon, cucumber, onion, 2 tsp of olive oil, salt, and pepper in a bowl. Place it in the frying basket and Air Fry for 4 minutes, tossing once. In a salad bowl, whisk the arugula, balsamic vinegar, honey, and the remaining olive oil until the arugula is coated. Add in watermelon mixture. Scatter with goat cheese, basil leaves and mint to serve.

Garlic-Parmesan Popcorn

Serves: 2 | Total Time: 15 minutes

2 tsp grated Parmesan cheese	1 tbsp lemon juice
¼ cup popcorn kernels	1 tsp garlic powder

Preheat air fryer to 400°F. Line the basket with aluminum foil. Put the popcorn kernels in a single layer and Grill for 6-8 minutes until they stop popping. Remove them into a bowl. Drizzle with lemon juice and toss until well coated. Sprinkle with garlic powder and grated Parmesan and toss to coat. Drizzle with more lemon juice. Serve.

Caraway Seed Pretzel Sticks

Serves: 4 | Total Time: 30 minutes

½ pizza dough   2 tbsp caraway seeds
1 tsp baking soda

Preheat air fryer to 400°F. Roll out the dough, on parchment paper, into a rectangle, then cut it into 8 strips. Whisk the baking soda and 1 cup of hot water until well dissolved in a bowl. Submerge each strip, shake off any excess, and stretch another 1 to 2 inches. Scatter with caraway seeds and let rise for 10 minutes in the frying basket. Grease with cooking spray and Air Fry for 8 minutes until golden brown, turning once. Serve.

Simple Carrot Chips

Serves: 4 | Total Time: 15 minutes

3 carrots, cut into coins   Salt and pepper to taste
1 tbsp sesame oil

Preheat air fryer to 375°F. Combine all ingredients in a bowl. Place carrots in the frying basket and Roast for 10 minutes, tossing once. Serve right away.

Cholula Onion Rings

Serves: 4 | Total Time: 30 minutes

1 large Vidalia onion   2 tbsp Cholula hot sauce
½ cup chickpea flour   1 tsp allspice
1/3 cup milk   2/3 cup bread crumbs
2 tbsp lemon juice

Preheat air fryer to 380°F. Cut ½-inch off the top of the onion's root, then cut into ½-inch thick rings. Set aside. Combine the chickpea flour, milk, lemon juice, hot sauce, and allspice in a bowl. In another bowl, add in breadcrumbs. Submerge each ring into the flour batter until well coated, then dip into the breadcrumbs, and Air Fry for 14 minutes until crispy, turning once. Serve.

Rich Spinach Chips

Serves: 4 | Total Time: 20 minutes

10 oz spinach   Salt and pepper to taste
2 tbsp lemon juice   ½ tsp garlic powder
2 tbsp olive oil   ½ tsp onion powder

Preheat air fryer to 350°F. Place the spinach in a bowl, and drizzle with lemon juice and olive oil and massage with your hands. Scatter with salt, pepper, garlic, and onion and gently toss to coat well. Arrange the leaves in a single layer and Bake for 3 minutes. Shake and Bake for another 1-3 minutes until brown. Let cool completely.

Balsamic Green Beans with Bacon

Serves 4 | Total Time: 15 minutes

2 cups green beans, trimmed
1 tbsp butter, melted   1 garlic clove, minced
Salt and pepper to taste   1 tbsp balsamic vinegar
1 bacon slice, diced

Preheat air fryer to 375°F. Combine green beans, butter, salt, and pepper in a bowl. Put the bean mixture in the frying basket and Air Fry for 5 minutes. Stir in bacon and Air Fry for 4 more minutes. Mix in garlic and cook for 1 minute. Transfer it to a serving dish, drizzle with balsamic vinegar and combine. Serve right away.

Provence French Fries

Serves: 4 | Total Time: 25 minutes

2 russet potatoes   1 tbsp herbs de Provence
1 tbsp olive oil

Preheat air fryer to 400°F. Slice the potatoes lengthwise into ½-inch thick strips. In a bowl, whisk the olive oil and herbs de Provence. Toss in the potatoes to coat. Arrange them in a single and Air Fry for 18-20 minutes, shaking once, until crispy. Serve warm.

Balsamic Stuffed Mushrooms

Serves: 4 | Total Time: 30 minutes

12 portobello mushroom caps
2 diced roasted red peppers   ½ lemon, zested
10 oz spinach, chopped   1 tsp garlic powder
2 tbsp chives, chopped   1 tbsp balsamic vinegar
¼ cup almond flour   1 fresh mozzarella ball, sliced

Preheat air fryer to 360°F. In a bowl, place the red peppers, spinach, chives, almond flour, lemon zest, and garlic powder and mix until well combined. Fill each mushroom cap with the spinach mixture, pressing down slightly. Top with mozzarella slices. Arrange the stuffed mushrooms on the greased frying basket and Bake in the fryer for 12-14 minutes until the cheese is melted. Drizzle with balsamic vinegar before serving.

Green Dip with Pine Nuts

Serves: 3 | Total Time: 30 minutes

10 oz canned artichokes, chopped
2 tsp grated Parmesan cheese   ½ cup milk
10 oz spinach, chopped   3 tbsp lemon juice
2 scallions, finely chopped   2 tsp tapioca flour
½ cup pine nuts   1 tsp allspice

Preheat air fryer to 360°F. Arrange spinach, artichokes, and scallions in a pan. Set aside. In a food processor, blitz the pine nuts, milk, lemon juice, Parmesan cheese, flour, and allspice on high until smooth. Pour it over the veggies and Bake for 20 minutes, stirring every 5 minutes. Serve.

Crunchy Green Beans

Serves: 4 | Total Time: 15 minutes

1 tbsp tahini   1 tsp allspice
1 tbsp lemon juice   1 lb green beans, trimmed

Preheat air fryer to 400°F. Whisk tahini, lemon juice, 1 tbsp of water, and allspice in a bowl. Put in the green beans and toss to coat. Roast for 5 minutes until golden brown and cooked. Serve immediately.

Cheesy Potato Skins

Serves: 4 | Total Time: 50 minutes

2 russet potatoes, halved lengthwise
1 tbsp grated Parmesan cheese
½ cup Alfredo sauce   2 scallions, chopped

Preheat air fryer to 400°F. Wrap each potato, cut-side down with parchment paper, and Roast for 30 minutes.

Carefully scoop out the potato flesh, leaving ¼-inch meat, and place it in a bowl. Stir in Alfredo sauce, scallions, and Parmesan cheese until well combined. Fill each potato skin with the cheese mixture and Grill for 3-4 minutes until crispy. Serve right away.

Turkish Mutabal (Eggplant Dip)

Serves: 2 | Total Time: 40 minutes

1 medium eggplant   1 tsp garlic powder
2 tbsp tahini   ¼ tsp sumac
2 tbsp lemon juice   1 tsp chopped parsley

Preheat air fryer to 400°F. Place the eggplant in a pan and Roast for 30 minutes, turning once. Let cool for 5-10 minutes. Scoop out the flesh and place it in a bowl. Squeeze any excess water; discard the water. Mix the flesh, tahini, lemon juice, garlic, and sumac until well combined. Scatter with parsley and serve.

Honey Brussels Sprouts

Serves: 4 | Total Time: 20 minutes

1 lb Brussels sprouts, quartered
2 tbsp olive oil   1 tbsp balsamic vinegar
1 tsp honey

Preheat air fryer to 400°F. Whisk the olive oil, honey, and balsamic vinegar in a bowl. Put in Brussels sprouts and toss to coat. Place them, cut-side up, in a single layer, and Roast for 10 minutes until crispy. Serve warm.

Cheesy Breaded Eggplants

Serves: 2 | Total Time: 35 minutes

4 eggplant slices   1 tbsp dried oregano
1 cup breadcrumbs   1 cup marinara sauce
½ tsp garlic powder   2 provolone cheese slices
2 eggs, beaten   1 tbsp Parmesan cheese
Salt and pepper to taste 6 basil leaves

Preheat air fryer to 350°F. Mix the breadcrumbs, oregano, garlic powder, salt, and pepper in a bowl. Dip the eggplant slices into the beaten eggs, then coat in the dry ingredients. Arrange the coated eggplant slices on the greased frying basket. Air Fry for 14-16 minutes, turning once. Spread half of the marinara sauce onto a baking pan. Lay the cooked eggplant on top of the sauce. Pour the remaining marinara sauce over the eggplant and top with the provolone cheese slices and grated Parmesan cheese. Bake in the air fryer for 5 minutes or until the cheese is melted. Serve topped with basil leaves.

Basil Spinach & Cheese Stuffed Shells

Serves: 4 | Total Time: 35 minutes

1 egg, beaten   4 cooked jumbo shells
1 tsp Italian seasoning   1 cup tomato sauce
1 cup shredded mozzarella 2 tbsp grated Parmesan
1 cup ricotta cheese   1 tbsp basil leaves
1 cup chopped spinach

Preheat air fryer to 360°F. Place the beaten egg, Italian seasoning, ricotta, mozzarella, and spinach in a bowl and mix until all the ingredients are combined. Fill the mixture into the cooked pasta shells. Spread half of the tomato sauce on a baking pan, then place the stuffed shells over the sauce. Spoon the remaining tomato sauce over the shells. Bake in the air fryer for 25 minutes or until the stuffed shells are wonderfully cooked, crispy on the outside with the spinach and cheeses inside gooey and delicious. Serve sprinkled with Parmesan and basil.

Ricotta & Broccoli Cannelloni

Serves: 4 | Total Time: 35 minutes

1 cup shredded mozzarella cheese
½ cup cooked broccoli, chopped
½ cup cooked spinach, chopped
4 cooked cannelloni shells   1 egg
1 cup ricotta cheese   1 cup passata
½ tsp dried marjoram   1 tbsp basil leaves

Preheat air fryer to 360°F. Beat the egg in a bowl until fluffy. Add the ricotta, marjoram, half of the mozzarella, broccoli, and spinach and stir to combine. Cover the base of a baking dish with a layer of passata. Fill the cannelloni with the cheese mixture and place them on top of the sauce. Spoon the remaining passata over the tops and top with the rest of the mozzarella cheese. Put the dish in the frying basket and Bake for 25 minutes until the cheese is melted and golden. Top with basil.

Cheese & Bacon Pasta Bake

Serves: 4 | Total Time: 35 minutes

½ cup shredded sharp cheddar cheese
½ cup shredded mozzarella cheese
4 oz cooked bacon, crumbled
3 tbsp butter, divided   ¼ cup heavy cream
1 tbsp flour   ½ lb cooked rotini
1 tsp black pepper   ¼ cup bread crumbs
2 oz crushed feta cheese

Melt 2 tbsp of butter in a skillet over medium heat. Stir in flour until the sauce thickens. Stir in all cheeses, black pepper and heavy cream and cook for 2 minutes until creamy. Toss in rotini and bacon until well coated. Spoon rotini mixture into a greased cake pan.

Preheat air fryer to 370°F. Microwave the remaining butter in 10-seconds intervals until melted. Then stir in breadcrumbs. Scatter over pasta mixture. Place cake pan in the frying basket and Bake for 15 minutes. Let sit for 10 minutes before serving.

LUNCH

Italian-Style Ratatouille

Serves: 4 | Total Time: 30 minutes

4 Roma tomatoes, seeded and chopped
3 garlic cloves, sliced   1 shallot, chopped
1 peeled eggplant, chopped   1 small fennel bulb, sliced
1 red bell pepper, chopped   1 tsp Italian seasoning
1 yellow bell pepper, minced   1 tsp olive oil

Preheat air fryer to 390°F. Put the tomatoes, garlic, eggplant, red and yellow bell peppers, shallot, fennel, Italian seasoning, and olive oil in a metal bowl and mix. Put the bowl in the air fryer and Roast for 12-16 minutes. Stir once about halfway through and cook until the veggies are soft. Serve and enjoy!

Kale & Cheese Sandwiches

Serves: 2 | Total Time: 25 minutes

1 ½ cups chopped kale   2 slices Gruyère cheese
2 garlic cloves, sliced   4 bread slices
2 tsp olive oil   1 dill pickle, sliced

Preheat air fryer to 400°F. Toss the kale, garlic, and some olive oil in a baking pan, then put the pan in the air fryer. Air Fry for 4-5 minutes until the kale is soft, making sure to stir at least once during cooking. Divide kale between two slices of bread and top with cheese and pickle slices, making 2 sandwiches. Spritz the outside of the bread slices with the remaining olive oil. Grill in the air fryer for 6-8 minutes, flipping once until the bread is browned and the cheese is melted. Serve warm.

Tuna & Mushroom Melts

Serves: 4 | Total Time: 30 minutes

1/3 cup chopped mushrooms
2 Cheddar cheese slices, halved
4 sandwich bread slices   2 spring onions, sliced
5 oz canned tuna, flaked   1/3 cup Greek yogurt
1 shredded carrot   2 tbsp yellow mustard

Preheat air fryer to 340°F. Set the bread slices in the fryer basket and Grill for 3-4 minutes, until crispy; reserve. Toss the tuna, carrot, mushrooms, spring onions, yogurt, and mustard in a bowl and stir until combined. Spread over 2 slices of bread, then top with cheese and sandwich with the remaining bread. Return to the air fryer and Air Fry for 4-7 more minutes. Serve warm.

Cheese & Vegetable Toasts

Serves: 4 | Total Time: 25 minutes

1 yellow bell pepper, cut into strips
1 cup sliced button mushrooms
1 small yellow squash, sliced
2 green onions, sliced   2 tbsp butter, softened
1 tbsp olive oil   ½ cup cream cheese
4 French bread slices

Preheat air fryer to 330°F. Add yellow pepper, mushrooms, squash, and green onions to the air fryer. Bake in the greased frying basket for 6-8 minutes, shaking once until the vegetables are tender. Remove and set aside. Spread the butter on the bread, then toast it butter-side up until golden, 2-4 minutes. Spread the cream cheese on the warm toast, then top with vegetables. Serve and enjoy!

Greek Eggplant Gyros

Serves: 4 | Total Time: 30 minutes

2 pita breads, halved crosswise
1 peeled eggplant, chopped   1 tsp olive oil
1 red bell pepper, sliced   1/3 cup hummus
½ cup red onion, diced   ½ Greek seasoning
1 baby carrot, shredded   6 Kalamata olives, sliced

Preheat air fryer to 390°F. Put the eggplant, red bell pepper, red onion, carrot, olive oil, and seasoning in a baking pan and mix. Put the pan into the frying basket and Bake for 7-9 minutes. Cook until the veggies are soft, making sure to stir once. Spread the hummus inside the pita bread pockets. Add the vegetables and olives. Put the sandwiches in the air fryer and Bake for 2-3 minutes, until the bread is browned to your taste. Serve warm.

Dijon Loaded New Potatoes

Serves: 4 | Total Time: 30 minutes

24 small new potatoes, scrubbed
1 tsp olive oil   3 tomatoes, chopped
½ cup mayonnaise   2 scallions, chopped
1 tbsp Dijon mustard   2 tbsp chopped chives
½ tsp dried basil

Preheat air fryer to 360°F. Coat the potatoes with olive oil, then put them in the frying basket and Roast for 20-25 minutes. Shake the basket once to ensure even cooking. Combine the mayonnaise, mustard, and basil in a small bowl. When the potatoes are done, move them to a large plate and mash each one lightly with the bottom of a glass. Put the mayonnaise mixture on top of the potatoes and add tomatoes, scallions, and chives. Serve.

Tandoori Chicken & Veggie Naan Pizzas

Serves: 2 | Total Time: 15 minutes

1 cup cooked chicken breasts, shredded
1 cup chopped button mushrooms
12 cherry tomatoes, halved   1 garlic clove, minced
2 naan breads   2 oz paneer, diced
¼ tsp tandoori seasoning   ¼ red bell pepper, sliced
2 tbsp pasta sauce   ¼ cup grated mozzarella

Preheat air fryer to 360°F. Combine the pasta sauce, garlic, and tandoori seasoning. Smear the mixture over the naan breads, then arrange the chicken, paneer, mushrooms, bell pepper, and cherry tomatoes on top. Sprinkle with mozzarella cheese. Place the pizzas in the air fryer and Bake for 3-6 minutes until the edges of the pita bread are golden and the cheese is melted. Serve.

Avocado & Spinach Melts

Serves: 4 | Total Time: 15 minutes

4 tbsp cheddar cheese, grated
2 brioche buns, halved   4 tomato slices
2 tbsp Dijon mustard   ½ peeled avocado, sliced
8 baby spinach leaves   8 basil leaves

Preheat air fryer to 390°F. Set the bun halves in the frying basket and Air Fry for 2 minutes until golden, then set them on a clean surface. Smear 1 ½ tsp of mustard on each bun piece, then put 2 spinach leaves, 1 tomato slice, ¼ of the avocado, 2 basil leaves and 1 tbsp of cheese on the top. Bake the sandwiches in the air fryer for 3-4 minutes. Make sure the cheese is melted. Serve hot.

Classic Falafel

Serves: 6 | Total Time: 25 minutes

1(16-oz) can chickpeas   ½ tsp allspice
1/3 cup flour   2 tbsp parsley, minced
1 red onion, chopped   1 tbsp olive oil
2 garlic cloves, minced   ½ tsp ground cumin
1 tsp ground coriander   ¼ tsp cayenne pepper

Smash the chickpeas into a smooth consistency using a masher, then add the flour, red onion, garlic, ground coriander, allspice, parsley, olive oil, cumin, and cayenne and stir until well-combined. Using your hands, make 12 balls from this mix. Preheat air fryer to 380°F. Put the balls in the air fryer, leaving space between and Air Fry for 11-12 minutes. Test for firmness and make sure they're golden. Repeat until all balls are cooked. Serve.

Hot Tomato & Spinach Scrambled Eggs

Serves: 4 | Total Time: 20 minutes

1 onion, chopped   8 eggs, beaten
1 red bell pepper, chopped   1 chili pepper, minced
2 tomatoes, diced   1 cup baby spinach
½ tsp dried marjoram

Preheat air fryer to 350°F. Toss the onion, bell pepper, tomatoes, marjoram, and chili pepper in a greased baking pan. Pour the eggs over the vegetables. Air Fry for 8-12 minutes. Stir 2-3 times during cooking to ensure they cook evenly. Serve warm.

Citrus Baked Scallops

Serves: 4 | Total Time: 15 minutes

1 tsp lemon juice   Salt and pepper to taste
1 tsp lime juice   1 lb sea scallops
2 tsp olive oil   2 tbsp chives, chopped

Preheat air fryer to 390°F. Combine lemon and lime juice, olive oil, salt, and pepper in a bowl. Toss in scallops to coat. Place the scallops in the greased frying basket and Bake for 5 -8 minutes, tossing once halfway through, until the scallops are just firm to the touch. Serve topped with chives and enjoy!

Tomatoes Stuffed with Ricotta & Spinach

Serves: 4 | Total Time: 30 minutes

¼ cup crumbled ricotta cheese
4 beef tomatoes   2 tsp olive oil
1 onion, chopped   2 cups fresh baby spinach
½ grated carrot   ½ tsp dried basil
1 garlic clove, minced

Slice the tops of each tomato off, but be careful not to cut too much, just about ½ an inch. With a spoon, carefully scrape out the insides, making sure about ½ inch walls are left. Place the tomatoes upside down on paper towels to drain. Preheat air fryer to 350°F. Combine the onion, carrot, garlic, and olive oil in a baking pan and put it into the air fryer. Bake for 4-6 minutes until the veggies are soft and crispy. Remove from the air fryer and add the spinach, ricotta cheese, and basil. Stir to combine. Spoon about ¼ of the mix into the drained tomatoes, then put them in the frying basket and Bake for 12-14 minutes.

Spring Rolls with Vegetables

Serves: 4 | Total Time: 25 minutes

2 asparagus, chopped   2 green onions, chopped
½ cup chopped mushrooms   8 egg roll wrappers
½ cup grated carrots   1 tbsp cornstarch
½ cup chopped zucchini   1 egg, beaten
1 tbsp soy sauce

Preheat air fryer to 390°F. Coat asparagus, mushrooms, carrots, zucchini, and green onions with soy sauce in a bowl. Set aside.

Mix together cornstarch and egg in a bowl. On a work surface, lay out the egg roll wrappers. Put about 3 tbsp of vegetable filling at the bottom of the wrapper. Brush the cornstarch/egg mixture on the edges of the wrapper before rolling the egg roll. Brush the cornstarch/egg mixture along the outside to seal the wrapper. Place the egg rolls in the greased frying basket and Air Fry until eggs rolls are brown and crispy, 7-10 minutes. Serve.

Parma Ham Pizza

Serves: 4 | Total Time: 30 minutes

¾ cup self-raising flour   3 cups baby spinach
½ tsp baking powder   4 oz Parma ham, torn
2 chopped tomatoes   ½ tsp dried oregano
2 tsp olive oil   1 cup grated mozzarella

Preheat air fryer to 350°F. Sift the flour and baking powder in a small bowl, then add 2 tbsp of water and olive oil. Stir until the mix is doughy. Transfer the dough to your floured work surface. Using your hands, make a circle out of the dough.

Place the pizza base in the frying basket. Spread the base with tomatoes, then scatter over the oregano, mozzarella cheese, and baby spinach. Bake for 10-15 minutes until the crust is golden and cheese is melted. Top with Parma ham and cut into slices to serve. Enjoy!

Italian-Style Stuffed Mushrooms

Serves: 4 | Total Time: 30 minutes

4 portobello mushroom caps
2 tbsp cream cheese, softened
3 tsp grated Parmesan cheese
1 tsp olive oil
2 cups fresh baby spinach
1 red bell pepper, chopped
1/3 cup chopped leeks
2 tsp fresh thyme, chopped

Preheat air fryer to 390°F. Coat the mushrooms in olive oil and put them in the frying basket, hole side up, and Air Fry for 3 minutes. Take them out carefully and set aside. Combine the spinach, red bell pepper, leeks, thyme, cream cheese, and Parmesan cheese in a bowl and stir together. Then, stuff the mushroom caps with a fourth of the mix and put them back in the fryer. Bake for 6-9 minutes until the mix is hot and the caps are softened.

Vegetable Egg Quiche

Serves: 4 | Total Time: 30 minutes

2 tbsp grated Gruyère cheese
4 eggs, whisked
1 zucchini, grated
1 red bell pepper, chopped
½ cup chopped mushrooms
1/3 cup minced red onion
1 tbsp mustard

Preheat air fryer to 320°F. Add the eggs, zucchini, red bell pepper, mushrooms, onion, and mustard to a bowl and mix well. Stir in the Gruyere cheese to combine. Pour the egg mix in a greased baking and set in the air fryer. Bake for 18-22 minutes, letting the mix get puffy and golden. When finished, let cool for a few minutes.

Meat-Free Burgers

Serves: 3 | Total Time: 30 minutes

¾ cup canned red kidney beans
¼ cup roasted red peppers
1 tbsp hot sauce
1 tbsp balsamic vinegar
½ tsp ground coriander
1 egg, beaten

Preheat air fryer to 360°F. In a food processor, blitz the beans, red peppers, hot sauce, balsamic vinegar, and ¼ cup of water until smooth. Remove to a bowl. Add coriander and egg and toss until well combined. Make 3 patties out of the mixture and Bake for 16 minutes until golden brown, turning once. Serve warm or chilled.

Party Zucchini Pita Pizzas

Serves: 4 | Total Time: 15 minutes

1 cup grated mozzarella cheese
4 pitas
1 tbsp olive oil
¾ cup passata
1 sliced zucchini
½ tsp dried oregano
2 green onions, minced
12 cherry tomatoes, halved

Preheat air fryer to 360°F. Brush one side of each piece of pita with oil. Spread the passata on top and cover with zucchini slices. Sprinkle with oregano and green onions. Lastly, top with the grated cheese. Place in the greased frying basket and Bake until the cheese is melted and golden. Remove fand top with cherry tomatoes to serve.

Prawn Croquettes

Serves: 4 | Total Time: 25 minutes

½ lb cooked prawns, minced
1/3 cup Greek yogurt
½ red onion, minced
2 celery stalks, minced
1 garlic clove, minced
½ tsp dried basil
2 egg whites
½ cup breadcrumbs

Preheat air fryer to 370°F. Combine the prawns, yogurt, red onion, celery, garlic, basil, and one egg white in a bowl, then use your hands to make 8 ovals. Whisk the rest of the egg white in a shallow bowl and put the breadcrumbs on a plate. Dip each oval first in the egg white, then in the breadcrumbs. Air Fry the croquettes in the fryer for 7-10 minutes, turning them regularly until they are golden brown. Serve hot.

Feta & Parmesan Stuffed Mushrooms

Serves: 4 | Total Time: 30 minutes

4 Portobello mushroom caps
½ cup feta, crumbled
1 tbsp olive oil
1 cup spinach, chopped
1/3 cup bread crumbs
¼ tsp minced rosemary
3 tbsp Parmesan cheese

Preheat air fryer to 390°F. After rubbing the mushroom caps with olive oil, place them in the air fryer with the hollowed side up. Bake for 3 minutes. Using tongs, carefully remove the caps and drain any liquid out of the caps. Set aside. Combine feta, spinach, bread crumbs, and rosemary in a bowl. Spoon the mixture into the mushroom caps and sprinkle with Parmesan cheese. Return the caps to the fryer. Bake until the filling is hot and the caps are tender, 4-6 minutes. Serve warm.

Asiago & Spinach Quichê

Serves: 3 | Total Time: 30 minutes

3 eggs
1 cup chopped spinach
1/3 cup heavy cream
2 tbsp honey mustard
½ cup grated Asiago cheese
½ tsp dried thyme
Salt and pepper to taste

Preheat air fryer to 320°F. Beat the eggs in a bowl. Then, stir in the remaining ingredients until completely combined. Pour into prepared pan. Bake until the egg mixture is puffed, set, and just golden, 18-22 minutes. Allow to cool for 5 minutes. Cut into wedges and serve.

Balsamic Lentil Patties

Serves: 4 | Total Time: 25 minutes

¼ cup canned diced tomatoes
1 (15.5-oz) can lentils
2 tbsp balsamic vinegar
2 tbsp hot sauce
1 tbsp allspice
1 tsp liquid smoke
1 egg white

Preheat air fryer to 360°F. Using a fork, mash the lentils in a bowl. Stir in tomatoes and their juice, balsamic vinegar, hot sauce, allspice, liquid smoke, and egg white with your hands. Make 4 patties out of the mixture. Bake them for 15 minutes until crispy, turning once. Serve immediately.

Italian Chicken Sandwiches

Serves: 4 | Total Time: 20 minutes

1/3 cup Italian dressing	4 pita pockets, split
2 chicken breasts, cubed	2 cups torn butter lettuce
1 small red onion, sliced	1 cucumber, sliced
1 red bell pepper, sliced	6 black olives, quartered
½ tsp dried thyme	16 chopped cherry tomatoes

Preheat air fryer to 380°F. In a bowl, combine chicken, onion, and bell pepper. Add 1 tbsp of Italian dressing and the thyme. Toss until chicken and vegetables are coated. Place the mixture into the frying basket and Bake for 10-12 minutes, tossing once halfway through. Remove the chicken and vegetables to a bowl. Add the remaining Italian dressing and toss to coat.

To assemble the sandwiches, add the chicken, vegetables, butter lettuce, cucumber, black olives, and cherry tomatoes inside the pita pocket. Serve and enjoy!

Grilled Cheese & Prawn Sandwiches

Serves: 4 | Total Time: 15 minutes

1 ¼ cups shredded halloumi cheese

1 (6-oz) can prawns, minced	4 bread slices
3 tbsp mayonnaise	2 tbsp butter, softened
2 tbsp minced green onion	

Preheat air fryer to 400°F. Mix together halloumi cheese, prawns, mayonnaise, and green onion. On a work surface, lay out the bread. Spread half of the mixture on one slice of bread and then half on another slice of bread. Cover each slice with the remaining bread to make sandwiches. Spread butter on both sides of each sandwich.

Place the sandwich into the air fryer and Bake until the bread is toasted and crisp while the cheese is melted. Remove from the air fryer, cut in half, and serve warm.

Carrot & Zucchini Cakes

Serves: 4 | Total Time: 25 minutes

3 oz ricotta cheese, crumbled

1 egg, beaten	1/3 cup grated carrots
½ tsp dried oregano	2/3 cup bread crumbs
Salt and pepper to taste	2 tbsp olive oil
1 zucchini, grated	

Preheat air fryer to 340°F. Combine ricotta cheese, egg, oregano, salt, and pepper in a bowl. Stir in zucchini and carrots until well mixed. Then stir in the bread crumbs. Shape the mixture into patties. Brush them with oil. Place the cakes into the frying basket and Air Fry until crisp and golden, about 8-10 minutes. Serve and enjoy!

Gnocchi al Pesto

Serves: 4 | Total Time: 25 minutes

1/3 cup grated Parmesan cheese

1 tbsp olive oil	16 oz pack gnocchi
1 shallot, finely chopped	1 cup basil pesto
3 cloves garlic, sliced	

Preheat air fryer to 390°F. Add oil, shallot, garlic, and gnocchi to a baking pan. Put the pan into the air fryer. Bake for 10 minutes, then stir. Continue to cook until golden and crisp, 8-13 minutes. Remove the pan from the fryer. Add basil pesto and Parmesan and stir in with the gnocchi. Serve and enjoy!

Tuna Melts with English Muffins

Serves: 4 | Total Time: 15 minutes

1 (6-oz) can tuna, drained	½ red onion, minced
¼ cup mayonnaise	2 English muffins, halved
2 tsp mustard	2 tbsp butter, softened
1 tbsp lime juice	4 Muenster cheese slices

Preheat air fryer to 390°F. Mix together tuna, mayonnaise, mustard, lime juice, and red onion in a small bowl. Set aside. Spread butter on the cut side of the English muffins. Place into the air fryer with the butter side up. Bake until lightly golden, 3 minutes. Remove from the air fryer. Top each muffin with one slice of cheese. Bake in the air fryer for another 2-4 minutes until the cheese melts. Remove the muffins to a serving plate. Top with tuna mixture and serve.

Cheddar Tuna Tacos

Serves: 4 | Total Time: 25 minutes

1 cup grated Cheddar cheese

3 tbsp butter, softened	
4 corn tortillas	1/3 cup mild salsa
1 (6-oz) can tuna, flaked	2 tbsp chives, minced
½ zucchini, shredded	1 red chili pepper, diced

Preheat air fryer to 340°F. Spread softened butter on one side of the tortillas. Place in the frying basket, butter side up, and Bake until crisp, 3 minutes. Remove and set aside.

Mix together tuna, zucchini, mild salsa, chives, and red chili pepper in a bowl. Top each tortilla with the tuna mixture and then some of the cheese. Return to the fryer and Bake until the tuna mix is hot and the cheese has melted, 3 minutes. Serve.

Basil Cod Croquettes

Serves: 4 | Total Time: 20 minutes

1 ½ cups bread crumbs	2 green onions, chopped
1 egg, beaten	2 tbsp chopped basil
2 tbsp lemon juice	Salt and pepper to taste
1 lb cooked cod, flaked	2 tbsp olive oil

Preheat air fryer to 390°F. Mix together ½ cup bread crumbs, egg, and lemon juice in a bowl. Then add the chopped cod, green onions, basil, salt, and pepper. Set aside. In a shallow plate, combine the 1 cup of bread crumbs and olive oil until well mixed. Take the cod mixture and form 1½-inch round, compact balls. Roll the croquettes into the bread crumb mixture. Place the croquettes into the frying basket, without overcrowding and Air Fry until brown and crisp, 6-8 minutes. Serve.

Chickpea & Bulgur Baked Dinner

Serves: 6 | Total Time: 55 minutes

1 cup bulgur
2 ¼ cups chicken stock
1 (15.5-oz) can chickpeas
½ cup diced carrot
½ cup green peas
1 tsp ground cumin
½ tsp ground turmeric
½ tsp ground ginger
½ tsp shallot powder
Salt and pepper to taste
¼ tsp ground cinnamon
¼ tsp garlic powder
2 tbsp cilantro, chopped

Preheat air fryer to 380°F. Add the bulgur, stock, chickpeas, carrot, peas, cumin, turmeric, ginger, shallot powder, salt, cinnamon, garlic powder, and black pepper to a greased casserole dish and stir well to combine. Cover loosely with aluminum foil. Put the casserole dish into the air fryer and bake for 20 minutes. Stir well and uncover. Bake for 25 more minutes. Fluff with a spoon. Garnish with cilantro. Serve and enjoy!

Winter Veggie Quinoa

Serves: 6 | Total Time: 45 minutes

2 potatoes, cubed
2 carrots, sliced
1 small rutabaga, cubed
2 celery stalks, chopped
½ tsp smoked paprika
3 tbsp olive oil
1 thyme sprig
1 cup quinoa
2 cups vegetable broth
2 garlic cloves, minced
½ yellow onion, chopped
1 tsp salt

Preheat air fryer to 380°F. Mix the potatoes, carrots, rutabaga, and celery with the paprika and 2 tbsp of olive oil in a bowl. Pour the vegetable mixture into a greased baking dish and top with the thyme sprigs. Put the casserole dish into the air fryer and bake for 15 minutes.

Warm the remaining olive oil in a medium saucepan over medium heat. Add the quinoa, broth, garlic, onion, and salt and bring the mixture to a boil. Simmer for 10-12 minutes. Slide-out the casserole dish from the air fryer. Remove thyme sprigs and discard. Pour the cooked quinoa into the dish with the vegetables and stir to combine. Cover with aluminum foil and bake for 15 more minutes. Stir and serve.

Italian Salad with Roasted Veggies

Serves: 4 | Total Time: 35 minutes

1 ½ cups quartered mushrooms
1 cup cherry tomatoes
1 green onion, thinly sliced
1 tbsp allspice
10 oz green beans, thawed
2 cups fingerling potatoes
½ lb baby spinach
½ cup Italian dressing
¼ cup pepitas

Preheat air fryer to 380°F. Combine mushrooms, tomatoes, green onion, and allspice in a bowl. Set aside. Arrange the green beans on a baking pan, then put in the veggie mixture, and finally top with potatoes. Roast for 25 minutes until the potatoes are tender. Let cool completely before removing to a bowl; toss to combine. Stir in spinach, drizzle with Italian dressing, and scatter with pepitas; toss to combine. Serve right away.

Creamy Green Peas

Serves: 6: | Total Time: 30 minutes

3 tsp grated Parmesan cheese
1 cup cauliflower florets
1 shallot, chopped
2 tbsp olive oil
½ cup heavy cream
3 cups green peas
3 garlic cloves, minced
2 tbsp thyme, chopped
1 tsp rosemary, chopped
Salt and pepper to taste
2 tbsp parsley, chopped

Preheat air fryer to 380°F. Toss the cauliflower florets and shallot with olive oil in a bowl. Put the cauliflower mixture into the frying basket in a single layer and Bake for 15 minutes. Remove the cauliflower and shallot to your food processor. Add the heavy cream and puree until smooth. Combine the cauliflower puree, peas, garlic, thyme, rosemary, salt, and pepper in a saucepan over medium heat and mix well. Cook for 10 minutes, stirring regularly. Serve sprinkled with Parmesan cheese and parsley. Enjoy!

Sage Wild Rice Risotto

Serves: 6 | Total Time: 40 minutes

1 cup Parmesan cheese
1 ½ cups wild rice
2 ½ cups chicken broth
1 cup tomato sauce
1 yellow onion, diced
3 garlic cloves, minced
1 tbsp sage, chopped
½ tsp salt
2 tbsp butter, melted

Preheat air fryer to 380°F. Add the wild rice, broth, tomato sauce, onion, garlic, sage, salt, butter, and ½ cup of the Parmesan to a bowl and stir to combine. Pour the rice mixture into a greased casserole dish and cover with aluminum foil. Bake for 20 minutes, then uncover and stir. Sprinkle with the remaining Parmesan and Bake for 15 minutes more. Stir well before serving. Enjoy!

Corn & Asparagus Salad

Serves: 4 | Total Time: 30 minutes

2 heads romaine lettuce, halved lengthwise
2 tbsp cottage cheese
1 tsp garlic powder
2 bread slices
1 cup corn kernels
1 lb asparagus, trimmed
16 cherry tomatoes, halved
½ sliced red onion
½ cup Ranch dressing

Preheat air fryer to 400°F. Combine the cottage cheese and garlic in a bowl. Spread one side of each bread slice with half of the mixture and place them, spread-side up, in the frying basket. Grill for 2 minutes until toasted. Let cool completely before slicing into croutons. Set aside. Put the corn kernels in a baking dish in the air fryer. Grill for 4 minutes. Slice each asparagus into 3 pieces and Grill in the air fryer for 6-8 minutes until crisp-tender.

Put the lettuce halves, cut-side up, in the fryer and Grill for 3 minutes until golden brown. Divide the lettuce halves between serving plates and add the croutons, corn, asparagus, tomatoes, and red onion. Sprinkle each with Ranch dressing and serve right away.

Cajun Cheese & Shrimp Open Pie

Serves: 4 | Total Time: 30 minutes

½ lb cooked shrimp, minced	2 eggs, slightly beaten
1 cup grated cheddar cheese	1 tbsp butter, melted
1 Cajun seasoning	1 refrigerated piecrust
2 tbsp chopped chives	½ cup hot sauce

Preheat air fryer to 390°F. Place all the ingredients except pie crust and pepper sauce in a bowl and toss to coat. Place the piecrust on a pie dish. Spread the shrimp mixture over the crust, leaving 1 inch of edge. Fold up the edges of the crust around the filling. Bake in the fryer for 15-20 minutes until the crust is golden. Let cool for 15 minutes. Serve warm with hot sauce.

Bacon 'n' Bell Pepper Pita Pockets

Serves: 4 | Total Time: 25 minutes

8 bacon slices, cut into thirds	2 pita pockets, cut in half
1/3 cup spicy BBQ sauce	2 cups torn romaine lettuce
2 tbsp honey	2 tbsp sliced scallions
1 red bell pepper, sliced	2 tomatoes, sliced
1 yellow bell pepper, sliced	

Preheat air fryer to 350°F. Mix together barbecue sauce and honey in a bowl. Lightly brush the pepper slices with the barbecue mix and then the bacon, but do not dip your brush back into the sauce. Place the peppers into the frying basket. Air Fry for 4 minutes, shake the basket and add the bacon. Grill until the bacon browns and peppers are tender, 2 minutes. To assemble the sandwiches, layer the bacon, peppers, lettuce, and tomatoes in the pita halves. Add remaining BBQ sauce and top with scallions.

Black Bean & Sweet Potato Burgers

Serves: 4 | Total Time: 20 minutes

1 cup mashed sweet potatoes	Salt and pepper to taste
1 (15-oz) can black beans	1 tbsp lemon juice
½ tsp dried oregano	1 cup cooked brown rice
¼ tsp dried thyme	¼ cup bread crumbs
¼ tsp cumin	1 tbsp olive oil
1 garlic clove, minced	1 avocado, sliced for serving

Preheat air fryer to 380°F. Mash the black beans in a large bowl with the back of a fork. Add the mashed sweet potato, oregano, thyme, cumin, garlic, salt, pepper, and lemon juice, and mix until well combined. Stir in the cooked rice. Stir in bread crumbs. Form the dough into 4 patties. Put them into the air frying basket in a single layer. Lightly brush half of the olive oil onto the patties and bake for 5 minutes. Flip the patties over, brush the other side with the remaining oil, and bake for an additional 4-5 minutes. Serve with avocado.

Stuffed Tomatoes with Cheese & Lentils

Serves: 4 | Total Time: 25 minutes

2 tbsp grated mozzarella	½ cup cooked red lentils
4 tomatoes, tops removed	1 garlic clove, minced
1 tbsp minced red onion	Salt and pepper to taste
4 basil leaves, minced	4 oz cottage cheese

Preheat air fryer to 380°F. Scoop out half of the tomatoes' flesh and put it into a bowl. Add the cooked lentils, garlic, onion, basil, salt, pepper, and cottage cheese. Stir until well combined. Spoon the filling into the prepared tomatoes. Top with mozzarella cheese. Arrange the tomatoes in a single layer in the air frying basket and Bake for 15 minutes. Serve and enjoy!

Poblano Lentil Patties

Serves: 4 | Total Time: 25 minutes

1 cup cooked brown lentils	2 tbsp lemon juice
¼ cup cilantro leaves	2 tbsp olive oil, divided
¼ red onion, minced	½ tsp onion powder
½ cup grated carrots	½ tsp smoked paprika
1 poblano pepper, minced	½ tsp dried oregano
¼ red bell pepper, minced	½ tsp mustard powder
2 garlic cloves, minced	Salt and pepper to taste
1 large egg	½ cup corn flour

Preheat air fryer to 380°F. In your food processor, blitz the lentils and cilantro until mostly smooth. Pour the lentils into a large bowl, and combine with the onion, carrots, poblano pepper, bell pepper, garlic, egg, lemon juice, and 1 tablespoon olive oil.

Add the onion powder, paprika, oregano, mustard powder, salt, pepper, and corn flour. Stir everything together until the seasonings and corn flour are well distributed. Form the dough into 4 patties. Put them into the air frying basket in a single layer and drizzle them with the remaining olive oil. Bake for 10 minutes, flipping once. Serve and enjoy!

Basil Green Lentil Balls

Serves: 6 | Total Time: 20 minutes

½ cup cooked green lentils	1 cup cooked millet
2 garlic cloves, minced	1 tbsp lime juice
¼ white onion, minced	1 tbsp olive oil
¼ cup parsley leaves	½ tsp salt
5 basil leaves	

Preheat air fryer to 380°F. Blitz the cooked lentils with the garlic, onion, parsley, and basil in your food processor until mostly smooth. Transfer the lentil mixture into a large bowl, and stir in millet, lime juice, olive oil, and salt. Stir until well combined. Form the lentil mixture into balls. Arrange the rice balls in a single layer in the frying basket. Air Fry for 10-12 minutes, turning once until the balls are browned on all sides. Serve and enjoy!

Chickpea Cakes

Serves: 4 | Total Time: 25 minutes

1 (14-oz) can chickpeas	½ tsp cayenne pepper
½ red bell pepper, chopped	2 tbsp lemon juice
3 scallions, chopped	2 tbsp mayonnaise
¼ tsp garlic powder	1 cup chickpea flour

Preheat air fryer to 400°F. Using a fork, mash the chickpeas. Combine them with bell pepper, scallions, garlic, cayenne pepper, lemon juice, and mayonnaise until well mixed in a bowl. Mix in chickpea flour until fully incorporated. Make 6 equal patties out of the mixture and Air Fry for 13-15 minutes until browned and crispy, turning once. Serve immediately.

Tasty Roasted Kidney Beans & Peppers

Serves: 4 | Total Time: 20 minutes

2 (15-oz) cans kidney beans	1 tbsp olive oil
1 green bell pepper, diced	Salt and pepper to taste
1 shallot, diced	1 rosemary sprig
3 garlic cloves, minced	1 bay leaf

Preheat air fryer to 360°F. Combine the beans, bell pepper, shallot, garlic, olive oil, salt, and pepper in a bowl. Pour the bean mixture into a greased casserole dish, put the rosemary and bay leaf on top, and then place the casserole dish into the air fryer. Roast for 15 minutes. Remove the rosemary and bay leaves, then stir. Serve.

Tomato-Bean Bake

Serves: 4 | Total Time: 35 minutes

2 oz feta cheese, crumbled	¼ cup olive oil
1 (15-oz) can white beans	2 garlic cloves, minced
1 (15-oz) can Navy beans	2 tbsp chopped dill
1 green onion, diced	Salt and pepper to taste
1 (8-oz) can tomato sauce	1 bay leaf
1 ½ tbsp honey	1 tbsp balsamic vinegar

Preheat air fryer to 360°F. Place all ingredients, except for the feta cheese, in a bowl and stir until well combined. Pour the bean mixture into a greased casserole dish. Bake for 30 minutes. Remove and discard the bay leaf. Sprinkle crumbled feta over the top, then serve.

White Bean Bake

Serves: 4 | Total Time: 35 minutes

1 (15-oz) can cooked white beans	
1 cup diced tomatoes	½ tsp salt
½ tbsp tomato puree	¼ cup olive oil
2 garlic cloves, minced	¼ cup chervil, chopped
½ yellow onion, diced	

Preheat air fryer to 380°F. Place the beans, tomatoes, tomato puree, garlic, onion, salt, and olive oil in a bowl and mix until all ingredients are combined. Pour the mixture into a greased casserole dish and top with the chopped chervil. Bake in the air fryer for 25-30 minutes, stirring once. Serve and enjoy!

Spicy Roasted Cauliflower

Serves: 4 | Total Time: 30 minutes

½ head cauliflower, cut into florets	
¾ cup chickpea flour	2 tbsp lime juice
2 tsp allspice	½ cup milk
3 tbsp enchilada sauce	

Preheat air fryer to 360°F. Beat the chickpea flour, allspice, 2 tbsp of hot sauce, 1 tbsp of lime juice, and milk in a shallow bowl. Add in cauliflower florets and toss until completely coated. Bake for 15 minutes until browned and crispy, turning once. Whisk 1 tbsp of enchilada sauce and 1 tbsp of lime juice until well combined. Drizzle over the cauliflower or use it as a dip.

Paprika Mushroom & Buckwheat Pilaf

Serves: 4 | Total Time: 45 minutes

8 oz button mushrooms, diced	
2 tbsp cilantro, chopped	2 cups vegetable broth
2 tbsp olive oil	1 tbsp thyme, chopped
½ onion, diced	½ tsp salt
2 garlic cloves, minced	¼ tsp smoked paprika
1 cup buckwheat	

Preheat air fryer to 380°F. Warm the olive oil in a skillet over medium heat. Add the mushrooms, garlic, and onion and cook, stirring occasionally, until tender, about 5 minutes. Remove the vegetables to a large bowl. Stir in the buckwheat, broth, thyme, salt, and paprika. Pour the mixture into a greased casserole dish and place the dish into the air fryer. Bake for 25-30 minutes. Allow to rest for 5 minutes. Fluf with a fork and sprinkle with cilantro.

Sriracha Spring Rolls

Serves: 4 | Total Time: 30 minutes

2 tbsp nut butter	4 scallions, sliced
2 tbsp lime juice	16 oz coleslaw mix
1 tbsp sriracha hot sauce	8 spring roll wrappers

Preheat air fryer to 350°F. Whisk the nut butter, lime juice, and hot sauce in a bowl. Stir in scallions and coleslaw until well coated. Lay the wrappers, face up, and fill each with 1/8 cup of filling onto the corner. Then fold up over the filling, pushing back to compact it, and finally fold the sides. Grease them with cooking spray and Bake for 17 minutes until golden brown and crispy, turning once. Serve warm.

White Bean Falafel Salad

Serves: 4 | Total Time: 30 minutes

1 cup cherry tomatoes, halved	
2 cups torn romaine lettuce	1 tsp garlic powder
1 (15.5-oz) can white beans	1 tsp ground cumin
½ sliced red onion	¼ cup chickpea flour
2 tbsp chopped cilantro	1 peeled cucumber, sliced
2 tbsp lemon juice	¼ cup Italian dressing

Preheat air fryer to 375°F. Using a fork, mash the white beans until smooth. Stir in ¼ cup of red onion, cilantro, lemon juice, garlic, cumin, and chickpea flour until well combined. Make 8 equal patties out of the mixture and Bake for 12 minutes until golden brown, turning once. Let cool slightly. Combine the lettuce, tomatoes, cucumber, and the remaining red onion in a bowl. Add in falafels and drizzle with Italian dressing; toss to combine. Serve.

Burritos Enmolados with Tofu

Serves: 2 | Total Time: 30 minutes

1 ½ cups shredded red cabbage

4 tbsp lime juice	2 scallions, finely sliced
2 tbsp mole hot sauce	1 ½ tbsp mayonnaise
½ tsp ground cumin	2 tbsp chopped cilantro
16 oz super-firm tofu	4 corn tortillas

Preheat air fryer to 400°F. Whisk 2 tbsp of lime juice, 1 tbsp of mole sauce and cumin until smooth. Set aside. Slice tofu into 4 pieces. Submerge the slices into the sauce and arrange them in a single layer. Drizzle with half of the sauce and Air Fry for 6 minutes. Turn the slices, drizzle with the remaining sauce, and Air Fry for another 6 minutes. Let cool slightly before cutting into strips.

Combine red cabbage, scallions, mayonnaise, cilantro, 2 tbsp of lime juice, and 1 tbsp of hot sauce. Set aside. Air Fry corn tortillas for 2-3 minutes in a single layer. For the tacos, fill each tortilla with ¼ of slaw and top each with ¼ of tofu strips. Serve immediately.

Nutty Brussels Sprouts Salad

Serves: 4 | Total Time: 25 minutes

4 cups sliced Brussels sprouts

1 ½ tbsp olive oil	⅛ tsp salt
1 ½ tbsp lemon juice	¼ cup chopped red onion
1 tsp maple syrup	3 tbsp cracker crumbs
½ tsp whole-grain mustard	½ tbsp walnuts, chopped

Preheat air fryer to 400°F. Whisk olive oil, lemon juice, maple syrup, mustard, and salt. Set the dressing aside. Combine Brussels sprouts, cracker crumbs, and onion in a greased baking dish and place in the frying basket. Bake for 5 minutes. Stir the vegetables and bake for another 5 minutes. Stir in walnuts and bake for 2 more minutes. Remove the dish from the air fryer. Pour the dressing over the cooked vegetables and toss to coat. Serve warm.

Original Grilled Cheese Sandwiches

Serves: 2 | Total Time: 15 minutes

¼ cup sliced roasted red peppers

¼ cup Alfredo sauce	¼ cup mozzarella cheese
4 bread slices	3 tbsp sliced red onions

Preheat air fryer to 400°F. Lay 2 bread slices on a flat surface, spread some Alfredo sauce on one side, and place them in frying the basket. Scatter with mozzarella cheese, roasted peppers, and red onion. Drizzle with the remaining Alfredo sauce and top with the remaining bread slices. Grill for 4 minutes, turn the sandwiches, and Grill for 3 more minutes until toasted. Serve warm.

Catalan-Style Bikini Sandwiches

Serves: 2 | Total Time: 30 minutes

4 bread slices	4 smoked ham
2 mozzarella cheese slices	2 tsp butter, melted
2 provolone cheese slices	

Preheat air fryer to 360°F. Smear both sides of the bread with butter and place them in the frying basket. Toast in the fryer for 6 minutes. Flip over each slice of bread. Cover 2 of the bread slices with a layer of mozzarella cheese, and the other two slices with a layer of the provolone and then the ham. Cook for 10 more minutes until the cheeses are melted and lightly bubbling, and the bread is golden brown. Bring them together, slice and serve.

Lentil & Bean Tacos

Serves: 6 | Total Time: 35 minutes

1 (15-oz) can red kidney beans

¼ cup chopped red onion	½ cup diced tomato
1 (15-oz) can red lentils	¼ cup chopped cilantro
2 tbsp taco seasoning	¼ cup lime juice
1 tbsp hot sauce	12 corn tortillas

Preheat air fryer to 360°F. Using a fork, mash the beans and lentils in a bowl. Mix in taco seasoning, hot sauce, red onion, tomato, cilantro, and lime juice. Fill each tortilla with 2 tbsp of bean mixture, keeping the filling close to one side, and roll them. Bake for 20 minutes until crispy. Serve right away.

Bacon & Bell Pepper Wraps

Serves: 4 | Total Time: 25 minutes

4 oz cooked bacon, crumbled	4 oz cream cheese, softened
1 red bell pepper, sliced	1 garlic clove, minced
1 green bell pepper, sliced	½ tbsp minced dill
½ red onion, sliced	½ tbsp minced chives
2 tbsp olive oil	4 warmed tortillas
Salt and pepper to taste	1 cup baby spinach

Preheat air fryer to 400°F. Toss bell peppers, onion, olive oil, and salt in a small bowl. Set to the side. Arrange peppers and onions in a single layer in the foil-lined frying basket. Bake for 5 minutes, then stir the vegetables. Bake for another 5 minutes and stir again. Bake for 2 more minutes. Combine cream cheese, garlic, dill, chives, and black pepper in a small bowl. Spread 1 tablespoon of the mixture on each tortilla, then add ¼ cup spinach, bacon, and ¼ of the pepper and onion mixture. Fold in the two sides and roll the tortilla over the filling. Serve.

Layered Cheese & Ham Casserole

Serves: 4 | Total Time: 25 minutes

¼ cup minced peeled sweet onion

1/3 cup shredded cheddar	1 tsp ground coriander
5 eggs	1 mashed clove of garlic
Salt and pepper to taste	¼ cup diced cooked ham
1 tsp Dijon mustard	2 bread slices, diced

Preheat air fryer to 325°F. Combine the eggs, salt, black pepper, coriander, garlic, mustard, onion, ham, cheddar cheese, and bread in a bowl. Pour it into a greased cake pan. Place cake pan in the frying basket and Air Fry for 14 minutes. Let cool onto a cooling rack for 5 minutes before slicing. Serve immediately.

BBQ Pork & Bacon Cheese Balls

Serves 4 | Total Time: 25 minutes

4 (1-oz) Pepper Jack cheese, cubes	
2 oz cooked bacon, crumbled	¼ cup grated yellow onion
1 lb ground pork	Salt and pepper to taste
1 tbsp barbecue sauce	1 tbsp capers

Preheat air fryer to 350°F. Combine all ingredients, except for bacon, capers, and cheese, in a bowl. Form the mixture into 4 balls. Press your thumb into the center of each ball. Add bacon crumbles, capers, and cheese cubes to the hole and seal them. Place patties in the lightly greased frying basket and Air Fry for 9 minutes or until you reach your desired doneness, flipping once. Serve.

Cilantro Falafel with Minty Yogurt Sauce

Serves: 4 | Total Time: 20 minutes

1 (15-oz) can chickpeas	Salt to taste
½ cup cilantro	1 cup Greek yogurt
3 garlic cloves, minced	1 tbsp chopped mint
½ tbsp ground cumin	2 tbsp lime juice
1 tbsp flour	

Preheat air fryer to 360°F. Place the chickpeas into your food processor and blitz until mostly chopped. Add the cilantro, 2 garlic cloves, and cumin and pulse for another 1-2 minutes until everything is well mixed and a dough is formed. Add the flour. Pulse a few more times until combined. Roll the dough into 8 balls, then flatten them slightly with the palm of your hand. Arrange the falafel patties in the greased frying basket and Air Fry for 15 minutes or until nicely browned on all sides. Mix the yogurt, remaining garlic, mint, and lime juice in a small bowl. Remove falafels from the fryer, season with salt and serve with the yogurt sauce.

Scallion Cheese & Ham Omelet

Serves: 4 | Total Time: 20 minutes

½ cup grated Parmesan	¼ cup chopped scallions
6 eggs	Salt and pepper to taste
1/3 cup cured ham, cubed	2 tbsp parsley, chopped

Preheat air fryer to 360°F. In a bowl, beat the eggs, and stir in ham, scallions, and Parmesan. Transfer to a greased baking pan and Bake in the air fryer for 15 minutes or until golden and crisp. Season to taste, top with parsley and serve immediately.

Homemade Spanakopita

Serves: 2 | Total Time: 25 minutes

3 tbsp olive oil	1 lemon, zested
2 tbsp minced onion	¼ tsp ground nutmeg
1 green onion, chopped	1 tsp dried Greek seasoning
2 garlic cloves, minced	½ tsp salt
4 cups spinach	1 cup carrot sticks
4 oz cream cheese, softened	
4 oz feta cheese	

Preheat air fryer to 360°F. Warm 1 tbsp of the olive oil in a large skillet over medium heat. Sauté the green onion and garlic for 2 minutes, stirring often. Mix in the spinach and 2 tbsp of water and cook for 2 -3 minutes until the spinach wilts. Set aside.

Combine the cream cheese, half of the feta, remaining olive oil, lemon zest, nutmeg, Greek seasoning, and salt in a bowl. Mix well. Stir in the vegetables to the cheese base. Pour the mixture into a greased ramekin and top with the remaining feta. Put the dip into the frying basket. Bake for 10 minutes or until bubbling. Serve with carrot sticks.

Ranch Chicken Salad

Serves: 2 | Total Time: 30 minutes

2 cups torn romaine lettuce	Salt and pepper to taste
1 peeled cucumber, diced	½ cup sliced almonds
½ cup Greek yogurt	1 tbsp olive oil
¼ cup buttermilk	1 tbsp lime juice
½ tbsp dried parsley	1 tsp paprika
½ tbsp dried chives	½ tsp chili powder
¼ tsp dried dill	½ tsp ground cumin
1 ⅛ tsp garlic powder	2 chicken breasts
⅛ tsp onion powder	2 Roma tomatoes, diced
2 stalk celery, diced	

Prepare ranch dressing. Whisk yogurt, buttermilk, parsley, chives, dill, garlic powder, onion powder, salt, and pepper in a small bowl. Cover and refrigerate.

Preheat air fryer to 360°F. Lightly grease the bottom of the frying basket with olive oil. Combine olive oil, lime juice, paprika, chili powder, cumin, and salt in a medium bowl. Coat the chicken in the oil mixture, then transfer it to the frying basket. Dispose of any leftover seasoning oil. Air Fry for 10 minutes, then flip the chicken. Air Fry for another 8 minutes. Transfer to a plate and loosely cover with foil to rest for 5 minutes. Place equal portions of lettuce and celery on two plates and top with tomatoes and cucumbers. Slice the chicken and arrange it on top of the salad. Serve with ranch dressing and almonds.

Pepperoni Pizza Bites

Serves: 4 | Total Time: 25 minutes

½ cup marinara sauce, warm	2 oz cream cheese, softened
3 tbsp shredded mozzarella	3 tbsp parmesan
1/3 cup flour	½ tsp Italian seasoning
¼ tsp salt	1 tsp of dried basil
¼ tsp baking powder	2 tbsp whole milk
½ cup diced pepperoni	1 tsp olive oil

Preheat air fryer to 325°F. Combine the flour, salt, and baking powder in a bowl. Toss the pepperoni, cream cheese, mozzarella cheese, Parmesan, Italian seasoning, basil, milk, and olive oil in another bowl. Add dry ingredients into the bowl with pepperoni mixture and toss until well combined. Form mixture into bite-sized pieces and place them on a pizza pan. Place pizza pan in the frying basket and Air Fry for 12 minutes. Remove it to a large plate. Serve with marinara sauce on the side.

Canadian-Style Pizza

Serves: 4 | Total Time: 30 minutes

8 Canadian bacon slices, chopped
1 ¼ cups shredded cheddar   ¾ cup marinara sauce
1 pizza dough   ½ tsp dried oregano
5 cloves garlic, minced   Garlic salt to taste

Preheat air fryer to 370°F. Lightly flour a work surface and roll out the pizza dough. Mix together garlic, marinara sauce, oregano, and garlic salt. Spread the sauce on the pizza crust, then top with bacon and cheddar cheese. Place in the frying basket and Bake until the crust is browned and the cheese is melted, about 8 minutes.

Black Bean Fajitas

Serves: 2 | Total Time: 20 minutes

1 (15.5-oz) black beans   ¼ cup salsa
1 tbsp fajita seasoning   2 scallions, thinly sliced
2 tbsp lime juice   1 tbsp hot sauce
2 flour tortillas

Preheat air fryer to 400°F. Using a fork, mash the beans until smooth. Stir in fajita seasoning and lime juice. Set aside. Place tortillas on a flat surface, spread half of the salsa on each tortilla, scatter with scallions, and top with the bean mixture. Drizzle with the hot sauce.

For the burritos, fold in the sides of the tortilla, then fold up the bottom, and finally roll-up. Grill for 10 minutes until crispy, turning once. Serve warm.

Picante Chickpea Salad

Serves: 2 | Total Time: 20 minutes

2 cups torn romaine lettuce   1 cucumber, sliced
3 tbsp chipotle hot sauce   3 radishes, sliced
1 tsp garlic powder   2 celery stalks, chopped
1 (15.5-oz) can chickpeas   2 scallions, sliced
12 cherry tomatoes   ¼ cup Ranch dressing

Preheat air fryer to 360°F. Whisk chipotle hot sauce and garlic in a bowl. Add in chickpeas and toss to coat. Bake chickpeas and tomatoes, in a single layer, for 8-10 minutes until tomatoes are blistered.

In the meantime, combine lettuce, cucumber, celery, radishes, and scallions in a bowl. Drizzle with Ranch dressing and toss to combine. Mix in baked chickpeas and tomatoes and serve.

Speedy Bean Salad

Serves: 4 | Total Time: 20 minutes

½ cup grated cheddar   ½ tsp dried sage
½ cup grated Parmesan   ⅛ tsp chili powder
2 garlic cloves, minced   ⅛ tsp paprika
½ cup diced red bell pepper   4 cups torn romaine lettuce
¼ cup diced red onion   1 cup baby spinach
1 (15-oz) can black beans   2 tomatoes, diced
2 tsp olive oil   1 lime, quartered
½ tsp ground cumin

Preheat air fryer to 375°F. Combine garlic, bell pepper, onion, black beans, olive oil, cumin, sage, chili powder, and paprika in a baking dish. Place the dish in the frying basket. Bake for 8 minutes, stirring once. Place the romaine lettuce and baby spinach in the center of a serving platter. When the beans are ready, put them on top, add the tomatoes, cheddar cheese, and Parmesan cheese. Garnish with a lime wedge to squeeze over. Serve.

Rich Cheese & Pesto Sandwiches

Serves: 4 | Total Time: 15 minutes

½ tbsp Asiago cheese, grated
½ tbsp Parmesan cheese, grated
1 garlic clove   1 tbsp vegetable broth
1 tbsp toasted pine nuts   1 tbsp olive oil
1 tomato, sliced   8 bread slices
1 cup basil leaves   8 mozzarella cheese slices
¼ tsp salt

Preheat air fryer to 400°F. Add garlic, pine nuts, basil, salt, and vegetable broth in a food processor. Pulse until finely chopped. Slowly pour in olive oil from the top while it is processing until combined and just thick. Pulse in Asiago and Parmesan cheeses until combined.

Fall Chicken Salad

Serves: 2 | Total Time: 30 minutes

2 boneless, skinless chicken thighs
1 cup cubed butternut squash
½ cucumber, peeled into ribbons
2 cups torn romaine lettuce   1 tbsp cilantro, chopped
¼ cup sliced red onion   1 tbsp olive oil
2 tbsp Dijon mustard   2 cups baby spinach
Salt and pepper to taste   ½ lime, juiced
¼ tsp ground sage   ½ lime, cut into wedges
¼ tsp smoked paprika

Preheat air fryer to 360°F. Combine mustard, salt, pepper, sage, and paprika in a small bowl. Coat the butternut squash with olive oil, salt, and pepper in a medium bowl. Brush half of the mustard mixture on the top of the chicken, then transfer the chicken to one side of the frying basket. Place the squash on the other side of the basket. Roast for 10 minutes, then flip the chicken and brush the top with the rest of the mustard mixture. Stir the squash. Roast for another 8 to 10 minutes.

Transfer the chicken to a plate to rest for about 5 minutes. Transfer the squash to a salad bowl and toss with lettuce, spinach, cucumber, onion, and lime juice. Slice the chicken and plate on top of the salad. Serve garnished with lime wedges and cilantro.

Bavarian Bratwurst with Sauerkraut

Serves: 4 | Total Time: 30 minutes

1 lb pork bratwurst, pierced with a fork
1 (12-oz) bottle lager beer   2 bay leaves
½ onion, sliced   2 tbsp ketchup
2 cups drained sauerkraut

Place bratwurst, beer, onion, bay leaves and 2 cups of water in a saucepan over high heat and bring it to a boil. Low the heat to and simmer for 15 minutes. Drain.

Preheat air fryer to 400°F. Place cooked bratwurst and onions in the greased frying basket and Air Fry for 3 minutes. Turn bratwurst, add in sauerkraut and cook for 3 more minutes. Serve with ketchup on the side.

Malaysian-Inspired Chicken Wraps

Serves: 4 | Total Time: 25 minutes

1 lb chicken breasts, cut into 2-inch pieces

¼ cup butter, melted	1 tbsp sesame oil
2 tbsp coconut aminos	1 tbsp honey
1 tbsp maple syrup	2 tsp apple cider vinegar
1 garlic clove, minced	Salt and pepper to taste
½ tsp ground ginger	2 cups grated cabbage
1 tsp chopped cilantro	¼ red onion, sliced
½ tsp turmeric powder	1 carrot, grated
¼ tsp red pepper flakes	4 warmed tortillas

Preheat air fryer to 375°F. Whisk butter, coconut aminos, maple syrup, turmeric, cilantro, garlic, ginger, red pepper flakes, and 2 tablespoons of water in a large bowl until well combined. Coat the chicken in the sauce, then transfer the chicken to the frying basket. Arrange them on a single layer and bake for 5 minutes. Stir the chicken and cook for another 5 minutes.

Mix together sesame oil, honey, vinegar, salt, and black pepper in a large bowl. Then add cabbage, onion, and carrot and toss. Stir in cooked chicken until just combined. Place ¼ of the chicken slaw on each tortilla. Fold in the sides and roll the tortilla over the filling. Serve.

German-Style Egg Salad on Toast

Serves: 4 | Total Time: 30 minutes

6 eggs	Salt and pepper to taste
¼ cup Greek yogurt	8 bread slices
1 tbsp whole-grain mustard	2 tbsp melted butter
1 scallion, minced	2 leaves butter lettuce
1 tbsp chopped dill	2 small tomatoes, sliced

Preheat air fryer to 300°F. Arrange the eggs on a single layer in the frying basket. Air Fry for 14 minutes. Remove from the fryer and run the eggs under cold water. When cool, peel the shells and discard them. In a medium bowl, place cooked eggs and mash them with a fork. Stir in yogurt, mustard, scallion, dill, salt, and pepper. Arrange bread slices on a single layer in the frying basket, butter each slice, and toast for 4 minutes at 400°F. Spread ¼ of the egg salad on a slice of toast and top with another slice of bread. Repeat for the other three sandwiches. Cut in half. Serve with lettuce and tomato slices and enjoy!

Authentic Three-Meat Pizza

Serves: 2 | Total Time: 20 minutes

½ cup shredded mozzarella	1/3 cup pizza sauce
1 pizza crust	2 oz grilled steak, sliced
2 oz soppressata, sliced	4 basil leaves, torn
2 oz pepperoni, sliced	

Preheat air fryer to 350°F. Place the pizza crust on the foil-lined frying basket. Spread the sauce evenly over the pizza base, allowing at least ½ inch border. Top with soppressata, pepperoni, and steak slices, then sprinkle the cheese on top. Bake for 10-12 minutes until the cheese is melted and lightly crisped and the pizza crust is golden brown. Top with basil leaves. Serve sliced.

Picnic Pasta Salad

Serves: 6 | Total Time: 40 minutes

2 tsp chopped tarragon	¼ cup apple cider vinegar
1 lb cooked rotini pasta	1 tsp whole-grain mustard
1 small zucchini, cubed	1 garlic clove, minced
1 red onion, chopped	1 tbsp chopped dill
1 cup broccoli florets	½ tsp cayenne pepper
1 tbsp olive oil	1 tsp chopped fresh thyme
Salt and pepper to taste	Salt and pepper to taste
1/3 cup olive oil	¼ tsp smoked paprika

Preheat air fryer to 375°F. Combine zucchini, squash, onion, broccoli, olive oil, salt, and pepper in a large bowl. Toss to coat. Add vegetables to the frying basket and Roast for 8 minutes. Shake the basket, then roast for another 4 minutes. Stir in with cooked rotini; set aside.

To prepare the dressing, whisk olive oil, cayenne pepper, tarragon, thyme, vinegar, mustard, garlic, dill, salt, pepper, and paprika. Pour over pasta salad and toss to coat. Serve right away or chill until another time.

Spread 1 tablespoon of pesto each on 4 slices of bread, then top with 2 slices of mozzarella cheese and tomato slices to each of them. Top each sandwich with another slice of bread. Arrange the sandwiches on a single layer in the frying basket. Toast for 5 minutes. Serve hot.

Teriyaki Meatloaf

Serves: 4 | Total Time: 45 minutes

¾ lb ground beef	2 tbsp white wine vinegar
½ lb ground pork	1 red chili, finely sliced
1/3 cup breadcrumbs	1 egg
4 tbsp pineapple juice	½ tsp garlic salt
4 tbsp brown sugar	½ tsp onion powder
3 tbsp ketchup	

Preheat the air fryer to 390°F. Combine the beef, pork, breadcrumbs, half of the pineapple juice, half of the brown sugar, half of the ketchup, white wine vinegar, egg, garlic salt, red chili, and onion powder in a bowl and mix. Shape the mixture into a loaf and place it inside the greased frying basket. Bake for 25 minutes. Mix the remaining pineapple juice, brown sugar, and ketchup. Remove the meat from the air fryer and glaze it with the pineapple mix. Return to the fryer and bake for 7-10 more minutes or nicely glazed and cooked. Transfer the meatloaf to a serving plate to rest for 10 minutes, then slice and serve.

Bacon & Egg Scramble Bake

Serves: 4 | Total Time: 30 minutes

½ diced green bell pepper	Salt and pepper to taste
¾ cup shredded Cheddar	½ cup diced red bell pepper
6 bacon slices	½ chopped leeks
6 eggs	½ tbsp chives, chopped

Cook the bacon in a skillet over high heat until crisp, 5 minutes. Drain on paper towels, then crumble and set aside. Whisk eggs with salt and pepper in a medium bowl.

Preheat air fryer to 400°F. Add the red and green peppers, bacon, leek, and egg mixture to a greased baking pan. Place the pan in the air fryer and Bake for 6 minutes. Slide-out, top the eggs with cheese and cook for 2 minutes until the cheese melts. Sprinkle with chives.

Salmon & Spinach Salad

Serves: 2 | Total Time: 30 minutes

¼ cup sliced red onion	¼ tsp cayenne pepper
¼ cup pecans	4 salmon fillets
2 tbsp olive oil	1 tsp apple cider vinegar
2 garlic cloves, minced	3 tbsp lemon juice
2 tbsp maple syrup	4 cups baby spinach
½ tbsp coconut aminos	2 tbsp chopped parsley
Salt and pepper to taste	1 tsp poppy seeds

Preheat air fryer to 400°F. Add pecans to the frying basket. Toast for 5 minutes, then shake the basket. Toast for another 5 minutes, then transfer to a large bowl. While the pecans are toasting, combine garlic, parsley, lemon juice, maple syrup, coconut aminos, salt, and cayenne pepper in a small bowl. Brush the sauce on the tops and sides of the salmon. Transfer the salmon to the greased frying basket. Air Fry for 8 minutes. Let it rest.

To prepare the salad, whisk olive oil, vinegar, salt, and black pepper. Pour the dressing over the pecans, then add spinach and onion. Toss everything until evenly coated. Arrange the salad equally between two plates and top with 2 pieces of salmon each. Serve immediately sprinkled with poppy seeds.

Meatball & Cabbage Bake

Serves: 4 | Total Time: 30 minutes

2 cups chopped green cabbage

1 shallot, chopped	2 tomatoes, chopped
2 tbsp olive oil	2 tbsp parsley, chopped
16 pre-cooked meatballs	Salt and pepper to taste
1 cup cooked rice	

Preheat air fryer to 370°F. Combine shallot and olive oil in a metal bowl. Place the bowl in the air fryer and Bake until the shallot is crispy and tender, 2-4 minutes. Stir in cabbage, meatballs, rice, tomatoes, parsley, salt, and pepper. Bake for 6-8 minutes. Stir the contents in the bowl, and then continue baking for another 6-8 minutes or until the meatballs are hot, the rice is warm, and the veggies tender. Serve warm.

Chihuahua Andouille Sausage Rice Bake

Serves: 4 | Total Time: 30 minutes

7 oz cooked andouille sausage, sliced

¼ cup crumbled queso fresco cheese

1 tbsp olive oil	1 cup canned corn, drained
¼ cup diced onion	¼ cup mayonnaise
1 green bell pepper, diced	2 tbsp sour cream
5 tbsp tomato paste	1 tsp chili powder
1 yellow bell pepper, sliced	Salt and pepper to taste
3 cups cooked wild rice	1 tbsp chopped parsley

Warm the olive oil in a skillet over high heat for 30 seconds. Add in onion and bell peppers and cook for 4 minutes until the onions are translucent. Turn the heat off. Combine cooked veggies and the remaining ingredients in a bowl. Preheat air fryer to 350°F. Spoon sausage mixture into a greased cake pan, place it in the frying basket, and Bake for 15 minutes. Let chill for 10 minutes before serving sprinkled with parsley.

Cheese & Beef Stuffed Peppers

Serves: 4 | Total Time: 40 minutes

2 halved bell peppers	1 tbsp thyme, chopped
1 lb lean ground beef	Salt and pepper to taste
½ cup cooked wild rice	¼ tsp ground allspice
2 tomatoes, diced	4 oz goat cheese
3 garlic cloves, minced	¼ cup parsley, chopped
½ yellow onion, diced	

Preheat air fryer to 360°F. Mix the ground beef, rice, tomatoes, garlic, onion, thyme, salt, pepper, and allspice in a bowl. Stuff the halved bell peppers with the beef mixture and top with goat cheese. Put the peppers into the frying basket in a single layer. Bake for 30 minutes. Sprinkle with parsley. Serve and enjoy!

Baked Squash with Bacon & Avocado

Serves 4 | Total Time: 40 minutes

1 (1 ½-lb) spaghetti squash, halved and seeded

3 tbsp grated Pecorino cheese

2 tsp olive oil	¼ tsp salt
1 avocado, peeled and pitted	½ lemon, zested
¼ cup chicken broth	2 bacon slices
1 egg	¼ cup chopped parsley

Preheat air fryer to 370°F. Brush the squash with olive oil on both sides. Place the flat sides down in the frying basket and Bake for 25 minutes. Meanwhile, mix the avocado, lemon zest, chicken broth, egg, Pecorino cheese, and salt in a bowl until blended. Set aside. Heat a large skillet over medium heat and cook bacon for 5 minutes until crispy. Let it cool for 5 minutes, and crumble it.

Let cool cooked squash onto a cutting board for 5 minutes until easy to handle. Using a fork, gently pull strands out of the squash and transfer strands to the same skillet. Pour in the avocado mixture, lemon zest, and parsley and cook over medium heat for 2 minutes until well coated, stirring often. Top with bacon and serve.

Breaded Cheese Tortellini with Mayo Dip

Serves: 4 | Total Time: 30 minutes

2 cups frozen cheese tortellini
¾ cup mayonnaise   ½ tsp dried oregano
2 tbsp chili sauce   2 cups bread crumbs
1 egg   2 tbsp olive oil
½ cup flour

Preheat air fryer to 380°F. Mix mayonnaise and chili sauce in a small bowl, then set aside. In a shallow bowl, beat the egg. In another bowl, mix together flour and oregano. And in a third bowl, mix bread crumbs and olive oil until well combined.

First, dip a few of the tortellini into the egg, then lightly dredge in the flour. Dip it in the egg again and then coat with the bread crumbs. Repeat this process for all of the tortellini. Place the tortellini in the greased frying basket and Air Fry for 10 minutes, shaking once halfway through, until the tortellini are hot and golden. Serve warm with chili-mayo dip.

Jacket Potatoes with Bacon

Serves: 4 | Total Time: 65 minutes

4 oz cooked bacon, crumbled
1 ¼ cups shredded Cheddar cheese
4 russet potatoes   Salt and pepper to taste
2 tbsp butter   2 spring onions, sliced
½ cup milk   2 tbsp sour cream
1 tsp garlic powder   ½ tsp ground fennel seeds

Preheat air fryer to 400°F. Poke the top of each potato three times with a fork. Put the potatoes into the air fryer and Bake for 40 minutes. Remove the potatoes and allow to cool for 10 minutes. Warm the butter with milk in a saucepan for 2-3 minutes. Cut the cooled potatoes in half lengthwise. Use a spoon to scoop out half of the flesh in each half, leaving room for filling but enough on the skins for support.

Transfer potato flesh to a large bowl and mash with a potato masher. Mix in the milk/butter mixture, garlic, salt, and pepper. Stir in bacon, fennel seeds, spring onions, sour cream, and 1 cup of cheddar cheese until combined. Stuff each potato shell with 1-2 tbsp of the potato filling. Top with the remaining cheddar and Bake for 2-3 minutes until the cheese melts. Let cool slightly.

Cheese & Chorizo Bake

Serves: 4 | Total Time: 35 minutes

1 cup shredded cheddar   4 eggs
6 oz chorizo sausage, sliced   Salt and pepper to taste
½ cup bread crumbs

Preheat air fryer to 350°F. In a saucepan, fry the sausage for 10 minutes, breaking it with a wooden spatula. Remove and set aside. Beat the eggs in a bowl until fluffy. Add the sausage meat, half cup of cheddar cheese, half of the crumbs, salt, and pepper.

Transfer the mixture to a baking dish and top with the remaining crumbs and cheese. Place into the air fryer and Bake for 20-22 minutes until golden and crunchy.

Piri Piri Frittata

Serves: 4 | Total Time: 30 minutes

4 oz mushrooms, sliced   1 garlic clove, minced
½ cup grated Gruyère cheese   2 cups baby spinach
8 eggs, beaten   1 shallot, diced
Salt and pepper to taste   1 cup Piri Piri spicy sauce

Preheat air fryer to 360°F. Whisk the eggs, salt, pepper, and garlic in a large bowl until well combined. Stir in the spinach, mushrooms, shallot, and half of Gruyere.

Pour the egg mixture into a greased cake pan and top with the remaining cheese. Place into the air fryer and Bake for 18-20 minutes, or until the eggs are set in the center. Leave to cool for 5 minutes. Drizzle with Piri Piri sauce and serve.

Hawaiian Pork Sausage Tacos

Serves: 3 | Total Time: 25 minutes

1 (12-oz) pack andouille smoked pork sausage, sliced
1 cup diced pineapples   ¼ cup chopped mint
½ cup lime juice   Salt and pepper to taste
1 tbsp lime zest   1 cup coleslaw mix
2 tomatoes, diced   1 batch Sriracha mayonnaise
¼ cup diced red onion   1 tbsp mustard
¼ cup chopped cilantro   6 flour tortillas

In a bowl, combine pineapple, lime juice, lime zest, tomatoes, red onion, cilantro, mint, salt, and black pepper. Let sit covered in the fridge until ready to use.

Preheat air fryer to 375°F. Place andouille sausage slices in the greased frying basket and Air Fry for 7 minutes, flipping once. Set aside. Add cooked sausage, coleslaw, pineapple salsa, and a squeeze of sriracha mayonnaise and mustard to flour tortillas. Serve immediately.

Tomato & Mushroom Hash

Serves: 4 | Total Time: 30 minutes

4 oz baby Bella mushrooms, diced
2 tbsp olive oil   1 tsp cornflour
1 spring onion, diced   Salt and pepper to taste
1 garlic clove, minced   1 tomato, diced
2 cups shredded potatoes   ½ cup grated mozzarella

Preheat air fryer to 380°F. Warm the olive oil in a small skillet over medium heat. Add the mushrooms, spring onion, and garlic and sauté for 4-5 minutes until softened. Remove from heat. Toss the potatoes, cornflour, salt, pepper, and the remaining olive oil in a large bowl until well coated. Spread half of the potatoes onto a greased cake pan. Top with the mushroom mixture, tomato, and mozzarella. Spread the remaining potatoes over the top. Bake in the air fryer for 12-15 minutes or until the top is golden brown. Allow to cool for 5 minutes. Serve sliced.

Pecan-Crusted Ravioli

Serves: 4 | Total Time: 30 minutes

12 oz premade frozen ravioli	2 cups flour
2 eggs, beaten	1 tsp lemon zest
1 cup ground pecans	Salt and pepper to taste

Preheat air fryer to 375°F. Whisk the eggs with salt and pepper in a bowl. Mix the flour with lemon zest in a separate bowl. Place the pecans on a shallow plate.

Dip the ravioli in the eggs, then dredge in the flour mixture. Dip again in the egg mixture and finally coat with ground pecans. Place them on the greased frying basket and Air Fry for 16-18 minutes, turning once until golden and crisp crust is formed. Serve and enjoy!

Bacon-Crab Button Mushroom Caps

Serves: 4 | Total Time: 25 minutes

4 brown button mushroom caps

1 cup lump crab meat	2 tbsp grated cheddar
4 oz cooked bacon, diced	1 tbsp olive oil
¼ cup bread crumbs	Salt and pepper to taste
1 green onion, minced	2 tbsp parsley, chopped

Preheat air fryer to 350°F. Put the crab meat, chopped bacon, bread crumbs, green onion, cheddar cheese, salt, and pepper in a bowl and mix thoroughly until all the ingredients are evenly combined. Brush the mushroom caps with olive oil. Divide the crab mixture among the mushroom caps and place them on the greased frying basket. Bake for 10-15 minutes or until the mushrooms are tender and the top is golden. Serve topped with parsley.

Beef Hot Dog Bread

Serves 4 | Total Time: 15 minutes

2 beef hot dogs, cut into sections

1 lb flour	1 tbsp tomato paste
1 tbsp granulated sugar	1 egg
½ tsp baking powder	½ tsp gelatin
¼ tsp salt	1 tsp dried thyme
2 tbsp butter, melted	

Preheat air fryer to 300°F. Sift the flour, sugar, baking powder, and salt in a bowl. In another bowl, whisk butter, tomato paste, egg, gelatin, and thyme. Add the butter mixture to the flour and stir until smooth.

Fold in the hot dogs. Spoon the mixture into a pizza pan, place the pan in the frying basket, and Bake for 10 minutes. Let chill for 5 minutes before slicing. Serve.

Spanish-Style Fried Rice Three Delights

Serves: 4 | Total Time: 25 minutes + chilling time

2 cups cooked rice	½ chopped onion
2 tsp sesame oil, divided	Salt and pepper to taste
2 oz deli ham, chopped	1 tbsp soy sauce
1 cup peas	2 eggs, scrambled
2 carrots, diced	

Preheat air fryer to 370°F. Coat a baking pan with 1 tsp of sesame oil. Set aside. Combine rice, deli ham, peas, carrots, and onions in a large bowl. Drizzle with 1 tsp of sesame oil and add salt and pepper. Stir. Pour the rice mixture into the prepared pan. Bake for 15 minutes in the air fryer. Remove the pan and drizzle the soy sauce on the rice. Stir in scrambled eggs. Serve.

Mexican-Style Chorzo Pizza

Serves: 4 | Total Time: 15 minutes

1 cup grated mozzarella cheese
½ cup grated Chihuahua cheese

4 oz chorizo, sliced	1 jalapeño pepper, sliced
¾ cup refried beans	4 pita breads
½ cup salsa	1/3 cup sour cream

Preheat air fryer to 370°F. Mix together chorizo, refried beans, salsa, and jalapeño pepper in a bowl. Top the pitas with the bean mixture, then with the mozzarella and Chihuahua cheeses. Bake until the pitas are crisp and the cheese is melted and just turning golden, 8-10 minutes. Serve warm with a dollop of sour cream.

Stuffed Mushrooms with Feta & Farro

Serves: 6 | Total Time: 15 minutes

24 button mushrooms, stemmed

2 tbsp diced red bell pepper	¼ tsp dried thyme
1 garlic clove, minced	2 oz crumbled feta
¼ cup cooked farro	3 tbsp bread crumbs
⅛ tsp salt	

Preheat air fryer to 360°F. Mix the bell pepper, garlic, farro, salt, and thyme in a bowl. Divide the farro stuffing between the mushroom caps. Top with feta cheese. Sprinkle a pinch of bread crumbs over the feta on each mushroom. Place the mushrooms into the greased frying basket and Bake for 8 minutes. Serve immediately.

Exotic Beef Kebabs

Serves: 4 | Total Time: 15 minutes

¾ lb beef sirloin tip, cubed	1 tsp ground ginger
2 tbsp balsamic vinegar	1 tsp chili powder
1 tbsp olive oil	Salt and pepper to taste
1 tbsp honey	1 mango, cubed
½ tsp dried marjoram	

Preheat air fryer to 390°F. In a bowl, toss the beef cubes in balsamic vinegar, olive oil, honey, marjoram, ginger, chili, salt, and pepper. Massage marinade onto beef, and set aside. Alternate the beef and mango cubes on metal skewers, starting with beef. Set the skewers in the frying basket and Bake until the beef is brown, 7 minutes, turning once. Serve warm.

SWEETS

Choco-Granola Bars with Cranberries

Serves: 6 | Total Time: 20 minutes

2 tbsp dark chocolate chunks
2 cups quick oats
2 tbsp dried cranberries
3 tbsp shredded coconut
½ cup maple syrup
1 tsp ground cinnamon
⅛ tsp salt
2 tbsp smooth peanut butter

Preheat air fryer to 360°F. Stir together all the ingredients in a bowl until well combined. Press the oat mixture into a parchment-lined baking pan in a single layer. Put the pan into the frying basket and Bake for 15 minutes. Remove the pan from the fryer, and lift the granola cake out of the pan using the edges of the parchment paper. Leave to cool for 5 minutes. Serve sliced and enjoy!.

Famous Chocolate Lava Cake

Serves: 4 | Total Time: 15 minutes

¼ cup flour
1 tbsp cocoa powder
⅛ tsp salt
½ tsp baking powder
1 tsp vanilla extract
¼ cup raw honey
1 egg, beaten
2 tbsp olive oil
2 tbsp icing sugar, to dust

Preheat air fryer to 380°F. Sift the flour, cocoa powder, salt, vanilla, and baking powder in a bowl. Add in honey, egg, and olive oil and stir to combine. Divide the batter evenly among greased ramekins. Put the filled ramekins inside the air fryer and Bake for 10 minutes. Remove the lava cakes from the fryer and slide a knife around the outside edge of each cake. Turn each ramekin upside down on a saucer and serve dusted with icing sugar.

Cheese & Honey Stuffed Figs

Serves: 4 | Total Time: 15 minutes

8 figs, stem off
2 oz cottage cheese
¼ tsp ground cinnamon
¼ tsp orange zest
¼ tsp vanilla extract
2 tbsp honey
1 tbsp olive oil

Preheat air fryer to 360°F. Cut an "X" in the top of each fig 1/3 way through, leaving intact the base. Mix together the cottage cheese, cinnamon, orange zest, vanilla extract and 1 tbsp of honey in a bowl. Spoon the cheese mixture into the cavity of each fig. Put the figs in a single layer in the frying basket. Drizzle the olive oil over the top of the figs and Roast for 10 minutes. Drizzle with the remaining honey. Serve and enjoy!

Pecan-Oat Filled Apples

Serves: 4 | Total Time: 20 minutes

2 cored Granny Smith apples, halved
¼ cup rolled oats
2 tbsp honey
½ tsp ground cinnamon
½ tsp ground ginger
2 tbsp chopped pecans
A pinch of salt
1 tbsp olive oil

Preheat air fryer to 380°F. Combine together the oats, honey, cinnamon, ginger, pecans, salt, and olive oil in a bowl. Scoop a quarter of the oat mixture onto the top of each half apple. Put the apples in the frying basket and Roast for 12-15 minutes until the apples are fork-tender.

Mini Carrot Cakes

Serves: 6 | Total Time: 25 minutes

1 cup grated carrots
¼ cup raw honey
¼ cup olive oil
½ tsp vanilla extract
½ tsp lemon zest
1 egg
¼ cup applesauce
1 1/3 cups flour
¾ tsp baking powder
½ tsp baking soda
½ tsp ground cinnamon
¼ tsp ground nutmeg
⅛ tsp ground ginger
⅛ tsp salt
¼ cup chopped hazelnuts
2 tbsp chopped sultanas

Preheat air fryer to 380°F. Combine the carrots, honey, olive oil, vanilla extract, lemon zest, egg, and applesauce in a bowl. Sift the flour, baking powder, baking soda, cinnamon, nutmeg, ginger, and salt in a separate bowl. Add the wet ingredients to the dry ingredients, mixing until just combined. Fold in the hazelnuts and sultanas. Fill greased muffin cups three-quarters full with the batter, and place them in the frying basket. Bake for 10-12 minutes until a toothpick inserted in the center of a cupcake comes out clean. Serve and enjoy!

Holiday Peppermint Cake

Serves: 4 | Total Time: 20 minutes

1 ½ cups flour
3 eggs
1/3 cup molasses
½ cup olive oil
½ cup almond milk
½ tsp vanilla extract
½ tsp peppermint extract
1 tsp baking powder
½ tsp salt

Preheat air fryer to 380°F. Whisk the eggs and molasses in a bowl until smooth. Slowly mix in the olive oil, almond milk, vanilla, and peppermint extract until combined. Sift the flour, baking powder, and salt in another bowl. Gradually incorporate the dry ingredients into the wet ingredients until combined. Pour the batter into a greased baking pan and place in the fryer. Bake for 12-15 minutes until a toothpick inserted in the center comes out clean. Serve and enjoy!

British Bread Pudding

Serves: 4 | Total Time: 30 minutes

4 bread slices
1 cup milk
¼ cup sugar
2 eggs, beaten
1 tbsp vanilla extract
½ tsp ground cinnamon

Preheat air fryer to 320°F. Slice bread into bite-size pieces. Set aside in a small cake pan. Mix the milk, sugar, eggs, vanilla extract, and cinnamon in a bowl until well combined. Pour over the bread and toss to coat. Bake for 20 minutes until crispy and all liquid is absorbed. Slice into 4 pieces. Serve and enjoy!

Lemon Iced Donut Balls

Serves: 6 | Total Time: 25 minutes

1 (8-oz) can jumbo biscuit dough
2 tsp lemon juice   ½ cup icing sugar, sifted

Preheat air fryer to 360°F. Divide the biscuit dough into 16 equal portions. Roll the dough into balls of 1½ inches thickness. Place the donut holes in the greased frying basket and Air Fry for 8 minutes, flipping once. Mix the icing sugar and lemon juice until smooth. Spread the icing over the top of the donuts. Leave to set a bit. Serve.

Healthy Chickpea Cookies

Serves: 6 | Total Time: 25 minutes

1 cup canned chickpeas   2 tbsp butter, melted
2 tsp vanilla extract   1/3 cup flour
1 tsp lemon juice   ½ tsp baking powder
1/3 cup date paste   ¼ cup dark chocolate chips

Preheat air fryer to 320°F. Line the basket with parchment paper. In a blender, blitz chickpeas, vanilla extract, and lemon juice until smooth. Remove it to a bowl. Stir in date paste and butter until well combined. Then mix in flour, baking powder, chocolate chips. Make 2-tablespoon balls out of the mixture. Place the balls onto the paper and flatten them into a cookie shape. Bake for 13 minutes until golden brown. Cool cookies slightly before serving.

Guilty Chocolate Cookies

Serves: 6 | Total Time: 25 minutes

3 eggs, beaten   1/3 cup sugar
1 tsp vanilla extract   ¼ cup cacao powder
1 tsp apple cider vinegar   ¼ tsp baking soda
1/3 cup butter, softened

Preheat air fryer to 300°F. Combine eggs, vanilla extract, and apple vinegar in a bowl until well combined. Refrigerate for 5 minutes. Whisk in butter and sugar until smooth, finally toss in cacao powder and baking soda until smooth. Make balls out of the mixture. Place the balls onto the parchment-lined frying basket. Bake for 13 minutes until brown. Using a fork, flatten each cookie. Let cool completely before serving.

Pumpkin Brownies

Serves: 4 | Total Time: 30 minutes + chilling time

¼ cup canned pumpkin   ¼ cup tapioca flour
½ cup maple syrup   ¼ cup flour
2 eggs, beaten   ½ tsp baking powder
1 tbsp vanilla extract

Preheat air fryer to 320°F. Mix the pumpkin, maple syrup, eggs, and vanilla extract in a bowl. Toss in tapioca flour, flour, and baking powder until smooth. Pour the batter into a small round cake pan and Bake for 20 minutes until a toothpick comes out clean. Allow to cool completely before slicing into 4 brownies. Serve and enjoy!

Peanut Butter-Banana Roll-Ups

Serves: 4 | Total Time: 20 minutes

2 ripe bananas, halved crosswise
4 spring roll wrappers   1 tsp ground cinnamon
¼ cup molasses   1 tsp lemon zest
¼ cup peanut butter

Preheat air fryer to 375°F. Place the roll wrappers on a flat surface with one corner facing up. Spread 1 tbsp of molasses on each, then 1 tbsp of peanut butter, and finally top with lemon zest and 1 banana half. Sprinkle with cinnamon all over. For the wontons, fold the bottom over the banana, then fold the sides, and roll up. Place them seam-side down and Roast for 10 minutes until golden brown and crispy. Serve warm.

Ricotta Stuffed Apples

Serves: 4 | Total Time: 25 minutes

½ cup cheddar cheese   2 apples
¼ cup raisins   ½ tsp ground cinnamon

Preheat air fryer to 350°F. Combine cheddar cheese and raisins in a bowl and set aside. Chop apples lengthwise and discard the core and stem. Sprinkle each half with cinnamon and stuff each half with 1/4 of the cheddar mixture. Bake for 7 minutes, turn, and Bake for 13 minutes more until the apples are soft. Serve immediately.

Banana-Almond Delights

Serves: 4 | Total Time: 30 minutes + cooling time

1 ripe banana, mashed   1 cup almond flour
1 tbsp almond liqueur   ¼ tsp baking soda
½ tsp ground cinnamon   8 raw almonds
2 tbsp coconut sugar

Preheat air fryer to 300°F. Add the banana to a bowl and stir in almond liqueur, cinnamon, and coconut sugar until well combined. Toss in almond flour and baking soda until smooth. Make 8 balls out of the mixture. Place the balls onto the parchment-lined frying basket, flatten each into ½-inch thick, and press 1 almond into the center. Bake for 12 minutes, turn and Bake for 6 more minutes. Let stand for 10 minutes before serving.

Holiday Pear Crumble

Serves: 4 | Total Time: 40 minutes

2 tbsp coconut oil   2 cups finely chopped pears
¼ cup flour   ½ tbsp lemon juice
¼ cup demerara sugar   ¾ tsp cinnamon
⅛ tsp salt

Combine the coconut oil, flour, sugar, and salt in a bowl and mix well. Preheat air fryer to 320°F. Stir the pears with 3 tbsp of water, lemon juice, and cinnamon into a baking pan until combined. Sprinkle the chilled topping over the pears. Bake for 30 minutes or until they are softened, and the topping is crispy and golden. Serve.

Nutty Banana Bread

Serves: 6 | Total Time: 30 minutes + cooling time

2 bananas	½ tsp ground cinnamon
2 tbsp ground flaxseed	2 tbsp honey
¼ cup milk	½ cup oat flour
1 tbsp apple cider vinegar	½ tsp baking soda
1 tbsp vanilla extract	3 tbsp butter

Preheat air fryer to 320°F. Using a fork, mash the bananas until chunky. Mix in flaxseed, milk, apple vinegar, vanilla extract, cinnamon, and honey. Finally, toss in oat flour and baking soda until smooth but still chunky. Divide the batter between 6 cupcake molds. Top with one and a half teaspoons of butter each and swirl it slightly. Bake for 18 minutes until golden brown and puffy. Leave to cool completely before serving.

Apple-Carrot Cupcakes

Serves: 6 | Total Time: 25 minutes + cooling time

1 cup grated carrot	1 tsp ground cinnamon
1/3 cup chopped apple	½ tsp ground ginger
¼ cup raisins	1 tsp baking powder
2 tbsp maple syrup	½ tsp baking soda
1/3 cup milk	1/3 cup chopped walnuts
1 cup oat flour	

Preheat air fryer to 350°F. Combine carrot, apple, raisins, maple syrup, and milk in a bowl. Stir in oat flour, cinnamon, ginger, baking powder, and baking soda until combined. Divide the batter between 6 cupcake molds. Top with chopped walnuts each and press down a little. Bake for 15 minutes until golden brown and a toothpick comes out clean. Leave to cool completely before serving.

Greek Pumpkin Cheesecake

Serves: 4 | Total Time: 35 minutes + chilling time

2 tbsp peanut butter	¼ cup canned pumpkin
¼ cup oat flour	1 tbsp vanilla extract
½ cup Greek yogurt	2 tbsp cornstarch
2 tbsp sugar	¼ tsp ground cinnamon
¼ cup ricotta cheese	

Preheat air fryer to 320°F. For the crust: Whisk the peanut butter, oat flour, 1 tbsp of Greek yogurt, and 1 tsp of sugar until you get a dough. Remove the dough onto a small cake pan and press down to get a ½-inch thick crust. Set aside. Mix the ricotta cheese, pumpkin, vanilla extract, cornstarch, cinnamon, ½ cup of Greek yogurt, and 1 tbsp of sugar until smooth. Pour over the crust and Bake for 20 minutes until golden brown. Let cool completely and refrigerate for 1 hour before serving.

Strawberry Donuts

Serves: 4 | Total Time: 55 minutes

¾ cup Greek yogurt	1 ½ cups all-purpose flour
2 tbsp maple syrup	3 tbsp milk
1 tbsp vanilla extract	½ cup strawberry jam
2 tsp active dry yeast	

Preheat air fryer to 350°F. Whisk the Greek yogurt, maple syrup, vanilla extract, and yeast until well combined. Then toss in flour until you get a sticky dough. Let rest covered for 10 minutes. Flour a parchment paper on a flat surface, lay the dough, sprinkle with some flour, and flatten to ½-inch thick with a rolling pin.

Using a 3-inch cookie cutter, cut the donuts. Repeat the process until no dough is left. Place the donuts in the basket and let rise for 15-20 minutes. Spread some milk on top of each donut and Air Fry for 4 minutes. Turn the donuts, spread more milk, and Air Fry for 4 more minutes until golden brown. Let cool for 15 minutes. Using a knife, cut the donuts 3/4 lengthwise, brush 1 tbsp of strawberry jam on each and close them. Serve.

Raspberry-Chocolate Cake

Serves: 6 | Total Time: 45 minutes + cooling time

2 eggs, beaten	¾ cup all-purpose flour
2 tbsp Greek yogurt	1 ½ tsp baking powder
¼ cup maple syrup	¼ cup dark chocolate chips
1 tbsp apple cider vinegar	1/3 cup raspberry jam
1 tbsp vanilla extract	1 tbsp heavy cream

Preheat air fryer to 360°F. Combine the eggs, milk, Greek yogurt, maple syrup, apple vinegar, and vanilla in a bowl. Toss in flour and baking powder until combined. Pour the batter into a greased cake pan, that fit in the fryer, distributing well. Bake for 20-25 minutes until a toothpick comes out clean. Let cool completely. When the cake is cold, carefully cut it in half horizontally. Set aside.

Adjust the temperature of the air fryer to 290°F. Add chocolate chips to a heat-proof bowl and Bake in the fryer for 2-3 minutes until fully melted. In the meantime, Spread a layer of raspberry jam over the bottom layer and top with the remaining layer. Once the chocolate is ready, stir in the heavy cream. Pour over the layer cake and spread well. Cut into wedges and serve right away.

Strawberry Donut Bites

Serves: 6 | Total Time: 25 minutes

2/3 cup flour	½ cup diced strawberries
A pinch of salt	1 tbsp butter, melted
½ tsp baking powder	2 tbsp powdered sugar
1 tsp vanilla extract	2 tsp sour cream
2 tbsp light brown sugar	¼ cup crushed pretzels
1 tbsp honey	

Preheat air fryer to 325°F. In a bowl, sift flour, baking powder, and salt. Add in vanilla, brown sugar, honey, 2 tbsp of water, butter, and strawberries and whisk until combined. Form dough into balls. Place the balls on a lightly greased pizza pan, place them in the frying basket, and Air Fry for 10-12 minutes. Let cool onto a cooling rack for 5 minutes. Mix the powdered sugar and sour cream in a small bowl, 1 tsp of sour cream at a time until you reach your desired consistency. Gently pour over the donut bites. Scatter with crushed pretzels and serve.

Cinnamon Pear Cheesecake

Serves: 6 | Total Time: 60 minutes + cooling time

16 oz cream cheese, softened
1 cup crumbled graham crackers
4 peeled pears, sliced   1 egg
1 tsp vanilla extract   1 cup condensed milk
1 tbsp brown sugar   2 tbsp white sugar
1 tsp ground cinnamon   1 ½ tsp butter, melted

Preheat air fryer to 350°F. Place the crumbled graham cracker, white sugar, and butter in a large bowl and stir to combine. Spoon the mixture into a greased pan and press around the edges to flatten it against the dish. Place the pan into the frying basket and Bake for 5 minutes. Remove and let it cool for 30 minutes to harden.

Place the cream cheese, vanilla extract, brown sugar, cinnamon, condensed milk and egg in a large bowl and whip until the ingredients are thoroughly mixed. Arrange the pear slices on the cooled crust and spoon the wet mixture over. Level the top with a spatula. Place the pan in the frying basket. Bake for 40 minutes. Allow to cool completely. Serve and enjoy!

Coconut Cream Roll-Ups

Serves: 4 | Total Time: 20 minutes

½ cup cream cheese, softened
1 cup fresh raspberries   1 egg
¼ cup brown sugar   1 tsp corn starch
¼ cup coconut cream   6 spring roll wrappers

Preheat air fryer to 350°F. Add the cream cheese, brown sugar, coconut cream, cornstarch, and egg to a bowl. Whisk until all ingredients are thoroughly mixed, fluffy, thick, and stiff. Spoon even amounts of the creamy filling into each spring roll wrapper, then top each dollop of filling with several raspberries. Roll up the wraps around the creamy raspberry filling, and seal the seams with a few dabs of water.

Place each roll on the foil-lined frying basket, seams facing down. Bake for 10 minutes, flipping them once until golden brown and perfect on the outside, while the raspberries and cream filling will have cooked together in a glorious fusion. Remove with tongs and serve hot or cold. Serve and enjoy!

Fall Caramelized Apples

Serves: 2 | Total Time: 25 minutes

2 apples, sliced   ¼ tsp nutmeg
1 ½ tsp brown sugar   ¼ tsp salt
¼ tsp cinnamon   1 tsp lemon zest

Preheat air fryer to 390°F. Set the apples upright in a baking pan. Add 2 tbsp of water to the bottom to keep the apples moist. Sprinkle the tops with sugar, lemon zest, cinnamon, and nutmeg. Lightly sprinkle the halves with salt and the tops with oil. Bake for 20 minutes or until the apples are tender and golden on top. Enjoy.

Dark Chocolate Cream Galette

Serves: 4 | Total Time: 55 minutes + cooling time

16 oz cream cheese, softened
1 cup crumbled graham crackers
1 cup dark cocoa powder   1 egg
½ cup white sugar   1 cup condensed milk
1 tsp peppermint extract   2 tbsp muscovado sugar
1 tsp ground cinnamon   1 ½ tsp butter, melted

Preheat air fryer to 350°F. Place the crumbled graham crackers in a large bowl and stir in the muscovado sugar and melted butter. Spread the mixture into a greased pie pan, pressing down to form the galette base. Place the pan into the air fryer and Bake for 5 minutes. Remove the pan and set aside.

Place the cocoa powder, cream cheese, peppermint extract, white sugar, cinnamon, condensed milk, and egg in a large bowl and whip thoroughly to combine. Spoon the chocolate mixture over the graham cracker crust and level the top with a spatula. Put in the air fryer and Bake for 40 minutes until firm. Transfer the cookies to a wire rack to cool. Serve and enjoy!

Chocolate Rum Brownies

Serves: 6 | Total Time: 30 minutes + cooling time

½ cup butter, melted   ½ cup flour
1 cup white sugar   1/3 cup cocoa powder
1 tsp dark rum   ¼ tsp baking powder
2 eggs   Pinch of salt

Preheat air fryer to 350°F. Whisk the melted butter, eggs, and dark rum in a mixing bowl until slightly fluffy and all ingredients are thoroughly combined. Place the flour, sugar, cocoa, salt, and baking powder in a separate bowl and stir to combine. Gradually pour the dry ingredients into the wet ingredients, stirring continuously until thoroughly blended, and there are no lumps in the batter. Spoon the batter into a greased cake pan. Put the pan in the frying basket and Bake for 20 minutes until a toothpick comes out dry and clean. Let cool for several minutes. Cut and serve. Enjoy!

Apple & Blueberry Crumble

Serves: 4 | Total Time: 20 minutes

5 apples, peeled and diced   1 tsp cinnamon
½ lemon, zested and juiced   ½ cup butter
½ cup blueberries   ½ cup flour
1 cup brown sugar

Preheat air fryer to 360°F. Place the apple chunks, blueberries, lemon juice and zest, half of the butter, half of the brown sugar, and cinnamon in a greased baking dish. Combine thoroughly until all is well mixed. Combine the flour with the remaining butter and brown sugar in a separate bowl. Stir until it forms a crumbly consistency. Spread the mixture over the fruit. Bake in the air fryer for 10-15 minutes until golden and bubbling. Serve and enjoy!

Caramel Blondies with Macadamia Nuts

Serves: 4 | Total Time: 35 minutes + cooling time

1/3 cup ground macadamia	½ cup all-purpose flour
½ cup unsalted butter	½ cup caramel chips
1 cup white sugar	¼ tsp baking powder
1 tsp vanilla extract	A pinch of salt
2 eggs	

Preheat air fryer to 360°F. Whisk the eggs in a bowl. Add the melted butter and vanilla extract and whip thoroughly until slightly fluffy. Combine the flour, sugar, ground macadamia, caramel chips, salt, and baking powder in another bowl. Slowly pour the dry ingredients into the wet ingredients, stirring until thoroughly blended and no lumps in the batter. Spoon the batter into a greased cake pan. Place the pan in the air fryer. Bake for 20 minutes until a knife comes out dry and clean. Let cool for a few minutes before cutting and serving.

Fall Pumpkin Cake

Serves: 6 | Total Time: 50 minutes

1/3 cup pecan pieces	½ cup granulated sugar
5 gingersnap cookies	½ tsp baking soda
1/3 cup light brown sugar	1 tsp baking powder
6 tbsp butter, melted	1 tsp pumpkin pie spice
3 eggs	6 oz mascarpone cheese
½ tsp vanilla extract	1 1/3 cups powdered sugar
1 cup pumpkin purée	1 tsp cinnamon
2 tbsp sour cream	2 tbsp butter, softened
½ cup flour	1 tbsp milk
¼ cup tapioca flour	1 tbsp flaked almonds
½ tsp cornstarch	

Blitz the pecans, gingersnap cookies, brown sugar, and 3 tbsp of melted butter in a food processor until combined. Press mixture into the bottom of a lightly greased cake pan. Preheat air fryer to 350°F. In a bowl, whisk the eggs, remaining melted butter, ½ tsp of vanilla extract, pumpkin purée, and sour cream. In another bowl, combine the flour, tapioca flour, cornstarch, granulated sugar, baking soda, baking powder, and pumpkin pie spice. Add wet ingredients to dry ingredients and combine. Do not overmix. Pour the batter into a cake pan and cover it with aluminum foil. Place the cake pan in the frying basket. Bake for 30 minutes. Remove the foil and cook for another 5 minutes. Let cool onto a cooling rack for 10 minutes. Then, turn the cake onto a large serving platter. In a small bowl, whisk the mascarpone cheese, powdered sugar, remaining vanilla extract, cinnamon, softened butter, and milk. Spread over cooled cake and cut into slices. Serve sprinkled with almonds and enjoy!

Mango-Chocolate Custard

Serves: 4 | Total Time: 40 minutes

4 egg yolks	3/4 cup chocolate chips
2 tbsp granulated sugar	1 mango, pureed
1/8 tsp almond extract	1 mango, chopped
1 ½ cups half-and-half	1 tsp fresh mint, chopped

Beat the egg yolks, sugar, and almond extract in a bowl. Set aside. Place half-and-half in a saucepan over low heat and bring it to a low simmer. Whisk a spoonful of heated half-and-half into egg mixture, then slowly whisk egg mixture into saucepan. Stir in chocolate chips and mango purée for 10 minutes until chocolate melts. Divide the mixture between 4 ramekins.

Preheat air fryer to 350°F. Place ramekins in the frying basket and Bake for 6-8 minutes. Let cool onto a cooling rack for 15 minutes, then let chill covered in the fridge for at least 2 hours or up to 2 days. Serve with chopped mangoes and mint on top.

Spanish Churro Bites

Serves: 5 | Total Time: 35 minutes

¼ tsp salt	1 cup flour
2 tbsp vegetable oil	½ tsp ground cinnamon
3 tbsp white sugar	2 tbsp granulated sugar

On the stovetop, add 1 cup of water, salt, 1 tbsp of vegetable oil and 1 tbsp sugar to a pot. Bring to a boil over high heat. Remove from the heat and add flour. Stir with a wooden spoon until the flour is combined and a ball of dough forms. Cool for 5 minutes. Put the dough ball in a plastic pastry bag with a star tip. Squeeze the dough to the tip and twist the top of the bag. Squeeze 10 strips of dough, about 5-inches long each, onto a workspace. Spray with cooking oil.

Preheat air fryer to 360°F. Place the churros in the greased frying basket and Air Fry for 22-25 minutes, flipping once halfway through until golden. Meanwhile, heat the remaining vegetable oil in a small bowl. In another shallow bowl, mix the remaining 2 tbsp sugar and cinnamon. Roll the cooked churros in cinnamon sugar. Top with granulated sugar and serve immediately.

Mom's Amaretto Cheesecake

Serves: 6 | Total Time: 35 minutes

2/3 cup slivered almonds	2 tbsp sour cream
½ cup Corn Chex	½ cup granulated sugar
1 tbsp light brown sugar	½ cup Amaretto liqueur
3 tbsp butter, melted	½ tsp lemon juice
14 oz cream cheese	2 tbsp almond flakes

In a food processor, pulse corn Chex, almonds, and brown sugar until it has a powdered consistency. Transfer it to a bowl. Stir in melted butter with a fork until butter is well distributed. Press mixture into a greased cake pan.

Preheat air fryer to 400°F. In a bowl, combine cream cheese, sour cream, granulated sugar, Amaretto liqueur, and lemon juice until smooth. Pour it over the crust and cover with aluminum foil. Place springform pan in the frying basket and Bake for 16 minutes. Remove the foil and cook for 6 more minutes until a little jiggly in the center. Let sit covered in the fridge for at least 2 hours. Release side pan and serve sprinkled with almond flakes.

Vanilla-Strawberry Muffins

Serves: 4 | Total Time: 25 minutes

¼ cup diced strawberries	1 egg
2 tbsp powdered sugar	1 tbsp butter, melted
1 cup flour	½ cup diced strawberries
½ tsp baking soda	2 tbsp chopped walnuts
1/3 cup granulated sugar	6 tbsp butter, softened
¼ tsp salt	1 ½ cups powdered sugar
1 tsp vanilla extract	1/8 tsp peppermint extract

Preheat air fryer to 375°F. Combine flour, baking soda, granulated sugar, and salt in a bowl. In another bowl, combine the vanilla, egg, walnuts and melted butter. Pour wet ingredients into dry ingredients and toss to combine. Fold in half of the strawberries and spoon the mixture into 8 greased silicone cupcake liners.

Place cupcakes in the frying basket and Bake for 6-8 minutes. Let cool onto a cooling rack for 10 minutes. Blend the remaining strawberries in a food processor until smooth. Slowly add powdered sugar to softened butter while beating in a bowl. Stir in peppermint extract and puréed strawberries until blended. Spread over cooled cupcakes. Serve sprinkled with powdered sugar.

Coconut-Carrot Cupcakes

Serves: 4 | Total Time: 25 minutes

1 cup flour	1 tbsp vegetable oil
½ tsp baking soda	¼ cup grated carrots
1/3 cup light brown sugar	2 tbsp coconut shreds
¼ tsp salt	6 oz cream cheese
¼ tsp ground cinnamon	1 1/3 cups powdered sugar
1 ½ tsp vanilla extract	2 tbsp butter, softened
1 egg	1 tbsp milk
1 tbsp buttermilk	1 tbsp coconut flakes

Preheat air fryer to 375°F. Combine flour, baking soda, brown sugar, salt, and cinnamon in a bowl. In another bowl, combine egg, 1 tsp of vanilla, buttermilk, and vegetable oil. Pour wet ingredients into dry ingredients and toss to combine. Do not overmix. Fold in carrots and coconut shreds. Spoon mixture into 8 greased silicone cupcake liners. Place cupcakes in the frying basket and Bake for 6-8 minutes. Let cool onto a cooling rack for 15 minutes. Whisk cream cheese, powdered sugar, remaining vanilla, softened butter, and milk in a bowl until smooth. Spread over cooled cupcakes. Garnish with coconut flakes and serve.

Berry Streusel Cake

Serves: 6 | Total Time: 60 minutes

2 tbsp demerara sugar	¾ cup milk
2 tbsp sunflower oil	2 tbsp olive oil
¼ cup almond flour	1 tsp vanilla
1 cup pastry flour	1 cup blueberries
½ cup brown sugar	½ cup powdered sugar
1 tsp baking powder	1 tbsp lemon juice
1 tbsp lemon zest	⅛ tsp salt
¼ tsp salt	

Mix the demerara sugar, sunflower oil, and almond flour in a bowl and put it in the refrigerator. Whisk the pastry flour, brown sugar, baking powder, lemon zest, and salt in another bowl. Add the milk, olive oil, and vanilla and stir with a rubber spatula until combined. Add the blueberries and stir slowly. Coat the inside of a baking pan with oil and pour the batter into the pan.

Preheat air fryer to 310°F. Remove the almond mix from the fridge and spread it over the cake batter. Put the cake in the air fryer and Bake for 45 minutes or until a knife inserted in the center comes out clean and the top is golden. Combine the powdered sugar, lemon juice and salt in a bowl. Once the cake has cooled, slice it into 4 pieces and drizzle each with icing. Serve.

Rich Blueberry Biscuit Shortcakes

Serves: 4 | Total Time: 35 minutes

1 lb blueberries, halved	1 egg yolk
¼ cup granulated sugar	1 tbsp baking powder
1 tsp orange zest	½ tsp baking soda
1 cup heavy cream	½ tsp cornstarch
1 tbsp orange juice	½ tsp salt
2 tbsp powdered sugar	½ tsp vanilla extract
¼ tsp cinnamon	½ tsp honey
¼ tsp nutmeg	4 tbsp cold butter, cubed
2 cups flour	1 ¼ cups buttermilk

Combine blueberries, granulated sugar, and orange zest in a bowl. Let chill the topping covered in the fridge until ready to use. Beat heavy cream, orange juice, egg yolk, vanilla extract and powdered sugar in a metal bowl until peaks form. Let chill the whipped cream covered in the fridge until ready to use.

Preheat air fryer to 350°F. Combine flour, cinnamon, nutmeg, baking powder, baking soda, cornstarch, honey, butter cubes, and buttermilk in a bowl until a sticky dough forms. Flour your hands and form dough into 8 balls. Place them on a lightly greased pizza pan. Place pizza pan in the frying basket and Air Fry for 8 minutes. Transfer biscuits to serving plates and cut them in half. Spread blueberry mixture to each biscuit bottom and place tops of biscuits. Garnish with whipped cream and serve.

Honey Tortilla Fritters

Serves: 8 | Total Time: 10 minutes

2 tbsp granulated sugar	8 flour tortillas, quartered
½ tsp ground cinnamon	2 tbsp butter, melted
1 tsp vanilla powder	4 tsp honey
Salt to taste	1 tbsp almond flakes

Preheat air fryer to 400°F. Combine the sugar, cinnamon, vanilla powder, and salt in a bowl. Set aside. Brush tortilla quarters with melted butter and sprinkle with sugar mixture. Place tortilla quarters in the frying basket and Air Fry for 4 minutes, turning once. Let cool on a large plate for 5 minutes until hardened. Drizzle with honey and scatter with almond flakes to serve.

Fruity Oatmeal Crisp

Serves: 6 | Total Time: 25 minutes

2 peeled nectarines, chopped	1/3 cup brown sugar
1 peeled apple, chopped	¼ cup flour
1/3 cup raisins	½ cup oatmeal
2 tbsp honey	3 tbsp softened butter

Preheat air fryer to 380°F. Mix together nectarines, apple, raisins, and honey in a baking pan. Set aside. Mix brown sugar, flour, oatmeal, and butter in a medium bowl until crumbly. Top the fruit in a greased pan with the crumble. Bake until bubbly and the topping is golden, 10-12 minutes. Serve warm and top with vanilla ice cream if desired.

Vanilla Cupcakes with Chocolate Chips

Serves: 2 | Total Time: 25 minutes + cooling time

½ cup white sugar	1 egg
1 ½ cups flour	2 tsp maple extract
2 tsp baking powder	¼ cup vanilla yogurt
½ tsp salt	1 cup chocolate chips
2/3 cup sunflower oil	

Preheat air fryer to 350°F. Combine the sugar, flour, baking powder, and salt in a bowl and stir to combine. Whisk the egg in a separate bowl. Pour in the sunflower oil, yogurt, and maple extract, and continue whisking until light and fluffy. Spoon the wet mixture into the dry ingredients and stir to combine. Gently fold in the chocolate chips with a spatula. Divide the batter between cupcake cups and Bake in the air fryer for 12-15 minutes or until a toothpick comes out dry. Remove the cupcakes and let them cool. Serve and enjoy!

Easy Bread Pudding

Serves: 4 | Total Time: 25 minutes+ cooling time

2 cups sandwich bread cubes	1 tsp vanilla extract
½ cup pecan pieces	2 tbsp bourbon
½ cup raisins	2 tbsp dark brown sugar
3 eggs	¼ tsp ground cinnamon
¼ cup half-and-half	½ tsp nutmeg
¼ cup dark corn syrup	¼ tsp salt

Preheat air fryer to 325°F. Spread the bread pieces in a cake pan and layer pecan pieces and raisins over the top. Whisk the eggs, half-and-half, corn syrup, bourbon, vanilla extract, cinnamon, nutmeg, and salt in a bowl. Pour egg mixture over pecan pieces. Let sit for 10 minutes. Place the cake pan in the frying basket and Bake for 15 minutes. Leave to cool onto a rack for 10 minutes before slicing. Serve immediately.

Fluffy Orange Cake

Serves: 6 | Total Time: 30 minutes

1/3 cup cornmeal	¼ cup safflower oil
1 ¼ cups flour	1 ¼ cups orange juice
¾ cup white sugar	1 tsp orange zest
1 tsp baking soda	¼ cup powdered sugar

Preheat air fryer to 360°F. Mix cornmeal, flour, sugar, baking soda, safflower oil, 1 cup of orange juice, and orange zest in a medium bowl. Mix until combined.

Pour the batter into a greased baking pan and set into the air fryer. Bake until a toothpick in the center of the cake comes out clean. Remove the cake and place it on a cooling rack. Use the toothpick to make 20 holes in the cake. Meanwhile, combine the rest of the juice with the powdered sugar in a small bowl. Drizzle the glaze over the hot cake and allow it to absorb. Leave to cool completely, then cut into pieces. Serve and enjoy!

Orange-Chocolate Cake

Serves: 6 | Total Time: 35 minutes

¾ cup flour	½ tbsp orange juice
½ cup sugar	2 tsp vanilla
7 tbsp cocoa powder	2 tsp orange zest
½ tsp baking soda	3 tbsp butter, softened
½ cup milk	1 ¼ cups powdered sugar
2 ½ tbsp sunflower oil	

Use a whisk to combine the flour, sugar, 2 tbsp of cocoa powder, baking soda, and a pinch of salt in a bowl. Once combined, add milk, sunflower oil, orange juice, and orange zest. Stir until combined. Preheat air fryer to 350°F. Pour the batter into a greased cake pan and Bake for 25 minutes or until a knife inserted in the center comes out clean.

Use an electric beater to beat the butter and powdered sugar together in a bowl. Add the remaining cocoa powder and vanilla and whip until fluffy. Scrape the sides occasionally. Refrigerate until ready to use. Allow the cake to cool completely, then run a knife around the edges of the baking pan. Turn it upside-down on a plate so it can be frosted on the sides and top. When the frosting is no longer cold, use a butter knife or small spatula to frost the sides and top. Cut into slices and enjoy!

Fruit Turnovers

Serves: 6 | Total Time: 25 minutes

1 sheet puff pastry dough	1 large egg, beaten
6 tsp peach preserves	1 tbsp icing sugar
3 kiwi, sliced	

Prepare puff pastry by cutting it into 6 rectangles. Roll out the pastry with a rolling pin into 5-inch squares. On your workspace, position one square so that it looks like a diamond with points to the top and bottom. Spoon 1 tsp of the preserves on the bottom half and spread it, leaving a ½-inch border from the edge. Place half of one kiwi on top of the preserves. Brush the clean edges with the egg, then fold the top corner over the filling to make a triangle. Crimp with a fork to seal the pastry. Brush the top of the pastry with egg. Preheat air fryer to 350°F. Put the pastries in the greased frying basket. Air Fry for 10 minutes, flipping once until golden and puffy. Remove from the fryer, let cool and dush with icing sugar. Serve.

Mixed Berry Pie

Serves: 4 | Total Time: 25 minutes

2/3 cup blackberries, cut into thirds
¼ cup sugar — 1 cup sliced strawberries
2 tbsp cornstarch — 1 cup raspberries
¼ tsp vanilla extract — 1 refrigerated piecrust
¼ tsp peppermint extract — 1 large egg
½ tsp lemon zest

Mix the sugar, cornstarch, vanilla, peppermint extract, and lemon zest in a bowl. Toss in all berries gently until combined. Pour into a greased dish. On a clean workspace, lay out the dough and cut it into a 7-inch diameter round. Cover the baking dish with the round and crimp the edges. With a knife, cut 4 slits in the top to vent.

Beat 1 egg and 1 tbsp of water to make an egg wash. Brush the egg wash over the crust. Preheat air fryer to 350°F. Put the baking dish into the frying basket. Bake for 15 minutes or until the crust is golden and the berries are bubbling through the vents. Remove from the air fryer and let stand for 15 minutes. Serve warm.

Chocolate Bars

Serves: 4 | Total Time: 30 minutes

2 tbsp chocolate toffee chips — 1/3 cup peanut butter
¼ cup chopped pecans — 2 tbsp chocolate chips
2 tbsp raisins — 2 tbsp butter, melted
1 tbsp dried blueberries — ½ tsp vanilla extract
2 tbsp maple syrup — Salt to taste
¼ cup light brown sugar

Preheat air fryer to 350°F. In a bowl, combine the pecans, maple syrup, sugar, peanut butter, toffee chips, raisins, dried blueberries, chocolate chips, butter, vanilla extract, and salt. Press mixture into a lightly greased cake pan and cover it with aluminum foil. Place cake pan in the frying basket and Bake for 15 minutes. Remove the foil and cook for 5 more minutes. Cool completely for 15 minutes. Turn over on a place and cut into 6 bars. Enjoy!

German Streusel-Stuffed Baked Apples

Serves: 4 | Total Time: 40 minutes

2 large apples — 1 tsp vanilla extract
3 tbsp flour — 1 tsp chopped pecans
3 tbsp light brown sugar — 2 tbsp cold butter
⅛ tsp ground cinnamon — 2 tbsp salted caramel sauce

Cut the apples in half through the stem and scoop out the core and seeds. Mix flour, brown sugar, vanilla, pecans and cinnamon in a bowl. Cut in the butter with a fork until it turns into crumbs. Top each apple half with 2 ½ tbsp of the crumble mixture.

Preheat air fryer to 325°F. Put the apple halves in the greased frying basket. Cook until soft in the center and the crumble is golden, 25-30 minutes. Serve warm topped with caramel sauce.

Banana-Lemon Bars

Serves: 6 | Total Time: 40 minutes

¾ cup flour — ¼ cup lemon juice
2 tbsp powdered sugar — ⅛ tsp salt
¼ cup coconut oil, melted — ¼ cup mashed bananas
½ cup brown sugar — 1¾ tsp cornstarch
1 tbsp lemon zest — ¾ tsp baking powder

Combine the flour, powdered sugar, and coconut oil in a mixing bowl. Place in the fridge. Mix the brown sugar, lemon zest and juice, salt, bananas, cornstarch, and baking powder in another bowl. Stir well.

Preheat air fryer to 350°F. Spray a baking pan with oil. Remove the crust from the fridge and press it into the bottom of the pan to form a crust. Place in the air fryer and Bake for 5 minutes or until firm. Remove and spread the lemon filling over the crust. Bake for 18-20 minutes or until the top is golden. Chill for an hour in the fridge. Once firm and cooled, cut into pieces and serve.

Magic Giant Chocolate Cookies

Serves: 2 | Total Time: 30 minutes

2 tbsp white chocolate chips — 2 eggs
½ cup flour — 2 tbsp milk chocolate chips
1/8 tsp baking soda — ¼ cup chopped pecans
¼ cup butter, melted — ¼ cup chopped hazelnuts
¼ cup light brown sugar — ½ tsp vanilla extract
2 tbsp granulated sugar — Salt to taste

Preheat air fryer to 350°F. In a bowl, combine the flour, baking soda, butter, brown sugar, granulated sugar, eggs, milk chocolate chips, white chocolate chips, pecans, hazelnuts, vanilla extract, and salt. Press cookie mixture onto a greased pizza pan. Place pizza pan in the frying basket and Bake for 10 minutes. Cool completely. Turn onto a plate and serve.

Mango Cobbler with Raspberries

Serves: 4 | Total Time: 30 minutes

1 ½ cups chopped mango — 1 tsp vanilla
1 cup raspberries — ½ cup rolled oats
1 tbsp brown sugar — 1/3 cup flour
2 tsp cornstarch — 3 tbsp coconut sugar
1 tsp lemon juice — 1 tsp cinnamon
2 tbsp sunflower oil — ¼ tsp nutmeg
1 tbsp maple syrup — ⅛ tsp salt

Preheat air fryer to 320°F. Place the mango, raspberries, brown sugar, cornstarch, and lemon juice in a baking pan. Stir with a rubber spatula until combined. Set aside.

In a separate bowl, add the oil, maple syrup, and vanilla and stir well. Toss in the oats, flour, coconut sugar, cinnamon, nutmeg, and salt. Stir until combined. Sprinkle evenly over the mango-raspberry filling. Bake for 20 minutes or until the topping is crispy and golden. Enjoy warm.

Oatmeal Blackberry Crisp

Serves: 6 | Total Time: 20 minutes

1 cup rolled oats	1 tsp cinnamon
½ cup flour	1/3 cup honey
¼ cup olive oil	4 cups blackberries
¼ tsp salt	

Preheat air fryer to 350°F. Combine rolled oats, flour, olive oil, salt, cinnamon, and honey in a large bowl. Mix well. Spread the blackberries on the bottom of a greased cooking pan. Cover them with the oat mixture. Place the pan in air fryer and Bake for 15 minutes. Leave to cool for a few minutes. Serve and enjoy.

Fast Brownies

Serves: 4 | Total Time: 25 minutes

½ cup flour	¼ tsp salt
2 tbsp cocoa	½ cup chocolate chips
1/3 cup granulated sugar	¼ cup chopped hazelnuts
¼ tsp baking soda	1 tbsp powdered sugar
3 tbsp butter, melted	1 tsp vanilla extract
1 egg	

Preheat air fryer to 350°F. Combine all ingredients, except chocolate chips, hazelnuts, and powdered sugar, in a bowl. Fold in chocolate chips and pecans. Press mixture into a greased cake pan. Place cake pan in the frying basket and Bake for 12 minutes. Let cool for 10 minutes before slicing into 9 brownies. Scatter with powdered sugar and serve.

Honey Apple-Pear Crisp

Serves: 4 | Total Time: 25 minutes

1 peeled apple, chopped	1/3 cup flour
2 peeled pears, chopped	3 tbsp sugar
2 tbsp honey	2 tbsp butter, softened
½ cup oatmeal	½ tsp ground cinnamon

Preheat air fryer to 380°F. Combine the apple, pears, and honey in a baking pan. Mix the oatmeal, flour, sugar, butter, and cinnamon in a bowl. Note that this mix won't be smooth. Dust the mix over the fruit, then Bake for 10-12 minutes. Serve hot.

Baked Caramelized Peaches

Serves: 6 | Total Time: 25 minutes

3 pitted peaches, halved	1 tsp vanilla extract
2 tbsp brown sugar	¼ tsp ground cinnamon
1 cup heavy cream	1 cup fresh blueberries

Preheat air fryer to 380°F. Lay the peaches in the frying basket with the cut side up, then top them with brown sugar. Bake for 7-11 minutes, allowing the peaches to brown around the edges. In a mixing bowl, whisk heavy cream, vanilla, and cinnamon until stiff peaks form. Fold the peaches into a plate. Spoon the cream mixture into the peach cups, top with blueberries, and serve.

Homemade Chocolate Chips Ahoy

Serves: 4 | Total Time: 25 minutes + cooling time

1 egg white, large	1 cup flour
1 tbsp coconut oil, melted	2 tbsp coconut sugar
2 tbsp honey	¼ tsp salt
2 tbsp milk, warm	¼ tsp baking powder
¼ tsp vanilla extract	4 tbsp chocolate chips

Preheat air fryer to 360°F. Combine the egg white, coconut oil, honey, milk, and vanilla in a bowl. Add the flour, coconut sugar, salt, and baking powder. Stir until combined. Fold in the chocolate chips. Roll the dough into balls, then flatten slightly. Place in a greased baking pan, leaving a little room in between. Bake for 12-15 minutes or until golden. Let cool before serving.

Brownies with White Chocolate

Serves: 6 | Total Time: 30 minutes

¼ cup white chocolate chips	2 tbsp sunflower oil
1 egg	1 tsp dark rum
¼ cup muscovado sugar	¼ cup cocoa powder
2 tbsp white sugar	1/3 cup self-raising flour

Preheat air fryer to 350°F. Beat the egg with muscovado sugar and white sugar in a bowl. Mix in the sunflower oil and rum. Next, stir in cocoa powder and flour until just combined. Gently fold in white chocolate chips. Spoon the batter into a lightly greased pan. Bake for 20-25 minutes or until a toothpick inserted comes out dry and clean. Remove from the air fryer and leave to cool for a few minutes in the pan. Cut into squares and serve.

Cinnamon Chips with Fruit Salsa

Serves: 4 | Total Time: 15 minutes

1 cup chopped mango	2 tbsp butter, melted
1 peeled kiwi, chopped	2 tsp brown sugar
1 (8-inch) tortilla	½ tsp cinnamon

Preheat air fryer to 380°F. Slice the tortilla into 8 triangles like a pizza. Brush the slices with butter. Sprinkle brown sugar and cinnamon on top. Place in the frying basket in a single layer. Air Fry for 8-10 minutes or until they are light brown. Mix the fruit in a bowl. Serve with chips.

Sultana & Walnut Stuffed Apples

Serves: 4 | Total Time: 30 minutes

4 apples, cored and halved	3 tbsp dried cranberries
2 tbsp lemon juice	2 tbsp packed brown sugar
¼ cup sultana raisins	1/3 cup apple cider
3 tbsp chopped walnuts	1 tbsp cinnamon

Preheat air fryer to 360°F. Spritz the apples with lemon juice and put them in a baking pan. Combine the raisins, cinnamon, walnuts, cranberries, and brown sugar, then spoon ¼ of the mix into the apples. Drizzle the apple cider around the apples and Bake for 13-18 minutes until softened. Serve warm.

Date Oat Cookies

Serves: 6 | Total Time: 20 minutes

¼ cup butter, softened	3/4 cup flour
2 ½ tbsp milk	¼ tsp salt
½ cup sugar	¾ cup rolled oats
½ tsp vanilla extract	¼ tsp baking soda
½ tsp lemon zest	¼ tsp baking powder
½ tsp ground cinnamon	2 tbsp dates, chopped

Use an electric beater to whip the butter until fluffy. Add the milk, sugar, lemon zest, and vanilla. Stir until well combined. Add the cinnamon, flour, salt, oats, baking soda, and baking powder in a separate bowl and stir. Add the dry mix to the wet mix and stir with a wooden spoon. Pour in the dates.

Preheat air fryer to 360°F. Drop tablespoonfuls of the batter onto a greased baking pan, leaving room in between each. Bake for 6 minutes or until light brown. Make all the cookies at once, or save the batter in the fridge for later. Let them cool. Serve and enjoy!

Dark Chocolate Cookies

Serves: 4 | Total Time: 35 minutes + cooling time

1/3 cup brown sugar	5 tbsp peanut butter
2 tbsp butter, softened	¼ tsp baking soda
1 egg yolk	1 tsp dark rum
2/3 cup flour	½ cup dark chocolate chips

Preheat air fryer to 320°F. Beat butter and brown sugar in a bowl until fluffy. Stir in the egg yolk. Add flour, 3 tbsp of peanut butter, baking soda, and rum until well mixed. Spread the batter into a parchment-lined baking pan. Bake in the air fryer until the cooking is lightly brown and just set, 8-10 minutes. Remove from the fryer and let cool for 10 minutes.

After, remove the cookie from the pan and the parchment paper and cool on the wire rack. When cooled, combine the chips with the remaining peanut butter in a heatproof cup. Place in the air fryer and Bake until melted, 2 minutes. Remove and stir. Spread on the cooled cookies and serve.

Maple Berry Crumble Bars

Serves: 4 | Total Time: 30 minutes

½ cup fresh blackberries	1 tbsp maple syrup
½ cup chopped strawberries	2/3 cup self-raising flour
½ cup raspberries	3 tbsp sugar
½ lemon, juiced and zested	2 tbsp butter, melted

Preheat air fryer to 370°F. Add the strawberries, blackberries, and raspberries to a baking pan, then sprinkle lemon juice and honey over the berries. Combine the flour, lemon zest, and sugar, then add the butter and mix; the mixture won't be smooth. Drizzle this all over the berries. Put the pan in the fryer and Bake for 12-17 minutes until the top is golden brown. Leave to cool for 5 minutes, then cut into bars to serve. Serve warm.

Nutella S'mores

Serves: 4 | Total Time: 15 minutes

2 tbsp Nutella chocolate	8 graham crackers
1 tsp chopped walnuts	8 marshmallows

Preheat air fryer to 360°F. Spread the Nutella onto the top of 4 crackers and sprinkle with walnuts. Add a marshmallow to each piece of crackers. Place in the air fryer. Bake for 2-3 minutes. Remove and top with another piece of cracker. Serve warm and enjoy!

Strawberry Wonton Bites

Serves: 4 | Total Time: 45 minutes

1 cup strawberry pie filling	8 wonton wrappers
3 tbsp sugar	2 tbsp butter, melted

Preheat air fryer to 370°F. Combine the strawberry pie filling, sugar, and butter in a bowl. Lay out wonton wrappers on a flat, clean surface. Divide the fruit mixture between the wontons. Fold each wrapper from one corner to another to create a triangle. Bring the 2 bottom corners together, but do not seal. Gently press out any air, then press the open edges to seal. Bake the wontons in the greased frying basket for 15-18 minutes, flipping once halfway through cooking, until golden and crisp. Let cool for a few minutes. Serve and enjoy!

Spiced Fruit Skewers

Serves: 4 | Total Time: 15 minutes

2 peeled peaches, thickly sliced	
3 plums, halved and pitted	½ tsp ground cinnamon
3 peeled kiwi, quartered	¼ tsp ground allspice
1 tbsp honey	¼ tsp cayenne pepper

Preheat air fryer to 400°F. Combine the honey, cinnamon, allspice, and cayenne and set aside. Alternate fruits on 8 bamboo skewers, then brush the fruit with the honey mix. Lay the skewers in the air fryer and Air Fry for 3-5 minutes. Allow to chill for 5 minutes before serving.

Cherry Cheesecake Rolls

Serves: 6 | Total Time: 30 minutes

1 (8-oz) can crescent rolls	1 tbsp cherry preserves
4 oz cream cheese	1/3 cup sliced fresh cherries

Roll out the dough into a large rectangle on a flat work surface. Cut the dough into 12 rectangles by cutting 3 cuts across and 2 cuts down. In a microwave-safe bowl, soften cream cheese for 15 seconds. Stir together with cherry preserves. Mound 2 tsp of the cherries-cheese mix on each piece of dough. Carefully spread the mixture but not on the edges. Top with 2 tsp of cherries each. Roll each triangle to make a cylinder.

Preheat air fryer to 350°F. Place the first batch of the rolls in the greased air fryer. Spray the rolls with cooking oil and Bake for 8 minutes. Let cool in the air fryer for 2-3 minutes before removing. Serve and enjoy

Raspberry Turnovers

Serves: 6 | Total Time: 35 minutes

1 (10-oz) can raspberry pie filling
1 puff pastry dough   1 egg white, beaten

Preheat air fryer to 370°F. Unroll the two sheets of dough and cut into 4 squares each, or 8 squares total. Scoop ½ to 1 tbsp of the raspberry pie filling in the center of each square. Brush the edges with egg white. Fold diagonally to form a triangle and close the turnover. Press the edges with the back of a fork to seal. Arrange the turnovers in a single layer in the greased basket. Spray the empanadas with cooking oil and Bake for 8 minutes. Let them sit in the air fryer for 3-4 minutes to cool before removing. Repeat for the other batch. Serve and enjoy!

Cinnamon Canned Biscuit Donuts

Serves: 4 | Total Time: 25 minutes

1 (8-oz) can jumbo biscuits   1 cup cinnamon sugar

Preheat air fryer to 360°F. Divide biscuit dough into 8 biscuits and place on a flat work surface. Cut a small circle in the center of the biscuit with a small cookie cutter. Place a batch of 4 donuts in the air fryer. Spray with oil and Bake for 8 minutes, flipping once. Drizzle the cinnamon sugar over the donuts and serve.

Banana Fritters

Serves: 6 | Total Time: 20 minutes

1 egg   3 bananas, halved crosswise
¼ cup cornstarch   ¼ cup caramel sauce
¼ cup bread crumbs

Preheat air fryer to 350°F. Set up three small bowls. In the first bowl, add cornstarch. In the second bowl, beat the egg. In the third bowl, add bread crumbs. Dip the bananas in the cornstarch first, then the egg, and then dredge in bread crumbs. Put the bananas in the greased frying basket and spray with oil. Air Fry for 8 minutes, flipping once around minute 5. Remove to a serving plate and drizzle with caramel sauce. Serve warm and enjoy.

Home-Style Pumpkin Pie Pudding

Serves: 4 | Total Time: 30 minutes

1 cup canned pumpkin purée
¼ cup sugar   1 orange, zested
3 tbsp all-purpose flour   2 tbsp milk
1 tbsp butter, melted   1 tsp vanilla extract
1 egg   4 vanilla wafers, crumbled

Preheat air fryer to 350°F. Beat the pumpkin puree, sugar, flour, butter, egg, orange zest, milk, and vanilla until well-mixed. Spritz a baking pan with the cooking spray, then pour the pumpkin mix in. Place it in the air fryer and Bake for 11-17 minutes or until golden brown. Take the pudding out of the fryer and let it chill. Serve with vanilla wager crumbs.

Nutty Cookies

Serves: 6 | Total Time: 25 minutes

¼ cup pistachios   ½ cup almond flour
¼ cup evaporated cane sugar   1 tsp pure vanilla extract
¼ cup raw almonds   1 egg white

Preheat air fryer to 375°F. Add ¼ cup of pistachios and almonds into a food processor. Pulse until they resemble crumbles. Roughly chop the rest of the pistachios with a sharp knife. Combine all ingredients in a large bowl until completely incorporated. Form 6 equally-sized balls and transfer to the parchment-lined frying basket. Allow for 1 inch between each portion. Bake for 7 minutes. Cool on a wire rack for 5 minutes. Serve and enjoy.

Carrot-Oat Cake Muffins

Serves: 4 | Total Time: 20 minutes

3 tbsp butter, softened   1/3 cup finely grated carrots
¼ cup brown sugar   ½ cup oatmeal
1 tbsp maple syrup   1/3 cup flour
1 egg white   ½ tsp baking soda
½ tsp vanilla extract   ¼ cup raisins

Preheat air fryer to 350°F. Mix the butter, brown sugar, and maple syrup until smooth, then toss in the egg white, vanilla, and carrots. Whisk well and add the oatmeal, flour, baking soda, and raisins. Divide the mixture between muffin cups. Bake in the fryer for 8-10 minutes.

Baked Stuffed Pears

Serves: 4 | Total Time: 15 minutes + cooling time

4 cored pears, halved   ½ stick butter, softened
½ cup chopped cashews   ½ tsp ground cinnamon
½ cup dried cranberries   ½ cup apple juice
¼ cup agave nectar

Preheat the air fryer to 350°F. Combine the cashews, cranberries, agave nectar, butter, and cinnamon and mix well. Stuff this mixture into the pears, heaping it up on top. Set the pears in a baking pan and pour the apple juice into the bottom of the pan. Put the pan in the fryer and Bake for 10-12 minutes or until the pears are tender. Let cool before serving.

Lemon Pound Cake Bites

Serves: 6 | Total Time: 20 minutes

1 (16-oz) pound cake, cubed 1 cup vanilla yogurt
1/3 cup cinnamon sugar   3 tbsp brown sugar
½ stick butter, melted   1 tsp lemon zest

Preheat the air fryer to 350°F. Drizzle the cake cubes with melted butter, then put them in the cinnamon sugar and toss until coated. Put them in a single layer in the frying basket and Air Fry for 4 minutes or until golden. Remove and place on a serving plate. Combine the yogurt, brown sugar, and lemon zest in a bowl. Serve with the cake bites.

INGREDIENT-BASED RECIPE INDEX

Asparagus

Gruyère Asparagus & Chicken Quiche, 70
Asparagus & Salmon Spring Rolls, 94
Honey-Mustard Asparagus Puffs, 126
Asparagus & Cherry Tomato Roast, 130
Asparagus Wrapped in Pancetta, 132
Roasted Thyme Asparagus, 134
Dilly Sesame Roasted Asparagus, 135
Easy Parmesan Asparagus, 136

Avocados

Avocado Toasts with Poached Eggs, 17
Bagels with Avocado & Tomatoes, 26
Avocado Balls, 50
Cholula Fried Avocado, 50
Crispy Avocados with Pico de Gallo, 64
Cheesy Salmon-Stuffed Avocados, 96
Smoked Avocado Wedges, 137
Avocado & Spinach Melts, 142

Apples

Morning Apple Biscuits, 21
Spiced Apple Roll-Ups, 32
Stunning Apples & Onions, 127
Pecan-Oat Filled Apples, 155
Ricotta Stuffed Apples, 156
Fall Caramelized Apples, 158
German Streusel-Stuffed Baked Apples, 162
Sultana & Walnut Stuffed Apples, 163

Bacon

English Breakfast, 18
Bacon & Egg Quesadillas, 22
Mini Bacon Egg Quiches, 34
Wrapped Smokies in Bacon, 38
Bacon-Wrapped Stuffed Dates, 40
Bacon & Blue Cheese Tartlets, 48
Bacon & Chicken Flatbread, 70
Chicken Breasts Wrapped in Bacon, 81
Stuffed Shrimp Wrapped in Bacon, 101
Cheese & Bacon Pasta Bake, 140
Bacon 'n' Bell Pepper Pita Pockets, 146
Bacon & Bell Pepper Wraps, 148
Bacon & Egg Scramble Bake, 152
Bacon-Crab Button Mushroom Caps, 154

Bananas

Banana-Strawberry Cakecups, 18
Smooth Walnut-Banana Loaf, 29
Banana Vegan French Toast, 68
Peanut Butter-Banana Roll-Ups, 156
Banana-Almond Delights, 156
Banana-Lemon Bars, 162

Broccoli

Creamy Broccoli & Mushroom Casserole, 65
Broccoli in Adobo, 126
Broccoli Au Gratin, 129
Sticky Broccoli Florets, 131
Buttered Garlic Broccolini, 135
Double Cheese-Broccoli Tots, 136
Ricotta & Broccoli Cannelloni, 140

Beans/Chickpeas

Fried String Beans with Greek Sauce, 36
Spicy Bean Patties, 55
Pinto Bean Casserole, 58
Tasty Roasted Kidney Beans & Peppers, 147
White Bean Bake, 147
Black Bean Fajitas, 150
Middle Eastern Roasted Chickpeas, 41
Meatless Kimchi Bowls, 63
Classic Falafel, 142
Chickpea & Bulgur Baked Dinner, 145
Chickpea Cakes, 146
Cilantro Falafel with Minty Yogurt Sauce, 149

Beef Steak

Flank Steak with Caramelized Onions, 17
Seedy Rib Eye Steak Bites, 116
Thyme Steak Finger Strips, 116
Sirloin Steak Flatbread, 116
Crispy Steak Subs, 116
Flank Steak with Chimichurri Sauce, 117
Fusion Tender Flank Steak, 118

Burgers/Patties

Cauliflower

Cheddar Cheese

Cheese

Chicken Breasts

Chicken Wings

Chicken Thighs

Chicken Drumsticks/Legs

More Chicken Recipes

Chili

Chips

Meatballs

Muffins

Mushrooms

Nuts/Seeds

Olives

Onion

Orange/Lemon

Shrimp

More Seafood Recipes

Skewers

Tofu

Tomatoes

Turkey

Vegetables

Zucchini

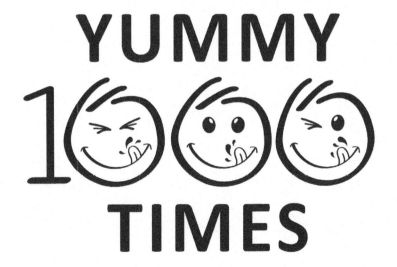

Made in the USA
Las Vegas, NV
17 September 2023

77686841R00098